Compact Textbooks in Mathematics

This textbook series presents concise introductions to current topics in mathematics and mainly addresses advanced undergraduates and master students. The concept is to offer small books covering subject matter equivalent to 2- or 3-hour lectures or seminars which are also suitable for self-study. The books provide students and teachers with new perspectives and novel approaches. They may feature examples and exercises to illustrate key concepts and applications of the theoretical contents. The series also includes textbooks specifically speaking to the needs of students from other disciplines such as physics, computer science, engineering, life sciences, finance.

- **compact:** small books presenting the relevant knowledge
- **learning made easy:** examples and exercises illustrate the application of the contents
- **useful for lecturers:** each title can serve as basis and guideline for a semester course/lecture/seminar of 2-3 hours per week.

Roberto Mantaci • Jean-Baptiste Yunès

Basics of Programming and Algorithms, Principles and Applications

Roberto Mantaci
Department of Computer Science, Institut
de Recherche en Informatique
Fondamentale (IRIF)
Université Paris Cité
Paris, France

Jean-Baptiste Yunès
Department of Computer Science, Institut
de Recherche en Informatique
Fondamentale (IRIF)
Université Paris Cité
Paris, France

ISSN 2296-4568 ISSN 2296-455X (electronic)
Compact Textbooks in Mathematics
ISBN 978-3-031-59800-5 ISBN 978-3-031-59801-2 (eBook)
https://doi.org/10.1007/978-3-031-59801-2

© The Editor(s) (if applicable) and The Author(s), under exclusive license to Springer Nature Switzerland AG 2024

This work is subject to copyright. All rights are solely and exclusively licensed by the Publisher, whether the whole or part of the material is concerned, specifically the rights of translation, reprinting, reuse of illustrations, recitation, broadcasting, reproduction on microfilms or in any other physical way, and transmission or information storage and retrieval, electronic adaptation, computer software, or by similar or dissimilar methodology now known or hereafter developed.

The use of general descriptive names, registered names, trademarks, service marks, etc. in this publication does not imply, even in the absence of a specific statement, that such names are exempt from the relevant protective laws and regulations and therefore free for general use.

The publisher, the authors and the editors are safe to assume that the advice and information in this book are believed to be true and accurate at the date of publication. Neither the publisher nor the authors or the editors give a warranty, expressed or implied, with respect to the material contained herein or for any errors or omissions that may have been made. The publisher remains neutral with regard to jurisdictional claims in published maps and institutional affiliations.

This book is published under the imprint Birkhäuser, www.birkhauser-science.com by the registered company Springer Nature Switzerland AG
The registered company address is: Gewerbestrasse 11, 6330 Cham, Switzerland

If disposing of this product, please recycle the paper.

Preface

This book is an outgrowth of several courses given in the context of thematic schools to various audiences in different countries over the years:

- Two weeks in Vontovorona/Antananarivo, Republic of Madagascar, for engineering students and mathematics teachers in various colleges in the country.
- Three weeks at the University of Nairobi, Republic of Kenya, for master and PhD students in mathematics in the East Africa area (mainly Republic of Kenya, United Republic of Tanzania, Republic of Zambia, Republic of Rwanda, Republic of Uganda, but also representatives from other parts of Africa such as Democratic Republic of Congo, Federal Democratic Republic of Ethiopia, Republic of Ghana, Republic of Senegal).
- Two weeks at the Royal University of Phnom-Penh, Kingdom of Cambodia, for mostly bachelor degrees and undergraduate students, as well as representatives of the academic staff of the university.

Obviously, the material used in the courses taught at our university, Université Paris Cité, throughout our respective careers, also inspired what is presented here.

While the audiences of the aforementioned schools were diverse, they shared a common motivation: the recognition that, in certain regions of the world, individuals engaged in mathematics across different levels lack access to fundamental knowledge in computer science, an essential requirement for any modern mathematician. However, although the content is primarily designed for mathematicians and scientists in the 'exact sciences', it is accessible to a broad range of readers seeking to embark on the journey of programming and algorithm design and who are comfortable enough with elementary mathematical formulas and proofs, irrespective of their background or expertise, including:

- Scientists and researchers from various fields who would like to use computers in their experiments.
- Teachers who would like to draw inspiration for setting up a course in the field of designing, programming, and analysing algorithms.
- Students of any degree, beginners or slightly experienced, who would like to enhance their expertise in writing programs.

This book is organised in two parts: programming and algorithms, one for each author:

Jean-Baptiste Yunès   Part I, Python Programming;
Roberto Mantaci   Part II, Algorithms.

Each chapter typically starts with examples to illustrate the ideas, and many exercises are spread over the content. Solutions to some exercises are included too.

As mentioned earlier, this volume is derived from lectures given in the context of thematic schools. Hence, we chose to use a style and a language that preserve the feeling of a presentation given in front of a live audience. We both give the highest importance to our mission as teachers and propagators of knowledge. In our courses, when it helps students grasp a concept, we do not hesitate to use images, intuition, figurative language, and whatever helps create in their minds a representation of those abstract objects. We have tried to transfer that into this book and assume that choice, even if we acknowledge that somebody may not find it academic enough.

For instance, do not be surprised if the writer switches between "you" and "we." If you have some teaching experience, you know that sometimes you want to take your students by the hand because "*we* walk through this together," while in other cases you want to tell them "*you* should do this" and let them advance alone through the difficulties.

There will certainly be some errors (beyond simple typos) in texts, proofs, and programs; alas, this is inevitable in a volume like this one. The authors hope that these errors will not pollute the reading too much. We humbly apologize in advance.

Thanks

Such work could never exist without the direct or indirect help of several individuals and organizations. We would like to thank, in particular, the many people and organizations involved in financing, managing, conducting, supporting, helping, teaching, etc., all these heavy tasks that no one wishes to do without having a bit of faith.

Organizations

CIMPA (Centre International de Mathématiques Pures et Appliquées, Nice, France), SIDA (Swedish International Development Cooperation Agency), IRIF/CNRS/Université Paris Cité, France, RUPP (Royal University of Phnom-penh, Cambodia), EAUMP/ITCP (East-African University Mathematics Program).

People

Alex Bamunoba, who deserves special credits for his careful reading of the text and his invaluable assistance in Kenya; Kanal Hun; Karl Julian Jaranilla for his support and for his revisions and suggestions; Wastalas Montognon, who, like Alex, deserves the same credits; Jared Ongaro; Fanja Rakotondrajao; Balázs Szendroi; Bengt-Ove Turesson; Paul Vaderlind, who introduced us to the Swedish development programs in Africa and in Asia and gave us the first impulse to write this book; Anna Vanden Wyngaerd, our dear companion in the Kenyan adventure; Mike Zabrocki, our dear companion in the Malagasy adventure.

Special Thanks

The authors would like to thank all the people we met and who touched our lives on the occasion of those schools. We have so many good memories of being here and there, teaching in and seeing a bit of these magnificent countries. Breathless...

We met so many people with so various profiles, experiences, cultural background, habits, cooking and drinking traditions... We were always welcomed with a heavy load of kindness. Our experiences were so great; we have been enriched in many aspects by the true feeling of embracing the humanity in its diversity. Speechless...

Thanks to you all.

Paris, France
2023

Roberto Mantaci
Jean-Baptiste Yunès

About This Book

Writing programs is a hard task that involves many different skills that are not necessarily part of the expertise acquired by undergraduate and even graduate students in scientific fields other than computer science. Here we will focus on: **algorithmic**, **algorithmic analysis** and **programming** (not necessarily in that precise order).

Algorithmic is the art[1] of designing an abstract procedure, the **algorithm**, that can be followed to solve a problem given any of its instances. Algorithmic is as old as hard science is. In the history of algorithms, it is commonly accepted that Babylonians designed two of the earliest algorithms: the Square rooting method and the Factorisation method (both 1600 BCE). We can at least say that Babylonians wrote the details of the procedure on a clay tablet that we found much later, but they had been probably inspired by ancient Egyptian's methods. Ancient Greeks, as Euclides or Eratosthenes for example, defined some other procedures: Euclidian division method (300 BCE), Eratosthenes' sieve (200 BCE) to compute prime numbers. Not to be western-centric, we should mention that there also exist old Chinese, Indian, Maya, etc. algorithms. The Persian Muḥammad ibn Mūsā al-Khwārizmī (800 CE) is commonly referred as the first algorithmician in the computer science folklore. He did not design algorithms as we often believe but classified them, and the term **algorithm** was forged from his name. This to say that algorithms existed even long before computing machines where invented. Whatever is used to apply such a procedure (a human, a computer or whatever) will obviously take time and necessitate resources.

Algorithmic analysis is the field that focuses on the way algorithms behave relatively to the time and memory used to solve a given problem on a given instance. This is called time and space complexity of the algorithm. Analysing algorithms is a very important task that is often neglected. Designing a procedure may not be difficult, but designing an efficient one is. Designing an efficient procedure is sometimes a necessity. How useful is a procedure that leads you to "predict" weather forecast for the next day but needs a week to give its results? On the contrary, it is sometimes very useful to know that a problem does not have any efficient procedure

---

[1] We used the term "art" to honour Donald Knuth who wrote the most famous book in computer science [14].

to solve its instances, which happens for some problems. One may think about cryptography, where one would like to encipher/decipher easily but make breaking the code a tremendously heavy task without an efficient procedure to do it.

Programming is the art of implementing an algorithm into a machine. Some may say that this task is more adequately called coding. We would not like to participate in this never-ending debate. Let us just say that programming is more wide/general/abstract than coding, in the sense that programming involves more engineering aspects while coding is a more technical matter. And to make this more complete, we may add that algorithmic is more a scientific matter, generally reserved to (computer) scientists. We know that this classification is too broad and that sometimes a technician may design algorithms. We would just like to emphasise the fact that the same person may use different level of abstractions when "programming" (in the very broad sense). One must be aware on this.

To roughly sum up the different levels of abstraction one can use the following:

- In **algorithmic** we can reason on the natural numbers (thus unbounded).
- In **programming** we reason knowing that the used numbers will be bounded.
- In **coding** we exactly know all the constraints.

We then propose to explain all of these, with a mix of theoretical and practical aspects. The reader will then find some formal definitions of notions, practical applications, exercises and many of their solutions. Applications and programming considerations will be based on the PYTHON programming language. PYTHON is freely available on every mainstream platform and widely used.

Notations

Throughout this book, we will use several typographical conventions.

Programs and algorithms will be illustrated like the following:

Algorithm 1: Sum of elements of an array

```
1  Sum(a: array of n integers): integer
2    for i from 0 to n-1 do
3      sum += a[i]
4    return sum
```

Program 1: A program

```
1  import math
2
3  print("Pi=",math.pi) # A very long comment that may wrap to the next ▷
                        ▷ line(s) by the use of a small triangle symbol. Note that line ▷
                        ▷ numbering respects the wrapping.
4  exit(0)
```

There are small numbers on the left that can be ignored, they are used to refer to them as line number through the text. Some words are represented in bold face, they are reserved/standard words of the language; this is just a visual representation, the faces have no meaning per se. All (but numbers on the left) can be copied verbatim to be tested by the reader. Note that some programs depend on others (modules), but that will be clear in the given explanations. Also note that some lines can be very long, they are wrapped to the next line(s) by the use of a small triangle (that can be ignored when copying). Line numbering respect the wrapping.

Execution of the program above will be depicted like this:

```
1  Pi= 3.141592653589793
```

Executions may depend on the current running environment (machine, operating system, etc.) so that the results can be slightly different. The reader is then invited to focus on the intention not on the exact produced values.

In Part I, "Python Programming," we will use, at several places, interactive sessions. In such an interactive session are parts that are inputed by the user and results given as answers by PYTHON:

REPL 1: An interactive Python session

```
1  >>> import math
2  >>> print("Pi=",math.pi)
3  Pi= 3.141592653589793
4  >>>
```

Everything that is represented as `foo bar` suggests a keyboard input from the user in front of the keyboard. That can be copied verbatim. Note that every input must be validated by typing an ending ⏎ (return key). That is never represented but is **mandatory**, that's the only way to let PYTHON answer the request. Inputs may also happen in executions of interactive programs.

In the flow of the text we will use fixed font like in print to represent portion of code, instructions, keywords, etc.

At different locations, we will give exercises to help the reader getting better expertise. They will look like:

Exercise 1
Solve the following equation: $x^2 = 1$.

Many solutions are provided (but not all) at the end of each chapter, most of the time each one in its own section/subsection.

Solutions

Solution to Exercise 1

In $\mathbb{R}$ that would lead to two solutions: $x = -1$ or $x = 1$.

Contents

Part I Python Programming

1 Introduction 3

2 First Steps in Python 9
    2.1   Interactive Mode 10
    2.2   Arithmetic, Types 12
            2.2.1   Integers and Floating Point Numbers 12
            2.2.2   Types Everywhere 14
            2.2.3   Some Mathematical Functions 16
    2.3   Variables 21
            2.3.1   Identifiers 22
            2.3.2   Definition and Assignment 23
            2.3.3   Deletion of a Variable 23
            2.3.4   Empty Variable, `None` 23
    2.4   Statements 24
            2.4.1   Sequential Composition 26
            2.4.2   Compound Assignments 26
    2.5   Booleans 27
    2.6   Solutions to Exercises 28

3 Programs 31
    3.1   Programs 31
    3.2   Sequence 33
            3.2.1   Flowchart of a Sequence 34
    3.3   Iteration, the `for` 34
    3.4   Input 38
    3.5   Strings 38
    3.6   Alternative, the `if` 40
    3.7   Conditional Loop, the `while` 43
    3.8   Early Exits and Continuations in Loops 45
            3.8.1   Early Exit, the `break` 46
            3.8.2   Early Continuation, the `continue` 48
    3.9   Solutions to Exercises 50

4 Functions and Recursion ... 55
4.1 Functions ... 55
4.1.1 Parameters ... 57
4.1.2 Local Variables ... 58
4.1.3 Returning a Value ... 59
4.1.4 Error Handling ... 59
4.1.5 Exception Handling ... 61
4.1.6 Closure ... 62
4.1.7 Variable Hiding ... 65
4.1.8 Documenting a Function ... 65
4.2 Modules ... 66
4.3 More on Parameters ... 67
4.3.1 Default Values ... 67
4.3.2 Positional and Keyword Arguments ... 69
4.4 Recursion ... 70
4.4.1 Loops vs Recursion ... 75
4.5 Solutions to Exercises ... 76

5 Data Structures ... 83
5.1 Tuples ... 83
5.1.1 Tuples as Parameters or Return Value ... 85
5.1.2 Length of a Tuple ... 88
5.1.3 Labeled Tuples ... 89
5.2 Arrays/Lists ... 89
5.2.1 List Concatenation ... 90
5.2.2 Access to Elements ... 91
5.2.3 Modification of Elements ... 92
5.2.4 Insertion and Removal of Elements ... 93
5.2.5 More on Accessing and Slicing ... 97
5.3 Variables, Objects and Values ... 99
5.4 More on Tuples, Lists, Strings: Sequences ... 102
5.5 More on Lists: Comprehension ... 104
5.6 Dictionaries ... 107
5.6.1 Iterating over Dictionaries ... 109
5.7 Objects ... 110
5.7.1 Methods ... 112
5.7.2 Printing ... 116
5.8 Solutions to Exercises ... 118

6 Drawings and More ... 127
6.1 Measuring Time ... 127
6.1.1 Wall Clock ... 128
6.1.2 CPU Clock ... 130
6.2 Counting Operations ... 132

	6.3	Drawing	136
		6.3.1 Generate an Image File	138
		6.3.2 Picture Properties	138
		6.3.3 Drawing Several Functions	141
		6.3.4 Scaling Axis	141
	6.4	File Handling	143
		6.4.1 Writing	144
		6.4.2 Reading	145
	6.5	Random Numbers	148
	6.6	Solutions to Exercises	152

Part II Algorithms

7 Algorithm Performance ... 161
- 7.1 Complexity in Time and Space ... 163
  - 7.1.1 Time Complexity ... 164
  - 7.1.2 Space Complexity ... 164
- 7.2 Complexity Functions (for Time Complexity) ... 165
  - 7.2.1 A First Example: The Sum of Entries of an Array ... 165
  - 7.2.2 Another Example: The Minimum Element of an Array ... 167
- 7.3 Asymptotic Notations of O, Θ and Ω ... 170
  - 7.3.1 Notation O (big-O) ... 170
  - 7.3.2 Notation Θ (big-theta) ... 172
  - 7.3.3 Notation Ω (big-omega) ... 174
- 7.4 Evaluating the Complexity of Algorithms ... 176
  - 7.4.1 Sequential Blocks ... 176
  - 7.4.2 Loops ... 177
  - 7.4.3 Examples ... 178
- 7.5 Solutions to Exercises ... 182

8 Introduction to Recursion ... 187
- 8.1 Factorial ... 188
  - 8.1.1 Space Complexity of Recursive Algorithms, Tree of Recursive Calls ... 190
- 8.2 Exponentiation ... 191
- 8.3 Searching ... 194
  - 8.3.1 Naive Search ... 194
  - 8.3.2 Binary Search ... 195
- 8.4 Fibonacci Numbers ... 199
- 8.5 Solution for Exercises ... 201

9 The Sorting Problem ... 209
- 9.1 Selection Sort ... 211
  - 9.1.1 Complexity of Selection Sort ... 212
- 9.2 Insertion Sort ... 213
  - 9.2.1 Complexity of Insertion Sort ... 215

	9.3	Merge Sort	217
		9.3.1 Time Complexity of Merge and Merge Sort	219
		9.3.2 Space Complexity and Other Features of Merge Sort	220
	9.4	Quick Sort	222
		9.4.1 Complexity of Quick Sort	225
	9.5	Is $n \log n$ Optimal?	228
	9.6	Sorting in Linear Time	230
		9.6.1 Counting Sort	230
		9.6.2 Radix Sort	232
		9.6.3 Bucket Sort	233
	9.7	Solutions to Exercises	235
10	**More on Recursion**		**243**
	10.1	Divide and Conquer Algorithms and the Master Theorem	244
	10.2	More Divide and Conquer Algorithms	246
		10.2.1 Minimum of an Array	246
		10.2.2 Longest Freezing Period	247
		10.2.3 Karatsuba's Multiplication	249
		10.2.4 Stooge Sort	251
	10.3	Dynamic Programming	253
		10.3.1 Memoisation (Top Down)	254
		10.3.2 Tabulation (Bottom-Up)	256
		10.3.3 Binomial Coefficients	257
		10.3.4 On the Order of the Filling of the Memoisation Table	259
	10.4	Tail Recursion	261
	10.5	Solutions to Exercises	266
11	**Trees as Data Structures**		**273**
	11.1	Definitions	274
		11.1.1 Key Components and Basic Properties of a Tree	274
	11.2	Implementation of Trees in Memory	276
		11.2.1 Implementations by Arrays	276
		11.2.2 Implementation by References/Pointers	277
		11.2.3 The .parent Attribute	280
	11.3	Tree Traversal	281
		11.3.1 Depth-First Traversal	281
		11.3.2 Breadth-First Traversal	285
	11.4	Recursive Functions on Trees	286
		11.4.1 Computation of the Size of a Tree	286
		11.4.2 Computation of the Height	287
		11.4.3 Another Exemple	288
	11.5	Heaps and Priority Queues	289
		11.5.1 Definition of Heaps	290
		11.5.2 Implications on Heap Implementation in Memory	292
		11.5.3 Insert and MinRemoval in Heaps	293
		11.5.4 A Step Back to the Aspect of the Implementation	294

	11.5.5	Insertion in a Heap	297
	11.5.6	MinRemoval in a Heap	297
11.6	Binary Search Trees (BST)		300
	11.6.1	BST Definition	301
	11.6.2	Testing That a Binary Tree Is a BST	302
	11.6.3	Search in a BST	304
	11.6.4	Insertion in a BST	305
	11.6.5	Deletion in a BST	307
11.7	AVL Trees		312
	11.7.1	Definition and Properties	312
	11.7.2	Rotations	315
	11.7.3	Rebalancing	318
	11.7.4	Complexity and Implementation Issues	319
	11.7.5	Insertions in AVL	320
	11.7.6	Deletions in AVL	321
11.8	Solutions to Exercises		322

12 Hashing ... 327

12.1	Separate Chaining		328
12.2	Hashing with Open Addressing		330
	12.2.1	Insertion in Tables with Opening Addressing	330
	12.2.2	Searching in Tables with Opening Addressing	332
	12.2.3	Deletion in Tables with Opening Addressing	333
	12.2.4	Complexity of Search, Insertion and Deletion with Open Addressing	334

List of Figures ... 337

List of Python Interactive Sessions (REPL) ... 341

List of Programs ... 345

List of Algorithms ... 349

References ... 353

Index ... 355

Part I
Python Programming

Introduction 1

What is **programming** all about?

In this book, **programming** will refer to the task of building a **finite sequence of basic instructions** (a **program**) that can be interpreted or executed by a computer, so that the execution on an input (usually an instance of a problem to solve) will produce a result as the output (usually a solution to the problem).

A **problem** could be "find the shortest path between two cities in a graph of cities and roads".

An **instance of that problem** could be "find the shortest path from Kigali (Rwanda) to Mombasa (Kenya) using East African roads". Note that this instance is different from "find the shortest path from Kigali (Rwanda) to Mombasa (Kenya) using only roads of Rwanda, Uganda and Kenya". Both have different answers.

A **programming paradigm** captures a way of thinking about the conceptualisation of a computation to achieve: "how to proceed to get a result?" (decomposing), "which bricks to assemble to get the desired result?" (composing). There is two main classes of programming paradigm: imperative and declarative, each one with its own refinements (procedural, object-oriented, functional, logic, reactive, etc.). The paradigm that will be used in this book is the imperative one. We chose to present it because it is the "most spread" paradigm.

In the **imperative paradigm**, one focuses on the sequencing of instructions needed to achieve the computations.[1] A **programming language** is a language to describe programs with a precise syntax (how to write) and semantic (what it does) of instructions.

Instructions are taken from a given finite subset, and it is the purpose of this part of the book to present the most used ones of the PYTHON language. Note that in programming languages, we focus more on instructions than on operations

---

[1] In the **declarative paradigm**, programmer focuses on what to achieve, forgetting many details and lets the "machinery" decide how to compute the goals.

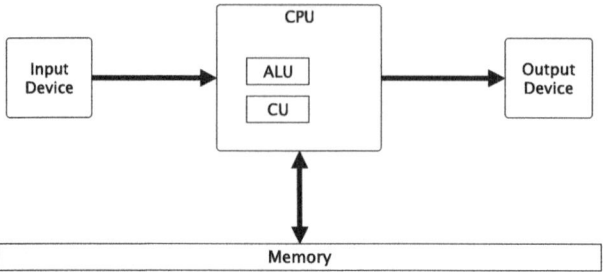

Fig. 1.1 von Neumann architecture of a computer

(a term used in calculus). An **instruction** finitely changes the state of the computer. For example an instruction may modify a memory cell or produce the result of an elementary arithmetic operation. There are also instructions that structure the sequencing of the execution. If programs were only linear sequences of instructions from the first to the last, then a computer would be no different from a basic calculator. What makes computers powerful is there ability to break the linear sequencing, jump back and forth to any instruction, thus possibly inducing feedback effects.[2]

A (standard) **computer** is an electronic machinery made of a memory (a collection of ordered memory cells, **RAM**) and a central processing unit (**CPU**), and obviously some input/output devices (ways to communicate to the external environment of the computer: screens, disks, keyboards, mouses, etc. This is illustrated in Fig. 1.1

A **memory cell** stores a finite amount of information (usually 8 bits, elementary units of value 0 or 1). A cell is accessed through its index (cell 0, cell 1, etc.). They are numerous but always in a finite number, and they can be accessed/read or modified/written/stored.

A **program** is a list of instructions somewhere in memory. That's the von Neumann architecture defined in the early years of computer engineering (see [20]), where program and data are both stored in the same memory.

The **CPU** or **processor** is in charge executing the program by looping over these three operations:

fetch   getting an instruction from the memory.
realize   the instruction: reading some memory cells, optionally applying some arithmetic operation on the values through its Arithmetic and Logical Unit (**ALU**), and storing the result on some memory cells; reading or writing from/to some device.
jump   to the next defined instruction through the Control Unit (**CU**).

---

[2] This is concomitant to the rise Control theory and Cybernetics.

1 Introduction

In a CPU there are basically two kinds of **instructions**, namely:

operation modifies a memory cell, storing the value produced applying an operation on values stored in memory and jumps to the next instruction of the program.

flow control is intended to break the linear flow of execution, permitting to jump (either conditionally or unconditionally) to another defined point in the program.

Computer instructions are very basic; writing programs in their language is a difficult task. This is why computer scientists and engineers designed **programming languages** more suitable to humans. Their purpose is to express computations in a more abstract way forgetting the many tricky details of the machine. There are tools to translate programs expressed in such a programming language to the language of the machine: **interpreters** and **compilers**. An interpreter translates high-level instruction (human description) to low-level ones (machine description) on-the-fly during the execution, while a compiler translates the whole high-level program (human description) to a corresponding low-level one (machine description) before any execution.

High-level programming language also have instructions:

basic instructions: produce a value from an expression, store it somewhere and jumps to the next high-level instruction of the program;

conditional branchings: depending on a boolean condition, jump to defined points of the program;

controlled loops: repeat a given subsequence of the program for number of times;

function calls: jump to some well-defined part of the program (say a sub-program or sub-routine), executes the code and comes back exactly where the jump occurred.

Executions of a program can be represented in a another abstract way by drawing a graph of the control flow (sometimes a picture worth a thousand words). A **flowchart** helps beginners to understand how control structures of high-level programming languages work by abstracting many technical details of program construction, focusing mainly on the possible flows. A flowchart is made of nodes and oriented (possibly labelled) edges. Executing the corresponding program is to start from the entry point of it, following the edges up to the ending point. We will not formally define the flowchart language but will introduce many different constructions on the flow of the text. Now, to illustrate how easy it is to understand what a flowchart can represent, we give an example in Fig. 1.2.

Fig. 1.2 Solving $ax^2 + bx + c$ over $\mathbb{R}$ (flowchart)

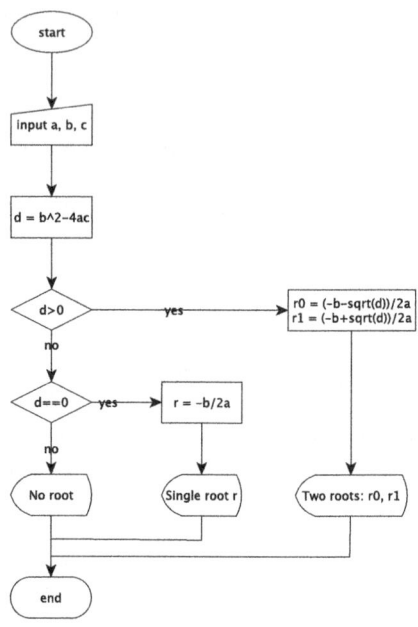

There is a lot of different programming languages, surely hundreds, probably thousands. For example and in no particular order: C, C++, JAVA, PYTHON, FORTRAN, MATHEMATICA, MATLAB, HASKELL, LISP, BASIC, PHP, PASCAL, ADA, ASSEMBLY, GO, KOTLIN etc. Each of them is as powerful as any other (any can be used to solve any problem solvable by any other). One may ask "why not only one programming language then?" Alas, that is a Graal. Each language as its own set of abstractions, instructions, its own addressable paradigm variant, etc, thus making it more suitable to be used in some kind of problems. For example:

C	mixes structured-procedural programming and fine control of the underlying machine. It is mainly used in operating system development.
C++	mixes C, object-oriented, part of functional programming. It is mainly used in embedded systems and control systems development.
Java	mixes object-oriented with part of functional programming. It is mainly used in general purpose applications and web back-ends development.
Mathematica	mixes symbolic computing with general-purpose programming. It is mainly use by scientists.
LISP	is a minimalist purely functional programming language. It was mainly used for AI applications.

Haskell	is a typed pure functional programming language. It covers various area of application development: from compiler writing to concurrent programming.
Go	is a kind of "secure" C mixed with good concurrent programming support. It is recommended for cloud services to command line tools development.
Kotlin	mixes object-oriented and functional programming with type inference, mainly used in Android application development.

We did not pretend to be exhaustive or completely exact in the (very) short descriptions given in this list. It is intended to show that languages use cases can be very different. Each language focus on the ease of some functionalities considered as more important than others.

We already said, that in this part, we will focus on the **Python** programming language. PYTHON is a multi-paradigm high-level language. It is used by many people over the world, and scientists in many fields; it is not intended to computerists only. It is a very general-purpose programming language provided with many extensions allowing to solve lots of very different problems. This is why we chose it.

A PYTHON program (corresponding to the flowchart of Fig. 1.2) could be:

Program 1.1: Solving a polynomial of degree 2 over $\mathbb{R}$ equation.py

```python
import math

a = float(input("a (not nul)? "))
b = float(input("b? "))
c = float(input("c? "))
d = b**2-4*a*c
if d > 0:
    r0 = (-b-math.sqrt(d))/(2*a)
    r1 = (-b+math.sqrt(d))/(2*a)
    print(f"Two roots: {r0}, {r1}")
else:
    if d == 0:
        r = -b/(2*a)
        print(f"Single root: {r}")
    else:
        print("No root")
```

This program is given for illustrative purpose, it has several flaws, rather strange constructions but discussing them here is irrelevant. We will learn this step by step.

First Steps in Python 2

Before addressing some more complex PYTHON's constructions used to build programs, we first need to understand some basics but essential concepts used in **Python** programming language. PYTHON can be used in two ways: interactive mode and script mode. Its **interactive mode** will let us experiment and explain what expressions, statements, types, identifiers, and variables are and how to use modules. Roughly:

Expressions are group of syntactic elements whose execution leads to a value.
Statements   are sentences that represents actions.
Types   are sets of values and their associated operators.
Identifiers are names affected to manipulate entities.
Variables   are storage entities.
Modules   are sets of functionalities that can be added at will when necessary.

Before starting we may need to install PYTHON on our computer. We refer the reader to the website python.org to find a suitable installation. Beware that PYTHON comes in many different flavours called versions. It is available to almost all operating systems and versions: WINDOWS™, LINUX™, MACOS™. We recommended to get the latest PYTHON version (at least 3.7). Version 2 is obsolete, do not use it, never. Even if it is already installed for technical reasons in your operating systems, rather install version 3.

While not mandatory, we recommend to install any suitable IDE. An **IDE** (**Integrated Development Environment**) is a tool (an application) that integrates functionalities that help writing programs such as: context-sensitive editing, integrated help, console output, run/debug functions, etc. Good IDEs for PYTHON are PYCHARM or VISUAL STUDIO CODE.

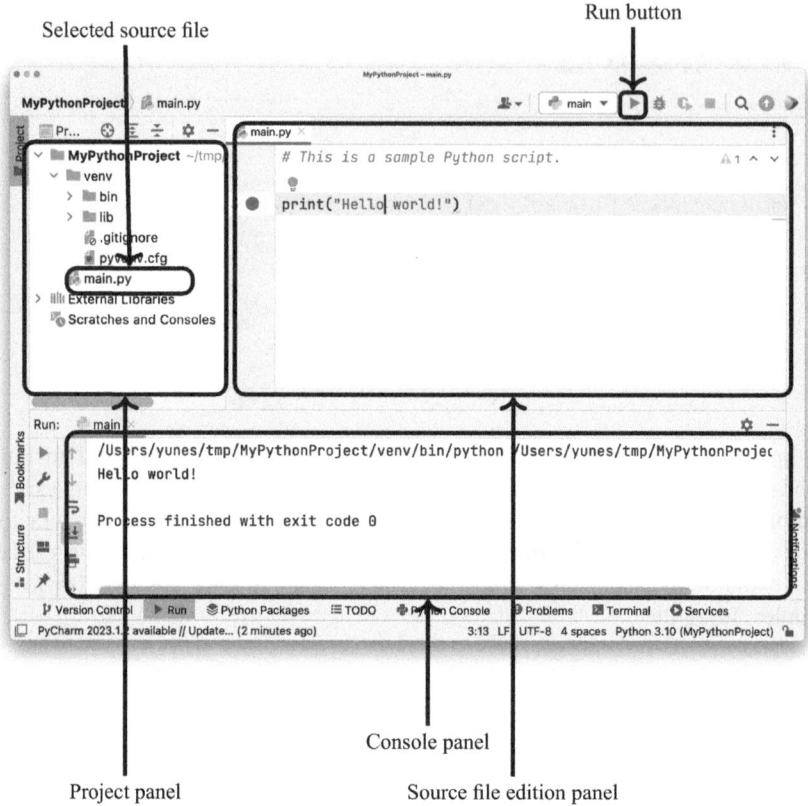

Fig. 2.1 A standard PyCharm window

An IDE always looks like Fig. 2.1.

It is not within the purposes of this book to describe how to obtain one or another IDE, even how to use it, and we let the reader refers to his knowledge and documentation or tutorials of the IDE of his choice.

2.1 Interactive Mode

The **interactive mode** is better known as **REPL mode** (Read-Evaluate-Print Loop). As the acronym suggests, it is a way of interacting with PYTHON such that it operates in a loop of two steps:

read wait for an order to be input (a **command**),
evaluate answers it (possibly giving back some output).

2.1 Interactive Mode

This mode is only usable for very simple computations, to test basic things. We will use it, in this chapter, to introduce some essential PYTHON concepts.

Here is a simple REPL session:

REPL 2.1: Hello world

```
1  Python 3.9.7 (default, Sep 16 2021, 08:50:36)
2  [Clang 10.0.0 ] :: Anaconda, Inc. on darwin
3  Type "help", "copyright", "credits" or "license" for more information↪
    ▷ .
4  >>> print('hello')
5  hello
6  >>> 3+4
7  7
8  >>> quit()
```

Be careful that running PYTHON in the REPL mode may take place in very different ways. We may use the command line interpreter of the hosting operating system (for example BASH on Linux/Mac OS, or CMD on Windows) and launch PYTHON, or we may use the appropriate functionality in our IDE (for PYCHARM: View ⟩ Tool Windows ⟩ Python Console or for VISUAL STUDIO CODE use Terminal ⟩ New terminal then type python).

As soon as REPL mode starts, it prints some information about PYTHON itself (lines 1 to 3). There is nothing really important there, except which version the language is running. A PYTHON version number is roughly made of three numbers separated by a dot as 3.9.7. The schema used by PYTHON is *major.minor.micro*. The first number (i.e. 3) is the major release.

After printing some information, PYTHON waits the user to input something by printing its **prompt** first, by default » (beginning of lines 4, 6 and 8). In this example we inputed print('hello') followed by a ⏎ (enter key). We will not insist on this later on, but the ⏎ key is a necessity, as it is used in almost all interactive modes to validate an input. Then, just after that, ending key is typed, PYTHON gets the input, evaluates the instruction and may print a result (line 5 is its answer to input off line4, and line 7 is that of the line 6). Line 8 contains a command to terminate the interpreter. As we shall see, PYTHON will try to evaluate anything typed, but only some typings are correct. The purpose of this learning course is to give the reader sufficient informations about what PYTHON is able to accept. Describing it formally is beyond the scope of this book.

It is probably not too mysterious that we asked PYTHON to do three things:

1. print a message on the console (the output device);
2. compute the result of an addition;
3. and terminate the session.

In the reminder of this book, we will never mention anymore (except if necessary) that quit is to be used to close the REPL session. From now, if you want to close the session type quit() at the prompt (and validate by pressing the enter key!).

2.2 Arithmetic, Types

We saw that it is easy to compute an addition, and one can imagine what will be the effect of using other operators like - - (substraction), * (product), % (modulus), etc. Again, we will not list every possible arithmetic operator, as it is easy to find them in the PYTHON documentation. We prefer to focus on more conceptual things.

▶ Beware of the operator /. As we experimented, it provides the result of a division, but we have some important things to discuss before understanding what is the nature of the value produced.

Obviously, we can write arithmetic expressions just like we do at primary school. Let us do it (avoiding / for the moment). A primary application of PYTHON could be to compute some integer arithmetic as in the following:

REPL 2.2: Basic arithmetic

```
1  >>> (5*6)+4
2  34
3  >>> 5*6+4
4  34
5  >>> 5*(6+4)
6  50
7  >>> 11**50
8  117390852879695316506666495990358319938982138987230001
```

We learned that:

- arithmetic can be expressed using standard notation for basic operators including parenthesis, in particular these expressions follow the BODMAS[1] rule,
- there exists an exponentiation operator **,
- integers are not bounded unlike in some other languages, they can be as huge as possible.

2.2.1 Integers and Floating Point Numbers

We used only integers, but PYTHON allows us to express arithmetic with **floating-point** numbers as in the following REPL session.

---

[1] BODMAS is an acronym for Brackets, Orders (powers and roots), Divisions, Multiplications, Additions and Subtraction. This to remember the order to follow when carrying out calculations of mathematical expressions.

2.2 Arithmetic, Types

> **REPL 2.3: Floating-point arithmetic**

```
1  >>> 1.5
2  1.5
3  >>> 4/2
4  2.0
5  >>> 1/3
6  0.3333333333333333
7  >>> (10**40)/3
8  3.333333333333333e+39
9  >>> 1.5+1/3
10 1.8333333333333333
11 >>> 1.20 - 1.18
12 0.020000000000000018
```

As one can see:

- division operator / provides a result as a floating point, even if operands are integers,
- printing of floating point values is not uniform (floating decimal point or scientific notation),
- arithmetic is not exact with floats.

Computers, as discrete finite machines, can not obviously manage real numbers, but only a finite subset of $\mathbb{D}$ (the set of decimal fractions). This set of possible values is referred as **floating-point** or `floats`. Arithmetic on floats has many surprising effects. **Use them with a lot of care!**

We refer the reader to the technical document to get details about the way these values are stored (see [12]). It is sufficient to say that floating-point is a way to represent numbers as a pair of a finite mantissa and a finite exponent: the float (5;16) represents the number 5×10^{16} and is usually printed as `5.0e+16`.

▶ There is a major fallacy here that one may first quietly ignore at first, but still should be very careful about it when making programs. The printed value does not reflect exactly the value stored in the machine. Always remember that printing is a process of representing something to (usually) a human. Thus the printing tries to adapt the representation in a way that the human would be happy with. That is exactly what PYTHON does. For example `0.3333333333333333` may correspond to what the reader think but may not be the exact stored value, which is neither the value of $\frac{1}{3}$ nor the exact value `0.3333333333333333`. It is the printing of a floating point number approximating $\frac{1}{3}$. At the first place, anyone may be satisfied with what was printed, but if we want to launch a rocket to the moon, we have to take a lot of care of this problem.

- Another major fallacy is the nature of the arithmetic on floating point numbers. Computations can very easily lead to wrong values (we just want to mean "unexpected values from the user's point of view"). For example:

REPL 2.4: Fallacies of arithmetic on floats
```
1 >>> 1.20-1.18
2 0.020000000000000018
3 >>> (1.20-1.18)*100000000000
4 2000000000.0000017
5 >>> .1 + .1 + .1 - .3
6 5.551115123125783e-17
```

We do not want to dig more on this, just warn and insist that, outside integer arithmetic, one must be very careful. A good paper on the subject is [8]. Mastering precise arithmetic is a scientific field by itself called **numerical analysis**.

We saw that PYTHON switches on floats from integer arithmetic with the "standard" division operator /. But there exists an **integer division** operator //:

REPL 2.5: Integer division
```
1 >>> 12345678910111213141516171819820/100000000000000
2 1.2345678910111214e+16
3 >>> 12345678910111213141516171819820//100000000000000
4 12345678910111213
5 >>> 5//3
6 1
7 >>> 5%3
8 2
```

The second and third computations provide exact results, the value of the **floor integer division** and the fourth expression is the **remainder of the integer division** by the use of the operator %. The floor integer division and integer remainder have the property that for any $x \in \mathbb{Z}, y \in \mathbb{Z}\setminus\{0\}$, $(x//y)*y+(x\%y) == x$.

A writing like 5, 13.5, etc., is called a **literal**, that is something that represent a fixed value or a constant.

2.2.2 Types Everywhere

Mathematicians (at least set theorists) know that really $\mathbb{Z}$ is not a subset of $\mathbb{R}$ (there are isomorphisms in between $\mathbb{Z}$ and some subsets of $\mathbb{R}$). That is the same for PYTHON values, some are integers, some others are floats. As we saw, we can use **literals** to express values, but values are elements of sets. For example, 15 is an integer literal while 15. (beware of the trailing dot) is a float literal.

2.2 Arithmetic, Types

In its core, PYTHON uses **type** or **data type** to refer to a set of values. A type is a set of representable values and operations permitted on them with a well defined behaviour. Every single "value" used during a computation is typed. Even if PYTHON programmers can almost forget about types, the language is said to be strongly and dynamically typed.

If one want to get the type of something there is a builtin function (`type`) that can be used to determine the type of an expression:

REPL 2.6: Types

```
1  >>> type(123)
2  <class 'int'>
3  >>> type(123.5)
4  <class 'float'>
5  >>> type(4/2)
6  <class 'float'>
7  >>> type(4//2)
8  <class 'int'>
```

`int` are arbitrary long precision integers. `float` are floating-point numbers but PYTHON also natively supports `complex` numbers:

REPL 2.7: Arithmetic on complex

```
1   >>> 2+3j
2   (2+3j)
3   >>> (2+3j)*(4+6j)
4   (-10+24j)
5   >>> (2+3j)*(4+6.5j)
6   (-11.5+25j)
7   >>> (2+3j)**3
8   (-46+9j)
9   >>> (2+3j)**2
10  (-5+12j)
11  >>> type(2+3j)
12  <class 'complex'>
```

Note that the imaginary part of a complex is specified with the suffix j. Of course it is not the standard mathematical way of writing complex but it is the PYTHON way. There is some debate "about why it is so?", "can not it be changed?", etc., but we just want to say that any language has its own proper syntax, we can complain about it but it is designed that way for some reason, bad or good. That's it, syntax is syntax.

It may be useful to convert values from a type to a corresponding value in another type. PYTHON provides such:

REPL 2.8: Type conversion

```
1  >>> int(5.6)
2  5
3  >>> float(5)
4  5.0
5  >>> complex(int(5.5))
6  (5+0j)
7  >>> int(5+3j)
8  Traceback (most recent call last):
9    File "<stdin>", line 1, in <module>
10 TypeError: can't convert complex to int
```

In general an expression like type(value) converts the given typed value to a corresponding one of the given type, with a significant loss of information in this particular case. Be aware that converting sometimes leads to "rounding" and that some conversions do not have any meaning.

An example would be to convert 3.5 to an int, which will produce the value 3 by rounding to the integer part (floor for positive number and ceil for negative numbers).

For example the last conversion (complex to int) has no standard meaning and PYTHON reported it. This is the way PYTHON tells the user that something is wrong, at least reporting the location where the error was encountered and the kind of error.

2.2.3 Some Mathematical Functions

PYTHON provides several useful mathematical functions. If it did not, we would be sentenced to use tables of logarithms, trigonometry or things like that, just like our forefathers did.[2] Again this is not intended to be exhaustive but to give a starting point to further exploration. Although arithmetic is available freely (we didn't asked for it, it is immediately available from the beginning), to have access to more mathematical functions we need to import them. They are not available as simply as arithmetic operators, because that would overload PYTHON unnecessarily. At start, PYTHON offers a minimal set of functionalities. So, when we need additional things we must ask PYTHON to load/import them if they are available in its environment. PYTHON is provided with a lot of **modules**, exploring them all would be a very intensive task! A **library** or a **module** is a set of definitions (functions, constants, etc.) belonging to some specific computing area, for example

---

[2] Remember how hard it was to compute something before machines and computers. Scientists made a lot of calculus by hand for many centuries.

2.2 Arithmetic, Types

math, drawing, algebra, etc. We will learn some of them through this part of the book.

So to use a given module we need to `import`[3] it into PYTHON such that its content becomes available in the current set of available functionalities. Let us try to use some mathematical functions of the standard module `math`.

REPL 2.9: Math functions

```
1  >>> import math
2  >>> math. ⇥⇥ ← ⇥ (tab) key twice!
3  math.acos(        math.erf(         math.isfinite(    math.pi
4  math.acosh(       math.erfc(        math.isinf(       math.pow(
5  math.asin(        math.exp(         math.isnan(       math.prod(
6  math.asinh(       math.expm1(       math.isqrt(       math.radians(
7  math.atan(        math.fabs(        math.lcm(         math.remainder(
8  math.atan2(       math.factorial(   math.ldexp(       math.sin(
9  math.atanh(       math.floor(       math.lgamma(      math.sinh(
10 math.ceil(        math.fmod(        math.log(         math.sqrt(
11 math.comb(        math.frexp(       math.log10(       math.tan(
12 math.copysign(    math.fsum(        math.log1p(       math.tanh(
13 math.cos(         math.gamma(       math.log2(        math.tau
14 math.cosh(        math.gcd(         math.modf(        math.trunc(
15 math.degrees(     math.hypot(       math.nan          math.ulp(
16 math.dist(        math.inf          math.nextafter(
17 math.e            math.isclose(     math.perm(
18 >>> math.factorial(50)
19 30414093201713378043612608166064768844377641568960512000000000000
20 >>> math.cos(math.pi)
21 -1.0
22 >>> math.cos(math.pi/3)
23 0.5000000000000001
24 >>> math.sqrt(17)
25 4.123105625617661
```

While many of these functions are very easy to use, to get all the power of them or get details on their behaviour we must read the documentation. The website docs.python.org is the best entry point to everything that is available in PYTHON's environment: definition of the language, modules, etc. For example, Library Reference ⟩ Numeric and Mathematical modules ⟩ math — Mathematical Functions leads to a page with all documented constructions of the corresponding module.

---

[3] If it is not a standard module, we need to install it first. Please refer to any tutorial on how to use `pip` or documentation of your IDE for module installation.

We can find:

math.**factorial**(n)

Return n factorial as an integer. Raises ValueError if n is not integral or is negative.
Deprecated since version 3.9: Accepting floats with integral values (like 5.0) is deprecated.

or

math.**gcd**(*integers)

Return the greatest common divisor of the specified integer arguments. If any of the arguments is nonzero, then the returned value is the largest positive integer that is a divisor of all arguments. If all arguments are zero, then the returned value is 0. gcd() without arguments returns 0.
New in version 3.5.
Changed in version 3.9: Added support for an arbitrary number of arguments. Formerly, only two arguments were supported.

We can note that the documentation sometimes refers to different versions of PYTHON. We must know that the language evolves regularly and that some things may differs in between versions. For example, it is said that `math.factorial` on floats is deprecated since PYTHON 3.9, that means that this functionality may disappear in the future, you may not rely on it when writing code. Another example is `math.gcd` which appears since PYTHON 3.5, which means that before that version the function was not available.

The documentation explain how the functions can be used. The **signature** or **prototype** of a function is the specification of the form by which the function can be called (identifier, number of parameters).

For example, when we see `math.factorial(n)` that means that the function must be called with exactly one argument, if we do not respect this an error is emitted:

REPL 2.10: Signature violation

```
1  >>> import math
2  >>> math.factorial()
3  Traceback (most recent call last):
4    File "<stdin>", line 1, in <module>
5  TypeError: math.factorial() takes exactly one argument (0 given)
6  >>> math.factorial(12,3)
7  Traceback (most recent call last):
8    File "<stdin>", line 1, in <module>
9  TypeError: math.factorial() takes exactly one argument (2 given)
10 >>>
```

When we see `math.gcd(*integers)`, the star (*) means that a variable number of arguments is accepted. In the specification of the function gcd, the

2.2 Arithmetic, Types

argument is prefixed by * which means "any number of". Thus, `math.gcd()` or `math.gcd(2,4,55)` are legitimate use of the function. So we can call it like:

REPL 2.11: Use of a math function

```
1  >>> math.gcd()
2  0
3  >>> math.gcd(34)
4  34
5  >>> math.gcd(34,17)
6  17
7  >>> math.gcd(40,8,24)
8  8
9  >>> math.gcd(5.5)
10 Traceback (most recent call last)
11   File "<stdin>", line 1, in <module>
12 TypeError: 'float' object cannot be interpreted as an integer
```

As said in the documentation, using a `float` argument is an error.
We may also use the on-the-fly help by the use of the function `help`:

REPL 2.12: On-the-fly help

```
1  >>> import math
2  >>> help(math.gcd)
3  Help on built-in function gcd in module math:
4
5  gcd(*integers)
6      Greatest Common Divisor.
```

Note that we can also use `help` to get the documentation for the module, for example `help(math)` (if imported first):

REPL 2.13: Help of a module

```
1  >>> import math
2  >>> help(math)
3  Help on module math:
4
5  NAME
6      math
7
8  MODULE REFERENCE
9      {https://docs.python.org/3.9/library/math}
10
11     The following documentation is ...
12
13 DESCRIPTION
14     This module provides access to the mathematical functions
15     defined by the C standard.
16
17 FUNCTIONS
```

```
18      acos(x, /)
19          Return the arc cosine (measured in radians) of x.
20
21          The result is between 0 and pi.
22
23      acosh(x, /)
24          Return the inverse hyperbolic cosine of x.
25
26      asin(x, /)
27          Return the arc sine (measured in radians) of x.
28
29          The result is between -pi/2 and pi/2.
30      ...
```

The / that appears in the prototype of some functions parameter list, as in asin(x, /) does not define a second argument but means that the preceding arguments are **positional arguments** only (we will explain later what that means, see Sect. 4.3.2). Thus we must call asin with a single argument.

Exercise 2.1
In REPL mode, compute the approximated value of

$$\sqrt{3} + \frac{53}{7} - \left| \left(\frac{-1}{4} \right)^{23} \right|$$

Hint: Absolute value is freely available with the function abs.

Exercise 2.2
Leonhard Euler (see [6]) demonstrated that the series

$$S_n = \sum_{i=1}^{n} \frac{1}{i^2}$$

converges to $\frac{\pi^2}{6}$.
In REPL mode, compute the approximated values of π given by S_3 and S_4.

Exercise 2.3
Gottfried Wilhelm Leibniz and James Gregory demonstrated that the series

$$S_n = \sum_{k=0}^{n} (-1)^k \frac{1}{2k+1}$$

converges to $\frac{\pi}{4}$.
In REPL mode, compute the approximated values of π given by S_3 and S_4?.

2.3 Variables

Exercise 2.4 (Tedious)
Srinivasa Ramanujan designed a series whose limit gives π:

$$\frac{1}{\pi} = \frac{2\sqrt{2}}{9801} \sum_{k=0}^{\infty} \frac{(4k)! \cdot (1103 + 26390k)}{(k!)^4 \cdot (396)^{4k}}$$

In REPL mode, compute the approximated values of π given by $k \leq 3$ and $k \leq 4$.

Exercise 2.5
We know that the Taylor expansion for e^x is $\sum_{k=0}^{\infty} \frac{x^k}{k!}$. So given

$$S_n = \sum_{k=0}^{n} \frac{x^k}{k!}$$

In REPL mode, compute the approximated values of e given by S_3 and S_4.

2.3 Variables

It may sometimes be necessary to catch results of intermediate computations or store a value to be used in some further computations. That is the purpose of **variables**. In Mathematics, a variable is a symbol that represents a mathematical object. It is also very often called an **unknown** in equations to be solved. In computer science, a variable is something different, it correspond to a **storage** (a chunk of memory) we can set to a value at any time and read back that value later.

In PYTHON, a **variable** is a **name** (symbolic name or **identifier**) that is **paired** with an **object** (a typed value). It is never an unknown. Whatever happens during a computation, a variable always has a defined value. We frequently confuse a variable and its name, but it is really the pairing (name,object) that defines a variable. This pairing may change over time, thus we say that the variable changed. Be careful that, in PYTHON only values are typed, symbolic names are not (never). Thus the same symbol may be used to denote several kinds of values over time (confusing, not recommended, but possible).

Let us try:

REPL 2.14: Use of variables

```
1  >>> age=39
2  >>> print(age//10, 'full decades since my birthday')
3  3 full decades since my birthday
4  >>> print(100-age, 'years to be centenary')
5  61 years to be centenary
```

The first command defines a variable pairing the name age with the int decimal value 39. The next two commands compute something with this variable. Notice that the print function can accept several arguments, separated by a , (comma).

Every argument is printed from the first to the last, all printings separated by a single spacing.

Exercise 2.6
Write a command to compute the number of decades to become centenary from the value of the variable age.

Exercise 2.7
Let S_n be the series defined in Exercise 2.2.
Write a sequence of commands to compute S_3 and S_4 using a variable to "accumulate" intermediate terms.

2.3.1 Identifiers

An **identifier** or a **name** can be made of letters (at least one), digits and _ (underscore). An identifier can not start with a digit. If authorised, the use of _ as the first or last character is not recommended and should be avoided (it is reserved for some technical usages). The character _ is generally used to separate meaning words. Let's see some examples:

invalid	`0a, 21foo;`
not recommended:	`_foo, _bar;`
good	`my_age, number_of_students, x, x23, foo.`

▶ Even accented characters, non English language characters or more weird ones like emojis can be used to make a valid identifier, but again this is not recommended as it will probably not help the editing and reading of your programs.

The choice of an identifier is not always easy. We can recommend to use one that is sufficiently meaningful in a given context. For example, if we do some physics calculus, almost everybody will understand that `v` may represent the velocity. But beware that it may not be so clear as there are some other quantities whose name also begins with letter v (viscosity for example). So a better choice would be `velocity` or `viscosity`. Longer verbose names are preferable, but try not to overdo it. For example, `velocity_of_the_vehicle` is probably too verbose. There is no strict rule, we just have to think about those who will read our PYTHON code later.

2.3.2 Definition and Assignment

To **define** a variable we just paired a **name** with a **value** using the operator =. That operator (=) is called the **assignment** operator. An assignment either defines a new variable if it does not exist, or pairs an existing identifier with a new object (value):

REPL 2.15: Assignment

```
1  >>> a = 12
2  >>> a
3  >>> a = 4.5
4  >>> a
5  4.5
```

Note that an assignment does not output anything, it is a statement. An assignment does not provide a result but produces a **side effect**,[4] the new pairing; silently.

2.3.3 Deletion of a Variable

Note that once defined a variable remains in memory; it exists. At least it exists for its defined lifetime as we will see later (see Sects. 4.1.1 and 4.1.2). We can explicitly ask for the removal of a variable by the use of del but that must be used with a lot of care.

REPL 2.16: Deleting a variable

```
1  >>> a
2  3
3  >>> del(a)
4  >>> a
5  Traceback (most recent call last):
6    File "<stdin>", line 1, in <module>
7  NameError: name 'a' is not defined
```

2.3.4 Empty Variable, None

Technically there is no empty variable, but we may sometime want that a variable exists but has "no value". That may seem rather strange to have a variable and want

---

[4] A **side effect** realises an action, later observable, other than returning a value.

to associate no data to it, it contradicts what we said above. There are different kind of scenarii to understand why we may need such:

- we may sometime be unable to attribute a correct value to an existing variable. Say we want to store the result of $\frac{1}{x}$, what to store if x equals 0?
- we may think about the case of a variable representing a relation in between data. For example an entry in an address book for which there is no associated data at some point; an empty entry. How to represent it?

PYTHON offers a special value to express these needs (we will see later that this will be very useful when representing lists or trees, for example see Sect. 11.2). That special value is None, of type NoneType. So it is common to test if a variable has the None value. That value is also used in return from function to say that there is no produced result in some cases (see Sect. 5.1.1).

REPL 2.17: None

```
>>> a=3
>>> a
3
>>> a=None
>>> a
>>> print(a)
None
```

2.4 Statements

A **statement** is a PYTHON sentence that expresses a computation to be done. For example, an assignment is a statement and not an expression, it has no value. An expression can be a literal, a variable, an arithmetic expression, a logical expression, etc. Every expression is a statement. Thus:
$$4+5*math.cos(math.pi/3)$$
is an expression.

We can use any expression in the right side of an assignment, as in:
$$v = 4+5*math.cos(math.pi/3)$$
An **identifier** that appears in an expression is replaced during the evaluation by its corresponding value at that time (i.e. the most recent value assigned to it).

Let's try:

REPL 2.18: Assignment

```
>>> v=45
>>> print(v)
45
>>> v=v+1
```

2.4 Statements

```
5  >>> print(v)
6  46
7  >>> v2=v+666
8  >>> print(v,v2)
9  46 712
10 >>> v=0
11 >>> print(v,v2)
12 0 712
```

One may be surprised by the statement v=v+1 (remember that this is not a mathematical equation!), but an assignment (=). What it does is:

- first evaluates the expression on the right side of =,
- pairs the value produced with the name on the left side of =.

This can be decomposed as:

1. computing the value of v+1 which is 46 (value of v at that time 45+1) and,
2. pair v with that new value.

Such a statement is usually written in the shorter form v += 1. Operator += is semantically equivalent to v = v+1. One can imagine what -=, *=, /=, %=, //=, etc., are for.

At the time we executed v2=v+666, the variable v already existed and had value 46. If we change the variable v after, that will not change v2 as we can check (after evaluating v+666, we have no link in between them).

We can log the variable values over time as illustrated in Table 2.1:

Any identifier used in an expression must be defined before the evaluation, if not that will be reported as an error:

REPL 2.19: Undefined variable error

```
1  >>> your_age = my_age
2  Traceback (most recent call last):
3    File "<stdin>", line 1, in <module>
4  NameError: name 'my_age' is not defined
```

Table 2.1 Evolution of variables over time

	v	v2
Line 1	45	Does not exist
Line 4	46	Does not exist
Line 7	46	712
Line 10	0	712

Exercise 2.8
Let S_n be the series defined in Exercise 2.2.
Using variables to catch intermediate computations, compute all values of $S_{1 \leq n \leq 6}$.

Exercise 2.9
Let S_n be the series defined in Exercise 2.3.
Using variables to catch intermediate computations, compute all values of $S_{1 \leq n \leq 6}$.

Exercise 2.10
Using variables to catch intermediate computations, compute approximations of π for all $k \leq 6$ with the formula of Exercise 2.4.

Exercise 2.11
Let S_n be the series defined in Exercise 2.5.
Using variables to catch intermediate computations, compute all values of $S_{1 \leq n \leq 6}$.

2.4.1 Sequential Composition

It is acceptable to sequence several statements on the same line. It is simply required to separate them with a ; (semi colon):

REPL 2.20: Sequential composition

```
1  >>> v = 99; a = 45; print(a,v)
2  45 99
```

Exercise 2.12
Using the sequential composition, rewrite the solutions of Exercise 2.8 to Exercise 2.11 so that each single line will compute a finer approximation of π or e (respectively).

2.4.2 Compound Assignments

It is possible to assign several values at the same time using the , (comma) operator. Let see an example:

REPL 2.21: Compound or parallel assignment

```
1  >>> a, b = 34, 56
2  >>> a
3  34
4  >>> b
5  56
6  >>> a, b = b, a
7  >>> a
```

```
8   56
9   >>> b
10  34
```

The first assignment assigns a (respectively b) with the value 34 (resp. 56).

The last assignment a,b=b,a may seems strange, but we have to remember that PYTHON first evaluates the expressions on the right side and then assign the evaluated objects to every name on the left respectively. This simple statement exchanges the value of a and b (a very common pattern to use). This kind of operation is called **swapping**.

Beware that a,b=b,a can not be replaced by the two sequenced assignments a=b; b=a! The first assignment makes an exchange of the values of the variables while the second makes a equals to b.

Of course, we can also assign more than two variables at the same time with an expression of the form:

$$var_1, \ldots, var_n = expr_1, \ldots, expr_n$$

2.5 Booleans

PYTHON has a predefined type to catch true/false, **boolean** values that satisfies the Booleans laws. The boolean Algebra is due to George Boole (see [3]). That type is bool with two literal values True and False. Operators on booleans are or, and and not.

Let's try some things:

REPL 2.22: Booleans

```
1  >>> True or False
2  True
3  >>> not True
4  False
5  >>> True and False
6  False
```

Some other operators produce boolean values as ==, <=, <, >=, > , etc. Let see:

REPL 2.23: Tests

```
1  >>> a=3; a==4
2  False
3  >>> b=3; a==b
4  True
5  >>> a==5 or a<=b
6  True
7  >>> a==5 or a>b
8  False
```

```
 9  >>> not a==4
10  True
11  >>> my_bool = not a==4
12  >>> my_bool
13  True
```

We will see later (Chap. 3) that these values are used to control the flow of execution in some complex instructions like `if`, or `while`.

Now that we have presented basics of PYTHON syntax, types, variables and assignments we are ready to jump to "programming".

2.6 Solutions to Exercises

Solution of Exercise 2.1

REPL 2.24: Some arithmetic expression

```
1  >>> import math
2  >>> math.sqrt(3)+(53/7)+abs((-1/4)**23)
3  9.303479378997448
```

Solution of Exercise 2.2

REPL 2.25: Approximation of π

```
1  >>> import math
2  >>> math.sqrt(6*(1+ (1/2)**2 + (1/3)**2))
3  2.8577380332470415
4  >>> math.sqrt(6*(1+ (1/2)**2 + (1/3)**2 + (1/4)**2))
5  2.9226129861250305
```

Solution of Exercise 2.6

REPL 2.26: Computing decades

```
1  >>> print((100-age)//10+1, 'decades to become centenary')
```

2.6 Solutions to Exercises

Solution of Exercise 2.8

REPL 2.27: Approximation of π

```
1  >>> i=0
2  >>> v=0
3  >>> print(i,math.sqrt(6*v))
4  0 0.0
5  >>> i=i+1
6  >>> v = v+ (1/i)**2
7  >>> print(i,math.sqrt(6*v))
8  1 2.449489742783178
9  >>> i=i+1
10 >>> v = v+ (1/i)**2
11 >>> print(i,math.sqrt(6*v))
12 2 2.7386127875258306
13 >>> i=i+1
14 >>> v = v+ (1/i)**2
15 >>> print(i,math.sqrt(6*v))
16 3 2.8577380332470415
17 >>> i=i+1
18 >>> v = v+ (1/i)**2
19 >>> print(i,math.sqrt(6*v))
20 4 2.9226129861250305
21 >>> i=i+1
22 >>> v = v+ (1/i)**2
23 >>> print(i,math.sqrt(6*v))
24 5 2.9633877010385707
25 >>> i=i+1
26 >>> v = v+ (1/i)**2
27 >>> print(i,math.sqrt(6*v))
28 6 2.9913764947484185
```

We can observe how repetitive this code is. We will see later how to factorise this.

Solution of Exercise 2.12

REPL 2.28: Approximation of π

```
1  >>> i = 0; v = 0; print(i,math.sqrt(6*v))
2  0 0.0
3  >>> i=i+1; v = v+ (1/i)**2; print(i,math.sqrt(6*v))
4  1 2.449489742783178
5  >>> i=i+1; v = v+ (1/i)**2; print(i,math.sqrt(6*v))
6  2 2.7386127875258306
7  >>> i=i+1; v = v+ (1/i)**2; print(i,math.sqrt(6*v))
8  3 2.8577380332470415
```

```
>>> i=i+1; v = v+ (1/i)**2; print(i,math.sqrt(6*v))
4 2.9226129861250305
>>> i=i+1; v = v+ (1/i)**2; print(i,math.sqrt(6*v))
5 2.9633877010385707
>>> i=i+1; v = v+ (1/i)**2; print(i,math.sqrt(6*v))
6 2.9913764947484185
```

Programs 3

A **program** is much more than a list of arithmetic or alike statements executed sequentially. What makes computers so powerful is their ability to control the sequencing of operations. "Powerful" is to be understood in the sense of computational power, i.e. the ability to perform complex calculations, not in the sense computing speed. One may want to execute some part of the program depending on a condition, or loop over it for a number of times, etc. High level languages such as PYTHON, provide several instructions to satisfy these needs. These instructions belongs to the set of **control flow** statements.

Another type of important functionalities are input/output instructions. In itself, a program that does not interact with its environment has no interest (that would be a closed system just consuming processor power and generating heat for nothing). There is no program that does not interact with its environment in some way during its execution, producing data in files, printing values, asking for input, pushing value on the network, etc.

In this chapter we will then cover the process of writing programs mainly focusing on control flow.

3.1 Programs

In PYTHON, a **program** (or a **script**) is stored in at least one **source file**, a simple text file whose content conforms to PYTHON syntax. While not strictly mandatory, it is highly recommended that the name of a PYTHON source file ends with .py (for example myprogram.py or myapp.py).

Writing a source file is not correlated with the execution of it. We write the program and then execute it as needed.

To **write a program** we can use any **text editor** we like to **produce a source file**. There are many IDEs that will help you very much (PYCHARM, or VISUAL STUDIO CODE for example, see Chap. 2).

▶ Don't confuse text editors with word processors. A **text editor** is a tool to edit a pure text file, a file which contains only sequence of characters. A **word processor** is a tool to **edit and lay out** text to be rendered in style. For example:

- VIM, EMACS are raw editors, there are very basics in their look as their interface is pure text.
- PYCHARM or VISUAL STUDIO CODE are text editors embedded in graphical interface with a lot of features to help writing PYTHON code.
- MS-WORD, LIBREOFFICE, GOOGLE DOCS are word processors, don't use them to write programs, you will not succeed.

Once a source file is produced, we may **execute the program** it contains by giving it to the PYTHON interpreter. The PYTHON interpreter intervenes in the non interactive mode or **script mode** (opposed to the REPL mode) of PYTHON that executes instructions provided in the source code. Of course, the source file can be executed any number of times we want, making it an application (an informal term used to denote something you can execute).

Suppose we have this source file (again, produced by any text editor or IDE of our choice):

Program 3.1: Hello program   p1.py

```
1  # A program to print hello, written in Python!
2  print('Hello')
```

Executions can take place like the following under the command line of our host operating system (or by pushing the [run] button in your IDE). The **command line mode** of **terminal mode** of the system works like the REPL mode, it is an interactive mode whose prompt is by default a line ending with $ (on Linux or Mac OS) or > (on Windows):

```
1  $ python p1.py
2  Hello
3  $ python p1.py
4  Hello
```

We used `python` command with a source file to be executed as an argument . We then executed (twice) our first PYTHON application! That may seem of no interest, but such an application, called "Hello world!" is usually the first we write to test if our environment is correctly installed.

3.2 Sequence

Note that the first line of the program is not a statement, but a **comment**. It has absolutely no effect, PYTHON ignores it. A comment starts with # (sharp) and ends at the end of line. It may be necessary to use comments in programs so that who reads the program may easily understand what is done there. Comments are part of the documentation of the code. There are some rules about making a comment, but the most important is that a good comment must be a semantic one. It must not describe detailed operating things like "The variable is incremented" (any PYTHON programmer can understand what an assignment like n+=1 does), but better as "one more student" (the reader will then understand what n+=1 really means).

3.2 Sequence

From now on, we can write any statement we already know in a source file. Remember the first program shown in the introduction of this part (see Program 1.1).

As another example, we can try to write a program that will compute the approximations of π as suggested in Exercise 2.12:

Program 3.2: Approximations of π pi.py

```
1  # computes approximations of pi
2  import math
3  i = 0; v = 0; print(i,math.sqrt(6*v))
4  i=i+1; v = v+(1/i)**2; print(i,math.sqrt(6*v))
5  i=i+1; v = v+(1/i)**2; print(i,math.sqrt(6*v))
6  i=i+1; v = v+(1/i)**2; print(i,math.sqrt(6*v))
7  i=i+1; v = v+(1/i)**2; print(i,math.sqrt(6*v))
8  i=i+1; v = v+(1/i)**2; print(i,math.sqrt(6*v))
9  i=i+1; v = v+(1/i)**2; print(i,math.sqrt(6*v))
```

which during its execution, produces the following outputs:

```
1  0 0.0
2  1 2.449489742783178
3  2 2.7386127875258306
4  3 2.8577380332470415
5  4 2.9226129861250305
6  5 2.9633877010385707
7  6 2.9913764947484185
```

While valid, it is not recommended to use the sequencing operator ; (semi colon) too much in programs. One statement in one line is much more readable and manageable. We can much more easily insert a statement between two, remove a statement, add a comment, etc. So a better writing of the program could be:

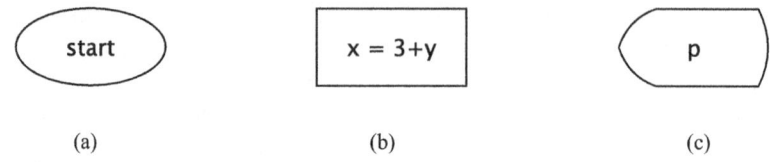

Fig. 3.1 Flowchart basic nodes. (**a**) Start of execution. (**b**) Instruction/Statement. (**c**) Output

Program 3.3: Formatted code   pi-good.py

```
1  # computes approximations of pi
2  import math
3  i = 0              # approximation index
4  v = 0              # first approximation
5  print(i,math.sqrt(6*v))
6  i=i+1              # next approx
7  v = v + (1/i)**2 # add one more term
8  print(i,math.sqrt(6*v))
9  i=i+1              # next approx
10 v = v + (1/i)**2 # add one more term
11 print(i,math.sqrt(6*v))
12 # to be continued...
```

We note that this program is too repetitive, we will present a solution very soon.

3.2.1 Flowchart of a Sequence

While the execution of the sequence of instructions/statements is very natural, this will let us introduce some flowchart elements (Fig. 3.1).

These let us depict (portion of) the Program 3.4 this way (Fig. 3.2).

Note that in the flowchart we said nothing about what happens after the last "node". There exists an ending node to represent the stopping of an execution, but we wanted to suggest that something else can be inserted after. What is important their is the representation of the sequence.

3.3   Iteration, the for

Observing Program 3.3 and Program 3.4 it is easy to see that the sequence includes groups of lines that are all exactly the same:

In Program 3.3   lines 5 to 9 are replicas of line 4;
In Program 3.4   groups of lines 9–11, and 12–14, etc are replicas of group 5–7.

3.3 Iteration, the for

Fig. 3.2 Flowchart of a simple sequence of instructions

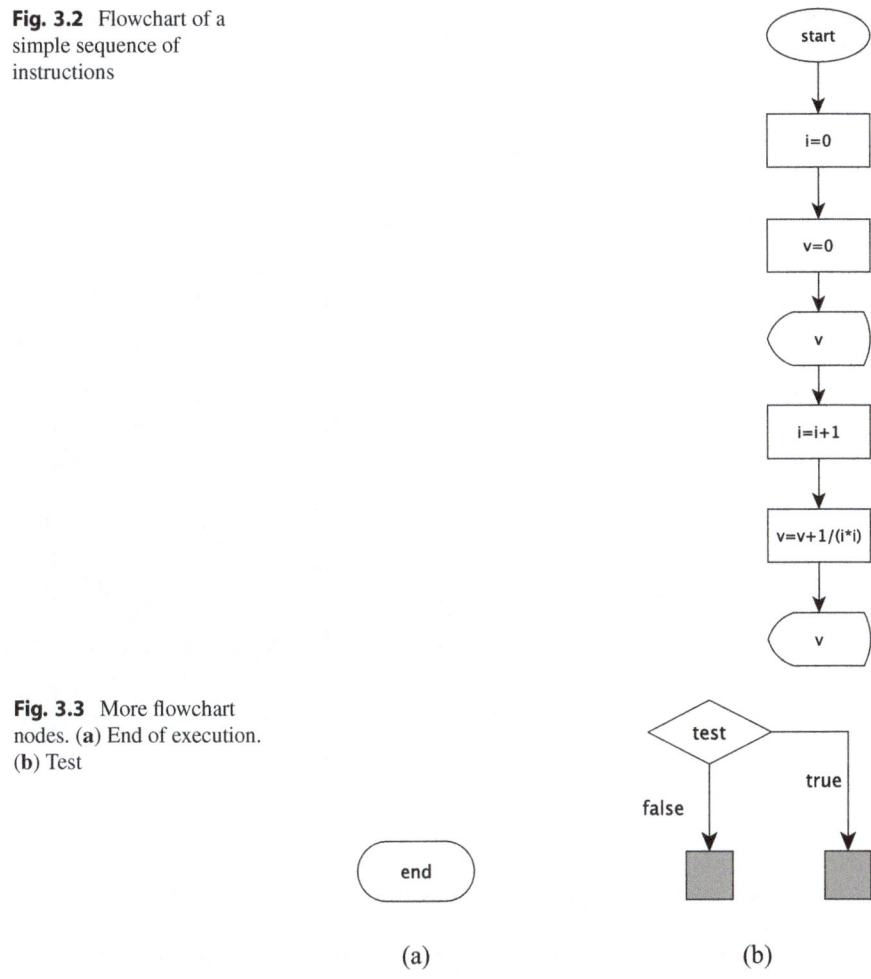

Fig. 3.3 More flowchart nodes. (**a**) End of execution. (**b**) Test

This is not surprising as we just want to repeat some computation over and over again, and we did it by replicating them. Of course, if the question would have required to compute the 10000-th approximation, anyone would have found that replicating 10,000 times the same line(s) may be stupid and obviously error-prone. More than this, the number of replicas required may not be constant, but determined by some computed value or a value given by some user input. This is precisely the purpose of the for **iteration statement**: to iterate (or to repeat) a given sequence of instructions a number of times.

Before being able to draw a flowchart for the for loop, we need to introduce two new elements (Fig. 3.3).

The **test node** evaluates an expression whose result must be a boolean value and redirects the flow to two different sub-sequences.

Fig. 3.4 Flowchart of a for iteration

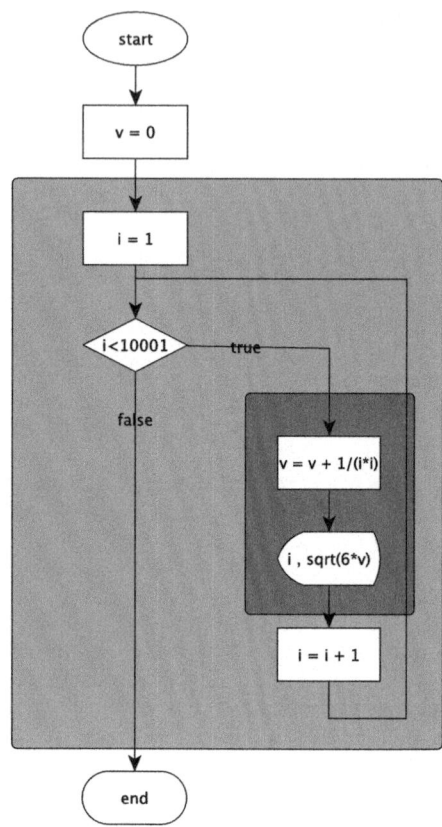

Given these two new elements, a flowchart for the for can be the one depicted in Fig. 3.4.

The idea is to have a variable (here i) which will take time after time all values from 1 to 10000 (this variable controls the loop), in that order; and then execute for each of the values the corresponding portion of code. The whole iteration takes place in the light gray box and the portion of code we want repeat is in the darker box. What is inside the light box and not in the dark box is the control structure of the loop, that is "automated" by PYTHON when we use such a for-loop; this is the kind of things high-level language offers.

There exist many different flavours of for iterations in PYTHON, but we will only introduce some more in the flow of the book. A for loop can be (we explicitly draw the spacing characters to exhibit the structuration of the code):

Program 3.4: Iterations with a range   pi-iterate.py

```
1  #␣computes␣approximations␣of␣pi
2  import␣math
3  v␣=␣0
```

3.3 Iteration, the for

```
4   for i in range(1,10001):
5       v = v + (1/i)**2
6       print(i,math.sqrt(6*v))
```

whose execution leads to:

```
1   1 2.449489742783178
2   2 2.7386127875258306
3   3 2.8577380332470415
4   4 2.9226129861250305
5   ...many lines...
6   9998 3.1414971448461304
7   9999 3.1414971543976273
8   10000 3.1414971639472147
```

Note that it is mandatory to have a : (colon) at then end of the line with the for to introduce the nested block. The nesting is expressed by the use of code **identation**.

The spacing characters exhibit the **indentation**. That indentation is mandatory, it is part of the PYTHON syntax. It is significant, we need to indicate what we want to loop over, just like the flowchart illustrates. The indentation reflects what was drawn in the flowchart, the block inside the iteration is on the right, so it is indented to the right in the code. Beware, while in a flowchart, positions of nodes are not significant, the syntax of PYTHON mandates that the block to be repeated must be indented to the right. In the flowchart, the whole for loop is in the light gray box; and the iterated block is in the dark gray box. One may also note that there exists a backward arrow in the flowchart, this is what makes the loop. In the source code, the for loop:

- starts with line for i in range(1,10001): which construct the light gray box mechanics ;
- and the next two indented lines that constitute the block of code that will be looped over (the dark gray box).

Be also aware that whatever we use for indentation must be uniform all along the indented block. Here, we used four spaces in line 5 and 6. We could have use 1 space, 23 spaces, a single tab, or 3 spaces and one tab, etc, provided we are consistent all over the block. Again don't be fool, always use the same kind of indentation in a given program, common is 4 spaces, or 1 tab. Any incorrect or inconsistent indentation will be reported as an error, PYTHON enforces the structure of the flows to be exactly reflected into the code; in almost all other languages, the structure is expressed much more freely.

We used the keyword for to introduce a loop, followed by a variable (the **control variable** that will pick its values in a range by the use of the function range), and executes the indented block of code that follows. PYTHON's ranges like range(a,b) are half-open ranges, i.e. $[a, b)$, and represent in increasing order all integer values from a to b (excluded) one by one.

Exercise 3.1

1. Draw the flowchart of the program that computes the 1000-th approximation of π as done before and that do not prints intermediate results but only the final value, such as:
   After 10000 iterations, pi≈3.1414971639472147
2. Write the corresponding PYTHON program.

Exercise 3.2
Modify the program of Exercise 3.1 such that it also prints the relative difference in between the computed approximation and the predefined value of π.

Hint: use module math to get the PYTHON's value of π.

3.4 Input

What if we want to compute the 10-th approximation? The 1000-th? Of course we can edit the source code for each need, but one solution is to rethink the problem. Why don't we ask the user for an input? That is the purpose of the function input.

Program 3.5: Interactive approximation of π pi-iterate3.py

```
# computes approximations of pi
import math
v = 0
n = int(input('# of iterations, please:'))
for i in range(1,n+1):
    v = v+ (1/i)**2
print('After',n,'iterations, approx. of pi is',math.sqrt(6*v))
```

Function input takes a message (a `string`) as a parameter and when executed prints that message on the console, then waits for the user to type something with the keyboard and return the `string` read. As we want the value as an `int`, we then convert the string.

An execution from the command line looks like:

```
$ python pi-iterate3.py
# of iterations, please: 100
After 100 iterations, approx. of pi is 3.1320765318091053
```

3.5 Strings

We already gave examples containing strings but almost said nothing about them. A `string` is a sequence of characters. A string literal (a constant of the `string` type)

3.5 Strings

is delimited either with ' (canonical delimiter) or " (must begin and end with the same delimiter character).

▶ Beware that outputs with functions like print always produce characters at the end. Thus print(123) has the same output as print('123'), but the objects that are being printed are not! The first one is the integer 123 whose standard representation (decimal) is 123 (character 1, followed by character 2, etc.) and the second the sequence of characters (character 1, followed by character 2, etc.) whose representation is 123 (character 1, followed by character 2, etc.).

This is why REPL mode gives different canonical representations of values if we do not print them but ask for their representations:

REPL 3.1: Canonical printing of typed values

```
1  >>> 123
2  123
3  >>> "123"
4  '123'
5  >>> '123'
6  '123'
```

There exist many **formatted strings** to ease the construction of strings depending on values. The one presented here is **interpolated strings** (or **string interpolation** or **f-strings**). Such a string is prefixed with letter f. The idea is to construct strings so that part of them contain expressions whose values will be printed in place:

REPL 3.2: f-strings

```
1  >>> a=3
2  >>> print(f"+++{a}+++"
3  +++3+++
4  >>> import math
5  >>> f"Pi ({math.pi}) is greater than 3 ({math.pi>3})"
6  'Pi (3.141592653589793) is greater than 3 (True)'
7  >>> print(f"Pi={math.pi} is greater than 3 ({math.pi>3})")
8  Pi=3.141592653589793 is greater than 3 (True)
```

Any expression enclosed in {} inside an f-string is replaced with the value of the expression. Such a mechanism is called **escaping**, we "escape" from the string to evaluate something and get its value.

Floating points number decimal part can be out-of-control when printed, so we may decorate the interpolation with a specification of a format:

REPL 3.3: Format in f-strings

```
1  >>> import math
2  >>> print(f"Pi≈{math.pi:10.2f} is > 3 ({math.pi>3})")
3  Pi≈      3.14 is > than 3 (True)
```

As one can see, an expression followed by : and a specifier (like 10.2f) can be used to format the expression. The specifier 10.2f means: print the value in a field of size 10 (filled with spaces), and with no more than 2 decimals. In this example, spacing characters have been printed in a "visible" way (a book effect).

Exercise 3.3
Rewrite your programs so that f-string are used when appropriate.

3.6 Alternative, the `if`

It is sometime useful to execute different portions of code depending on a condition.

> What if we want our program to answer if the computed approximation is good or not (given a criterion to determine this, with say less than 1% error)? We have to test a condition (is the error less than 1%?) and execute different instructions depending on the value of that condition.

PYTHON offers an instruction (in the set of control flow ones) that let us execute a block of code or (optionally) a different one, depending a given condition (an expression evaluated as a boolean): `if`. There are two flavours of this instruction: if-then-else or if-then, both are illustrated in the cases of Fig. 3.5.

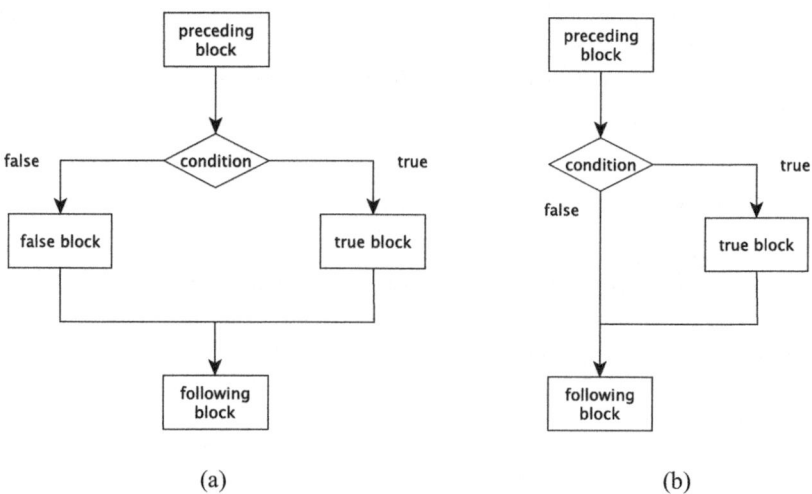

Fig. 3.5 If-then-else flowcharts. (**a**) If-then-else. (**b**) If-then

3.6 Alternative, the `if`

Their PYTHON counterparts are the following:

Program 3.6: if-then-else

```
1  #preceding block
2  if boolean expression:
3      #true block
4  else:
5      #false block
6  #following block
```

Full alternative uses two keywords: `if` and `else`. The first one let us introduce the condition and let us introduce the "true" block. The second one that should be on the same indentation level as the first, ends the "true" block and let us introduce the "false" block.

Program 3.7: if-then

```
1  #preceding block
2  if boolean expression:
3      block
4  #following block
```

This second form is to be used if we have nothing special to do in the "false" part.

Note that exactly as with the `for` loop, `if` and `else` lines end with a : (colon) to introduce their respective blocks of instructions.

Exactly as in the for loop, inner block(s) ("true"/"false") must be indented to the right. What is important to note is that the blocks must be indented to the right of the `if` and the `else` (if it exists).

So we can write a program of the approximation of π like this:

Program 3.8: Approximation of π pi-iterate4.py

```
1   # computes approximations of pi
2   import math
3   v = 0
4   n = int(input('# of iterations, please:'))
5   for i in range(1,n+1):
6       v = v + (1/i)**2
7   pi_approx = math.sqrt(6*v)
8   print(f'After {n} iterations, pi approx. equals to {pi_approx}')
9   error = math.pi-pi_approx
10  percent_error = abs(error/math.pi)*100
```

```
11  if percent_error < 1:
12          print("Good approximation")
13  else:
14          print("Bad approximation")
```

Execution can lead to:

```
1  $ python pi-iterate4.py
2  # of iterations, please: 10
3  After 10 iterations, pi approx. equals to 3.04936163598207
4  Bad approximation
5  $ python pi-iterate4.py
6  # of iterations, please: 100
7  After 100 iterations, pi approx. equals to 3.1320765318091053
8  Good approximation
```

Sometimes we need to nest several if-else. While there is nothing special with the nesting of ifs, the combination of else-if can be syntactically heavy. Suppose we want to do different things given many different values of the same variable, we can write:

Program 3.9: if else if else if else if

```
1  if i==0:
2      # do something for 0
3  else:
4      if i==1:
5          # do something for 1
6      else:
7          if i==2:
8              # do something for 2
9          else:
```

As we can see, the more cases we need to tackle, the more non useful indentation we need! PYTHON offers the elif that let us chain else with an if without the penalty of the indentation. We can use it like this:

Program 3.10: elif

```
1  if i==0:
2      # do something for 0
3  elif i==1:
4      # do something for 1
5  elif i==2:
6      # do something for 2
7  else:
```

As we can observe all cases are then aligned.

There is another if-else variant. If we need to assign different values to a variable depending on a condition we can write:

Program 3.11: if-else and assignment

```
1  if condition:
2      r = expression1
3  else:
4      r = expression2
```

PYTHON provides the **conditional expression** that let us write:
$$r = expression1 \text{ if } condition \text{ else } expression2$$
So lines 11–14 of Program 3.6 could have been written:

Program 3.12: Conditional expression

```
1  # The Good, The Bad and The Ugly?
2  gob = "Good" if percent_error<1 else "Bad"
3  print(f"{gob} approximation")
```

Exercise 3.4
Modify the Program 3.6 such that at the end a diagnostic is printed stating if the approximation is good or bad. An approximation will be considered good if two consecutive computed approximations are equals up to the first three decimal places.

3.7 Conditional Loop, the while

In some of the previous programs, we asked the user to input a value, but what if the given value is incorrect? At this point, we have to consider two kind of errors:

- incorrect value from the type point of view (user inputs a string where an integer is expected)
- incorrect value from the logic of the computation (user inputs a negative value where a positive is expected).

In general, we would like to keep asking the user for an input until he provides a correct one (having a correct input is a necessary condition to go further in the computation of π, is it not?).

For the first kind of error, we will see later how to catch them (see Sect. 4.1.5) as it is related to control flow structure.

For the second, we just have to repeat asking the question until the input is correct or, symmetrically while the input is incorrect. Many programming languages propose while and until loops. PYTHON only has one (since they are very symmetrical only one of them suffice), the **while loop** using the keyword `while`:

Program 3.13: while loop

```
1  while condition:
2      #while true block
3  #remaining "main" flow
```

The flowchart of a `while` is in Fig. 3.6.
Let us use `while` to validate user inputs:

Program 3.14: Input validation   pi-validate.py

```
1   # computes approximations of pi
2   import math
3   v = 0
4   n = int(input('# of iterations, please:'))
5   while n < 0:
6       print('Bad input, positive or 0 please.')
7       n = int(input('# of iterations, please:'))
8   for i in range(1,n+1):
9       v = v + (1/i)**2
10  pi_approx = math.sqrt(6*v)
11  print(f'After {n} iterations, pi approx. equals to {pi_approx}')
```

The logic is then the following:

line 4   input is required;
line 5   correctness is verified. If ok, the control passes over the loop and jumps to line 8 (same indentation level). If bad, inner block (lines 6–7) (on one more indentation level) is executed once and control goes back to line 5 for a new verification.

▶   Beware that **we may loop infinitely** if the condition is never met. For example in the case where the user never inputs a correct value.
    In general, introducing a while loop may lead to a non terminating computation. There is no way to ensure that such a loop ends. While surprising at the first time, we can think about a condition for which we have no proof that it will be false at some time. For example a condition related to a conjecture that is true? A conjecture can be of mathematical nature but also more "human": we cannot assert that a user will, at some point in time, input a correct value. One may say that humans are not so stupid but some just like to play).

Fig. 3.6 Flowchart of a `while`

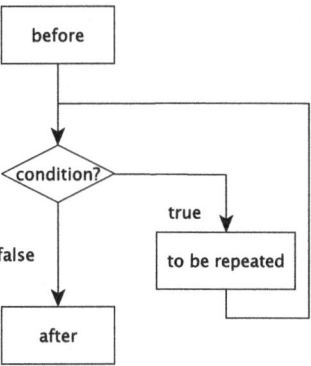

Another trap is that if no instruction in the block changes something used in the condition, then the condition will never change and the loop will never stop.

So be really careful, while loops are very powerful but also dangerous.

Exercise 3.5
Modify the validation part of the Program 3.7 so that the user will be asked no more than 3 times, at which point a default correct value defined by the program will be used.

Hint: use a counter and an `if`.

Exercise 3.6
Modify the program made in Exercise 3.5 such that after having computed an approximation, the user is asked if he wants another one (yes/no).

Hint: use a `while` to encompass the "input/approximation" block.

3.8 Early Exits and Continuations in Loops

We sometimes need to exit a loop prematurely or to shortcut the flow inside the inner block. While such constructions are strictly not mandatory, many programming languages offer such instructions because it will ease very much the writing/reading of programs. Without such, conditions and blocks would be much more complex to express.

These instructions are related to the (in)famous `goto`. There is a well-known paper from the computer scientist Edgar Dijkstra, entitled "Goto considered Harmful" (see [5]) explaining why jumping over code in an uncontrolled manner is a very bad practice that leads to "Spaghetti code". The type of code whose possible execution flows are too complex to be understandable and that is nearly unreadable or hardly maintainable. At least it is good to know that there are non harmful non conditional jumps in the form of `break` and `continue` instructions.

Fig. 3.7 Possible flowchart for a break in a for

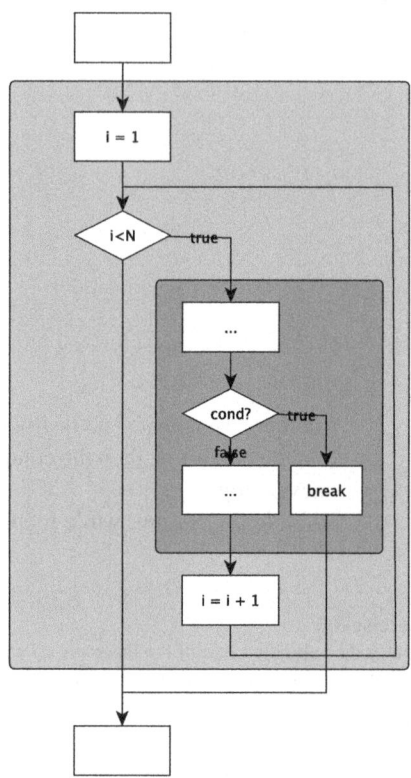

3.8.1 Early Exit, the break

What if we want to approximate π such that either we reached the total number of the expected iteration or when an intermediate approximation is good enough? In any loop we can use break to exit the loop immediately and give the control to the instruction following the loop (the next one at the same level of the loop). A flowchart for a break could be the one of Fig. 3.7.

Thus we can write a program to either stops after a number of given iterations or if the approximation is good enough:

Program 3.15: break   pi-break1.py

```
# computes approximations of pi
import math
v = 0
n = int(input('# of iterations, please:'))
for i in range(1,n+1):
```

3.8 Early Exits and Continuations in Loops

```
6      v = v + (1/i)**2
7      pi_approx = math.sqrt(6*v)
8      error = math.pi-pi_approx
9      percent_error = abs(error/math.pi)*100
10     if percent_error < 0.01:
11         break           # no need to continue, goal is reached
12 print(f'After {i} iterations, pi approx. equals to {pi_approx}')
```

Inside the `for` loop we computed the relative error, and when this error is less than our criterion we "stop" the loop by executing a `break`. This is easy to write and understand. Without such an instruction, it would be much more difficult to get the same computation. Either we would need, for a given criterion, to determine what will be the smallest value in the range for which the condition is met and iterate up to that value, or mix both conditions in a `while` loop. In general and in the first case, it may be not possible or at least not easy to determine that value! The second case can be written like this:

Program 3.16: While to replace break   `pi-breakwhile.py`

```
1  # computes approximations of pi
2  import math
3  v = 0
4  n = int(input('# of iterations, please:'))
5  i = 1
6  pi_approx = math.sqrt(6*v)
7  error = math.pi-pi_approx
8  percent_error = abs(error/math.pi)*100
9  while i < n+1 and percent_error >= 0.01:
10     v = v + (1/i)**2
11     pi_approx = math.sqrt(6*v)
12     error = math.pi-pi_approx
13     percent_error = abs(error/math.pi)*100
14     i += 1
15 print(f'After {i} iterations, pi approx. equals to {pi_approx}')
```

Exercise 3.7
Rewrite the solution of Exercise 3.6 using `break`.

Fig. 3.8 Possible flowchart for a continue in a for

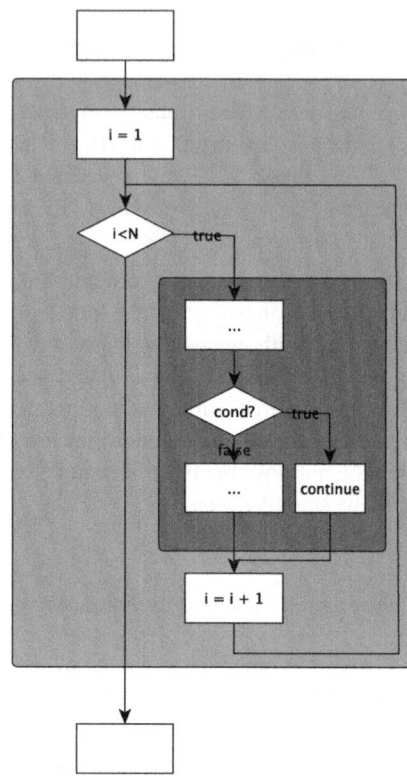

Exercise 3.8
Results of Program 3.8 and Program 3.9 are not exactly the same, the number of iterations is not consistent. Which one is correct? Why? How to correct it?

3.8.2 Early Continuation, the `continue`

In some other cases we want to skip some portion of the inner iterated block or take a short-circuit for some iterations. For example, suppose we want to sum all prime numbers up to a given number n. A simple solution is to iterate over all numbers from 2 to n and skip numbers that are not prime. The skip is expressed by continue which forgets the remaining of the block and jumps back immediately to the next iteration of the loop. A flowchart is given in Fig. 3.8.

3.8 Early Exits and Continuations in Loops

Thus we can write the following program that will also compute the approximation of this same sum using:

$$\sum_{k=1}^{k=N} p_k \approx \frac{N^2}{2} \log N$$

where p_k is the k-th prime number.

Program 3.17: Sum of prime numbers · sumprimes.py

```
1  # Sum of primes up to n
2  import sympy
3  import math
4  n = int(input("Up to? "))
5  sum_primes = 0
6  n_primes = 0
7  for i in range(1,n+1):
8      if not sympy.isprime(i):    # skip non prime numbers...
9          continue                # stop current iteration, go next
10     n_primes += 1
11     sum_primes += i
12 print(f"Sum of primes up to {n} equals to {sum_primes}")
13 print(f"Approx {n_primes**2/2*math.log(n_primes)}")
```

Note that we used a PYTHON's module: sympy. This module is not included in the standard PYTHON's distribution and needs to be installed.[1] We used it to test if a number is prime. We will see later (see Chap. 4) how we could have written such a function by ourselves. An execution could be:

```
1  Up to? 1000000
2  Sum of primes up to 1000000 equals to 37550402023
3  Approx 34725061735.73368
```

---

[1] In command line mode we may use `pip install sympy`.

3.9 Solutions to Exercises

Solution to Exercise 3.1

The flowchart:

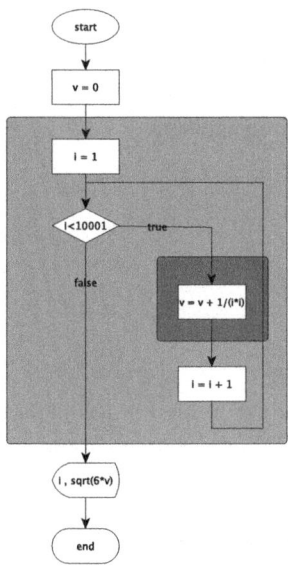

The program:

Program 3.18: Final approx. of π — pi-iterate2.py

```
# computes approximations of pi
import math
v = 0
for i in range(1,10001):
    v = v+ (1/i)**2
print('After',i,'iterations, pi≈',math.sqrt(6*v))
```

Solution to Exercise 3.2

Program 3.19: Final approx. of π — pi-iterate2-1.py

```
# computes approximations of pi
import math
v = 0
for i in range(1,100001):
```

3.9 Solutions to Exercises

```
5          v = v+ (1/i)**2
6   my_pi = math.sqrt(6*v)
7   print('After',i,'iterations, approximation of pi is',my_pi)
8   error = abs(math.pi-my_pi)/math.pi
9   print('Relative error is',error*100,'%')
```

Solution to Exercise 3.4

Program 3.20: π to the 4th decimal place   pi-4decimal.py

```
1   # computes approximations of pi
2   import math
3   n = int(input('# of iterations, please:'))
4   v = 0
5   for i in range(1,n+1):
6       v = v + (1/i)**2
7   pi_approx = math.sqrt(6*v)
8   print(f'After {n} iterations, pi≈{pi_approx}')
9   error = abs(int(math.pi*1000)-int(pi_approx*1000))
10  if error == 0:
11      print("Good approximation")
12  else:
13      print("Bad approximation")
```

Solution to Exercise 3.5

Program 3.21: Controlled validation   pi-validate3times.py

```
1   # computes approximations of pi
2   import math
3   n = int(input('# of iterations, please:'))
4   n_inputs = 1
5   while n < 0:
6       if n_inputs < 3:                    # try at most 3 times
7           print('Bad input, positive or 0 please.')
8           n = int(input('# of iterations, please:'))
9           n_inputs += 1                   # one more user input
10      else:                     # no good input, default value then
11          print('Too many bad inputs. Now using a default value.')
12          n = 10
```

```
13  v = 0
14  for i in range(1,n+1):
15      v = v + (1/i)**2
16  pi_approx = math.sqrt(6*v)
17  print(f'After {n} iterations, pi≈{pi_approx}')
```

Solution to Exercise 3.6

Program 3.22: Asking for continuation   pi-yesno.py

```
1   # computes approximations of pi
2   import math
3
4   more = 'yes' # we want to enter the loop at least once
5   while more == 'yes':
6       v = 0
7       n = int(input('# of iterations, please:'))
8       n_inputs = 1
9       while n < 0:
10          if n_inputs < 3:
11              print('Bad input, positive or 0 please.')
12              n = int(input('# of iterations, please:'))
13              n_inputs += 1
14          else:
15              print('Too many bad inputs. Now using a default value.')
16              n = 10
17      for i in range(1,n+1):
18          v = v + (1/i)**2
19      pi_approx = math.sqrt(6*v)
20      print(f'After {n} iterations, pi≈{pi_approx}')
21      more = input('Continue (yes/no)? ')
```

Solution to Exercise 3.7

Program 3.23: Validation loop using a break   pi-yesnobreak.py

```
1   # computes approximations of pi
2   import math
3
4   while True:                                  # A never ending loop?
```

3.9 Solutions to Exercises

```
5     n = int(input('# of iterations, please:'))
6     n_inputs = 1
7     while n < 0:
8         if n_inputs < 3:
9             print('Bad input, positive or 0 please.')
10            n = int(input('# of iterations, please:'))
11            n_inputs += 1
12        else:
13            print('Too many bad inputs. Now using a default value.')
14            n = 10
15    v = 0
16    for i in range(1,n+1):
17        v += (1/i)**2
18    pi_approx = math.sqrt(6*v)
19    print(f'After {n} iterations, pi≈{pi_approx}')
20    if input('Continue (yes/no)? ') == 'no': # break ?
21        break
22 print('Bye...')
```

What may surprise the reader is the `while True` loop. Such a loop is a very standard idiom in programming. Of course, a true never-ending loop is very rare; here we just want to express that:

- basically we want to iterate an unknown number of times,
- the stopping condition will be determined inside the loop and the loop is broken using a break.

Another solution would be to use a `for` loop for the input validation:

Program 3.24: Loops and break   pi-yesnobreak2.py

```
1  # computes approximations of pi
2  import math
3
4  while True:                                 # A never ending loop?
5      n = 10                                  # default value
6      for i in range(3):                      # max 3 times...
7          inp = int(input('# of iterations, please:'))
8          if inp>=0:                          # break if ok
9              n = inp
10             break
11         print('Bad input, positive or 0 please.')
12     v = 0
13     for i in range(1,n+1):
14         v = v + (1/i)**2
```

```
15      pi_approx = math.sqrt(6*v)
16      print(f'After {n} iterations, pi≈{pi_approx}')
17      if input('Continue (yes/no)? ') == 'no':    # break ?
18          break
19  print('Bye...')
```

Solution to Exercise 3.8

The bad value is produced with the `while`. We replace:

```
1  for i in range(a,b):
2      do_something
```

with:

```
1  i = a
2  while i < b:
3      do_something
4      i += 1
```

But at the end of the while, variable i equals to b. A more correct implementation (in this exact case) could be:

```
1  i = a
2  while i < b:
3      do_something
4      i += 1
5  i -= 1 # reconstruct the last ''correct'' value...
```

Functions and Recursion 4

Factorisation is a very common process in Mathematics. The idea is to write or define something once to be reused as needed. One may think about how we write complex proofs of theorem: we use definitions, lemmas, etc., many intermediate things to ease the writing and the reading (the verification) of the theorem.

One should know that there is a correspondence in between logical proofs and programs. This is known as the Curry-Howard isomorphism from the mathematician Haskell Brooks Curry and the logician William Alvin Howard. In programming, factorisation takes place with the help of functions. As program variables very roughly looks like mathematical variables, program functions are roughly like mathematical functions. In programs, functions may not be pure, they can have side effects.

4.1 Functions

A **function** is a block of instructions that is executed as-needed when called. Data can be transmitted to a function that can, in return give some data back. These mechanisms of pushing and getting data in/from function are known as **parameter passing** and **returning value**.

Let's take an example. Suppose, given $n, k \in \mathbb{N}$ that we need to compute the **binomial**:

$$\binom{n}{k} = \frac{n!}{k!\,(n-k)!}$$

© The Author(s), under exclusive license to Springer Nature Switzerland AG 2024
R. Mantaci, J.-B. Yunès, *Basics of Programming and Algorithms,*
Principles and Applications, Compact Textbooks in Mathematics,
https://doi.org/10.1007/978-3-031-59801-2_4

Of course, we can write a portion of code that computes the factorial for a given number, then copy-paste it and modify the copy to adapt it to the local needs:

Program 4.1: Binomial   binomial.py

```
 1  # Binomial (with cut-n-paste)
 2
 3  n = int(input("n="))
 4  k = int(input("k="))
 5
 6  n_fact = 1              # n!
 7  for i in range(1,n+1):
 8      n_fact *= i
 9
10  k_fact = 1              # k!
11  for i in range(1,k+1):
12      k_fact *= i
13
14  nk_fact = 1             # (n-k)!
15  for i in range(1,n-k+1):
16      nk_fact *= i
17
18  cnk = n_fact//(k_fact*nk_fact)
19  print(f"C({n},{k})={cnk}")
```

We can easily imagine that is very inefficient in terms of reading and writing, and worst, if the first definition is wrong, we then copied multiple times that bad definition. In case we want to correct the problem, we have to remember exactly where the copies are. In our example, we can observe that the range used in for loops could start at 2 for instance, we then need to make that correction at three different places.

We just prefer to define a new function that computes the **factorial** of a given value and use it when needed:

Program 4.2: Binomial using function   binomialfunction.py

```
 1  # Binomial with a definition to compute n!
 2
 3  def fact(v):
 4      f = 1
 5      for i in range(1,v+1):
 6          f *= i
 7      return f
 8
 9  n = int(input("n="))
```

4.1 Functions

```
10  k = int(input("k="))
11
12  cnk = fact(n) // ( fact(k) * fact(n-k) )
13  print(f"C({n},{k})={cnk}")
```

A function definition begins with def identifier(...)::; note the : (colon) at the end. Immediately after, there is a indented block of statements: the instructions of the function, that will be executed when needed. Without any surprise, looking at line 12, we can deduce that an expression like fact(n) will compute the factorial of n. Such a statement is a **function call**. The **function call** fac(n) executes the block of the code defined with def fact(v) in the following manner:

1. at the call point, the expression in parenthesis is evaluated (in this case the value of the simple expression n);
2. a **variable** (**parameter**) v is created and assigned to the value obtained at the call point;
3. statements in the definition are executed accordingly to their semantics until a return statement is encountered; If the end of the block is reached the function exits immediately, just like with an empty return (see the next point).
4. the expression just after return is evaluated, the execution of the block terminates and the control returns back to the call point replacing the call point with the returned value. If the return statement is empty (no expression on its right), the special None value is returned.

The general definition of a function has the following pattern:

Program 4.3: Definition of a function

```
1  def identifier(parameter_list):
2      block_of_the_function
```

The (possibly empty) *parameter_list* is a list of identifiers separated by , (comma). The *block_of_the_function* may be as arbitrary as possible and may contains return statements.

4.1.1 Parameters

Note that parameter v in Program 4.19 is a **bound (local) variable**. That means:

bound because its name is of no interest outside the function, it is an identifier used to catch the value of the expression given at the call point. Bound as in mathematics where $x \mapsto x^2$ is the exact same function as $y \mapsto y^2$.

local because this variable has the **lifetime** of a call and no existence outside it. It is created when control enters the function and destroyed on returning.

A function may have any number of parameters, even no parameter at all:

Program 4.4: Several parameters — funcparam.py

```
1  def add(a, b):
2      return a+b
3
4  def hello():
5      print('Hello')
6
7  hello()
8  c = add(3,5)
9  hello()
10 print(c)
```

Note that the function call must provide as much values as the parameter list of the definition specifies. There can be other possibilities, like functions with unbounded number of parameters, but we will not describe this in this book.

4.1.2 Local Variables

The variable f which appears in the block of the function fact in Program 4.19 is also a **bound (local) variable**, as the parameter v is. That means that this variable does not exists outside this block. Its purpose is to catch intermediate results inside the function; it is an inner mechanism not to be revealed outside. It is created at the time it is first used, and disappears when the function call exits:

REPL 4.1: Local variable

```
1  >>> def my_func(v):
2  ...     a = 5
3  ...     return a
4  ...
5  >>> my_func(100)
6  5
7  >>> a
8  Traceback (most recent call last):
9    File ``<stdin>'', line 1, in <module>
10 NameError: name 'a' is not defined
```

Variable a is confined in the function. This is called **variable lifetime**.

4.1.3 Returning a Value

We sometimes distinguish **function** and **procedure**. A **function** computes a value while a **procedure** does something as a side effect. For example:

math.sin is a function that computes and then returns the sinus of a given angle,
print   is a procedure, it returns no value, it has a side effect (display something on the output).

When we want to return from a procedure we may use a simple `return` statement:

Program 4.5: A procedure   procedure.py

```
1  def my_print(v):
2      print("The value is:",v)
3      return
4
5  my_print(666)
```

For a function we can use a `return value` statement:

Program 4.6: A function returning a value   function.py

```
1  def my_add(a,b,c):
2      return a+b+c
3
4  v = my_add(6,60,600)
5  print(v)
```

Exercise 4.1
We already proposed to compute an approximation of π (see Exercise 2.8 for example).
Write a program that uses a function to compute the n-th approximation of π and another one to get input from the user.
Use those functions to let the user chose any value for n, compute the appropriate approximation if this value is not nul, and stop the program when this value is 0.

4.1.4 Error Handling

Handling errors is a difficult task, mainly because there are many kinds of errors. We do not want to dig too much on that problem but at least give some basic solutions.

An example could be to try to implement the function $\frac{1}{x}$. As we know, it is not defined for $x = 0$ so we have to make something in the case the user of the function calls it with 0. Of course we can stop the execution suddenly by calling `quit`:

Program 4.7: Stop in case of bad input   badinput.py

```python
def inverse(x):
    if x==0:
        print("Wrong parameter")
        quit()
    return 1/x

v = int(input("Give me a value:"))
print(inverse(v))
```

But that may not be a good choice because the caller could be very surprised that the callee stopped the program. The caller may want use a fallback strategy in case it is impossible to compute the requested value. That solution puts too much burden on the implementor of the function: what to do in case of error? Think about that:

> When the oil level gets too low does an engine stop? No! A light comes on the dashboard so that the driver is able to take the right decision.

A better choice is then to return None value and let the caller take the problem into account:

Program 4.8: Error handling with None   nonereturn.py

```python
def inverse(x):
    if x==0:
        return None
    return 1/x

v = int(input("Give me a value: "))
inverse_v = inverse(v)
if inverse_v==None:
    print("Something's wrong, fallback to...")
else:
    print(inverse_v)
```

Another solution is to return a tuple as we will see in Sect. 5.1.1.1.

4.1.5 Exception Handling

Exception handling is a special kind of error handling. We already encountered exceptions, remember what happened when we tried to convert a string that do not represent an int to an int value as in the following:

REPL 4.2: Exception not catched

```
1  >>> i = int(input("Give me a number please: "))
2  Give me a number please: gfd
3  Traceback (most recent call last):
4    File "<stdin>", line 1, in <module>
5  ValueError: invalid literal for int() with base 10: 'gfd'
```

That mechanism is a little bit complex and mastering it is out the scope of this book. We just want to give elementary solution to tackle exceptions.

An **exception** is a kind of an alarm. When something is very bad, so that the normal computation cannot be continued, an alarm (an exception) is emitted (thrown) and the normal flow of the execution is interrupted. At this point, PYTHON search for a block of code that declares to be able to take (catch) that alarm in account. If there is not such catching block, execution ends with a message.

The general form of exception handling is through `try-except` blocks:

Program 4.9: Try-except block

```
1  try:
2      #block to execute that may throw an exception
3  except:
4      #bloc to execute in case an exception is thrown
```

`try` means: try to execute the nested block. In the case a exception is thrown in that block, the execution of the block is immediately interrupted and an `except` block is searched to be executed. If the try block is executed without any exception up to its end, the except block is ignored.

In our small preceding example we can then set a default value in case the user input something wrong:

Program 4.10: Example of a try-except

```
1  try:
2      i = int(input("Please, give me a number: "))
3  except:
4      i = 0
5  print(i)
```

4.1.6 Closure

An identifier not used as a parameter or as a local one can be referenced in a function, but needs to be bound to some variable existing "outside" the function. A **closure** or **lexical closure** is the binding of the **free variables** used in a function to its environment.

4.1.6.1 Reading a Variable "Outside"
A function can use variables defined outside of it, provided we only access them for reading:

Program 4.11: Closure   closure1.py

```
1  my_var = 666
2
3  def my_func(v):
4          return my_var+v
5
6  print(my_func(0))
7  print(my_func(333))
```

An execution will lead to:

```
1  666
2  999
```

The function `my_func` is bound to the variable `my_var` which is defined outside it. We insist that in this case, only reading the variable is admitted (to modify the variable see the next section). We say that `my_var` is in the closure of `my_func`.

While it is authorised to do so, it is recommended to avoid as much as possible to define such functions:

- that leads to functions that may behave differently depending on the call point, producing programs very hard to read and understand. Such functions are then far away from mathematical functions that always maps the same value given the same entries.

Program 4.12: Effect of a closure   closure2.py

```
1  my_var = 666
2
3  def my_func(v):
4          return my_var+v
5
6  print(my_func(0))
```

4.1 Functions

```
7  my_var = 333
8  print(my_func(0))
```

which leads to:

```
1  666
2  333
```

Same call, different values...

Try to never define context dependent functions (unless you know why you need it), or you will have serious problem at some point. Prefer the definition of **pure functions** (functions that do not depend on something "outside").

- it leads to functions that depend on the existence of some external things to be able to run correctly.

Program 4.13: Context dependent   closure3.py

```
1  def my_func(v):
2          return my_var+v
3
4  print(my_func(0))
5  my_var = 333
6  print(my_func(0))
```

which leads to an error:

```
1  Traceback (most recent call last):
2    File ".../closure3.py", line 4, in <module>
3      print(my_func(0))
4    File ".../closure3.py", line 2, in my_func
5      return my_var+v
6  NameError: name 'my_var' is not defined
```

my_func depends on the existence of my_var but the function is called before that variable exists!

4.1.6.2 Modifying a Variable "Outside"

We saw that reading a variable defined outside the function is possible without any effort. If we want to modify a variable in the closure then we need to specify it:

Program 4.14: Modifying a global variable   global.py

```
1  my_var = 10
2  def f():
3      global my_var
4      my_var += 1
5
6  print(my_var)
7  f()
8  print(my_var)
```

which produces:

```
1  10
2  11
```

If we do not specify `global`, then PYTHON will assume that it should be a local variable, but since this variable is not yet defined locally it complains:

Program 4.15: Bad usage of variable in closure   globbad.py

```
1  my_var = 10
2  def f():
3      my_var += 1
4
5  print(my_var)
6  f()
7  print(my_var)
```

produces at execution:

```
1  10
2  Traceback (most recent call last):
3    File "/Users/yunes/TeX/book/AlgoProg/book/examples/globbad.py", ▷
         ▷ line 6, in <module>
4      f()
5    File "/Users/yunes/TeX/book/AlgoProg/book/examples/globbad.py", ▷
         ▷ line 3, in f
6      my_var += 1
7  UnboundLocalError: local variable 'my_var' referenced before ▷
         ▷ assignment
```

The message seems misleading as there exists a variable `my_var`. That variable is defined outside, and inside the function we tried to modify a variable (without declaring `my_var` as global), so PYTHON just says that such a variable is missing.

4.1.7 Variable Hiding

If a local variable uses the same identifier as a variable defined in the closure, the former hides the latter. If we don't use variables in the closure then this is not a problem:

Program 4.16: Local hides global   globallocal.py

```
1  n = 10
2  print(n)
3
4  def a_function():
5      n = 666
6      print(n)
7
8  a_function()
9  print(n)
```

which leads to:

```
1  10
2  666
3  10
```

4.1.8 Documenting a Function

It is recommended to **document** a function so that its users can have information about its correct usage. To do so, we just have to insert as the first line of the block a **docstring**. A docstring is either an ordinary string or a text delimited by """ (triplet of double quotes) if the documentation is long. Here we use the REPL mode to get the help of a documented function:

REPL 4.3: Documenting a function

```
1  >>> def my_func(v):
2  ...     """this function returns the
3  ...     square of its parameter v"""
4  ...     return v*v
5  ...
6  >>> help(my_func)
7  Help on function my_func in module __main__:
8
9  my_func(v)
10     this function returns the square of its parameter v
```

4.2 Modules

Functions help the writing of programs by decomposing definitions as reusable and parametrisable portions of code. We sometimes want to reuse functions across different programs. The solution is to make **modules** containing functions. A **module**, in its simple form, is just a source file containing only functions (that could be much more complex, but we will not talk about this in this book).

Suppose we want to compute the n-th approx of e (Euler's number) using the infinite series due to Leonhard Euler himself:

$$e = \sum_{k=0}^{\infty} \frac{1}{k!}$$

We can write a module containing the definition of the computation of the series up to a parameter N:

$$e_N = \sum_{k=0}^{k=N} \frac{1}{k!}$$

and use it in another module (the main one).

We first define a module containing our function:

Program 4.17: Module of approximation functions — approx.py

```
import math

def e_approx(n):
    e = 0
    for i in range(0,n+1):
        e += 1/math.factorial(i)
    return e
```

and use it in another source file:

Program 4.18: Main module using external functions — e-approx.py

```
import approx

print(approx.e_approx(50))
```

As we can see, a module is nothing more than a collection of function definitions.[1] As the function e_approx needs the `factorial` function of the module math, we simply import the math module.

In the main program (the one we execute), we need to use the function e_approx defined externally in the module approx whose source file is named approx.py). So we need to import it. That is the purpose of the directive import, to import all definitions of the module.

One has to note that functions defined in a module are contextualised by the module, that means that the function e_approx of the module approx has as its real name approx.e_approx.

Exercise 4.2
Define a module (series) that contains two functions, one to approximate π and another one to approximate e for a given parameter n using previously defined series.
Write a program (pieapprox) that wait the user to input a value and then computes both the approximations of π and e.

Exercise 4.3
Rewrite the previous program such that the function which gets input from the user is in a module userinput.
Also parametrise the function such that one can choose the number of tries before returning a default value also given as a parameter.

4.3 More on Parameters

4.3.1 Default Values

Suppose we need to compute cosine of angles expressed in radians, degrees or gradians. A first solution could be to define three different functions:

Program 4.19: Cosines for different units   angles.py

```
1  import math
2
3  def cosine_radian(a):
4      "eats angles in radians"
5      return math.cos(a)
6
7  def cosine_degree(a):
8      "eats angles in degrees"
9      return math.cos(a/180*math.pi)
10
```

---
[1] It can be much more complex, but this is out of scope of this book.

```
11  def cosine_gradian(a):
12      "eats angles in gradians"
13      return math.cos(a/200*math.pi)
14
15
16  print(cosine_radian(math.pi/4))
17  print(cosine_degree(45))
18  print(cosine_gradian(50))
```

Another way could be to factorise this into a single function by introducing another parameter that represents the unit:

Program 4.20: Cosine for different units   angles1.py

```
1   import math
2
3   def cosine(angle,unit):
4       """unit: 1: radians, 2: degrees, 3: gradians"""
5       if unit == 1:
6           return math.cos(angle)
7       if unit == 2:
8           return math.cos(angle/180*math.pi)
9       if unit == 3:
10          return math.cos(angle/200*math.pi)
11      print("Bad unit for angle")
12      quit()
13
14
15  print(cosine(math.pi/4,1))
16  print(cosine(45,2))
17  print(cosine(50,3))
```

As radians is the standardised unit of the International System of Units, it is likely we mostly all the time call it as `cosine(angle,1)`, which may be considered painful. PYTHON let us define default values for parameters:

Program 4.21: Parameter default value   angles2.py

```
1   import math
2
3   def cosine(angle,unit=1):
4       "cosine of the angle expressed in radians (1), degrees (2), ▷
              ▷ gradians (3)"
5       if unit == 1:
6           return math.cos(angle)
```

4.3 More on Parameters

```
7      if unit == 2:
8          return math.cos(angle/180*math.pi)
9      if unit == 3:
10         return math.cos(angle/200*math.pi)
11     print("Bad unit for angle")
12     quit()
13
14
15 print(cosine(math.pi/4))
16 print(cosine(45,2))
17 print(cosine(50,3))
```

We introduced a default value for the last parameter by defining the function as `def cosine(angle, unit=1)`. Thus we can also call the function giving only one parameter, the second one is then defaulted to 1, i.e. `cosine(some_value)` is equivalent to `cosine(some_value,1)`.

We cannot define default values at random places, it is mandatory that the list of parameters begins with the list of non defaulted parameters and ends with the list of defaulted parameter. It is possible that there is no non-defaulted or no defaulted parameter lists. Thus `def f(a=1,b)` is forbidden. If default values are defined when calling the function, missing values are always completed to the right: `def f(a,b=1,c=2)` is callable in three ways:

- `f(4)` will generate a call to `f(4,1,2)`;
- `f(4,56)` will generate a call to `f(4,56,2)`;
- `f(4,56,78)` will generate a call to `f(4,56,78)`.

4.3.2 Positional and Keyword Arguments

We used variables to capture values passed at a function call. The calls we previously made use **positional arguments**, which means that values passed are orderly mapped to the parameter list (first value to first parameter, second to second, etc.). We can use identifiers to name parameters at the call point, in this case the ordering at the call point is no more mandatory:

Program 4.22: Keyword arguments   kargs.py

```
1  import math
2
3  def cosine(angle,unit):
4      if unit == 1:
5          return math.cos(angle)
6      if unit == 2:
```

```
7        return math.cos(angle/180*math.pi)
8    if unit == 3:
9        return math.cos(angle/200*math.pi)
10   print("error")
11   quit()
12
13 print(cosine(unit=3,angle=50))
```

4.4 Recursion

Recursion is the most powerful tool in programming, as we mentioned in the introduction of this chapter, that is what makes its computational power. That does not mean that without recursion programs are trivial; it just means that from the point of view of theoretical computer science we can compute a larger set of functions if we use recursion.

Loops are just special patterns of recursion, which every programming language offers to ease the design of programs. As we will see, basic loops (for, while) are more convenient in many cases. **Recursion** is sometimes defined as (excerpt from Wikipedia):

> Recursion occurs when the definition of a concept or process depends on a simpler version of itself. [...] The most common application of recursion is in mathematics and computer science, where a function being defined is applied within its own definition. While this apparently defines an infinite number of instances (function values), it is often done in such a way that no infinite loop or infinite chain of references ("crock recursion") can occur.

A basic iterative definition of factorial is:

$$n! = \prod_{k=1}^{k=n} k, \text{ with } 0! = 1$$

That definition is easily translated into the following PYTHON code:

Program 4.23: Factorial as iteration   fact.py

```
1 def fact(n):
2     f = 1
3     for i in range(1,n+1):
4         f *= i
5     return f
6
7 for i in range(0,11):  # A simple loop to test several calls
8     print(f"{i}!={fact(i)}")
```

4.4 Recursion

We already said that `for` loop is an iteration.
We also know that a definition of factorial could be:

$$n! = n \times (n-1)!, \text{ with } 0! = 1, n \geq 1$$

That is a **recursive** definition of it, a definition that uses itself. We also easily translated it in PYTHON like this:

Program 4.24: Factorial as recursion   factrec.py

```
1  def fact(n):
2      if n == 0:
3          return 1
4      return n * fact(n-1)
5
6  for i in range(0,11):    # a simple loop to test several calls
7      print(f"{i}!={fact(i)}")
```

There is no restriction on calling a function. We can call a function everywhere it is defined, even in the body of its definition.

We have to be very careful with recursive functions. A call to such a function can call that function too, and that is fine. In some way, we have a kind of *snake bitting its own tail*. A vicious circle that needs to be broken at some point, if not we will have a never ending computation (a thing we need to avoid at least when talking about algorithms—see Part II). Let's see what happens:

Program 4.25: Bad recursion   viciouscircle.py

```
1  def fact(n):
2      return n*fact(n-1)
3
4  print(fact(10))
```

An execution will produce:

```
1  Traceback (most recent call last):
2    File "/Users/yunes/TeX/book/AlgoProg/book/examples/viciouscircle.py▷
         ▷ ", line 4, in <module>
3      print(fact(10))
4    File "/Users/yunes/TeX/book/AlgoProg/book/examples/viciouscircle.py▷
         ▷ ", line 2, in fact
5      return n*fact(n-1)
6    File "/Users/yunes/TeX/book/AlgoProg/book/examples/viciouscircle.py▷
         ▷ ", line 2, in fact
7      return n*fact(n-1)
8    File "/Users/yunes/TeX/book/AlgoProg/book/examples/viciouscircle.py▷
         ▷ ", line 2, in fact
```

```
9       return n*fact(n-1)
10  [Previous line repeated 996 more times]
11  RecursionError: maximum recursion depth exceeded
```

A call to fact(10), generates a call to fact(9) which in turn calls fact(8), ..., fact(0), fact(-1), etc. There is no stopping condition! PYTHON generates an error, saying that RecursionError: maximum recursion depth exceeded after the 1000-th recursive call. That can be changed as we will see a little bit later. But why PYTHON arbitrarily stops the recursion at the 1000-th recursive call? Answer is "Recursion is powerful but dangerous" so PYTHON tries to protect us against abuse of recursion.

Recursion is powerful because some functions cannot be handled with for loops. Functions that can be expressed with only for loops where we know an upper bound for the iterations are called **primitive recursive functions** (see [18]). Even if some functions can be expressed with for loop, it is sometime much more convenient or simple to write them in their recursive form. Alas, some functions are not recursive primitive. The simplest example is the Ackermann function due to the mathematician and logician Wilhelm Friedrich Ackermann (see [1]). It is a function that is computable[2] but cannot be computed with bounded for loops:

$$\begin{cases} A(0, n) & = n + 1 \\ A(m + 1, 0) & = A(m, 1) \\ A(m + 1, n + 1) & = A(m, A(m + 1, n)) \end{cases}$$

Recursion is dangerous because it consumes memory too easily and computers have finite amount of memory. To understand why memory is consumed, let us analyse the way a computer can tackle **function calls**. First remark, an iteration loop in itself does consume some memory but only a finite slight amount of it, roughly only for the control variable. The loop for i in range(a,b) is roughly like:

```
1  i = a
2  while i<b:
3      ...
4      i += 1
```

Only one variable to control the loop, thus a small finite amount of memory.
A call to a function consume memory in two ways:

- every parameter is realised as a variable on a call. Remember that on a call, parameters are created and, when returning parameters are destroyed.

---

[2] Informally, a computable function is a function that can be realised in a computer and produces a result on any input in a finite amount of time. There exists non computable functions, for example the one that determines if a given program stops or not on a given input. This is known as the Halting Problem, Alan Turing proved that it has no solution as an algorithm, see [19].

4.4 Recursion

- calls can appear at any place in a program, thus it is necessary to remember the place where the call took place to be able to return back to then same place when the code of the function returns.

Thus in a recursive function call, for example with fact, we first call fact(i) from some place (inside print of line 7 of Program 4.38), and then we have to remind where this call is to be able to return at that exact place after the computation to finally execute print. But inside this call we call fact(n-1) (inside line 4 of Program 4.38), so we need to remember that place to be able to compute $n \times$ the returned value of fact(n − 1). Inside this call we call fact(n-1) again (with another value of n of course), etc.

The data structure behind this is a **stack** (as we will see later in Sect. 5.2.4.1). A stack behaves like a pile (stack) of plates: storing plates on top (storing the return point on top) and removing plates from the top (get return point from the top).

Then, we can see that a recursive function consume more memory each time it calls itself. So if there is no break in a recursion not only this function will never end but in practice the computer will consume more and more memory, until exhaustion. This phenomenon is called **stack overflow**. This is why PYTHON tries to protect us against memory exhaustion on recursion. By default, PYTHON considers that after 1000 recursive calls there is a doubt that the recursion will end. Beware, that is just a guess PYTHON makes, their designers could have chosen 2000 or 10,000. PYTHON is not able to analyse your program and see if there is such bugs as "never ending loops", etc., (in fact there is no program able to determine if any given program given will stop or not).

So, at least, we need to break the recursion at some point. The mathematical property behind this is that arguments on which the recursion takes place must be in a well-founded relation. If most of the cases, recursion takes place with a single integer descending argument, any well-founded relation is usable.

In our previous example, the recursive mathematical definition has a terminal case:

$$\begin{cases} 0! = 1 \\ n! = n \times (n-1)! \end{cases}$$

This is why we first test for terminal case $0! = 1$ (to ensure the recursion will end at some point) and then make the recursive call (to make the whole recursion of the function to apply).

If needed, we can change PYTHON's maximum recursion depth. Again, we must think twice, and a lot of care should be applied with recursion:

Program 4.26: Recursion limit in Python — factrec2.py

```
1  import sys
2
3
```

```
4    def fact(n):
5        if n == 0:
6            return 1
7        return n * fact(n-1)
8
9    sys.setrecursionlimit(3000)
10   for i in range(2000,2300):
11       print(f"{i}!={fact(i)}")
```

Exercise 4.4
Write a recursive function to compute e_n as defined in Sect. 4.2.
Write a program to test it for many different values of n.

Exercise 4.5
Write a program that asks the user to input a number in decimal and then writes its binary representation (for example 37 $\longrightarrow$ '100101') using recursion.

Exercise 4.6
Write a function that calculates the Ackermann function.
Caution: Do not to try to get answer for high values of the parameters. Especially for values of $m \geq 4$, for which the values of the function are so huge that it defies our imagination. Just try $A(2, 50)$ or $A(3, 30)$.

Exercise 4.7
Find the minimum of a list using recursion: find element of the first half and the minimum of the second half, then return the minimum of both. That method is sometimes called the **tournament method**.
Modify it so that both the minimum and the maximum of the list are returned at the end.
If you need random elements to fill a list, you can then use the module random and the function randint.

Exercise 4.8
Write a program that asks the user to input a positive integer n and generates the n first rows of the Pascal triangle modulo 2. Pascal triangle modulo 2 is defined as:

$$P_{i,n} = \begin{cases} 1, & \text{if } i = 0 \text{ and } n = 0 \\ 0, & \text{if } i \neq 0 \text{ and } n = 0 \\ (P_{i,n-1} + P_{i+1,n-1}) \bmod 2, & \text{else} \end{cases}$$

For $n = 30$ it looks like (where character '1' is replaced by 'X' and '0' as a space for better visual effect):

```
X
XX
X X
XXXX
X   X
XX  XX
X X X X
XXXXXXXX
X       X
XX      XX
```

```
X X     X X
XXXX    XXXX
X   X   X   X
XX XX  XX XX
X X X X X X X X
XXXXXXXXXXXXXXXX
X               X
XX              XX
X X             X X
XXXX            XXXX
X   X           X   X
XX XX           XX XX
X X X X         X X X X
XXXXXXXX        XXXXXXXX
X       X       X       X
XX      XX      XX      XX
X X     X X     X X     X X
XXXX    XXXX    XXXX    XXXX
X   X   X   X   X   X   X   X
XX XX  XX XX   XX XX   XX XX
X X X X X X X X X X X X X X X X
XXXXXXXXXXXXXXXXXXXXXXXXXXXXXXXX
```

(**hard**) Observing what is "drawn", write a program that generates (for $n = 2^p$) the same picture using recursion on elementary patterns.

Hint: recurse using the "rewriting rule" P$\to \dfrac{\text{P}}{\text{PP}}$

4.4.1 Loops vs Recursion

Any loop can be translated into recursion. For example a loop like:

```
for i in range(a,b):
    block of code
```

can be translated into the recursive function:

```
def for_loop(current_iteration,last):
    if current_iteration==last:
        return
    block of code
    for_loop(current_iteration+1,last)

for_loop(a,b)
```

Note that this translating schema does not tackle the way a result is built and returned. That gives only the general idea of translating any for loop into a recursion.

If any for loop is translatable into a recursion, the converse is false (Ackermann's function is a counterexample). Anyway, some recursion schemes can be easily translated into for loops, they are known as **tail recursive functions**.[3] The translated

---

[3] A recursive function is tail recursive if the recursive call is the last instruction executed in the current call. Tail recursion means "the recursive call is at the tail".

recursive function that mimics the for loop is tail recursive, i.e. for_loop is called as the last instruction of the definition block of for_loop. So, that surely could be reverted as a for loop. Some compilers and interpreters are able to unfold tail recursion to for loops.

Anyway, recursion is a more general tool than for loops. On the contrary a while loops (with the help of a stack) can be used to emulate recursion. Recursion in itself could have been the only given tool in a programming language, but in practice that would lead to a too rude programming language. This is why, so often, for and while loops are also available, to capture simple recursion cases in a more convenient way. Readers may be interested by the link in between recursion and fixed-point theory (see [18]).

Exercise 4.9
Using the given translation schema, rewrite the program that computes the factorial using a for loop to a program that uses a recursion.

Hint: recursion goes bottom-up and not top-down like in the mathematical definition.

Exercise 4.10
Construct the translation of a while loop into a recursive function.

4.5 Solutions to Exercises

Solution to Exercise 4.1

Program 4.27: With functions   pi-func.py

```
1  # computes approximations of pi
2  import math
3
4  def approx_pi(n):
5      v = 0
6      for i in range(1,n+1):
7          v = v + (1/i)**2
8      return math.sqrt(6*v)
9
10 def get_value_from_user():
11     n = int(input('# of iterations, please:'))
12     n_inputs = 1
13     while n < 0:
14         if n_inputs < 3:                    # try at most 3 times
15             print('Bad input, positive or 0 please.')
16             n = int(input('# of iterations, please:'))
17             n_inputs += 1                   # one more user input
```

4.5 Solutions to Exercises

```
18      else:                          # no good input, default▷
                   ▷ value then
19          print('Too many bad inputs. Now using a default value.')
20          n = 10
21      return n
22
23  n = get_value_from_user()
24  pi_approx = approx_pi(n)
25  print(f'After {n} iterations, pi approximatively equals to {pi_approx▷
           ▷ }')
```

Solution to Exercise 4.2

Program 4.28: Module of series for π and e series.py

```
1   import math
2
3   def e_approx(n):
4       e = 0
5       for i in range(0,n+1):
6           e += 1/math.factorial(i)
7       return e
8
9   def pi_approx(n):
10      v = 0
11      for i in range(1,n+1):
12          v = v + (1/i)**2
13      return math.sqrt(6*v)
```

Program 4.29: Program to compute n-th approximation of π and e pieapprox.py

```
1   import series
2
3   def get_user_input():
4       n = int(input('# of iterations, please:'))
5       n_inputs = 1
6       while n < 0:
7           if n_inputs < 3:               # try at most 3 times
8               print('Bad input, positive or 0 please.')
9               n = int(input('# of iterations, please:'))
10              n_inputs += 1              # one more user input
```

```
11      else:                           # no good input, default▷
                ▷ value then
12          print('Too many bad inputs. Now using a default value.')
13          n = 10
14    return n
15
16  n = get_user_input()
17  print(f"{n}-th approximation of pi is {series.pi_approx(n)}")
18  print(f"{n}-th approximation of e is {series.e_approx(n)}")
```

Solution to Exercise 4.3

Program 4.30: Module to get user input   userinput.py

```
1   def get(max_input,default_value):
2       n = int(input('# of iterations, please:'))
3       n_inputs = 1
4       while n < 0:
5           if n_inputs < max_input:         # try at most 3 times
6               print('Bad input, positive or 0 please.')
7               n = int(input('# of iterations, please:'))
8               n_inputs += 1                # one more user input
9           else:                            # no good input, default▷
                    ▷ value then
10              print('Too many bad inputs. Now using a default value.')
11              n = default_value
12      return n
```

Module `series` is the one designed for Exercise 4.2.

Program 4.31: Program to compute n-th approximation of π and e
pieapprox1.py

```
1  import series
2  import userinput
3
4  n = userinput.get(3,10)
5  print(f"{n}-th approximation of pi is {series.pi_approx(n)}")
6  print(f"{n}-th approximation of e is {series.e_approx(n)}")
```

4.5 Solutions to Exercises

Solution to Exercise 4.5

Program 4.32: Binary representation of a decimal — binary.py

```
1  def binary_rep(n):
2      if n<2:
3          return "0" if n==0 else "1"
4      return binary_rep(n//2) + ("0" if n%2==0 else "1")
5
6
7  print(binary_rep(int(input("n? "))))
```

Solution to Exercise 4.7

Program 4.33: Tournament method for min and max — tour.py

```
1   import random
2
3   def tournament_aux(l, begin, end):
4       if begin==end-1:
5           return l[begin], l[begin]
6       mid = (begin+end)//2
7       min, max = tournament_aux(l, begin, mid)
8       minr, maxr = tournament_aux(l, mid, end)
9       if min > minr:
10          min = minr
11      if max < maxr:
12          max = maxr
13      return min, max
14
15  def tournament(l):
16      if len(l)==0:
17          return None, None
18      return tournament_aux(l, 0, len(l))
19
20  l = [random.randint(0,100) for i in range(20)]
21  print(l)
22  print(tournament(l))
```

Solution to Exercise 4.8

Program 4.34: Pascal triangle   pascal.py

```
1  def special_print(l):
2      for i in range(len(l)):
3          print(' ' if l[i]==0 else 'X',end='')
4      print()
5
6  def next_pascal_mod_2(l):
7      return [1]+[(l[i]+l[i+1])%2 for i in range(len(l)-1)]+[1]
8
9  def pascal_mod_2_aux(l,level):
10     if level==0:
11         return
12     special_print(l)
13     pascal_mod_2_aux(next_pascal_mod_2(l),level-1)
14
15 def pascal_mod_2(level):
16     pascal_mod_2_aux([1],level)
17
18 pascal_mod_2(int(input("n? ")))
```

Program 4.35: Pascal triangle by recursing on pattern   pascalpattern.py

```
1  n = int(input("n? "))
2  n = 2**n
3
4  def pascal_pattern(level):
5      if level==1:
6          return ["X"]              # elementary triangle
7      r = pascal_pattern(level//2)  # get a triangle
8      for i in range(len(r)):       # copy the triangle...
9          sep = " "*(level//2-len(r[i]))
10         r.append(r[i]+sep+r[i])   # ...twice with separators
11     return r
12
13 figure = pascal_pattern(n)
14
15 for l in figure:
16     print(l)
```

Solution to Exercise 4.9

Program 4.36: Factorial, iteration as recursion — `factrecsol.py`

```python
def fact_for_loop_rec(f,i,n):
    if i>n:
        return f
    return fact_for_loop_rec(f*i,i+1,n)

def fact_for_loop(n):
    return fact_for_loop_rec(1, 1,n)

for i in range(0,11):
    print(f"{i}!={fact_for_loop(i)}")
```

Data Structures 5

High-level programming languages offer several kind of data structures. PYTHON is not different. A **data structure** is a way to group data for both efficient storage and easy access/read/write to their elements. There is a wide range of data structures including: records, arrays, lists, trees, maps, graphs, etc.

We will mainly focus here on three data structures that PYTHON offers, namely:

records (also called **structures** or **tuples**) are aggregates of several data that may be of different type, each one accessible by an index or a label.
lists are ordered collections of data commonly of the same type, each one accessible by an index.
dictionaries are collections of non ordered (key,value) pairs. A value is accessible given its key.

At the end of this chapter we also discuss about **objects**. They belong to the field of **Object Oriented Programming** (OOP), a programming paradigm whose description is beyond the scope of the book. We will only provide basic notions of objects because they are very useful to implement easy-to-manage data structures like lists, trees or graphs.

5.1 Tuples

PYTHON native **tuples** are aggregation of values of possibly different types. A mathematician would say that tuples are elements of Cartesian products. Tuples are **immutable data structures**, i.e., represent values. That means that a tuple cannot be modified once built.

A **tuple** is a collection of values of any type each separated with , (commas) and possibly enclosed in parenthesis. To access the i-th element of the tuple, we can use the [] operator to index it (beware that in computer science, elements are always indexed starting from 0).

REPL 5.1: Tuples

```
1  >>> t = 34, 35, 99
2  >>> t
3  (34, 35, 99)
4  >>> card = (3, '♣')
5  >>> card
6  (3, '♣')
7  >>> card[1]
8  '♣'
9  >>> card[1] = "foo"
10 Traceback (most recent call last):
11   File "<stdin>", line 1, in <module>
12 TypeError: 'tuple' object does not support item assignment>>> t[0]="▷
     ▷ foo"
13 Traceback (most recent call last):
14   File "<stdin>", line 1, in <module>
15 TypeError: 'tuple' object does not support item assignment
```

Line 1 defines a tuple (in this case a triplet) associated to the identifier t. That could have been written as t=(34, 35, 99), with the help of parenthesis. Line 3 show that the canonical representation of tuples uses parenthesis. Line 4 shows that any value can be used in a tuple, and that the canonical representation can be used to specify a tuple. The constructed tuple is a pair of a number (3) and a character (club). Line 7 shows how we can extract element from a tuple using the operator [] and an integer index. Finally, line 9 exhibits the fact that tuples are **immutable** objects, trying to modify one of its element generates an error.

Special attention is needed for tuples of one element:

REPL 5.2: Tuples

```
1  >>> t=(5)
2  >>> t
3  5
4  >>> type(t)
5  <class 'int'>
6  >>> t=(5,)
7  >>> t
8  (5,)
9  >>> type(t)
10 <class 'tuple'>
```

Surprisingly, t=(5) does not define a tuple, it is a very common mistake. Syntax analysis has its mysteries, and designers of programming language have to choose among many options to disambiguate the interpretation of lines of code. To

5.1 Tuples

understand why this does not define a tuple, we must remember that t=(5) is the definition of a variable pairing an identifier t with the value of the expression (5). The expression (5) is an arithmetic expression as one can always use parenthesis to enclose such expression. Thus it evaluates to integer 5; this is not very different than writing (3+2) or 5.

If we want to express a tuple of only one element (singleton) we have to express our need by adding a comma: (5,). As it contains a comma, it is not a valid arithmetic expression and PYTHON interprets it as a tuple. The empty tuple is identified by ().

5.1.1 Tuples as Parameters or Return Value

Remember that tuples are values, i.e., that implies that passing a tuple to a function is just like passing any value, thus the catching parameter catches the value:

Program 5.1: Passing a tuple to a function   tupleasparameter.py

```
# passing a tuple

def my_func(t):
    t = (1,2,3)

my_tuple = ("ready","steady","go")
print(my_tuple)
my_func(my_tuple)
print(my_tuple)
```

whose execution produces:

```
('ready', 'steady', 'go')
('ready', 'steady', 'go')
```

At the call, the function catches the value associated to my_tuple and pair it with t, thus both identifiers refers to the same tuple. The instruction t=(1,2,3) changes the pairing of t, but this does not change anything to the initial pairing. This is the **call by value** semantic of parameter passing.

Without any surprise a function may return a tuple. For example:

Program 5.2: Return a tuple   tuplereturn.py

```
def reorder(t):
    if t[0]<t[1]:
        return t
    else:
```

```
5        return t[1],t[0]
6
7   print(reorder((3,4)))
8   print(reorder((4,3)))
```

which leads to:

```
1   (3, 4)
2   (3, 4)
```

5.1.1.1 Error Handling with Tuples

A possible approach to manage errors is to return a tuple and not a single value. That tuple is a pair made of:

value   the value of the result in case the computation was possible, or None if not;
error   None is no problem occurred during the execution of the function, or a value representing an error on the contrary.

Then we can solve the problem of Sect. 4.1.4 this way;

Program 5.3: Error handling with tuples   nonereturn2.py

```
1   def inverse(x):
2       if x==0:
3           return None, "Bad value 0"
4       return 1/x, None
5
6   v = int(input("Give me a value: "))
7   inverse_v, error = inverse(v)
8   while error!=None:
9       print("Wrong!", error)
10      v = int(input("Give me a value: "))
11      inverse_v, error = inverse(v)
12
13  print(inverse_v)
```

As we can see, the second member of the returned tuple is an error (None if no error) which we can test and take any decision we like depending on its value. Respective responsibilities are much clearly defined:

on the callee side: we can detect the incident to report it;
on the caller side: we can take any decision we want in case of a problem.

Observing Program 5.53 we can see that lines 6–7 are exactly the same as lines 10–11.

5.1 Tuples

As we already said, copying statements is always a bad idea. Then how to factorise this? PYTHON has a very special operator := (colon followed by equal sign is called the **Walrus operator**) that allows to make an assignment inside a condition (standard assignments are forbidden in conditions). Alas, we cannot use tuple destructuring with Walrus assignment, so we need to catch the whole tuple and get its element individually:

Program 5.4: Walrus operator   nonereturn3.py

```
1  def inverse(x):
2      return (1/x, None) if x!=0 else (None, "Bad value 0")
3
4  while (r:=inverse(int(input("Give me a value: ")))) and r[1]!=None:
5      # r is a tuple: (value,error)
6      print("Wrong!",r[1])      # print the error
7  print(r[0])                   # get the result
```

Please note how concise (albeit a bit cryptic for beginners) this code is, using both the Walrus operator and the conditional expression.

Exercise 5.1
Write a function compare that takes two pairs as arguments, compares them lexicographically and returns:

−1 if the first is less than the second,
 0 if they are equals
 1 if the first is greater than the second.

The lexicographic order on pairs is defined as:

- $(x, y) < (x', y') \iff x < x' \lor (x = x' \land y < y')$.
- $(x, y) = (x', y') \iff x = x' \land y = y'$.
- $(x, y) > (x', y') \iff x > x' \lor (x = x' \land y > y')$.

Test your program with several couples.

Exercise 5.2
Considering a triplet of floats as point in the 3D space, write a function compare that takes three such points and returns

−1 if the distance between the first and the third is smaller than distance between the second and the third,
 0 if first and second are at the same distance from the third,
 1 in other cases.

Distance can be the Euclidean distance. Test with different points.

Exercise 5.3
Modify the program obtained in Exercise 5.2 so that the return value also includes the closest point.

Hint: return a tuple!

5.1.2 Length of a Tuple

PYTHON has a versatile function called `len` that can be also used on many kind of data structures to get the number of elements in:

REPL 5.3: Length of a tuple

```
1  >>> t=4,5,6,7
2  >>> len(t)
3  4
4  >>> t=()
5  >>> len(t)
6  0
7  >>> t=5,
8  >>> len(t)
9  1
```

The function `len` is then usable to extract all elements of any tuple by the use of an index:

REPL 5.4: Extracting elements of a tuple

```
1  >>> def print_all(t):
2  ...     for i in range(len(t)):
3  ...         print(t[i])
4  ...
5  >>> singleton = (5,)
6  >>> triplet = (1, 2, 3)
7  >>> print_all(singleton)
8  5
9  >>> print_all(triplet)
10 1
11 2
12 3
```

Exercise 5.4
Modify the program obtained for Exercise 5.2 so that the `compare` function is able to compare points in any n-dimensional space.

5.1.3 Labeled Tuples

Elements of native tuples are not labeled but only indexed, however PYTHON provides a module named `collections` allowing to use labels in tuples:

REPL 5.5: Labeled tuples

```
1  >>> import collections
2  >>> Point = collections.namedtuple('Point2D','x y')
3  >>> p = Point(3,4)
4  >>> p
5  Point2D(x=3, y=4)
6  >>> p[0]
7  3
8  >>> p.x
9  3
10 >>> p.u
11 Traceback (most recent call last):
12   File "<stdin>", line 1, in <module>
13 AttributeError: 'Point2D' object has no attribute 'u'
```

As we already know, the first line imports all the definitions of the module `collections`, so that they can be used later. Line 2 is more complex and we will not explain everything, but the identifier `Point` now belongs to a new type of data whose name is `Point2D`. That type of data is a tuple (actually a pair) with two labels, respectively `x` and `y`. The identifier `Point` (with an upper case, as it denotes a type and not a standard variable) is used to construct values of the referred type, as in line 3. Line 4 shows what was constructed, a pair of two labeled values. Next lines show how to extract values from the tuple, either by index or by label. And the last try is to show that the use of non existing labels leads to errors.

Exercise 5.5
Create a labeled tuple so that each card will be of type `Card` and its elements are `value` and `suit`.
Write a function to compare cards (by their value) with clubs as trump cards.
Test with different cards.

5.2 Arrays/Lists

Technically, PYTHON's native types do not include the array type. This is due to the fact that arrays have many drawbacks. The main one is that they are not dynamic: it is not possible to add or remove elements from an array. PYTHON lists behave mostly like arrays (including in term of performance), so PYTHON only offers lists. By some abuse of language we sometimes use "array" to designate lists.

A list is a **mutable sequence**, that means that we can modify the values inside a list or add/remove elements.

To create a list we can use the following:

REPL 5.6: Lists

```
1  >>> a_list=[1,2,3]
2  >>> a_list
3  [1, 2, 3]
4  >>> a_list=["Hi",3,"Georgia",4.5]
5  >>> a_list
6  ['Hi', 3, 'Georgia', 4.5]
```

To construct a list we just simply list the values, separating them with , (commas), the whole enclosed in [] (brackets). An **empty list** can be defined by the simple expression [].

We can observe that elements of lists can be of any type, mixing everything we want. Even a list or tuple can be an element of a list:

REPL 5.7: More lists

```
1   >>> list_1=[2, 3, 4]
2   >>> list_2=[1, list_1, 5]
3   >>> list_2
4   [1, [2, 3, 4], 5]
5   >>> list_1
6   [2, 3, 4]
7   >>> list_2=[1, [2, 3, 4], 5]
8   >>> list_2
9   [1, [2, 3, 4], 5]
10  >>> t=("hi", "ciao")
11  >>> list=[1, 2, 3, t, 4, 5, 6]
12  >>> l
13  [1, 2, 3, ('hi', 'ciao'), 4, 5, 6]
```

It is important to say that lists are not values but objects. The consequences of this are detailed in Sect. 5.3.

5.2.1 List Concatenation

Two lists can be concatenated to get a new one by the use of the operator +:

REPL 5.8: Concatenation of lists

```
1  >>> list_1 = [1, 2, 3]
2  >>> l2ist_ = [10, 11, 12]
3  >>> list_1+list_2
4  [1, 2, 3, 10, 11, 12]
```

5.2 Arrays/Lists

Of course this operator is not commutative as it construct a list made of all elements of the first with all elements of the second.

There exists another way to construct a list with the help of the operator * which let duplicates a given list *n* times:

REPL 5.9: List repetition

```
1  >>> a_list=[1,2]
2  >>> a_list
3  [1, 2]
4  >>> a_list*10
5  [1, 2, 1, 2, 1, 2, 1, 2, 1, 2, 1, 2, 1, 2, 1, 2, 1, 2, 1, 2]
6  >>> 10*a_list
7  [1, 2, 1, 2, 1, 2, 1, 2, 1, 2, 1, 2, 1, 2, 1, 2, 1, 2, 1, 2]
```

We can observe that this operator is commutative, i.e. 1*n is equivalent to n*1. The last construction is a frequent practice to construct a list of a given length with elements initialised to a given value:

REPL 5.10: Initializing a long list

```
1  >>> a_list=[0]*100
2  >>> a_list
3  [0, 0, 0, 0, 0, 0, 0, 0, 0, 0, 0, 0, 0, 0, 0, 0, 0, 0, 0, 0, 0, 0,▷
   ▷ 0, 0, 0, 0, 0, 0, 0, 0, 0, 0, 0, 0, 0, 0, 0, 0, 0, 0, 0, 0, ▷
   ▷ 0, 0, 0, 0, 0, 0, 0, 0, 0, 0, 0, 0, 0, 0, 0, 0, 0, 0, 0, 0,▷
   ▷ 0, 0, 0, 0, 0, 0, 0, 0, 0, 0, 0, 0, 0, 0, 0, 0, 0, 0, 0, ▷
   ▷ 0, 0, 0, 0, 0, 0, 0, 0, 0, 0, 0, 0, 0, 0, 0]
```

There exists a third form of list construction as we will see in Sect. 5.5.

5.2.2 Access to Elements

A list is an ordered structure whose elements are indexed and can be accessed through their index (remember that computers always start counting from 0):

REPL 5.11: Accessing elements of a list

```
1  >>> l=["andy","bernie","charlie"]
2  >>> l[0]
3  'andy'
4  >>> l[3]
5  Traceback (most recent call last):
6    File "<stdin>", line 1, in <module>
7  IndexError: list index out of range
```

If there is no element at a given index (here 3 for example) an error stops the program with an appropriate message. The versatile function len can be used to get the number of elements in a list (as in a tuple or any other data structure):

REPL 5.12: Length of a list

```
>>> a_list=[1,2,3,4,"hi"]
>>> len(a_list)
5
```

We can then use it to get all elements of a list in a loop (there is a better way to do this, see Sect. 5.4):

REPL 5.13: Extracting elements from a list

```
>>> a_list=[1,2,3,4,"hi"]
>>> for i in range(0,len(a_list)):
...     print(i, a_list[i])
...
0 1
1 2
2 3
3 4
4 hi
```

5.2.3 Modification of Elements

Lists are mutable objects whereas tuples are immutable, which means that we can modify the value of any element:

REPL 5.14: Modifying a list

```
>>> def change(l):
...     l[0] = 666
...
>>> a_list = [1,2,3,4,5]
>>> a_list[3]=333
>>> a_list
[1, 2, 3, 333, 5]
>>> change(a_list)
>>> a_list
[666, 2, 3, 333, 5]
```

5.2 Arrays/Lists

We can observe that lists are not values. Indeed when we pass a list to a function, if the function modifies the list, that modification can be observed after the return to call point. Remember that this does not work with values of primitives types (`int`, etc) nor with tuples that are value objects.

5.2.4 Insertion and Removal of Elements

Lists are dynamic objects. Not only that values inside can be modified, but even the list size can be changed as it is possible to remove or add elements. A list can be used as a stack; just adding and removing elements at one of its ends. A list can be used as a queue; just adding elements to one end and removing from the other.

The way elements are added and removed in a structure defines an **abstract data type**. An abstract data type (ADT) is just a model type.

The description of an ADT focuses on the semantic of the operations. Stacks, queues, even lists or arrays are ADT, they are defined by the set of operations that is it to perform on them. The way the elements are truly stored is of no interest to the user of the structure. For example, we used PYTHON lists but we don't know how their elements a stored in the memory, and we don't need to! After all, do we know how our car really works? All details of it? No, we do not! Do you know how integers are represented in memory? That is the same in programming, in general we focus on the use of objects, not on their concrete implementation.

5.2.4.1 List as Stack
A **stack** is an ADT. It is a abstract dynamic data structure on which basically three operations are defined:

`is_empty`	a predicate to determine if there is no elements in the stack;
`push`	an operation to add an element on top of the others;
`pop`	an operation to remove the element on top.

This structure acts as a pile of plates: we can always put new plates on top of others, and get the first plate from the top. It is also known as **LIFO** structure, Last-In-First-Out. Be aware that the name of the operations is not relevant per se, we could have named them respectively `of_null_size`, `add_on_top`, `remove_from top`.

To use a **list** as a **stack** we can, for example, restrict its usage to `append` and `pop` (Fig. 5.1):

Fig. 5.1 A list used as a stack

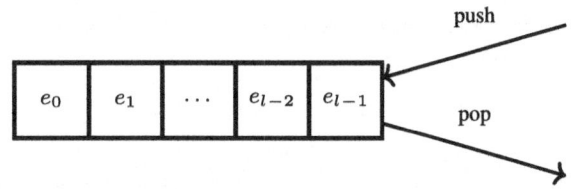

> **REPL 5.15: List as a stack**

```
>>> l=[]
>>> l.append("hello")
>>> l.append(4)
>>> l.append("hi")
>>> l.pop()
'hi'
>>> l
['hello', 4]
>>> l.pop()
4
>>> l.pop()
'hello'
>>> l.pop()
Traceback (most recent call last):
  File "<stdin>", line 1, in <module>
IndexError: pop from empty list
```

Note that we could have used other operations to get a stack from a list, for example: pop(0) and insert(0,e) which respectively remove the first element and insert an element at the first place.

Exercise 5.6

There exist calculators[1] that use the **Reverse Polish Notation** or **Polish Postfix Notation**. One of the advantages of this system is that there is no need for parenthesis in arithmetic expressions. In this system, an expression like a op b (whatever is op) is written a b op, for example 3 4 +; operators always follow their operands. To implement it we need a stack that is used this way:

- every time a number is input, it is pushed onto the stack;
- every time an operator is input, we need to pop two values from the stack, apply the operator on them and, push the result onto the stack.

Write a program to implement such a calculator. A simple session of its usage could be:

```
integer, operator or 'print' ('stop' to stop): 12
[12]
integer, operator or 'print' ('stop' to stop): 23
[12, 23]
integer, operator or 'print' ('stop' to stop): 11
[12, 23, 11]
integer, operator or 'print' ('stop' to stop): +
[12, 34]
integer, operator or 'print' ('stop' to stop): -
[-22]
```

---

[1] Famous calculators of this kind are those in the family of Hewlett-Packard calculators. The first German computer, the Konrad Zuse Z3, also used that system. There are also programming languages based on this notation, whose the most famous is FORTH.

5.2 Arrays/Lists

```
11  integer, operator or 'print' ('stop' to stop): stop
12  [-22]
```

Hint: to test if a string s contains only digits, you can use s.isdigit().

5.2.4.2 List as Queue

There also exist **queues** with three basic operations:

- is_empty   a predicate to test if there is something in the data structure;
- enqueue   an operation to add an element to the rear;
- dequeue   an operation to remove an element from the front.

This structure behave like a pipe of data. It is also known as **FIFO** structure, First-In-First-Out.

There are many ways to use a **list** as a **queue**, but the most frequent pattern is to use append and pop with a given argument (Fig. 5.2):

REPL 5.16: List as a queue

```
1   >>> l=[]
2   >>> l.append("hi")
3   >>> l.append(999)
4   >>> l.append("ho")
5   >>> l.pop(0)
6   'hi'
7   >>> l.pop(0)
8   999
9   >>> l.pop(0)
10  'ho'
```

See how elements are pushed to the end and removed from the beginning.

Exercise 5.7
Use a list as a queue implementing enqueue by adding element in the first place and dequeue by removing the last element.

5.2.4.3 Removal of an Element

There are two ways of removing an element:

- either by its value, with method remove;
- either by its index, with function del.

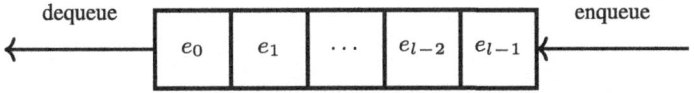

Fig. 5.2 A list as a queue

REPL 5.17: Removing or deleting an element from a list

```
1  >>> l=[9,8,7,6,5,4,3,2,1]
2  >>> l.remove(7)
3  >>> l
4  [9, 8, 6, 5, 4, 3, 2, 1]
5  >>> del l[5]
6  >>> l
7  [9, 8, 6, 5, 4, 2, 1]
```

Note that `remove` removes the first element that matches its argument.

`del` is more versatile than we may think. It is a function that can be used to suppress any variable (and the object denoted by if necessary).

5.2.4.4 Tests
We can also test if an element is `in` the list or `not in`:

REPL 5.18: Is an element in a list or not?

```
1  >>> l=[9,8,7,6,5,4,3,2,1]
2  >>> 99 in l
3  False
4  >>> 99 not in l
5  True
```

5.2.4.5 Other Operations on Lists
The method `clear` can be used to remove all elements from a list:

REPL 5.19: Clearing a list

```
1  >>> l=[3,45,5]
2  >>> l.clear()
3  >>> l
4  []
```

The method `sort` can sort the elements in the list. Elements are sorted by their natural order[2] and it is guaranteed that the sorting algorithm behind the scene is stable (for details on this see Chap. 9).

REPL 5.20: Sorting a list

```
1  >>> l=[6,5,7]
2  >>> l.sort()
```

---

[2] We can defined what natural order is for custom types, but this is beyond the scope of the book.

5.2 Arrays/Lists

```
3  >>> l
4  [5, 6, 7]
```

The method copy can be used to get a copy of the list. Remember that lists are mutable objects, so it is sometimes necessary to use a copy of the original list to preserve it from further modifications. The effect of a simple variable assignment for list may be surprising as it does not provide a copy but an alias, we will talk about this a little bit later in Sect. 5.3. When using copy, the copy and the original are then two independent lists:

REPL 5.21: Copying a list

```
1  >>> l=[5,6]
2  >>> l2=l.copy()
3  >>> l.append(100)
4  >>> l
5  [5, 6, 100]
6  >>> l2
7  [5, 6]
```

5.2.5 More on Accessing and Slicing

We have seen how to access an element through its index, which in principle is a positive one. In PYTHON, we can also use **negative indexing**. A negative index means to determine the position counting backward from the end: -1 is the index of the last element, -2 the before the last, etc. A negative index i is equivalent to the positive index $l + i$ (where l is the length of the data structure) (Fig. 5.3):

REPL 5.22: Negative indexing

```
1  >>> li=[1,2,3,4,5,6]
2  >>> li[-2]
3  5
```

There is a more complex way to index sequences, that is **slicing**. A slice is specified by two values separated by operator : (colon). It constructs a new structure

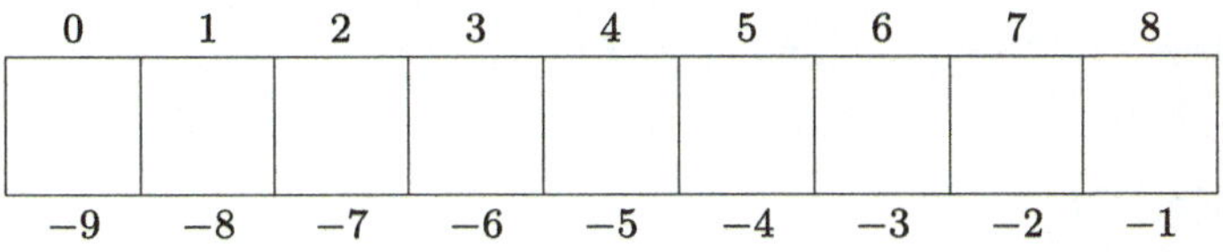

Fig. 5.3 Negative indexing

containing the elements of the original one whose indexes are in the range defined by the two values:

REPL 5.23: Slicing a list

```
>>> l=[9,8,7,6,5,4,3,2,1]
>>> l[3:6]
[6, 5, 4]
```

A slice can then construct a sub list from a list given the specification of the position range. As usual in PYTHON, a slice like [n:m] includes all element of indices in the open interval $[n, m)$. If the left bound of a slice is omitted, the default value is 0 (i.e. starts from the beginning of the list). If the right bound is omitted, the default value is the length of the original structure (i.e. up to the end of the list).

REPL 5.24: Slicing defaults

```
>>> l=[9,8,7,6,5,4,3,2,1]
>>> l[4:]
[5, 4, 3, 2, 1]
>>> l[:6]
[9, 8, 7, 6, 5, 4]
>>> l[:]
[9, 8, 7, 6, 5, 4, 3, 2, 1]
```

The definition of a slice may also contain a third parameter representing a step:

REPL 5.25: Slice step

```
>>> l=[0, 1, 2, 3, 4, 5, 6, 7, 8, 9]
>>> l
[0, 1, 2, 3, 4, 5, 6, 7, 8, 9]
>>> l[::2]
[0, 2, 4, 6, 8]
>>> l[3::2]
[3, 5, 7, 9]
```

Negative steps can also be used:

REPL 5.26: Negative step

```
>>> l=[0, 1, 2, 3, 4, 5, 6, 7, 8, 9]
>>> l[6:4:-1]
[6, 5]
>>> l[6:2:-1]
[6, 5, 4, 3]
```

5.3 Variables, Objects and Values

In PYTHON, an identifier denotes a (small) storage (in memory) that contains the address (id) of an object, the actual representation of the value currently associated to. When we write a=5, we can represent it as (Fig. 5.4):

There is a function named id that lets us get the id of an object denoted by an identifier:

REPL 5.27: id of an object

```
1  >>> a = 1234
2  >>> id(a)
3  140659488875568
```

What is interesting is that the id of two variables denoting the same integer value are not (necessarily) the same:

REPL 5.28: Two variables with two objects of the same value

```
1  >>> a=1234
2  >>> b=1234
3  >>> id(a)
4  140659488875568
5  >>> id(b)
6  140659524697968
```

A picture of this is in Fig. 5.5.

There are two copies of the representation of the same integer value 1234.

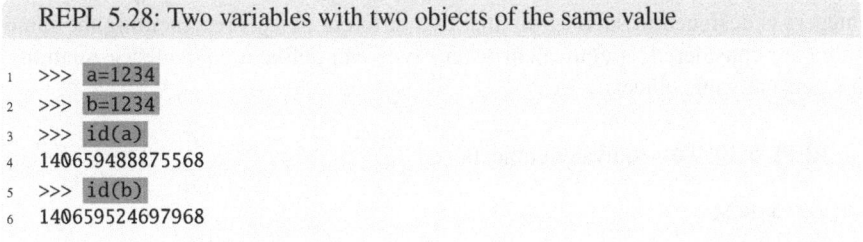

Fig. 5.4 A variable in Python

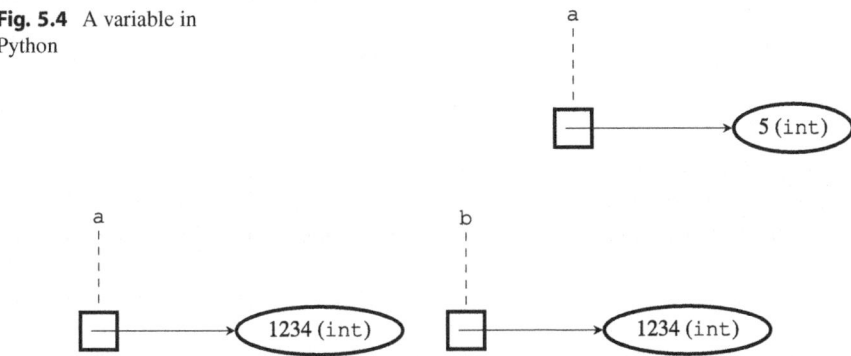

Fig. 5.5 Two variables and two objects of the same value

Fig. 5.6 Two variables and one object

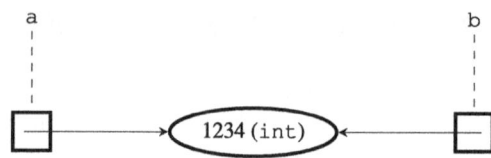

We can determine if two identifiers are associated to the same value object or not. It is the operator `is`:

REPL 5.29: Are objects the same?

```
>>> a=1234
>>> b=1234
>>> a is b
False
```

The identifiers a and b do not denote the same object. The equality operator == on integers is designed in such a way that two different objects representing the same value are considered as equivalent (every type can define a equivalence relation). Integers are value objects:

REPL 5.30: Two equivalent objects

```
>>> a=1234
>>> b=1234
>>> a == b
True
```

Beware that the assignment operator makes something very special:

REPL 5.31: Assignment

```
>>> a=1234
>>> b=a
>>> a is b
True
```

The object is shared as depicted in Fig. 5.6.

For common primitive value types like arithmetic types and tuples, we can ignore these sort of details, everything is made so that numbers behave the way we learn

5.3 Variables, Objects and Values

Fig. 5.7 Two variables and one object

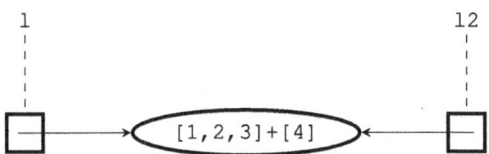

early at school. They are value objects. But, this has consequences on objects that are mutable, like the lists. For example:

REPL 5.32: Mutable objects and variables

```
1  >>> list_1 = [1, 2, 3]
2  >>> list_2 = list_1
3  >>> print(list_1,list_2)
4  [1, 2, 3] [1, 2, 3]
5  >>> list_1.append(4)
6  >>> print(list_1,list_2)
7  [1, 2, 3, 4] [1, 2, 3, 4]
```

We changed list 1 and l2 also changed! A picture of this is in Fig. 5.7.

There is a single object indirectly denoted by two identifiers and we modified the shared object. Now if we write:

REPL 5.33: Two variables and two objects

```
1  >>> l = [1, 2, 3]
2  >>> l2 = [1, 2, 3]
3  >>> print(l,l2)
4  [1, 2, 3] [1, 2, 3]
5  >>> l.append(4)
6  >>> print(l,l2)
7  [1, 2, 3, 4] [1, 2, 3]
```

We have two objects (Fig. 5.8).

Modifying one does not change the other. When we write an expression to get a actual value, we obtain a new object. Remember that this was the case even for the integers. The expression 5 constructs an integer object representing the value 5. The expression [1, 2, 3] constructs a list object representing the ordered collection of values 1, 2 and 3.

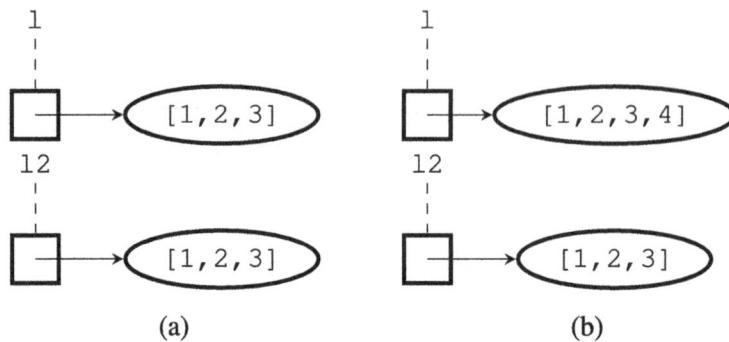

Fig. 5.8 Two variables and two list objects. (**a**) Before append. (**b**) After append

5.4 More on Tuples, Lists, Strings: Sequences

Tuples, lists, strings contain elements. Indeed, a string can be seen as a list of characters... All these structures are ordered collections. PYTHON calls them **sequences**. The for loop accepts any sequence to define the span of the loop control variable:

REPL 5.34: Looping over sequences

```
1  >>> a_list=[1,2,3]
2  >>> for i in a_list:
3  ...     print(i)
4  ...
5  1
6  2
7  3
8  >>> t=('a','b','c')
9  >>> for i in t:
10 ...     print(i)
11 ...
12 a
13 b
14 c
15 >>> for i in "hello":
16 ...     print(i)
17 ...
18 h
19 e
20 l
21 l
22 o
```

5.4 More on Tuples, Lists, Strings: Sequences

It is sometimes necessary to iterate over two sequences at the same time (in parallel). PYTHON offers a function to iterate over tuples whose values are constructed from several sequences. As it works like a zipper that binds two edges, the function is called `zip`:

REPL 5.35: Zip sequences

```
>>> fnames = ["Barak","Donald"]
>>> names = ["Obama","Trump"]
>>> for t in zip(fnames,names):
...     print(t)
...
('Barak', 'Obama')
('Donald', 'Trump')
```

If the sequences are not of the same length, `zip` stops after the exhaustion of the shorter one.

In fact, `range` that we have used so far in many for loops constructs a sequence.[3]

Exercise 5.8
Print every possible card in a 52 cards deck. Each card being a tuple (v,c), where $v \in [1, 13]$ and $c \in \{\clubsuit, \spadesuit, \heartsuit, \diamondsuit\}$.
Note: if you do not know how to type the symbols, replace each with chars 'c', 's', 'h', 'd' or strings 'club','spade','heart','diamond'.

Exercise 5.9
With the use of list repetition and `zip` construct a deck of all possible cards.

Exercise 5.10
Write a program that plays the Battle (or War) card game automatically.
Start by generating a shuffled deck of 52 cards. To shuffle elements of a list l you can use `random.shuffle(l)` the function `shuffle` of the module `random`.
Then, distribute cards in two hands. Each hand is considered as a queue of cards.
A turn of the game is defined like this:

- get one card from each hand (dequeue) and put them on a table,
- compare them. In case of equality, cards are stored in some auxiliary deck. In case their are not equal, the player that had the largest card wins and enqueues the cards on the table as well as the ones in the auxiliary deck.

The game will end either when a player has no card or 1000 turns have been played.
The winner is the player with the largest number of cards. In case of equality there is no winner.

---

[3] This is technically false, PYTHON distinguish sequences and iterables. A sequence is iterable, but an iterable may not be a sequence.

5.5 More on Lists: Comprehension

In Mathematics, we can define a set by **extension** giving all its elements one by one like {1, 2, 3, 4} or by **intension** giving the properties of the elements like

$$\{a : a \in \mathbb{R} \land a > \sqrt{2}\}$$

Very similarly PYTHON can do both. We already know how to construct a list by extension, for example as in a_list=[1,3,5,7]. The term used by PYTHON to construct list by intention is list by **comprehension**. The syntax is not easy to describe in its entirety, we will just give some examples. The simplest one is to construct a list of values, let says some even numbers:

```
[2*i for i in range(1,1000)]
```

The PYTHON construction for something like $\{2p \,/\, p \in [1, 1000)\}$ is called **comprehension list**. The simplest comprehension list has the general form of:

```
[expression for i in iterable]
```

The expression is evaluated for each value extracted in order from the iterable.[4] The bound variable i can be used as we want in the expression, and the expression itself can be as complex as we need. Thus:

```
l=[2*i for i in range(1,1000)]
```

constructs the ordered list of values of the set $\{2p \,/\, p \in [1, 1000)\}$.

One can observe that we can have two equivalent definitions of the same set:

$$\{2p \,/\, p \in \mathbb{N}\}$$

is the same set as

$$\{p \,/\, p \in \mathbb{N} \land \exists p' \in \mathbb{N},\ p = 2p'\}$$

If we want to use the latter form, which uses some kind of predicate or filter then we can use the following syntax:

```
[expression for i in iterable if condition]
```

The expression is evaluated only if the condition holds.

For example, we can get the set of odd numbers in the interval $[1, 8)$ with :

```
l=[i for i in range(1,8) if i%2 != 0]
```

---

[4] An iterable is something PYTHON can iterate over in a for loop.

5.5 More on Lists: Comprehension

Remember how we computed the sum of the first prime numbers (see Program 3.10). Knowing the comprehension lists, we can rewrite it as:

Program 5.5: Sum of n first primes   sumprime2.py

```
1  # Sum of primes up to n
2  import sympy
3  import math
4  n = int(input("Up to? "))
5  primes = [i for i in range(1,n+1) if sympy.isprime(i)]
6  s = sum(primes)
7  print(f"Sum of primes up to {n} equals to {s}")
8  n_primes = len(primes)
9  print(f"Approx {n_primes**2/2*math.log(n_primes)}")
```

We can observe how the list of primes is built by comprehension. Surprising is the way we calculate the sum, we used a convenient PYTHON standard function sum that is able to compute the sum of any iterable sequence whose elements can be added to each other. We wrote a simple but non trivial program without using any explicit loop. Remember that loops are useful and necessary constructions but they are error-prone, so using appropriate constructions and functions may lead to more secure programs. Of course that necessitates some expertise, knowledge and quite long practice.

We can use comprehension list to construct two or more dimensional structures. For example we can build the multiplication table of numbers from 1 to 9:

REPL 5.36: Multi-dimensional and comprehension list

```
1  >>> mt = [[i*j for i in range(0,10)] for j in range(0,10)]
2  >>> mt
3  [[0, 0, 0, 0, 0, 0, 0, 0, 0, 0], [0, 1, 2, 3, 4, 5, 6, 7, 8, 9], [0, ▷
      ▷ 2, 4, 6, 8, 10, 12, 14, 16, 18], [0, 3, 6, 9, 12, 15, 18, 21, ▷
      ▷ 24, 27], [0, 4, 8, 12, 16, 20, 24, 28, 32, 36], [0, 5, 10, 15,▷
      ▷  20, 25, 30, 35, 40, 45], [0, 6, 12, 18, 24, 30, 36, 42, 48, ▷
      ▷ 54], [0, 7, 14, 21, 28, 35, 42, 49, 56, 63], [0, 8, 16, 24, ▷
      ▷ 32, 40, 48, 56, 64, 72], [0, 9, 18, 27, 36, 45, 54, 63, 72, ▷
      ▷ 81]]
4  >>> mt[5][7]
5  35
```

Of course as this table is symmetrical, we can build "half" of it to get a triangular structure:

REPL 5.37: Triangular structure

```
1  >>> mt = [[i*j for i in range(0,j+1)] for j in range(0,10)]
2  >>> mt
```

```
3  [[0], [0, 1], [0, 2, 4], [0, 3, 6, 9], [0, 4, 8, 12, 16], [0, 5, 10, ▷
      ▷ 15, 20, 25], [0, 6, 12, 18, 24, 30, 36], [0, 7, 14, 21, 28, ▷
      ▷ 35, 42, 49], [0, 8, 16, 24, 32, 40, 48, 56, 64], [0, 9, 18, ▷
      ▷ 27, 36, 45, 54, 63, 72, 81]]
4  >>> mt[7][5]
5  35
```

To build the 5×5 identity matrix we can use the following:

REPL 5.38: Ternary expression

```
1  >>> l=[[0 if i!=j else 1 for i in range(0,5)] \
2  ...    for j in range(0,5)]
3  >>> l
4  [[1, 0, 0, 0, 0], [0, 1, 0, 0, 0], [0, 0, 1, 0, 0], [0, 0, 0, 1, 0], ▷
      ▷ [0, 0, 0, 0, 1]]
```

Note that line 1 and 2 make a single line of code. As it is too long to fit, we broke it using a trailing slash \ at the end.

Beware that in line 1 the `0 if i!=j else 1` is before the loops, not after, we can not write it on the right part. That if-else is not a predicate. It is not a standard if-else, we can see that the if part has no instruction.

The expression `0 if i!=j else 1` is called a **ternary expression**. We want to put 0 or 1 (depending on some condition) but this for all numbers in the given ranges. We don't want to filter some numbers in the range, that is not the same. So an expression like :

```
value if condition else value_else
```

is evaluated to `value` if the `condition` is true but to `value_else` if the condition is false. It is often used to build conditional messages, like:

```
"odd" if is_odd else "even"
```

Which loop do you prefer?

REPL 5.39: if-else vs ternary expression

```
1   >>> for i in range(1,4):
2   ...     if i%2==0:
3   ...         print(f"{i} is even")
4   ...     else:
5   ...         print(f"{i} is odd")
6   ...
7   1 is odd
8   2 is even
9   3 is odd
10  >>> for i in range(1,4):
11  ...     print(f"{i} is {'even' if i%2==0 else 'odd'}")
```

```
12  ...
13  1 is odd
14  2 is even
15  3 is odd
```

Almost all good programmers would prefer the second: less redundant, shorter, clearer.

Exercise 5.11
Write a program that multiplies two 3×3 matrices by the use of a function `matrixmult` using for loops.
Rewrite it using comprehension lists as `matrixmultcomp`.

Exercise 5.12
Write a module `matrix` to manipulate 3×3 matrices with operations as `mult`, `add`, `inverse`, `det`, etc.
Try to use comprehension list as much as possible.

5.6 Dictionaries

Lists or tuples are ordered data structures. Values are sequenced one after the other, and commonly are all of the same type. It is sometimes more convenient to access data by keys and not by indexes.

For example, if we want to have a data structure to represent an individual with his name and his age, we can obviously use a tuple or a list to represent it as in:

REPL 5.40: Printing a tuple
```
1  >>> def print_individual(ind):
2  ...     print(f"Name: {ind[0]} age: {ind[1]}")
3  ...
4  >>> i = ("Smith",35)
5  >>> print_individual(i)
6  Name: Smith age: 35
```

Note that the function `print_individual` would also accept a list as argument:

REPL 5.41: List is usable in place of a tuple
```
1  >>> another = [ "Murdoch", 23 ]
2  >>> print_individual(another)
3  Name: Murdoch age: 23
```

But this is too much error-prone:

- the `print_individual` function uses 0 and 1 as index to represent the name and the age respectively. While perfectly correct, it is not easy to remember which index represents what (think of a more complex data structure), and not so readable.
- the construction of the data structure also needs to know the convention used in the indexing. For example, one may construct a bad structure like:

REPL 5.42: Wrong data is usable

```
1 >>> a = [ 17, "Lyndon" ]
2 >>> print_individual(a)
3 Name: 17 age: Lyndon
```

Code is executed without any error but it is logically inconsistent.

To construct a **dictionary** (other languages use the term **map** or **hashmap**), we can pair keys (values of any type) with associated values (of any type), as in:

REPL 5.43: Constructing a dictionary

```
1 >>> s = { "name": "Smith", "age": 35 }
```

At least, it is more readable and we can construct it in any order. The following construction is equivalent:[5]

REPL 5.44: Constructing a dictionary

```
1 >>> s = { "age": 35, "name": "Smith" }
```

Now, a function to tackle this kind of data structure could be written as:

REPL 5.45: Accessing data in dictionary

```
1 >>> s = { "age": 35, "name": "Smith" }
2 >>> def print_individual(i):
3 ...     print(f"{i['name']} is {i['age']} years old.")
4 ...
5 >>> print_individual(s)
6 Smith is 35 years old.
```

---

[5] This no more true since PYTHON 3.7 in which some ordering (but no indexing) is preserved in the structure. But saying more on this is out of scope of this book.

5.6 Dictionaries

To access a value in an array we used brackets like `array[index]`, to access a value in a dictionary we specify the key: `dictionary[key]`. In some way the indexing with integers is generalised a value of any type.

Any value type can be used as a key, and each key has its own type:

REPL 5.46: Keys can be of any type

```
1 >>> d = { 3: 33, "name": "foo" }
```

While this is possible, one must not abuse of such.

A dictionary is a mutable data structure. We can change the value associated to an existing key, add or remove a key/value pair:

REPL 5.47: Modifying a dictionary

```
1  >>> d = { 3: 33, "name": "foo" }
2  >>> d
3  {3: 33, 'name': 'foo'}
4  >>> d[3]="bar"
5  >>> d
6  {3: 'bar', 'name': 'foo'}
7  >>> d[6]=445
8  >>> d
9  {3: 'bar', 'name': 'foo', 6: 445}
10 >>> d.pop(3)
11 'bar'
12 >>> d
13 {'name': 'foo', 6: 445}
```

Again, try not to abuse of adding/removing key/value pairs, as it will change the logic of the structure.

5.6.1 Iterating over Dictionaries

To iIterate over a dictionary one needs to choose among:

- iterating over keys by extracting the set of keys with `keys`,
- iterating over values by extracting the set of values with `values`
- iterating over key/value pairs by extracting the set of key/value pairs with `d.items`.

For example:

REPL 5.48: Iterating over a dictionary

```
1 >>> s = { "age": 35, "name": "Smith"}
2 >>> for k in s.keys():
```

```
 3  ...         print(k)
 4  ...
 5  age
 6  name
 7  >>> for v in s.values():
 8  ...         print(v)
 9  ...
10  35
11  Smith
12  >>> for k,v in s.items():
13  ...         print(k,v)
14  ...
15  age 35
16  name Smith
```

Exercise 5.13
Rewrite exercises on cards with dictionaries like:
$$\text{"a\_card = \{'color': '♣', 'value': 3\}"}$$

5.7 Objects

Data structures like tuples, lists or dictionaries are more than enough to represent any complex data we need. The reader may feel free to not read this part, but it will help him to better understand what is covered in Chap. 11.

Technically, objects are not part of data structures, at least in the classical meaning. Objects are a very tight way to put together data and functions on these data. **Object oriented programming** (OOP) is a programming paradigm on its own (with its advantages and disadvantages, OOP is not a panacea for all code diseases). While in this book we focus on functions and data structures, a very classical point of view of algorithmics, we need to say some few things about objects.

A major flaw with the use of tuples, lists or dictionaries is that they require a lot of attention. We need to remember either the order or the key/values pairs during construction and usage of theses constructs. That puts too much burden on the programmer. This kind of programming is referred as the **anemic domain model** anti-pattern (we refer the reader to the internet about these considerations).

In PYTHON, ultimately everything is an object (a value of a type). Object programming is a way to define new types. A type is a set of values and the semantic of possible operations on values; `int` type defines all representable values and operations like +, -, etc, with their behaviour.

5.7 Objects

In PYTHON, every type is described by a **class**, and we already encountered classes (without knowing anything about them):

REPL 5.49: Classes

```
1  >>> type(3)
2  <class 'int'>
3  >>> type(3.5)
4  <class 'float'>
5  >>> type([1, 3])
6  <class 'list'>
7  >>> type((1, 3))
8  <class 'tuple'>
9  >>> type({"name": "smith"})
10 <class 'dict'>
```

To define a new type, we have to define a **class**. A class can define:

- ways to initialise values of that type,
- ways to manipulate values of that type.

Imagine we need to implement a type to represent points in a 2D plane with Cartesian coordinates:

Program 5.6: Type Point   point.py

```
1  class Point:              # definition of a new type of data
2      def __init__(self,x,y): # constructor
3          self.abs = x         # definition of a field
4          self.ord = y         # definition of a field
5
6  p = Point(4,5)            # creation of an object
7  print(p.abs,p.ord)        # reading fields of that object
```

whose execution leads to:

```
1  4 5
```

Line 1 introduces a new type of data named Point.
Lines 2–4 define a special method named __init__. A function is called a **method** when it is defined in the context of a class, and we will see quickly what are the consequences. That function is referred to as the **initialiser** or **constructor**. It takes three arguments. At least it is easy to understand what the last two are used for; they provide values for initialising the point coordinates. The first one (usually named self) is more tricky to understand. It is a parameter we do not need to provide as argument at the call point. It represents the name of the object

being constructed. In some way, it is a parameter used to name the object itself. In every human language there are words we can use to talk about ourselves: me, I, myself, etc. That is the same for PYTHON objects, that argument is the name an object can use to denote itself during execution of some method. This is why it is highly recommended to name it `self` (some also use `this` inspired by other object oriented languages).

▶ We can remark that the name of `__init__` violates the rules we gave for identifiers in Sect. 2.3.1, i.e. that identifiers must start with a letter. PYTHON objects are special constructions that offer many useful and tricky functionalities. Object methods that have predefined behaviour have their name prefixed with one _ (underscore), and some have two like `__init__`. These identifiers are reserved by PYTHON. We may use them provided we know what are their exact purpose. We will see another one of such useful specific methods slightly later, `__str__`.

In `__init__` we can see how `self` is used (lines 3 and 4). Remind that what we want is to store into an object some values (here the coordinates of the `Point` under construction). An instruction like `self.abs = x` in the constructor:

- adds a new **field** (a data stored inside the object) called `abs`,
- initialises that field with the parameter `x`.

In line 6, we construct an object of that type and bind it to the identifier p. The call `Point(4,5)` constructs a new object by calling implicitly the `__init__` method of the class `Point` with three parameters, the object in construction and the values provided for initialisation.

As the object contain two fields `abs` and `ord`, we access them by the use of the dot notation: `p.abs` (resp. `p.ord`), as shown in line 7.

Note that the data structure is induced by the execution of `__init__` method. That is the place where the object is constructed.

5.7.1 Methods

We can enrich a class by providing methods for it. A method is just a function defined in the context of a class whose purpose is to make something with the data encapsulated in the objects. **Data encapsulation** is a major concern in OOP. For example:

Program 5.7: Objects with methods   point2.py

```
1  class Point:
2      def __init__(self,x,y):
```

5.7 Objects

```
3           self.abs = x
4           self.ord = y
5       def get_abscissa(self):
6           return self.abs
7       def get_ordinate(self):
8           return self.ord
9
10
11  p = Point(4,5)
12  print(p.get_abscissa(),p.get_ordinate())
```

whose execution leads to:

```
1   4 5
```

We defined two methods, `get_abscissa` and `get_ordinate`:[6]

- that are defined in the context of an object, so that they receive the object in the context of the call as their first argument (judiciously named `self`),
- that can be called on an existing object: `p.get_abscissa()` which provides p as the context. Remind how we used `l.append(v)` to add a new value at the end of a list! The function `append` is a method provided by the class `list`.

One may ask why we add all these mechanics and not use a simple tuple to represent a point? The answer is that in some way, at least the usage of this new type is much more explicit and clear than using, for example a tuple (4,5), which may represent anything but a point in the plane.

To get a bit further in this direction, we can add more methods to these objects. For example two methods to get the polar coordinates of a point (even if its internal representation is the cartesian one):

Program 5.8: Point with methods for polar   point3.py

```
1   import math
2
3   def print_point(p):
4       print(p.get_abscissa(),p.get_ordinate())
5       print(p.get_radius(),p.get_angle())
6
7   class Point:
8       def __init__(self,x,y):
```

---

[6] Note that both respect the recommended syntax of identifiers, both start with a letter. This is not the case for `__init__` that is a method with pre-defined behavior.

```
 9          self.abs = x
10          self.ord = y
11     def get_abscissa(self):
12          return self.abs
13     def get_ordinate(self):
14          return self.ord
15     def get_radius(self):
16          return math.sqrt(self.abs**2+self.ord**2)
17     def get_angle(self):
18          if self.abs == 0:
19              return 0
20          angle = math.atan(self.ord/self.abs)
21          if self.abs > 0:
22              return angle if self.ord > 0 else angle+math.pi*2
23          else:
24              return angle+math.pi
25
26  p = Point(4,4)
27  print_point(p)
28  p2 = Point(0,5)
29  print_point(p2)
30  p3 = Point(-4,4)
31  print_point(p3)
32  p4 = Point(-4,-4)
33  print_point(p4)
34  p5 = Point(4,-4)
35  print_point(p5)
```

whose execution leads to:

```
1  4 4
2  5.656854249492381 0.7853981633974483
3  0 5
4  5.0 0
5  -4 4
6  5.656854249492381 2.356194490192345
7  -4 -4
8  5.656854249492381 3.9269908169872414
9  4 -4
10 5.656854249492381 5.497787143782138
```

5.7 Objects

What if we want to initialise a Point either by using Cartesian coordinates or polar ones? We can modify the initialiser and add a default argument:

Program 5.9: Polar/Cartesian   point4.py

```
 1  import math
 2
 3  def print_point(p):
 4      print(p.get_abscissa(),p.get_ordinate(),p.get_radius(),p.▷
            ▷ get_angle())
 5
 6  class Point:
 7      def __init__(self,x,y,unit=0):
 8          if unit==0:
 9              self.abs = x
10              self.ord = y
11          else:
12              self.abs = math.cos(y)*x
13              self.ord = math.sin(y)*x
14      def get_abscissa(self):
15          return self.abs
16      def get_ordinate(self):
17          return self.ord
18      def get_radius(self):
19          return math.sqrt(self.abs**2+self.ord**2)
20      def get_angle(self):
21          if self.abs == 0:
22              return 0
23          angle = math.atan(self.ord/self.abs)
24          if self.abs > 0:
25              return angle if self.ord > 0 else angle+math.pi*2
26          else:
27              return angle+math.pi
28
29  print_point(Point(0,5))
30  print_point(Point(4,4))
31  print_point(Point(5.656854249492381,0.7853981633974483,1))
32  print_point(Point(-4,4))
33  print_point(Point(5.656854249492381,2.356194490192345,1))
34  print_point(Point(-4,-4))
35  print_point(Point(5.656854249492381,3.9269908169872414,1))
36  print_point(Point(4,-4))
37  print_point(Point(5.656854249492381,5.497787143782138,1))
```

whose execution leads to:

```
1  0 5 5.0 0
2  4 4 5.656854249492381 0.7853981633974483
3  4.000000000000001 4.0 5.656854249492381 0.7853981633974482
4  -4 4 5.656854249492381 2.356194490192345
5  -4.0 4.000000000000001 5.656854249492381 2.356194490192345
6  -4 -4 5.656854249492381 3.9269908169872414
7  -4.000000000000001 -4.0 5.656854249492381 3.9269908169872414
8  4 -4 5.656854249492381 5.497787143782138
9  4.0 -4.000000000000001 5.656854249492381 5.497787143782138
```

Note how we can construct a point by specifying either its cartesian or polar coordinates, and for any point we can get its cartesian and polar coordinates, however inside a point the coordinates are stored in cartesian system. That is the point of Object Programming: hiding representation to the user of the type. After all, do we know how lists (for example) are implemented behind the scene? We don't have to and we don't need to use them. The collections of the methods defined in an class makes it an **abstract data type** (see Sect. 5.2.4). Programs using abstract data types are much easier to read and manage.

5.7.2 Printing

As is, if we print an object with an instruction like print(p), we would have a message like:

```
1  <__main__.Point object at 0x7f9684c4dfd0>
```

PYTHON just informs that it is an object of type Point defined in the main module whose identity is 0x7f9684c4dfd0. Remember that each object has an identity. That message is not very useful, this is why we provided a function called print_point in the previous examples. We may need to get a good printing of it just like any other predefined type. To get it, we just have to define a special method whose name is __str__ intended to return a string representing the object. When the method __str__ is defined an instruction like print(p) will call it and then print the returned string and not the id of the object:

Program 5.10: Printing objects   point5.py

```
1  import math
2
3  class Point:
4      def __init__(self,x,y,unit=0):
5          if unit==0:
```

```
6            self.abs = x
7            self.ord = y
8        else:
9            self.abs = math.cos(y)*x
10           self.ord = math.sin(y)*x
11    def __str__(self):
12        return f"x:{self.abs} y:{self.ord} r:{self.get_radius()} a:{▷
              ▷ self.get_angle()}"
13    def get_abscissa(self):
14        return self.abs
15    def get_ordinate(self):
16        return self.ord
17    def get_radius(self):
18        return math.sqrt(self.abs**2+self.ord**2)
19    def get_angle(self):
20        if self.abs == 0:
21            return 0
22        angle = math.atan(self.ord/self.abs)
23        if self.abs > 0:
24            return angle if self.ord > 0 else angle+math.pi*2
25        else:
26            return angle+math.pi
27
28 print(Point(4,4))
29 print(Point(5.656854249492381,0.7853981633974483,1))
```

whose execution leads to:

```
1  x:4 y:4 r:5.656854249492381 a:0.7853981633974483
2  x:4.000000000000001 y:4.0 r:5.656854249492381 a:0.7853981633974482
```

Exercise 5.14
Use a class to define card objects: with an appropriate constructor, a good printing method and methods to get color and value.
Add a method to compare two cards with the following syntax c1.compare(c2), which will return -1 if $c1 < c2$, 0 if $c1 == c2$ and 1 if $c1 > c2$.
To compare two cards, we just need to compare their values ignoring their colours.

Exercise 5.15
Hard.
A simple a common way to implement a list is by chaining its elements. This structure is called a **linked list**. Here is a figure of such a list of two elements v_1 and v_2 (Fig. 5.9).
Define two classes: MyList and Element.
A MyList object will point to the first element of the list by the use of a field named first.
An Element will contain a value field and a next field that will point (respectively) to the value of this element and the next element in the list.

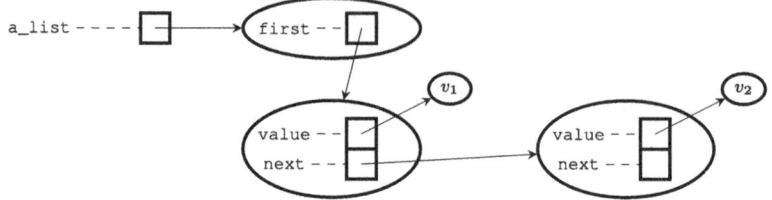

Fig. 5.9 A possible list implementation in Python

Methods on a MyList object could be: len, to_front (to add an element at the front), get (to get the element at a given position).
Could you add a method to_tail to add an element at the tail?
Could you add a method remove to remove an element at a given position?

5.8 Solutions to Exercises

Solution to Exercise 5.1

Program 5.11: Comparing tuples   compare.py

```
 1  def compare(t1,t2):
 2      if t1[0]==t2[0]:
 3          if t1[1]==t2[1]:
 4              return 0
 5          elif t1[1]<t2[1]:
 6              return -1
 7          else:
 8              return 1
 9      elif t1[0]<t2[0]:
10          return -1
11      else:
12          return 1
13
14
15  print(compare( (1,1), (1,1) ))
16  print(compare( (1,2), (1,1) ))
17  print(compare( (1,1), (1,2) ))
18  print(compare( (2,1), (1,1) ))
19  print(compare( (1,1), (2,1) ))
```

Solution to Exercises 5.2 and 5.3

Program 5.12: Comparing points   comparepoints.py

```
1  def sq_distance(t1,t2):
2      return (t1[0]-t2[0])**2 + (t1[1]-t2[1])**2 + (t1[2]-t2[2])**2
3
4  def compare(t1,t2,t3=(0,0,0)):
5      d1 = sq_distance(t1,t3)
6      d2 = sq_distance(t2,t3)
7      if d1<d2:
8          return -1,t1
9      elif d1==d2:
10         return 0,t1
11     else:
12         return 1,t2
13
14 p1 = (5,5,5)
15 p2 = (10,10,10)
16 p3 = (4,5,5)
17
18 print(compare(p1,p2,p3))
19 print(compare(p2,p1,p3))
20 print(compare(p1,p1,p3))
21 print(compare(p1,p2))
22 print(compare(p2,p1))
```

Solution to Exercise 5.4

Program 5.13: Comparing points in any n-D space   comparepointsnd.py

```
1  def sq_distance(t1,t2):
2      d = 0
3      for i in range(len(t1)):
4          d += (t1[i]-t2[i])**2
5      return d
6
7  def compare(t1,t2,t3):
8      d1 = sq_distance(t1,t3)
9      d2 = sq_distance(t2,t3)
10     if d1<d2:
11         return -1,t1
```

```
12      elif d1==d2:
13          return 0,t1
14      else:
15          return 1,t2
16
17  p1 = (5,5,5,5)
18  p2 = (10,10,10,10)
19  p3 = (4,5,5,4)
20
21  print(compare(p1,p2,p3))
22  print(compare(p2,p1,p3))
23  print(compare(p1,p1,p3))
```

Note that this does not work well if points are not in the same dimensional space. Would you be able to correct it and generate an error in this case?

Solution to Exercise 5.5

REPL 5.50: Labeled cards

```
1  >>> import collections
2  >>> K = collections.namedtuple('Card','value suit')
3  ... c = K(3,'♠')
4  ... print(c)
5  Card(value=3, suit='♠')
```

Solution to Exercise 5.6

Program 5.14: Reverse Polish calculator   basicpolishcalc.py

```
1   stack = []
2
3   while (v:=input("integer, operator or 'print' ('stop' to stop): ")) ▷
        ▷ != "stop":
4       if v=="print":
5           print(stack)
6           continue
7       r = 0
8       if v.isdigit():
9           r = int(v)
10      else:
```

5.8 Solutions to Exercises

```
11      n2 = stack.pop()
12      n1 = stack.pop()
13      if v == '+':
14          r = n1+n2
15      elif v == '-':
16          r = n1-n2
17      elif v == '*':
18          r = n1*n2
19      elif v == '/':
20          r = n1//n2
21  stack.append(r)
22  print(stack)
23
24 print(stack)
```

Solution to Exercise 5.8

REPL 5.51: 52 cards deck

```
1  >>> for v in [1, 2, 3, 4, 5, 6, 7, 8, 9, 10, 11, 12, 13]:
2  ...     for c in ['♣','♠','♡','♢']:
3  ...         print( (v,c) )
```

or

REPL 5.52: 52 cards, using range

```
1  >>> for v in range(1,14):
2  ...     for c in ['♣','♠','♡','♢']:
3  ...         print( (v,c) )
```

Solution to Exercise 5.9

Program 5.15: Generating a deck of 52 cards   deck.py

```
1  colors = ['♣','♠','♡','♢']*13      # 4 colors for 13 cards
2
3  values = [i for i in range(1,14)]*4 # 13 cards of 4 colors
4  # or
5  #values = [c for c in [i for i in range(1,14)] for j in range(4)]
6
```

```
 7  deck = []
 8  for c in zip(values,colors):
 9      deck.append(c)
10  print(deck)
```

Solution to Exercise 5.10

Program 5.16: A robot playing the Battle game   battle.py

```
 1  import random
 2
 3  def generate_shuffled_hands():          # distribute the cards
 4      colors = ['♣','♠','♡','◇']*13      # 4 colors for 13 table
 5      values = [c for c in [i for i in range(1,14)] for j in range(4)]
 6      deck = []
 7      for c in zip(values,colors):
 8          deck.append(c)
 9      random.shuffle(deck)
10      return [deck[:26], deck[26:]]
11
12  players = generate_shuffled_hands()
13
14  def turn(i,players,aux_deck):           # A turn
15      print("Turn", i+1)
16      print("Player1: ", players[0])
17      print("Player2: ", players[1])
18      print("Auxiliary deck: ",aux_deck)
19      table = [p.pop(0) for p in players]
20      print("Table: ", table)
21      if table[0][0]==table[1][0]:
22          print("Equality")
23          aux_deck.extend(table)
24      elif table[0][0]>table[1][0]:
25          print("Player 1 wins")
26          players[0] += table + aux_deck
27          aux_deck.clear()
28      else:
29          print("Player 2 wins")
30          players[1] += table + aux_deck
31          aux_deck.clear()
32      print()
33
```

5.8 Solutions to Exercises

```
34    aux_deck = []                          # The Game...
35    for i in range(1000):
36        if len(players[0])==0 or len(players[1])==0:
37            break
38        turn(i,players,aux_deck)
39
40    if len(players[0])==len(players[1]):
41        print("No winner")
42        quit()
43    if len(players[0])>len(players[1]):
44        print("Player1 is the final winner")
45    else:
46        print("Player2 is the final winner")
```

Solution to Exercise 5.11

Program 5.17: 3×3 matrix multiplication   matrixmult.py

```
1   def printmatrix(m):
2       print()
3       for row in range(0,3):
4           for col in range(0,3):
5               print(f"{m[row][col]:3}",end=' ')
6           print()
7
8   def rowcol(m1,i,m2,j):
9       res = 0
10      for k in range(0,3):
11          res += m1[i][k]*m2[k][j]
12      return res
13
14
15  def matrixmult(m1,m2):
16      m = []
17      for row in range(0,3):
18          r = []
19          for col in range(0,3):
20              r.append(rowcol(m1,row,m2,col))
21          m.append(r)
22      return m
23
24  def matrixmultcomp(m1,m2):
```

```
25      return [[sum([m1[row][k]*m2[k][col] for k in range(0,3)]) for col▷
               ▷ in range(0,3)] for row in range(0,3)]
26
27  m1 = [ [1,0,0], [1,1,0], [2,2,2] ]
28  m2 = [ [1,2,3], [4,5,6], [7,8,9] ]
29  printmatrix(m1)
30  printmatrix(m2)
31  m = matrixmult(m1,m2)
32  printmatrix(m)
33  m = matrixmultcomp(m1,m2)
34  printmatrix(m)
```

Solution to Exercise 5.15

Program 5.18: A primitive implementation of a chained list   mylist.py

```
1   class Element:
2       def __init__(self, value=None, next=None):
3           self.value = value
4           self.next = next
5       def __str__(self):
6           return repr(self.value)
7
8   class MyList:
9       def __init__(self):
10          self.first = None
11          self.length = 0
12      def __str__(self):
13          s = f"MyList (length={self.len()})["
14          p = self.first
15          while p is not None:
16              s += p.__str__()+","
17              p = p.next
18          s += "]"
19          return s
20      def len(self):
21          return self.length
22      def to_front(self,value):
23          if self.first is None:
24              self.first = Element(value)
25          else:
26              self.first = Element(value,self.first)
```

5.8 Solutions to Exercises

```
27              self.length += 1
28         def get(self,idx):
29             p = self.first
30             for i in range(idx):
31                 if p is None:
32                     return None
33                 p = p.next
34             return p.value if p is not None else None
35         def to_tail(self,value):
36             if self.first is None:
37                 self.first = Element(value)
38             else:
39                 p = self.first
40                 while p.next is not None:
41                     p = p.next
42                 p.next = Element(value)
43             self.length += 1
44         def remove(self,idx):
45             if idx >= self.length:
46                 return False,None
47             if idx == 0:
48                 e = self.first
49                 self.first = e.next
50                 self.length -= 1
51                 return True,e.value
52             previous = self.first
53             for i in range(1,idx):
54                 previous = previous.next
55                 if previous is None:
56                     return False,None
57             if previous.next is None:
58                 return False,None
59             e = previous.next
60             previous.next = e.next
61             self.length -= 1
62             return True,e.value
63
64     a_list = MyList()
65     print(a_list)
66     a_list.to_front(6)
67     print(a_list)
68     a_list.to_front(9)
69     a_list.to_front('foo')
70     a_list.to_front(666)
```

```
71  print(a_list)
72  for i in range(a_list.len()):
73      print(a_list.get(i))
74  print(a_list.get(2))
75  print(a_list.get(3))
76  a_list.to_tail(10)
77  print(a_list)
78  print(a_list.remove(5),a_list) # must be False
79  print(a_list.remove(4),a_list)
80  print(a_list.remove(1),a_list)
81  print(a_list.remove(0),a_list)
82  print(a_list.remove(0),a_list)
83  print(a_list.remove(0),a_list)
84  print(a_list.remove(0),a_list) # must be False
```

Drawings and More 6

PYTHON is provided with a lot of useful modules. As it is by no means a question of being exhaustive through this book, we have chosen, in this chapter, to present a few modules which could be useful for pragmatic algorithmic. Since in Part II we will focus on the study of algorithms and their possible implementations in PYTHON:

- it may be interesting to present results of some computations as drawings. For example, if we want to measure the time used by some algorithm, we may want to draw that time function to observe its behaviour. We may also want to measure how many times a given operation is executed during computations, etc. We will then see how measure time, how to add counting probes in a program, and how to draw something on the screen or an image file.
- as an aside it may be also useful to gather results into a file or read inputs from a file. We will then see how to read/write from/into files.
- we may also need to test our programs. As it is not always easy to prove that a program behave exactly the way we wanted, we can, at least, test them. A good test could be to try a program over a set of random inputs (a random choice other all possible valid inputs). We will then see how to tackle randomness.

6.1 Measuring Time

Measuring the speed of a program (or function) is called **benchmarking** (refer to Wikipedia entry "benchmark (computing)"). We must say that benchmarking is an hard task to do with high accuracy:

- First, because there may exists different clocks that can be used in a computer: CPU clock, wall clocks, system clocks, process clocks, etc. Each one has its advantages and drawbacks.

- Second, because of the **observer effect** (well know by physicists) stating that "observing a phenomenon disturbs the phenomenon itself".
- Third, because executions take place in fluctuant contexts (computer machinery is a wizardry) that may alter computation time. If executions took place on bare-metal machines that would be easy to measure time with accuracy. Alas, executions are managed by the operating system which, for good reasons, may alter a run being interrupted in the middle to manage a mouse move, a disk, the network, etc., thus modifying its execution time in some way.

6.1.1 Wall Clock

The first clock we can use is the **wall clock** to get a time as we would have been able to use a chronometer watch (but slightly more accurately). The idea is to catch the time on a watch just before the computation to be measured begins and the time just after it ends.

PYTHON provides a module time and a function time_ns to get such time expressed in nanoseconds.[1] The value returned is the number of nanoseconds elapsed from the EPOCH (January 1st, 1970, 00h00:00, the standard beginning of times in computer era):

Program 6.1: Wall clock measure   timeexp.py

```
import time

def fact(n):
    r = 1
    for i in range(2,n+1):
        r2 = 0
        for j in range(i): # multiplication made of adds to be slow
            r2 += r
        r = r2
    return r

start = time.time_ns()
fact(1000)
end = time.time_ns()
print(end - start)
```

---

[1] Prior to PYTHON 3.7, use time, which returns current time in fraction of seconds expressed in a float.

6.1 Measuring Time

An execution may lead to:

```
1  120249000
```

Some other executions (on the same machine) may give: 122482000 or 122961000. We may then ask what is the correct value? After all, the instructions executed are exactly the same, so why such differences? We already said that the context of execution (conditions on the machine at the time of execution) may vary and alter the elapsed time. At least, the order of magnitude of these measures seems to be consistent, but beware that may not be the case in general! Anyway, in standard conditions, the order of magnitude is preserved.

To be more accurate we may try to repeat the experiment several times and take the mean for example. Alas, it may not be possible to experiment the same computation several times! If the computation has border effects or depends on some context, it may not be possible to reproduce exactly the context. If we are not in that situation, for example if our system is not overladed with many running applications, we can safely try:

Program 6.2: Repeating experiments   timeexp2.py

```
1   import time
2
3   def fact(n):
4       r = 1
5       for i in range(2,n+1):
6           r2 = 0
7           for j in range(i): # multiplication made of adds to be slow
8               r2 += r
9           r = r2
10      return r
11
12  def experiment(): #time used to compute 1000!
13      start = time.time_ns()
14      fact(1000)
15      end = time.time_ns()
16      return end-start
17
18  n_experiments = int(input("Number of repetitions ? "))
19  t = 0
20  for i in range(n_experiments):
21      t += experiment()
22  print(t/n_experiments)
```

An execution in which we chose to repeat the computation hundred times may lead to:

```
1  Number of repetitions ? 100
2  117272200.0
```

Some other tries may give: 119715270.0 or 118540660.0, and we can then observe that this is not very consistent, too. One remark is that these average computed times are slightly less than the ones got by the former experiment. The reason is that for PYTHON to execute a portion of code necessitate some warming up, at least repeating again and again the experiment in the same execution smooths that overhead.

We can try again repeating the computation 500 times. Three runs may leads to 114694862.0, 117141384.0 and 115944956.0. So it looks like using this clock does not provide a very good accuracy. From these experiments we can at least deduce that the computation time of fact(1000) is around 115–120 ms on our machine.

Exercise 6.1
Would you be able to eliminate the overhead of the warm up? Try to see if it gives you better results.
Hint: do not take in account the first executions.

6.1.2 CPU Clock

Another clock available in PYTHON is provided by the use of process.time_ns. This clock is "internal" to the execution, it tries to measure the time spent in this run only. Time is not measured by getting time from an wall clock, but from a clock that ticks only when the execution is effective. OSes use time-sharing strategies to manage executions, thus the CPU clock counts only portions of "global" time allocated to the execution.. Thus it is potentially less sensible to some external conditions. We can then rewrite our program this way:

Program 6.3: CPU time   timeexp3.py

```
1  import time
2
3  def fact(n):
4      r = 1
5      for i in range(2,n+1):
6          r2 = 0
7          for j in range(i): # multiplication made of adds to be slow
8              r2 += r
9          r = r2
```

6.1 Measuring Time

```
10      return r
11
12  def experiment():
13      start = time.process_time_ns()
14      fact(1000)
15      end = time.process_time_ns()
16      return end-start
17
18  n_experiments = int(input("Number of repetitions ? "))
19  t = 0
20  for i in range(n_experiments):
21      t += experiment()
22  print(t/n_experiments)
```

On three different experiments (with a repetition factor of 100) we obtained: 116228800.0, 114797980.0 and 117841090.0. Alas these results seems not to be better than the ones got from the wall clock, but values are consistent with the previous results. Beware that there exist cases where CPU and wall clocks differ drastically. For example, wall clock counts time passed in user inputs (the time passed by the user to input something from the keyboard):

Program 6.4: Wall clock vs CPU clock on inputs   timeexpinp.py

```
1   import time
2
3   start_time = time.time_ns()
4   start_process = time.process_time_ns()
5   input("Tell me something: ")
6   end_time = time.time_ns()
7   end_process = time.process_time_ns()
8
9   print(end_time-start_time)
10  print(end_process-start_process)
```

An execution could lead to:

```
1   Tell me something: blabla  ⟵ we took some time to type the chars
2   5947894000
3   76000
```

We can observe that the wall clock measure is around 6 s while the CPU clock got 76 µs.

Exercise 6.2
We can shuffle a list with the help of the function shuffle of the module random:

> Program 6.5: Shuffling a list

```
1  import random
2  l = [1, 2, 3, 4]
3  random.shuffle(l)
```

Using this function measure the average time used to sort lists (using l.sort()) of different lengths (say from 1 to 100,000 by step 1000).
The average time may be obtained by shuffling and sorting 10 lists of the same size.
The result may looks like:

```
1   1 1 μs
2   1001 90 μs
3   2001 198 μs
4   3001 311 μs
5   4001 380 μs
6   5001 491 μs
7   6001 627 μs
8   7001 677 μs
9   ...
10  92001 12928 μs
11  93001 13226 μs
12  94001 13358 μs
13  95001 13716 μs
14  96001 13814 μs
15  97001 14025 μs
16  98001 14258 μs
17  99001 14373 μs
```

6.2 Counting Operations

We will see later in Part II that we will sometimes need to be finer in doing measures. For example, we may ask how many multiplications, additions, tests are executed in a given computation. Unfortunately there is no built-in tool to get these answers. We need to construct our own.

The Syracuse or Collatz function is defined for any positive integer n as:

$$C(n) = \begin{cases} n/2, & \text{if } n \text{ is odd.} \\ 3n+1, & \text{if } n \text{ is odd.} \end{cases}$$

The Collatz conjecture states that for any positive integer n, there exists an integer p such that $C^p(n) = \overbrace{C(C(\ldots C(n)))}^{p} = 1$.

6.2 Counting Operations

Consider the following program that stops only if the Syracuse sequence associated to a given integer reaches 1:

Program 6.6: Syracuse   syracuse.py

```
1  def syracuse(n):
2      while n != 1:
3          if n%2 == 0:
4              n = n/2
5          else:
6              n = 3*n+1
7  
8  syracuse(100)
```

Obviously this program do not print anything, but we can measure the time spent before it stops. What what to do if we want to know how many times we looped in the `while`?

We can add some variable to count the number of times we looped:

Program 6.7: Number of loops in Syracuse   syracuse2.py

```
1   def syracuse(n):
2       count = 0            # add instrument
3       while n != 1:
4           count += 1       # measure
5           if n%2 == 0:
6               n = n/2
7           else:
8               n = 3*n+1
9       return count         # return the final measure
10  
11  n = 100
12  print(f"Syracuse({n}) looped {syracuse(n)} times.")
```

The execution will give:

```
1  Syracuse(100) looped 25 times.
```

If we now want to know how many multiplications are involved? We need another counter:

Program 6.8: Number of multiplications in Syracuse   syracuse3.py

```
1  def syracuse(n):
2      count = 0            # add "loop" instrument
```

```
3    mult = 0              # add "*" instrument
4    while n != 1:
5        count += 1        # measure
6        if n%2 == 0:
7            n = n/2
8        else:
9            n = 3*n+1
10           mult += 1      # measure
11   return count,mult      # return the final measures
12
13 n = 100
14 loops, mults = syracuse(n)
15 print(f"Syracuse({n}) looped {loops} times with {mults} ▷
       ▷ multiplications.")
```

The execution will give:

```
1 Syracuse(100) looped 25 times with 7 multiplications.
```

We note that introducing more "instruments" (the counters) alters the code and obviously its execution time! We have to be careful in modifying a code this way, we introduced new variables and need to be sure that none will interfere with existing ones.

Alas, this can be more complicated if we want to count the number of comparisons. We need to destructure the code as in the following:

Program 6.9: Number of tests in Syracuse   syracuse4.py

```
1  def syracuse(n):
2      count = 0           # add "loop" instrument
3      mult = 0            # add "*" instrument
4      test = 0            # add "test" instrument
5      test += 1           # a test will be evaluated just after!
6      while n != 1:
7          count += 1      # measure
8          if n%2 == 0:
9              n = n/2
10         else:
11             n = 3*n+1
12             mult += 1   # measure
13         test += 1       # a test will be executed just after!
14     return count,mult,test # return the final measures
15
16 n = 100
```

6.2 Counting Operations

```
17  loops, mults,tests = syracuse(n)
18  print(f"Syracuse({n}) looped {loops} times with {mults} ▷
          ▷ multiplications, {tests} tests.")
```

The execution will give:

```
1  Syracuse(100) looped 25 times with 7 multiplications, 26 tests.
```

This last counter is tricky as we must ensure that for every comparison it will be incremented. In this case, we increment it before the comparison (but the symmetric case can be used).

A variant could be to use the Walrus operator (see Sect. 5.1.1.1) as in the following:

Program 6.10: Number of tests in Syracuse   syracuse4bis.py

```
1   def syracuse(n):
2       count, mult, test = 0, 0, 0 # add instruments
3       while (test := test+1, n != 1)[1]: # (increment,test) tuple
4           count += 1
5           if n%2 == 0:
6               n = n/2
7           else:
8               n = 3*n+1; mult += 1
9       return count,mult,test # return the final measures
10
11  n = 100
12  loops, mults, tests = syracuse(n)
13  print(f"Syracuse({n}) looped {loops} times with {mults} ▷
          ▷ multiplications, {tests} tests.")
```

That solution may seem more tricky than the previous but it has the advantage that the increment of the counter will take place at a single point in the code, and is then less error-prone.

Exercise 6.3
Add counters to the program Syracuse to get the number of additions and divisions.

Hint: take care of not counting the operations used by the counters themselves!

6.3 Drawing

The most common module used to make drawings is matplotlib.[2] It provides many ways of representing data in graphics and allows to save them in many different formats.

To draw something we need data (roughly, coordinates of points in some space). The data to be used with matplotlib are list of values, one for each coordinates. So to represent the $\sin(x)$ (resp. $\cos(x)$) function in the interval $[-2\pi, 2\pi]$, we can use the following module to create two lists of coordinates (x and $y = \sin(x)$ coordinates, resp. $y = \cos(x)$):

Program 6.11: Generate data to plot — generate.py

```python
import math

def generate_sin_data(step=0.05):
    begin = int(-2*math.pi/step)
    end = int(2*math.pi/step)
    x = [i*step for i in range(begin,end)]
    y = [math.sin(v) for v in x]
    return x,y

def generate_cos_data(step=0.05):
    begin = int(-2*math.pi/step)
    end = int(2*math.pi/step)
    x = [i*step for i in range(begin,end)]
    y = [math.cos(v) for v in x]
    return x,y
```

We need to tweak the range to get the values on the x-axis because range operates only on integers.[3] Now to draw this set of points, interpolated by lines, we can simply use:

Program 6.12: Plot some data — plotdata.py

```python
import matplotlib.pyplot
import generate
x,y = generate.generate_data()
```

---

[2] It is not part of the basic PYTHON installation, so we may need to install it with a command like pip install matplotlib (or any equivalent if we use an IDE).

[3] Many examples on the internet use the numpy module to generate such data. We did not want to use such module as it is not necessary for our basic needs. We refer the reader to the many available tutorials on the subject if needed.

6.3 Drawing

```
4  matplotlib.pyplot.plot(x,y)
5  matplotlib.pyplot.show()
```

whose execution opens a new window with the drawing inside, like in Fig. 6.1.

We should not be fooled by the result, it looks like a continuous drawing but it is not. The plot function simply draws a line in between successive points, so if points are sufficiently closed one to each other the final results looks like continuous. For example, if we call the function with a rougher step over x coordinates like generate_sin_data(0.7), we obtain the drawing in Fig. 6.2.

One can observe that the window contains several buttons to get some functionalities: pan, zoom, save to file, etc.

Note that showing the picture on screen by calling show will pause the execution until the window is closed. The execution will then resume at the instruction just after the call.

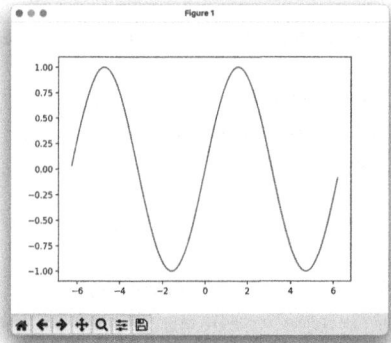

Fig. 6.1 Drawing of sin(x) with short segments

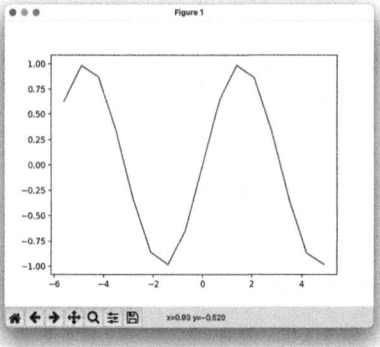

Fig. 6.2 Drawing of sin(x) with long segments

Fig. 6.3 Drawing saved in an image file

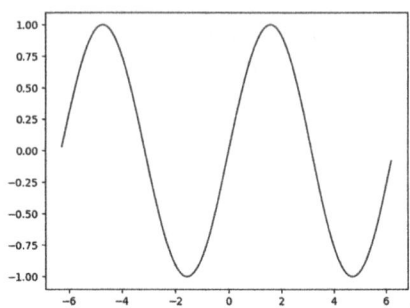

6.3.1 Generate an Image File

We may want not to display the picture in a window but to get an image file. The submodule pyplot has a function called savefig that can be used to generate an image file:

Program 6.13: Save picture as an image file   sinplot2.py

```
import math
import matplotlib.pyplot
import generate

x,y = generate.generate_sin_data()

matplotlib.pyplot.plot(x,y)
file_name = 'sin.png' # name of the image file
matplotlib.pyplot.savefig(file_name)
```

The generated file will then not contain any window decoration as illustrated in Fig. 6.3.

Available formats include: JPEG, PNG and PDF, with respective file extensions .jpg, .png and .pdf.

6.3.2 Picture Properties

We can customise the drawings in several ways. For example we may want to add labels on axis:

Program 6.14: Adding labels on axis   sinplot3.py

```
import math
import matplotlib.pyplot
```

6.3 Drawing

```
3  import generate
4
5  x,y = generate.generate_sin_data()
6
7  matplotlib.pyplot.plot(x,y)
8  matplotlib.pyplot.xlabel('angle in radians')
9  matplotlib.pyplot.ylabel('sin')
10 matplotlib.pyplot.savefig('sinlabel.png')
```

which produces an image like the one in Fig. 6.4.

If we want to change the colour of the plotting; the function `plot` accepts a third argument to specify it.

Program 6.15: Changing colours   sinplot4.py

```
1  import math
2  import matplotlib.pyplot
3  import generate
4
5  x,y = generate.generate_sin_data()
6
7  matplotlib.pyplot.plot(x,y,color='red')
8  matplotlib.pyplot.xlabel('angle in radians')
9  matplotlib.pyplot.ylabel('sin')
10 matplotlib.pyplot.savefig('sincolor.png')
```

Colours can be specified in many ways:

- by the use of standard colours specification: `black`, `gray`, `red`, `green`, etc. We cannot be exhaustive here and refer the reader to the documentation.

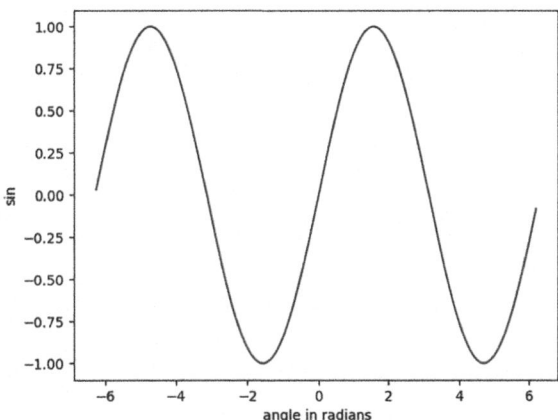

Fig. 6.4 Label a drawing

- by the use of RGB specification. There is at least two formats:
  - triples of floats in the interval [0, 1], like (0.5,0.5,0.5) for a gray or (0.0,0.0,1.0) for blue. Beware that in this case we must not pass a string but the tuple itself like: color=(0.5,0.5,0.5),
  - hexadecimal literal value of the colour where each channel is in the range [0, 256[thus from 00 to FF. Examples can be: #777777 for gray, or #0000FF for blue.

Refer to "Specifying colors in matplotlib" for more information about these representations.

We may also change the thickness of the drawing:

Program 6.16: Changing the thickness   sinplot5.py

```
1  import math
2  import matplotlib.pyplot
3  import generate
4
5  x,y = generate.generate_sin_data()
6
7  matplotlib.pyplot.plot(x,y,color='red',linewidth=10)
8  matplotlib.pyplot.xlabel('angle in radians')
9  matplotlib.pyplot.ylabel('sin')
10 matplotlib.pyplot.savefig('sinthick.png')
```

which produces the drawing of Fig. 6.5.

Fig. 6.5 Controlling the thickness of a drawing

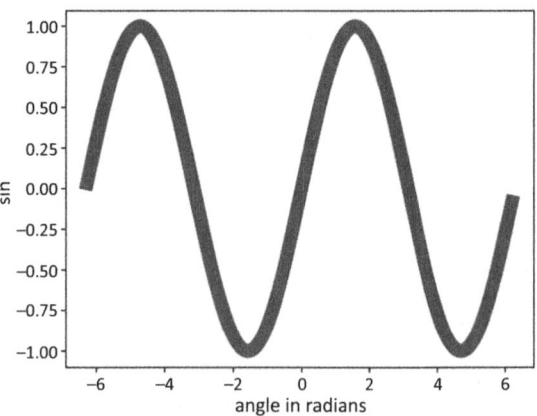

6.3.3 Drawing Several Functions

We can use the function plot several time to get many drawings on the same picture. In this case it may be better to label the curves and show a legend for each one:

Program 6.17: Adding labels on axis sinplot6.py

```
import math
import matplotlib.pyplot
import generate

x,y = generate.generate_sin_data()
t,z = generate.generate_cos_data()

matplotlib.pyplot.plot(x,y,color='black',label='sin',linewidth=10)
matplotlib.pyplot.plot(t,z,color='gray',label='cos',linewidth=10)
matplotlib.pyplot.xlabel('angle in radians')
matplotlib.pyplot.legend()
matplotlib.pyplot.savefig('sinmultiple.png')
```

which produces the picture in Fig. 6.6.

6.3.4 Scaling Axis

Some functions cannot easily be drawn in with linear scale on axis, for example the growth rate of the exponential is too large to let such a function correctly represented. A logarithmic scale on the y-axis can then be used:

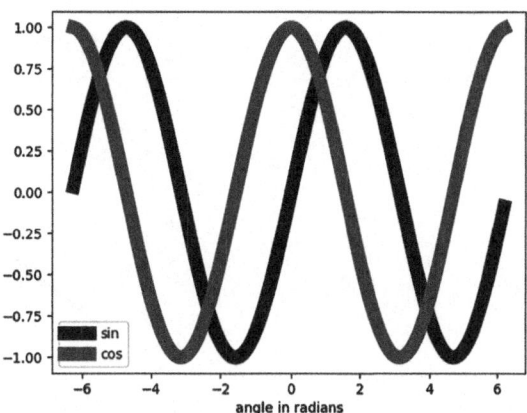

Fig. 6.6 Multiple drawings on the same picture

Program 6.18: Logarithmic scale on y-axis   sinplot7.py

```
import math
import matplotlib.pyplot

def generate_data():
    x = [i for i in range(10)]
    y = [2**v for v in x]
    return x,y

x,y = generate_data()

matplotlib.pyplot.title("A plot")
matplotlib.pyplot.plot(x,y,color='black',linewidth=3)
matplotlib.pyplot.xlabel('x')
matplotlib.pyplot.ylabel('$2^x$')
matplotlib.pyplot.yscale('log')
matplotlib.pyplot.savefig('sinscale.png')
```

This program produces the picture in Fig. 6.7. The representation of the function $y = 2^x$ is a straight line as we use a variable change for a unknown logarithmic base b:

$$Y = \log_b y = \log_b 2^x = \frac{\log_2 2^x}{\log_2 b} = K.x$$

We can figure out how to set up a logarithmic scale on the x-axis. We refer the reader to the documentation of `matplotlib` to find how to control the scaling of the axis.

Fig. 6.7 Axis scaling

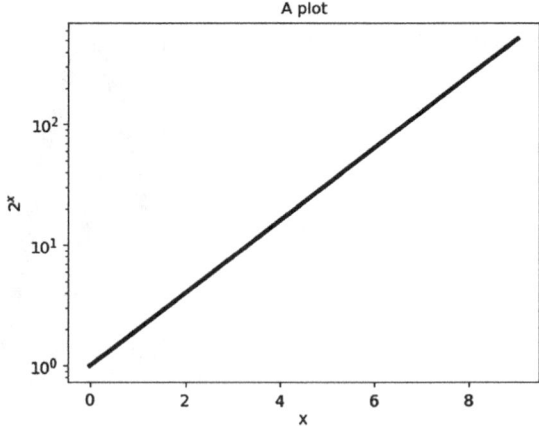

Note how we set the title of the whole picture with the use of `title()` function.

Also note that we used a special construct to get 2^x as the label on the y-axis. If you have a good LaTeX installation on your system then you can use any LaTeX formula for labels. Please read "Matplotlib Rendering math equations using TeX".

6.4 File Handling

Sometimes we need to store data in files, or to read data from files. Here we will just give some quick recipes to do this and will not dig into the complexity of input/output functionalities.

The most difficult part of this is to clearly define the way things are represented in the file, in computer engineering we call this the **file format**. If we do not specify very carefully the format of data, then soon or later we will face difficulties. In the following, we will only focus on reading and writing data as text strings. We must be aware that analysing a text, or simply a string of characters, to get values from it[4] is an hard task for beginners.

Suppose we want to generated some data like some pairs of points in 2D, for example the four points (12,23), (13,22), (14,33) and (15,19). How we will write them in a file?

- Each value in a single line of text?
- A pair of values in a single line of text?
- All values on a single line?

How are values separated: by a single space, sequence of tabs, mix of spaces and tabs, etc.?

We can choose any format we want to represent data in a file, but the point is that we have to be consistent for each use of the file, every time we read or write from/into it. At least at the beginning, we have to chose a format that will ease reads and writes.

In the following, we choose a pair of integer values on the same line of text, separated by a single space, to represent a point, something like:

```
1    12 23
2    13 22
3    14 33
4    15 19
```

---

[4] This is called parsing, or syntax analysis.

Let us suppose that, in PYTHON, the points are represented as two lists of coordinates values (any other representation would be fine too):

```
1  x = [12, 13, 14, 15]
2  y = [23, 22, 33, 19]
```

6.4.1 Writing

To write data into a file following the chosen file format, we can proceed as follows:

Program 6.19: Write data into a file   write.py

```
1  x = [12, 13, 14, 15]
2  y = [23, 22, 33, 19]
3
4  with open("data.txt","w") as f_key:
5      for i in range(len(x)):
6          f_key.write(f"{x[i]} {y[i]}\n")
```

The first new construct is the with. It is a new kind of control flow structure. Its primary goal is to automate the closing of resources. A **resource** is something external to a program, whose availability and usage are possible under some conditions (for example, in real life a resource could be a room). To manipulate a resource we always have to follow the pattern: acquire, use, then release it (for a room that could be get its key, use the room and then release its key). As a file is a resource, the pattern: acquire, use, release corresponds to the file functions open, read/write, close. As it is too common to forget to release a resource, PYTHON offers the control flow instruction with to release it automatically (in real life that could be a watchdog waiting you at the exit door of the building and picking the room key you have in your pocket when you exits the building). In the block of instructions under the with, the acquired resource is represented by the variable named f_key (in real life that would be the key of the room). We can use it as needed as we requested and gained an access to it with open. At the end of the block it will be implicitly released (by an implicit call to close on it).

The function open is to request access to a file (acquire the resource). Its first parameter is the name of the file. If we use a relative name then it will be relative to the directory the execution takes place. A relative name could be 'afile.txt' or 'mydata/myfile.txt'.[5] If we use an absolute name, the file is uniquely determined as it will not depend on the directory we are working in. An absolute

---

[5] Beware of the separator to be used for directories. In the Unix world it is / (slash) while in Windows world it is \ (backslash).

name is something like /home/user/smith/data/file.txt (Unix world), while in Windows world it could be like C:\Users\smith\data\file.txt. In general, relative names are preferred. The second parameter is the kind of opening (usage) we need on the file. The value 'w' specifies to open the file for writing. The file will be created if needed, or emptied first if it already exists. There is a lot of other possible accesses to be requested: overwrite, append, read, etc. (refer to the documentation).

In lines 5–6, we loop in parallel over the two lists of values and write what we want into the file with the help of the write function. Remark we add \n at the end of the string to be written. This is a special character, not two, only a single one, that represents an end of line (EOL) or what is inserted in a file when we type a ⏎ (return) key. There are several other special characters like \t (tab), \\ (\) and many others.

After the execution, we should be able to display the content of the file named data.txt:

```
1  12 23
2  13 22
3  14 33
4  15 19
```

That is exactly what we initially wanted.

Beware that a call to open may fail for many different reasons: no more space on disk, bad name, no permission to open it, etc. If it happens, an error will be reported and the script will immediately end, for example:

```
1  Traceback (most recent call last):
2    File "/home/yunes/examples/write.py", line 4, in <module>
3      with open("data.txt","w") as f:
4  PermissionError: [Errno 13] Permission denied: 'data.txt'
```

6.4.2 Reading

Intuitively reading may seem easier than writing. However it is not the writing or reading, per se, that are easy or difficult, it is the parsing (the analysis) of what was read that adds more complexity on the subject. As humans we learn how to read and write but that was very long and difficult to process. A computer is not smart in any way so we have to describe to it every basic operation needed to read and decode something.

Now, what if we want to read the content of a file? Without big surprise there is a mode to open the file for reading and if the file simply contains lines of text, we can iterate other them with a `for` loop:[6]

Program 6.20: Reading a file, iterating over the lines of text   read.py

```
1  with open("data.txt","r") as f:
2      for l in f:
3          print(f"I read the line [{l}]")
```

What will be printed (if the file was generated as in the previous section) is:

```
1  I read the line [12 23
2  ]
3  I read the line [13 22
4  ]
5  I read the line [14 33
6  ]
7  I read the line [15 19
8  ]
```

A opened file is an iterable of lines. Remember that an opened file is not the file, but a "key" to use the file.

The printing is somehow weird, but the program exactly did what it was instructed to. We read the text file line by line through the iteration, but a line is a sequence of characters ending with EOL (end of line special character). That character is inserted in the string returned by `read`, so PYTHON printed [, the whole sequence of chars read as a line (including the noisy EOL) and then a].

We can remove that last character, which is not important to us by the use of the function `strip`:

Program 6.21: Stripping strings   read2.py

```
1  with open("data.txt","r") as f:
2      for l in f:
3          stripped_l = l.strip()
4          print(f"I read the line [{stripped_l}]")
```

---

[6] Remember that we will only discuss about reading/writing text files in this book.

6.4 File Handling

What will now be printed is:

```
1  I read the line [12 23]
2  I read the line [13 22]
3  I read the line [14 33]
4  I read the line [15 19]
```

A call to the method `strip` removes any spacing character at the beginning and at the end of a given string. The character EOL is considered a spacing character, so it is removed by the call to `strip`.

Now that we get a string like `'12 23'` we need to extract the two numbers 12 and 23. We insist, it is very easy for humans, but for a computer we have to tell it how to get integers from the string. We will not do it, but in the hidden details of what we will present, a procedure similar to the following one as to be applied:

1. set current number to value 0,
2. get the first character, transform it as a number in [0, 9], set current number to value: old value × 10 + value of the character,
3. get the second, transform it as a number in [0, 9], set current number to value: old value × 10 + value of the character,
4. get the third, it's a space, then the current number is the value we are looking to,
5. etc.

In general this is not so simple (numbers do not have fixed length, a variable number of spaces may be present, etc.). Parsing is hard, at least if we don't know an appropriate theory to use.[7]

Anyway, our data format is very basic and we do not need such an heavy hammer. Our parsing strategy will be what is called **marshalling/unmarshalling**, a procedure to write a value in some external representation (marshall) and read it back (unmarshall). This is also called **serialisation/deserialisation**.

In our case we know that a line is made of two strings separated by a single space, so we can get the strings with the help of the `split` function. That function gets a string and returns a list of its words. By default, this function consider words as sequence of non-spacing characters separated by spacing characters. We can then use it:

Program 6.22: Splitting strings into list of words   read3.py

```
1  with open("data.txt","r") as f:
2      for l in f:
3          stripped_l = l.strip()
4          words = stripped_l.split()
5          print("Got:",words)
```

---

[7] It is one of the topics of **formal languages theory**.

We then get:

```
1  Got: ['12', '23']
2  Got: ['13', '22']
3  Got: ['14', '33']
4  Got: ['15', '19']
```

We already know how to convert a string representing a number to a python type (integer or float) value, hence we can write the final code:

Program 6.23: Splitting strings into list of words   read4.py

```
1   x = []
2   y = []
3   with open("data.txt","r") as f:
4       for l in f:
5           stripped_l = l.strip()
6           words = stripped_l.split()
7           x.append(int(words[0]))
8           y.append(int(words[1]))
9   print(x)
10  print(y)
```

We then get:

```
1  [12, 13, 14, 15]
2  [23, 22, 33, 19]
```

Beware that if there is a single mistake in the file (a missing number, a float and not an integer representation, a string not representing a number, etc.), this parsing will fail. Sometimes it will fail generating a non recoverable error and the execution will stop emitting a message, but sometimes it will fail generating some inconsistencies in the data (that is the worst situation).

Always remember: reading data necessitates parsing, which is not easy.

6.5 Random Numbers

To experiment, it is often required to get a bunch of random data. The term **random** is somehow misleading, there is no algorithm to generate truly random data. There is a contradiction between "being random" (unpredictable) and "being generated by an algorithm" (thus perfectly predictable). Algorithms can generate only **pseudo-random numbers**. These algorithms are called **pseudo-random number generators** (**PRNG**). That means that the generated sequences are not truly random but have some good "random" properties, i.e. they verify some good

6.5 Random Numbers

statistical properties. The only way to produce true randomness is by the use of external true random source, or by the help of some physical non deterministic phenomenon (mouse moves, network activity, etc.). Even in these cases there can be some biases that are hard to eliminate. True randomness is difficult to obtain but is almost mandatory in fields like cryptography. We then refer the reader to literature on the subject needed. Regardless, there exist many algorithms which can produce pseudo-random sequences.

Pseudo-random sequences have two major advantages:

- they are easy to construct and they looks like random, so we can use them to make some statistical tests on algorithms (we will have such a need in the algorithmic part);
- they are deterministic, so we can exactly reproduce any experience made, provided we know the parameters used by the generators. Remind that reproducibility is an important concern in science.

A major drawback of PRNG is that they ultimately generate periodic sequences, at some point the sequence falls into a cycle of values. That is the consequence of using finite deterministic machines. By the way, for the purpose of this book, PRN (pseudo-random number) sequences will be sufficient.

Usually a pseudo random sequence is obtained by the use of a **seed**. The seed and the PRNG used uniquely determine a sequence of pseudo-random numbers. Very simple PRNG are **LCG (Linear Congruential Generator)**. They are of the form:

$$x_{n+1} = (a \cdot x_n + b) \mod m$$

starting from a value x_0 called the **seed**. The choice of a, b and m have been subject of many studies. Today, nobody will use such generators, they are considered as too bad, but the reader may try to play with it.

A better choice is to use **LFSR (Linear-Feedback Shift Registers)**. PYTHON has a module named random which provides several ways of getting pseudo-random numbers. The PRNG used by python is known as the "Mersenne Twister" (in Honor of the sixteenth century mathematician **Marin Mersenne**, see [16]), an LFSR-based generator whose period is $2^{19937} - 1$. A very simple example of its use could be:

Program 6.24: Generating a pseudo-random sequence   rand1.py

```
import random

random.seed(12)

for i in range(100):
        print(random.randint(0,9),end=' ')
print()
```

Its execution will **always** produces the same result:

```
1  7 4 8 5 2 6 0 5 7 4 7 9 3 8 0 9 2 7 5 ... 3 9 1 8 3 2 1 4 0 6 4 7 5
```

We used the `seed` function to set the seed, and each time we need a new "random" integer we used `randint` which needs a (closed) interval in which a value is chosen.

Note that we used a variant of the function `print` to get print all the value on the same line. By default `print` prints its parameters followed by an EOL character to terminate the line. The function `print` accepts a named parameter end whose value is used (as a replacement of the default EOL) at the end of the printing of the other arguments. We used end=' ' to separate all the calls to `print` by a space character.

If we need to get different numbers on each execution, we can then call seed without providing a value, PYTHON will use the current time as the seed, thus generating an different sequence each time we execute the program. This is sufficient to get the illusion of randomness:

Program 6.25: Illusion of randomness   rand2.py

```
1  import random
2
3  random.seed()
4
5  for i in range(100):
6      print(random.randint(0,9),end=' ')
7  print()
```

A first execution could generate:

```
1  3 3 0 2 9 7 5 0 7 8 2 5 4 3 3 3 7 4 1 ... 3 5 9 9 8 7 3 5 8 9 3 8 2
```

and a second one:

```
1  5 1 4 2 1 6 8 8 9 4 3 0 0 7 4 8 1 0 8 ... 5 7 6 7 0 0 2 8 1 5 1 6 9
```

Exercise 6.4
Modify the program 6.91 such that, in place of printing the numbers, the average ($\bar{x}$) and the standard deviation (σ) of the values will be printed at the end.

Hint: store the generated numbers in a list to compute $\bar{x} = \frac{\sum x_i}{N}$ and $\sigma = \sqrt{\frac{\sum (x_i - \bar{x})^2}{N}}$.

Exercise 6.5
Use the formula

$$\sigma = \sqrt{\frac{\sum x_i^2}{N} - \left(\frac{\sum x_i}{N}\right)^2}$$

to compute the standard deviation on-the-fly (without storing the generated numbers in a list).

Exercise 6.6
Write a program that writes in a file a sequence of random numbers.
Write another program that reads these numbers and computes their average and standard deviation.

Exercise 6.7

1. Write a function `generate(n)` that generates a random list of n integers in $[0, n[$ and returns it.
2. Write a function `experiment(l)` that sorts a list `l` of integers with the predefined function `sort` and returns the time needed for.
3. Write a function `repeat_experiment(n,m)` that (in m loops): generates a random list of length n, accumulates the time needed to sort it; and then computes the mean of these times at the end.
4. Write a function `time_complexity(m)` that generates several calls to `repeat_experiment(,m)` and returns a table of values for several lengths of lists (for example: all powers of 2 from 2 to 2^{23} or little less if your computer is too slow).
5. Plot the curve of the times against the lengths, and compare it with functions n and $n \cdot log(n)$.
6. How the PYTHON list sorting function behave relatively to their lengths?

Exercise 6.8
There is a very simple way to get an approximation of π that uses the Monte-Carlo method (a general tool to get numerical results from random samplings). While the method has a very bad convergence in this case, we can try to simulate it.
To get an approximation of π, we can pick n random points in a square of length l and, count number m of them that are inside the circle inscribed in the square. As the surface of the square is l^2 and the one of the circle is $\frac{\pi \cdot l^2}{4}$, we will have $\frac{m}{n} \approx \frac{\pi}{4}$ and hence $\pi \approx 4\frac{m}{n}$.

1. Write a program to implement this method that will let the user chose the number n.
2. Add the code to get the picture of the picked points.

Hint: to plot single points and not lines, use `scatter` and not `plot` of `pyplot` module. To control the size of the plotted points, use the parameter s to `scatter`.

Exercise 6.9
Hard
Fractals are (roughly) self-similar structures, so some of them are eligible to recursive algorithms approximation.
The Sierpiński carpet is a **fractal** designed by a polish mathematician named Waclaw Franciszek Sierpiński in 1911.
The carpet is defined by subdividing a square into 9 subsquares of equal size, "removing" the central one and repeating the process on the others.
The first step is illustrated like Fig. 6.8 (the removal is replaced by a black filling).

Fig. 6.8 Removal in the Sierpiński carpet

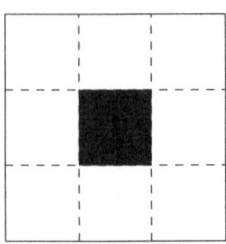

Fig. 6.9 A Sierpiński carpet after some recursions

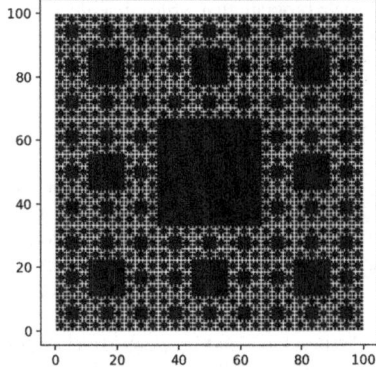

To better understand how it could looks, here is a carpet after some level of recursion (Fig. 6.9).
Write a program to generate a Sierpiński carpet for a given recursion depth.
How many calls are generated if the level of recursion is n?
Play with it: try several combinations of recursion and removals. Search for the Sierpiński gasket or the Wallis sieve, try to implement them.

Hint: to fill an area with a color we can use `fill` function of `pyplot` (look at the documentation).

6.6 Solutions to Exercises

Solution to Exercise 6.2

Program 6.26: Measure time to sort shuffled lists   cpu.py

```
import time
import random

def exp(n):
    l = [i for i in range(n)]
    random.shuffle(l)
    start = time.process_time_ns()
    l.sort()
    end = time.process_time_ns()
    return end-start
```

6.6 Solutions to Exercises

```
12  def rep_exp(n,r):
13      t = 0
14      for i in range(r):
15          t += exp(n)
16      return int(t/r)
17
18
19  for i in range(1,100000,1000):
20      print(i,rep_exp(i,10)//1000,"µs")
```

Solution to Exercise 6.4

Program 6.27: Average and standard deviation   randsol1.py

```
1   import random
2   import math
3
4   random.seed()
5
6   values = [random.randint(0,9) for i in range(100)]
7   sum = 0
8   for v in values:
9       sum += v
10  average = sum / len(values)
11  sum = 0
12  for v in values:
13      sum += (v-average)**2
14  deviation = math.sqrt(sum/len(values))
15
16  print(f"Average: {average}, standard deviation: {deviation}")
```

Solution to Exercise 6.5

Program 6.28: Average and standard deviation on-the-fly   randsol2.py

```
1   import random
2   import math
3
4   random.seed()
```

```
 5
 6  sum_squares = 0
 7  sum = 0
 8  N = 1000000
 9  for i in range(N):
10      v = random.randint(0,9)
11      sum_squares += v**2
12      sum += v
13  average = sum/N
14  deviation = math.sqrt(sum_squares/N - average**2)
15  print(f"Average: {average}, standard deviation: {deviation}")
```

Solution to Exercise 6.7

Program 6.29: Measure Python sort execution time — timemeasure.py

```
 1  import random
 2  import matplotlib.pyplot
 3  import time
 4  import math
 5
 6  r = random.seed(0)
 7
 8  def generate(n):
 9      return [random.randint(0,n) for i in range(n)]
10
11  def experiment(l):
12      start = time.process_time_ns()
13      l.sort()
14      end = time.process_time_ns()
15      return end-start
16
17  def repeat_experiment(n,m):
18      time = 0
19      for i in range(m):
20          time += experiment(generate(n))
21      return time//m
22
23  def time_complexity():
24      lengths = []
25      times = []
26      for n in range(25):
```

```
27          l = 2**n
28          print("Trying length",l)
29          lengths.append(l)
30          times.append(repeat_experiment(l,1))
31      return lengths, times
32
33  l, t = time_complexity()
34  matplotlib.pyplot.plot(l,t)
35
36  factor = 20    # Handy factor to "close" curves togetther
37  tn = [int(v*factor) for v in l]
38  matplotlib.pyplot.plot(l,tn)
39
40  tnln = [int(factor*v*math.log(v)) for v in l]
41  matplotlib.pyplot.plot(l,tnln)
42
43  matplotlib.pyplot.show()
```

Solution to Exercise 6.8

The proposed solution simulates the picks in the north-east quarter of the original figure as it is much more easy to implement. It is left to the reader to be convinced or to prove that this does not change anything at the end (Fig. 6.10).

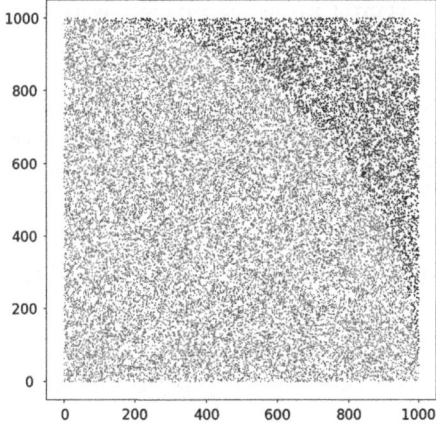

Fig. 6.10 Monte-Carlo picking to get π=3.1482666666666668

Program 6.30: π by Monte-Carlo   pimonte.py

```
1  import random
2  import math
3  import matplotlib.pyplot
4
5  random.seed() # new sequence each time
6
7  def is_in_circle(x,y,r):
8      return x**2+y**2 < r**2
9
10 def pick(n,l):
11     inside = 0
12     ox, oy, ix, iy = [], [], [], []
13     for i in range(n):
14         x, y = random.randint(0,l), random.randint(0,l)
15         if is_in_circle(x,y,l):
16             inside += 1
17             ix.append(x); iy.append(y)
18         else:
19             ox.append(x); oy.append(y)
20     return inside, ox, oy, ix, iy
21
22 n = int(input("Number of picks? "))
23 square_side = 1000
24
25 inside, ox, oy, ix, iy = pick(n,square_side)
26
27 print(f"pi approximatively equals {4*inside/n}")
28
29 dot_size = 0.2
30 matplotlib.pyplot.scatter(ox,oy,s=dot_size,color='black')
31 matplotlib.pyplot.scatter(ix,iy,s=dot_size,color='gray')
32 matplotlib.pyplot.axis('scaled')
33 matplotlib.pyplot.show()
```

The program can produce something like:

```
1  Number of picks? 30000
2  pi approximatively equals 3.1482666666666668
```

Solution to Exercise 6.9

Program 6.31: Drawing a Sierpiński carpet   sierpinskicarpet.py

```python
import matplotlib.pyplot

def rectangle(x,y,size):
    return [x, x+size, x+size, x, x], [y, y, y+size, y+size, y]

def sierpinski_carpet(x,y,size):
    if size<1:
        return
    for i in range(3):
        sx = x+i*size/3
        for j in range(3):
            sy = y+j*size/3
            if (i==1 and j==1):
                xs, ys = rectangle(sx,sy,size/3)
                matplotlib.pyplot.fill(xs,ys,color='black')
            else:
                sierpinski_carpet(sx,sy,size/3)

sierpinski_carpet(0,0,100)
matplotlib.pyplot.axis('scaled')
matplotlib.pyplot.show()
```

Each call to the function generates 8 recursive calls, one for each sub-square except the inner one. Thus, if there is n level of recursions, there will be $\sum_{i=0}^{n} 8^i = \frac{8^{n+1}-1}{7}$ calls.

Part II
Algorithms

Algorithm Performance

What Is an Algorithm? How Do We Measure Its Performances?

An **algorithm** is a procedure described in terms of elementary steps, allowing to determine the solution of a **problem** starting from any of the possible data (also called **instances of the problem**). An algorithm must always provide the correct answer/solution after carrying out a finite number of such elementary steps. We say that the algorithm *solves* the problem.

We will certainly have to formalise better the notion of "elementary steps" but let us first note that problems may take different forms and may have different kinds of instances and different kinds of answers or solutions they are expected to return. For example:

IsPrime?

The problem: given an integer number, determine if it is a prime number.
An instance: an integer number.
Expected answer: yes or no/true or false (a boolean).

Max

The Problem: given an array of integers, find the maximum of its values.
An instance: an array of integers.
Expected answer: an integer.

> ### Sort
> **The Problem:** given an array of integers, compute the array obtained by rearranging its values in increasing order.
> **An instance:** an array of integers.
> **Expected answer:** an array of integers.

> ### IsSubword?
> **The Problem:** given a text and a pattern (a word), determine if the text contains the pattern as a subword.
> **An instance:** a pair of sequences of characters (strings).
> **Expected answer:** a boolean.

> ### ShortestPath
> **The Problem:** given the map of a city find the shortest itinerary to go from point A to point B.
> **An instance:** a (weighted) graph.
> **Expected answer:** a path made of edges of the graph.

An **algorithm** is a simple transcription of a conceptual object: the procedure to follow to go from the data to the solution. In that sense algorithms are often compared to cooking recipes. An algorithm is not the same thing as a program. An algorithm can even be described using natural languages as long as the instructions are expressed in a clear and unambiguous way. Most of the time we use an hybrid language in between a natural language and an imperative programming language. Such hybrid language is used to write the **pseudocode** of the algorithm (more or less a sketch of the program). It is good practice to lay down on paper (or even just in your mind, for simpler problems) your algorithm before starting typing the code of a program. This way, you focus on the procedural aspects and difficulties of the problem and not on the syntactic issues related to the programming language. A well written algorithm can always be translated easily into a program using your favorite programming language later.

Algorithmics is the branch of computer science interested in:

- the analysis of the performances of algorithms, in particular in terms of computation time and amount of used memory;
- the conception and design of correct and efficient algorithms;
- proving that a given algorithm is correct, that is, that it always stops and it always provides the right answer to the problem.

In general, verifying/proving that an algorithm is correct is a difficult task and goes beyond the scope of this book. You should at least know however about a standard technique, call **invariant method** applied to prove the correctness of iterative algorithms (that is, algorithms that use only loops and no recursion). A **loop invariant** is a property that:

- if it is true before the execution of any iteration of the loop, in remains true after the iteration;
- if it is true at the end of the loop, that implies that the algorithm returns the correct answer.

Proofs of correctness by invariants are classical mathematical proofs because they are basically proofs by induction. You can easily find ample literature on invariants. The reader interested in invariant theory in logic and its application to algorithms is invited to read [10].

The conception and design of correct and efficient algorithms can turn out to be difficult too, because obviously there is no universal recipe to solve all kind of problems. Very often, groundbreaking algorithms are the result of deep and long investigations on a specific problem conducted by some ingenious researchers. Designing algorithms is a skill you acquire with experience when you start noticing that several problems do share some common approach and that it is possible to apply a strategy you have already used.

There are however some approaches, strategies or techniques such as **divide and conquer**, **dynamic programming** or **greedy approach** that in some cases (but not always) provide an efficient algorithm to solve the problem at hand. These are knowledges that is good to have in an algorithm designer's toolbox, even as beginner. Some of them will be presented in this book (see Chap. 10).

In other cases, more efficient (faster) algorithms can be obtained by using an appropriate data structure to store your data. This will be further shown in Chap. 11 where we present tree-like data structures.

None of this however can be done before we agree about how we measure the efficiency/performances of an algorithm or about how we compare the "performances" of two algorithms solving the same problem.

7.1 Complexity in Time and Space

As we anticipated, it is reasonable to focus on two specific aspects:[1]

- the time of computation necessary to obtain the answer/solution after entering the data. This measure is called the **time complexity** of the algorithm;
- the amount of machine memory necessary for executing the algorithm (or rather for executing the program the algorithm is translated into), which is called the **space complexity** of the algorithm.

---

[1] Although for some specific problems it may be interesting to look at other criteria of "efficiency".

In general, the two measures of complexity in time and space are, in a sense, complementary to each other. Most of the time, in order to have a faster algorithm, you need to use more memory and economising memory often comes with higher computation time. This is known as the **space-time tradeoff**.

7.1.1 Time Complexity

This brings us to the next question: how is time measured?

You may think that with the accurate clocks we all have on our computers, we may just let the computer itself tell us how much time passed from the moment you pushed the enter button to the moment the solution appeared on the screen. In other terms, we would be using the second (or its fractions) as unity of measure of time. This approach has, however, several flaws. Not to mention the fact that it is totally dependent on machine on which you run the experiment (the speed of the processor, for instance), it assumes that there is a program ready to be executed, whereas our goal is to analyse the performances of the algorithms itself, regardless of the language it will be translated into and the machine on which it will be executed.

Since computers can only perform some simple operations, we use these operations as the "elementary steps" in which we decompose an algorithm. Typically, the following operations are considered *elementary operations*:

- Assignments
- Arithmetic operations
- Comparisons
- Inputs/outputs (read/print)
- Functions calls
- Functions returns...

Each of these operations can be assumed to be performed in constant time (comparisons and inputs/outputs can be considered in constant time only on data of scalar/primitive type), it is then natural to take the elementary operation) as unity of measure of time: one elementary operation is one tick of our stopwatch hand.

It should be clear that in practice all these elementary operations do not take exactly the same time. A multiplication for instance takes longer than an addition. It can be assumed however that there is a constant that dominates the actual time of execution of all of them.

We will then evaluate the time complexity of an algorithm in terms of the number of elementary operations it performs.

7.1.2 Space Complexity

As you know, memory is classically measured in bytes (1 byte = 8 binary digits or bits) and according to common standards:

- A character is stored using 1 byte (8 bits).
- An integer number is stored using 4 bytes.
- An array of integers of length n hence needs $4n$ bytes of memory to be stored.
- A long integer number or a real (float) number in double precision is stored using 8 bytes.

Note that the fact that numbers have fixed size implies that there is a bound for the numbers of that type that you can represent in the machine. With the type int, since one of the 32 bits is used for the sign, you can only represent an integer between -2^{31} and $2^{31}-1$ (between $-2{,}147{,}483{,}648$ and $2{,}147{,}483{,}647$). Negative numbers are represented using the **two's complement** rule, that is, the first of the 32 bits is set at 1, and the absolute value of the number is be obtained by changing everyone of the 32 bits into its complement to 2. Some languages like Python allow to manipulate integers whose size is not bounded (other than by the memory capacity of your machine).

7.2 Complexity Functions (for Time Complexity)

The number of operations executed by an algorithm clearly depends on the size of the data. In almost all cases, the larger is that size, the largest is the number of elementary operations to be performed. There are cases however when this number may depend also on other properties than the size of the data.

If the number of elementary operations depends uniquely on the size, then this number is the same for all the data having the same size n. In this case we can define a function f such that $f(n) :=$ the number of elementary operations carried out by the algorithm on any data of size n.

Such function is called **(time) complexity function** of the algorithm.

7.2.1 A First Example: The Sum of Entries of an Array

Consider the following simple algorithm that computes the sum of all entries in a linear array of n integers.

Algorithm 7.1: Sum of elements of an array

```
1  Sum (T: array of n integers): integer
2      i, result: integer
3
4      result = 0
5      for i from 0 to n-1 do
6          result = result + T[i]
7      return(result);
```

Since this is the first algorithm written in the pseudocode used in this part of the book, we present some of the features and conventions of the chosen pseudocode.

In the first line we use to include:

- the name of the algorithm (Sum);
- between parentheses, the list of its **parameters** (arguments) and their type; in this case we indicated that there is only one parameter called T and that it is an array of integers with positions numbered from 0 to $n-1$ (and hence of size n);
- after a colon, the type of the object the algorithm is expected to **return** (in the case the algorithm is expected to return a result, some algorithms perform some actions without necessarily returning a result), here an integer.

Although in some programming languages like Python you do not have to specify the type of the parameters nor the type of the returned result, it is good practice to do so when you write algorithms and it is even mandatory in several other programming languages.

The lines immediately after the first generally contain the declarations of the variables that will be used by the algorithm, followed by their type. The algorithm Sum uses two variables: i and result and they are both of type integer. Neither the declaration of variables is required in Python however, as we will see, it is useful to do it in order to evaluate the space complexity of the algorithm.

Finally note that unlike some languages and pseudocode models that represent nesting by using symbols like opening and closing wiggles {...} or tags such as begin...end, we chose to use simple indention to represent nesting. The instruction result = result + T[i] for instance is nested in the for loop. Instructions will also be indented for nesting in if...then...else... instructions or other conditional instructions. As well as correct indention is essential for the correctness (both syntactic and semantic) of a Python program, it is equally essential for the design and the understanding of an algorithm.

We want to count the number of elementary operations executed by this algorithm. We should then count the assignment in line 4 and the return in line 7 as one elementary operation each. Furthermore, at a first look, at least two elementary operations are performed for each iteration of the for loop: an addition and an assignment. Since the loops turns n times, that counts for $2n$ elementary operations, for a total of $2n + 2$.

A more detailed analysis however may show that some "loop maintenance" operations should also be taken into account (see also Flowcharts in Part I, Sect. 3.3). Indeed, at the end of each iteration and before starting the next, the variable i needs to be incremented (one elementary operation) and its current value needs to be compared with $n - 1$ (one comparison of integers) to determine whether or not another iteration of the loop needs to be performed. It is therefore more precise to count four elementary operations for each iteration of the loop.

The total number of elementary operations is therefore $4n + 2$. The function $f(n) = 4n + 2$ is the **time complexity function** of the algorithm. In this case, $f(n)$

7.2 Complexity Functions (for Time Complexity)

is a polynomial function and more precisely a polynomial of degree 1. We say that the time complexity of the algorithm is **linear**.

Now we evaluate the **space complexity**.

A general rule when computing the space complexity of the algorithm is that we never take into account the space used for storing the data (parameters or arguments) and the result. The reason is simply that any algorithm needs to allocate memory space for data and for the result (if it returns one). What we take into account is just the *auxiliary* memory used by the algorithm (or by the program it translates into).

The only memory space used by algorithm Sum is the space used for the integer variable i (which takes exactly 4 bytes). Note that this amount of memory does not depend on n since it is the same (always 4 bytes) regardless of the size n of the array. The space complexity of this algorithm is therefore **constant**.

7.2.2 Another Example: The Minimum Element of an Array

The following algorithm obviously computes and return the minimum value in an array of integers.

Algorithm 7.2: Minimum of an array

```
1  Min (T: array of n integers): integer
2      i, min : integer
3
4      min = T[0];
5      for i from 1 to n-1 do
6          if (T[i] < min) then
7              min = T[i]
8      return(min)
```

In addition to the assignment of line 4 and the return of line 8, like the algorithm Sum of Sect. 7.2.1, this algorithm performs one incrementation and one comparison for each of the $n-1$ iterations of the for loop (loop maintenance). For each iteration, it also executes one comparison (T[i] < min). All this counts for a total of $3(n-1) + 2 = 3n - 1$ elementary operations. However the assignment min = T[i] is not always executed as its execution depends on the truth value of T[i] < min.

For this algorithm the number of elementary operations is not the same for all arrays of size n. Unlike the case of algorithm Sum, it is therefore impossible to write a function expressing the number of elementary operations executed for all data having size n.

In such a case, it is useful to analyse the complexity in the **best** and in the **worst** possible cases, that is, the minimum and the maximum number of elementary operations that may be executed by the algorithm to solve the problem for any possible data of size n. This will provide a lower and an upper bound for the complexity.

The worst case obviously occurs when the comparison T[i] < min is true for all i, in this case the assignment min = T[i] is always executed. This occurs when the array is non increasing. We need to count one more elementary operations for each iteration, for a total of $3n - 1 + n - 1 = 4n - 2$ elementary operations.

The best case occurs when the comparison T[i] < min is false for all i, in this case the assignment min = T[i] is never executed. This occurs when the minimum is in the first position T[0]. The total number of elementary operations in then $3n - 1 + 1$.

A more accurate analysis of the algorithm would require an evaluation of the complexity in an average case (**average complexity** of the algorithm). The average complexity is defined as the average of the complexities of all different cases weighted by the probability of occurrence of each case. In other terms, if there are m possible cases $\{1, 2, \ldots, m\}$, for each case $j \in \{1, 2, \ldots, m\}$ you need to know its complexity $f_j(n)$ and its probability to occur p_j and compute:

$$\sum_{i=1}^{m} p_j f_j(n).$$

This is in general difficult, both for the identification of the different cases and for the evaluation of the probability that each case can occur. Evaluating the average complexity sometimes requires some deep combinatorics and therefore goes beyond the extent of this book. Both the identification of the cases and the evaluation of the probability that each case can occur can be a hard task. In Exercise 7.1 you will be asked to prove that the best case of the algorithm Min is much more likely to occur than the worst case.

However for this algorithm we can at least deduce that the complexity is linear in all cases (and therefore that the average complexity is linear too) because it is linear both in the best and in the worst (we have a polynomial of degree 1 in both cases).

There are several algorithm whose best-case complexity and worst-case complexity are of a different order of magnitude (in the sense that will be described in the next section). For instance the best-case complexity may be linear while the worst-case complexity may be quadratic (a polynomial of degree 2). In such a situation, anything can happen to the average complexity, it may be linear, quadratic, or something in between.

Exercise 7.1
Consider the set of arrays of size n containing the integers $1, 2, \ldots, n$ (in any order).
What is the size of this set?
Compute the probability that an array of this set has the value 1 in the first cell.
Compute the probability that an array of this set is increasing.
Deduce the probability of the best and of the worst case of the algorithm researching a minimum of an array of size n.

7.2 Complexity Functions (for Time Complexity)

Exercise 7.2
Let's consider the following multiplication algorithm, said of the **Russian Peasant**:

```
def russian_multiplication (m, n):
    res = 0
    while n != 0 :
        if n%2 == 1 : res += m
        m *= 2
        n //= 2
    return res
```

1. Test this algorithm for the values m = 13, n = 14.
2. Show that this algorithm computes the multiplication of m by n.
3. Compute the number of additions, of multiplications by 2 and of divisions by 2 carried out by this algorithm in the worst case as a function of n.
4. In base 2, how do you perform the multiplication by 2? The division by 2? How do we test if a binary number is even or odd?
   Write the numbers 13 et 14 in base 2 and apply the algorithm of the above multiplication to these numbers.
5. Compare with the usual multiplication algorithm.

Exercise 7.3

1. Propose an algorithm is_prime(p) *as naive as possible* allowing to determine if an integer p is prime.[2] What is its complexity? How can we improve it?
2. Now, consider the following algorithm (known as the **Sieve of Eratosthenes**):

```
def eratosthene(n) :
    tab = [False, False] + [True]*(n-1)    # tab = [False,False,True,True,▷
        ▷ ...,True]
    for i in range(2, n+1) :
        if tab[i] :
            for k in range(2*i, n+1, i) : # from 2i, by steps of i
                tab[k] = False
    return tab
```

Run the algorithm for n = 10.
3. What does the table computed by eratosthene(n) represent? Justify.
4. Calculate an upper bound of the number of additions and of multiplications of integers carried out by the algorithm for an input n.
5. To witness the practical impact of complexity differences, you can compare on your machine the computing times of
   [p for p in range(10**6) if is_prime(p)]
   and of
   [p for p,b in enumerate(eratosthene(10**6)) if b].

---

[2] Reminder: a prime number is a positive integer having exactly two dividers (they are then 1 and itself).

7.3 Asymptotic Notations of O, Θ and Ω

7.3.1 Notation O (big-O)

Suppose we have two algorithms solving the same problem, one has complexity function $f(n)$, the other $g(n)$. How to compare the two functions f and g to determine which of the two algorithms is more efficient (in terms of computation time)?

Intuitively, the more efficient algorithm will be the one whose complexity function has the slower growth rate, because it will require fewer elementary operations (and hence less time) to solve the problem as the size n of data increases. We are going to express this concept of slower or faster growth rate by the formal definition of an order (**dominance** order) on the set of functions.

The mathematical tools and the techniques presented in the remainder of this chapter will also allow us to estimate the growth rate of a complexity function without computing the complexity function itself. For instance, instead of determining whether the complexity function is $2n + 2$ or $4n + 2$ as we did for algorithm Sum, we will simply estimate that the complexity is linear (that is, it grows linearly, like a polynomial of degree 1).

Complexity functions of algorithms express the number of elementary operations executed on data having size (an integer) n, therefore they are functions defined over the set of positive integers and with positive integer values, however, the next definition is given for a wider class of functions, defined over the set of real numbers and with real values.[3]

> **Definition 7.1**
>
> Let f, g be functions defined over the set real numbers and with real values: $f, g : \mathbb{R} \to \mathbb{R}$. We say that $f \in O(g)$ (usually read "f is big O of g" or simply "f is O of g") if there exist a positive integer n_0 and a positive (real) constant c such that:
>
> $$f(n) \leq c \cdot g(n) \text{ for all } n \geq n_0.$$

Figure 7.1 may help to visualise this definition. If $f \in O(g)$, then for n sufficiently large (namely for all $n > n_0$) the graph of the function $y = f(x)$ is always below the graph of the function $y = c \cdot g(x)$. This expresses indeed that the growth rate of f is smaller than or equal to the growth rate of g. In this case we say that f *is dominated by* g (or that g *dominates* f).

---

[3] If a function f defined over $\mathbb{R}$ and with values in $\mathbb{R}$ has a certain asymptotic behaviour then its restriction to $\mathbb{N}^+$ has the same asymptotic behaviour. This is why, instead of plotting the graph of complexity functions dot-by-dot as it should be done for discrete functions, we plot the graph of the corresponding continuous function $\mathbb{R} \longrightarrow \mathbb{R}$.

7.3 Asymptotic Notations of O, Θ and Ω

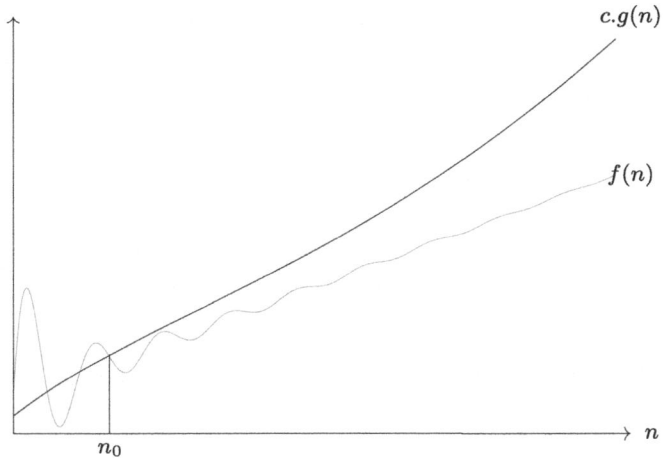

Fig. 7.1 $f(n) \in O(g(n))$

Thus $O(g)$ denotes the set of all functions dominated by g, in other words $O(g)$ is the set all functions whose growth rate is smaller than or equal to the growth rate of g.

Example 7.1
Let $f(n) = n$ and $g(n) = 2n + 4$, is $f \in O(g)$?
In this case, for any positive integer n we have $n < 2n + 4$, so if we choose $n_0 = 0, c = 1$ we have: $f(n) \leq c \cdot g(n)$ for all $n \geq n_0$, therefore $f \in O(g)$.

Example 7.2
Let $f(n) = n$ and $g(n) = n^2$, is $f \in O(g)$?
Since for all $n \geq 1$ we have $n \leq n^2$, if we choose $n_0 = 1, c = 1$ we have: $f(n) \leq c \cdot g(n)$ for all $n \geq n_0$, therefore $f \in O(g)$.

Example 7.3
Let $f(n) = n$ and $g(n) = n^2 - 6$, is $f \in O(g)$?
The two curves $y = f(x) = x$ and $y = g(x) = x^2 - 6$ intersect in two points (Fig. 7.2).
For computing n_0 we can determine the point of intersection having positive abscissa. Solving the equation $n^2 - 6 = n$ we obtain $n = -2$ or $n = 3$. Since for all $n \geq 3$ we have $f(n) \leq g(n)$, if we choose $n_0 = 3, c = 1$, we have that: $f(n) \leq c \cdot g(n)$ for all $n \geq n_0$, therefore $f \in O(g)$.

In the previous examples we have always chosen $c = 1$, which may make you wonder why such constant c is even necessary in the definition. Why not to compare directly the functions f and g rather than the functions f and $c \cdot g$? In fact the definition of $O()$ includes that constant c to ensure that when two functions have the same growth rate, neither of them strictly dominates the other, but rather they dominate each other. This is illustrated in the following example.

Fig. 7.2 $f(x) = x$ and $g(x) = x^2 - 6$

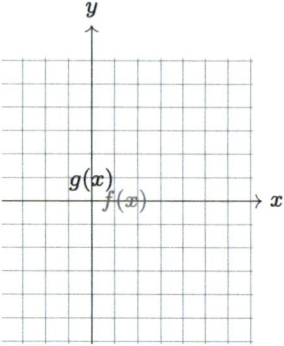

Fig. 7.3 $g(x) = 2x + 4 \in O(f(x))$

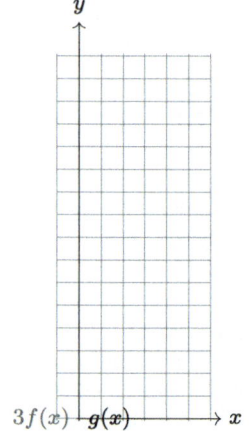

Example 7.4

Let us take the same two functions of Example 7.1, $f(n) = n$ and $g(n) = 2n + 4$, but this time we ask whether $g \in O(f)$.

We need to show that there exist $n_0 \in \mathbb{N}^+$ and $c \in \mathbb{R}^+$ such that $g(n) \leq c \cdot f(n)$ for all $n \geq n_0$. Indeed, if we take $c = 3$, the straight lines $y = g(x) = 2x + 4$ and $y = 3f(x) = 3x$ cross at the point of abscissa $n_0 = 4$ and for all values n larger than 4, the value $3n$ is always larger than $2n + 4$ (Fig. 7.3).

So $g(n) \leq 3f(n)$ for all $n \geq 4$, that is, $g \in O(f)$.

7.3.2 Notation Θ (big-theta)

The last example shows that two functions may dominate each other ($f \in O(g)$ and $g \in O(f)$).

Definition 7.2

We say that $f \in \Theta(g)$ if $f \in O(g)$ and $g \in O(f)$.

7.3 Asymptotic Notations of O, Θ and Ω

Thus $f \in \Theta(g)$ if there exist a positive integer n_0 and two positive constants c_1 and c_2 such that:

$$c_1 \cdot g(n) \leq f(n) \leq c_2 \cdot g(n) \text{ for all } n \geq n_0.$$

▶ **Remark 7.1** $f \in \Theta(g)$ iff $g \in \Theta(f)$ (this is false in general for O).

We noted that the set $O(g)$ includes all functions having growth rate smaller than or equal to g, the set $\Theta(g)$ includes instead all functions having *exactly* the same growth rate as g. Two sets $\Theta(g_1)$ and $\Theta(g_2)$ are either equal or disjoint. The relation R defined by $f R g$ if $f \in \Theta(g)$ is an equivalence relation, hence it is sensible to refer to the sets $\Theta()$ as Θ *classes*.

We already saw that $f(n) = 2n + 4$ is in the class $\Theta(n)$, the class of *linear growth*, algorithms having complexity functions with linear growth are considered very good.

More generally, for every positive integer k, all polynomials of degree k are in the class $\Theta(n^k)$. These are classes of functions having *polynomial growth*. Algorithms having complexity functions with polynomial growth are generally considered acceptable.[4]

It can be proven that if $f(n) = n$ and $g(n) = n^2$ then $g(n) \notin O(f(n))$. Indeed for any value of the constant c, the inequality $n^2 \leq c \cdot n$ is verified for $n \leq c$, therefore it is impossible to find an integer n_0 such that the inequality is true for all n larger then n_0.

In general, if two polynomials have different degrees, the one with larger degree always strictly dominates the other. This is also true for non integer exponents: if $\alpha > \beta \in \mathbb{R}^+$ then $n^\beta \in O(n^\alpha)$ (and $n^\alpha \notin O(n^\beta)$)

It's a simple exercise to verify that all constants are in the class $\Theta(1)$ (the class of functions with null growth rate).

It is well known that logarithmic functions have a very slow growth rate. Indeed the function $\log n$ (regardless of the basis of the logarithm, see Exercise 7.4) is strictly dominated by any polynomial, and in fact is dominated (strictly) by any function n^α with $\alpha > 0 \in \mathbb{R}^+$. Algorithms having complexity functions with logarithmic growth are therefore excellent.

On the other hand, it is well known that exponential function have a very fast growth rate. For instance the function 2^n dominates strictly all polynomials, and in fact it dominates any function n^α with $\alpha > 0$. Algorithms having complexity functions with exponential growth are very, very bad from a time efficiency point of view, because even for data of relatively small size, the number of elementary operations and hence the computation time are so large that it can take days, years or even centuries for the algorithm/program to return its answers.

---

[4] They can be considered acceptable if k is "small". In practice, when the exponent k is 5 or more, the computation time becomes unacceptably long even for data whose size is smaller than what you need.

Table 7.1 Execution time for a computer executing 10^9 instructions per second

Function (n)	n				
	20	40	60	100	300
n^2	0.4 µs	1.6 µs	3.6 µs	10 µs	90 µs
n^5	3.2 ms	102 ms	777 ms	10 s	40 mn
2^n	1 ms	18 mn	36 years	40.10^9 mil.	(71) Ky
n^n	(7) Ky	(45) Ky	(88) Ky	(181) Ky	(724) Ky

While algorithms with exponential complexity have very little practical interest, you should know that there exists nevertheless a large number of problems in very diversified areas (such as graph theory or optimisation problems) for which only algorithms having exponential complexity are known. Furthermore, for these problems we are also unable to prove that a solving algorithm with polynomial complexity does not exists. Finding an algorithm with polynomial complexity for one of these problems would solve the so called "$P = NP$?" question that you might have heard about and about which you may find a lot of literature.

Substantially, in some situations exponential complexity is unavoidable. In particular if you are working with mathematical sets having exponential size. For instance, if you study combinatorial property of permutations, you work on a set of $n!$ elements. It can be proven (see Exercise 7.6) that $2^n \in O(n!)$ and that $n! \notin O(2^n)$ therefore $n!$ grows even faster than an exponential function, so any loop of the kind `for all permutations of size n ...` is going to turn a number of times that is at least exponential.

Another noteworthy class that we will encounter often in this book is the class $\Theta(n \log(n))$, which includes functions whose growth rate is (slightly) larger than linear and (much) smaller than quadratic.

Table 7.1 shows how changing class of complexity can have extreme effects on the computation time.

In Table 7.1, the symbol "µs" represents one microsecond, that is, one millionth (0.000001 or 10^{-6} or 1/1,000,000) of a second, the symbol "ms" represents one millisecond, that is, one thousandth (0.001 or 10^{-3} or 1/1000) of a second, the symbol "Ky" represents one millennium, that is, one thousand years. The notation (x) means a number made of x digits in base 10. Hence "(7) Ky" is not equal to 7 millennia but a number in the order of $10^7 = 10,000,000$ millennia.

To realise how huge these numbers are, we may just recall that the estimated age of the universe is (8) millennia, the estimated age of the earth is (7) millennia and that the earth is expected to disappear in about (7) millennia.

7.3.3 Notation Ω (big-omega)

Sometimes, the following definition can be useful as well.

7.3 Asymptotic Notations of O, Θ and Ω

Definition 7.3

Let f, g be functions defined over the set of real numbers and with real values: $f, g : \mathbb{R} \to \mathbb{R}$. We say that $f \in \Omega(g)$ ("f is omega of g") if there exist a positive integer n_0 and a positive (real) constant c such that:

$$f(n) \geq c \cdot g(n) \text{ for all } n \geq n_0.$$

In other terms, if $f \in \Omega(g)$ then the growth rate of f is *at least* as large as the growth rate of g.

Exercise 7.4
Prove that $\log_2 n \in \Theta(\log_3 n)$. Generalise by proving that $\log_a n \in \Theta(\log_b n)$ for all pair of positive real numbers a and b.

Exercise 7.5
Prove that $2^n \in O(3^n)$ but $3^n \notin O(2^n)$. Generalise by proving that if $a < b$ then b^n strictly dominates a^n for all pair of positive real numbers a and b.

Exercise 7.6
Prove that $2^n \in O(n!)$ and that $n! \in O(n^n)$. Prove that these dominations are stricts, that is, $n! \notin O(2^n)$ and that $n^n \notin O(n!)$.

Exercise 7.7
Classify the following functions depending on their magnitude in the classes $\Theta_1 - \Theta_7$ respecting the following conditions:

- two functions appear in the same class Θ_i if and only if they have the same order:

$$\forall f, g, \quad f \in \Theta(g) \iff \exists i, \; f, g \in \Theta_i$$

- the classes Θ_i are arranged in increasing order of magnitude:

$$\forall i, \forall f, g, \quad f \in \Theta_i \text{ et } g \in \Theta_{i+1} \implies f \in O(g)$$

Functions to classify: $2n^2 + 3n$, $n^2 + \frac{1}{8}n^3$, $n^2 + \sqrt{n}$, $n^2\sqrt{n}$, $\sqrt{n}$, 2^n, 4^n, 2^{n+4}, $\log n$, $\log(n^2)$

Exercise 7.8
Order the following functions in asymptotic order of magnitude. (If $f(n) \in O(g(n))$, we will write $f \ll g$).
$n^2, \log_2(n), n \cdot \sqrt{n}, 3^n, \log_2(\log_2(n)), n, n^3, 2^n, n!, n \cdot \log_2(n), \sqrt{n}, n^n, \log_{10}(n)$.

Exercise 7.9
Yes or No?

1. If $f(n) \in O(g(n))$, then $g(n) \in \Omega(f(n))$
2. If $f(n) \in \Omega(g(n))$, then $g(n) \in O(f(n))$

3. $n \in O(n), n \in \Theta(n), n^2 \in O(2^n)$
4. $n \in O(n^2), n \in \Theta(n^2), n^2 \in \Theta(2^n)$,
5. $n^2 \in O(n), n^2 \in \Theta(n), \sqrt{n} + n \in \Theta(n)$
6. $3 \cdot log_2(n) \in \Theta(log_2(n)), n \cdot log_2(n) \in O(n^2), n + log(n) \in O(n)$
7. If $f(n) \in \Theta(g(n))$, then $g(n) \in \Theta(f(n))$
8. If $f(n) \in O(g(n))$, then $g(n) \in O(f(n))$
9. If $f(n) \in O(h(n))$ and $g(n) \in O(h(n))$, then $f(n) + g(n) \in O(h(n))$
10. If $f(n) + g(n) \in O(h(n))$, then $f(n) \in O(h(n))$ and $g(n) \in O(h(n))$
11. If $f(n) + g(n) \in \Theta(h(n))$, then $f(n) \in \Theta(h(n))$ and $g(n) \in \Theta(h(n))$

Exercise 7.10
Prove that for all functions $f, g : \mathbb{N} \longrightarrow \mathbb{R}^+$ one has:

$$(f+g)(n) \in \Theta(\max(f, g)).$$

The function $(f + g)(n)$ is defined as $f(n) + g(n)$ for all $n \in \mathbb{N}$ and the function $\max(f, g)(n)$ is defined as $\max(f(n), g(n))$ for all $n \in \mathbb{N}$.

Exercise 7.11
A few years ago, the **Pokémon Go** game on smartphones was a big success. One of the principles of this game is to physically go to certain locations to capture pokémons using your smartphone. Suppose we know in advance the geographical position (coordinates x and y on a map) of each of the pokémons that interest us (only the first 42 of course!). We also know our starting position x_0, y_0.

- Can you write an algorithm that computes the shortest path to capture them all and return to the starting position? Your algorithm does not need to be efficient.
- Can you evaluate its complexity?
- Is it possible to create a significantly better algorithm?

Exercise 7.12
Twenty-five years ago, a computer performed ten million operations per second and executed a sorting algorithm requiring $50 \times n \times \log_{10} n$ operations for an array of lengths n. Let's compare it with a computer 100 times faster, but executing a (weaker) sorting algorithm requiring n^2 operations. What is the computing time for each on an input of size $n = 10^6$? And $n = 10^7$?
On the other hand, what is the maximum size of a table that can be processed in an hour for each of the two configurations?

7.4 Evaluating the Complexity of Algorithms

7.4.1 Sequential Blocks

Suppose that an algorithm can be decomposed into two blocks of instructions, B_1 and B_2, to be executed sequentially (one after the other) and suppose that $f_1(n)$ is the complexity function counting the number of elementary operations for the execution of block B_1 and $f_2(n)$ is the complexity function counting the number of elementary operations for the execution of block B_2, we will say also that the block B_1 has a cost of $f_1(n)$ while the block B_2 has a cost of $f_2(n)$ (cost in terms of time

7.4 Evaluating the Complexity of Algorithms

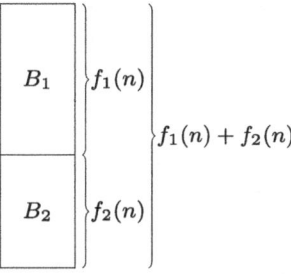

Fig. 7.4 Complexity of sequential composition, B_1 then B_2

spent). Clearly, the total number of elementary operations executed by the algorithm is expressed by the function $f_1(n) + f_2(n)$ (Fig. 7.4).

In some cases, you do not know precisely the complexity functions of the two blocks but you can determine without computing the actual functions that the complexity function of the first block is in $O(g_1)$ and that the complexity function of the second block is in $O(g_2)$, for two specific functions g_1 and g_2. Then you can obviously conclude that the complexity function of the sequential execution of both blocks is dominated by $g_1(n) + g_2(n)$ and hence it is in $O(g_1 + g_2)$. The same is true if you replace O by Θ: if the complexity function of the first block is in $\Theta(g_1)$ and the complexity function of the second block is in $\Theta(g_2)$ then the complexity function of the entire algorithms is in $\Theta(g_1 + g_2)$.

However, for any two functions h_1 and h_2 one can easily prove that $\Theta(h_1+h_2) = \Theta(\max(h_1, h_2))$ (see Exercise 7.10), hence, in the above paragraph, you can replace the sum of the two functions with the maximum of the two functions. This implies that the Θ class of an algorithm is determined uniquely by the block(s) having the largest[5] complexity function and that the contribution of all the rest of the algorithm to the growth of the complexity function is irrelevant.

7.4.2 Loops

Suppose you have a loop containing a block of instructions B whose complexity function (for *one* execution of the block B) is $f(n)$ and suppose that you can determine that the loop is executed $g(n)$ times, then the complexity function of the entire loop is exactly $(f \cdot g)(n) = f(n) \cdot g(n)$ (Fig. 7.5).

In some cases, you can determine that the block B has a complexity function in $O(f)$ and that the number of iterations of the loop is in $O(g)$, then you can easily deduce that the complexity function of the entire loop is dominated by $f(n) \cdot g(n)$, that is, it is in $O(f \cdot g)$.

The same is true for the Θ classes: if the block B has a complexity function in $\Theta(f)$ and that the number of iterations of the loop is in $\Theta(g)$, then the complexity function of the entire loop is in $\Theta(f \cdot g)$.

---

[5] In the sense of the dominance order.

Fig. 7.5 Complexity of a loop including a block of instructions

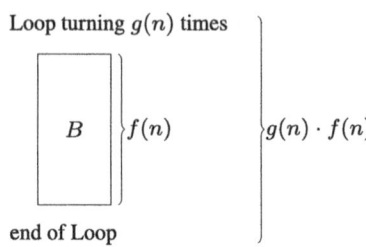

7.4.3 Examples

Example 7.5
If we are only interested in the Θ class and not the precise complexity functions of the two algorithms Sum and Min of Sects. 7.2.1 and 7.2.2, we can observe that for both of them, the block of instruction determining the total complexity is a for loop making $\Theta(n)$ iterations and containing a block having constant cost (in $\Theta(1)$). So both algorithms have complexity in $\Theta(n)$.

Example 7.6
Consider the following algorithm:

Algorithm 7.3: Example

```
1  Algo1 (n: integer): integer
2    i, x : integer
3
4    x = 0;
5    i = 1;
6    while i < n do
7      x = x + 1
8      i = i * 2
9    return(x)
```

The block inside the while loop is composed of a constant number of elementary operations. Precisely four of them: two arithmetical operations and two assignments, but we do not need to evaluate this number precisely). It is therefore in $\Theta(1)$.

How many times does the while loop turn? Since the value of i is doubled at every iteration of the loop, by the definition of logarithms the value of i will become larger than or equal to n after $\lfloor \log_2 n \rfloor$ iterations and at the point the loop stops. The function $\lfloor \log_2 n \rfloor$ is clearly in $\Theta(\log n)$. The total complexity of the algorithms is therefore in $\Theta((\log n) \cdot 1) = \Theta(\log n)$. This is the first example of an algorithms having **logarithmic complexity**.

Example 7.7
The following algorithm computes the sum of two matrices A and B having n rows and m columns.

7.4 Evaluating the Complexity of Algorithms

Algorithm 7.4: Sum of matrices

```
1  Algo2 (A, B: matrix of n x m integers): matrix of n x m integers
2     i, j: integer
3     C: matrix of n x m integers
4
5     for i from 0 to n-1 do
6        for j from 0 to m-1 do
7           C[i][j]= A[i][j]+ B[i][j]
8     return(C)
```

The block of instructions including only the instruction in line 7 is in constant time so it is in $\Theta(1)$, therefore the complexity function of the for j loop of lines 6–7 is in $\Theta(n)$.
The loop for i of lines 5–7 contains a block in $\Theta(n)$ (the for j loop) and it turns also $\Theta(n)$ times, so its complexity is in $\Theta(n^2)$. The instruction return(C) of line 8 is in $\Theta(1)$ and thus it is irrelevant for the purposes of computing the complexity class of the algorithm, hence the total complexity of the algorithm is in $\Theta(n^2)$.

Exercise 7.13
Express as a function of n the number of instructions carried out by the following loops:

1.
```
for i in range(n) :
  for j in range(n) :
    for k in range(n) :
      # instruction in constant time
```

2.
```
for i in range(n) :
  for j in range(i) :
    # instruction in constant time
```

3.
```
for i in range(n) :
  for j in range(i, n - i) :
    # instruction of constant time
```

Exercise 7.14
Compute the complexity class of the following programs extracts:

1.
```
s = 0
i = 1
while (i < n) do
  for j from 0 to n-1 do
      s = s + 1
  i = i * 2
```

2.
```
s = 0
i = 1
while (i < n) do
    j = 1
    while (j < n) do
        s = s + 1
        j = j * 2
    i = i * 2
```

3.
```
s = 0
i = n
while (i > 1)
    for j from 0 to i-1
        s = s + 1
    i = i / 2
```

Exercise 7.15
Compute the complexity class for the functions below.

1.
```
f1(n: int): int
    i,j,res: int
    res=0
    for i from 1 to n do
        for j from 1 to i do
            res= res+i*j
    return(n)
```

2.
```
f2(n: int): int
    i: int; i=0
    if (n<=0) then return(-1)
    while (n>1) do
        i++; n=n/2
    return(i)
```

3.
```
f3(n: int): int
    i,j,res: int
    res=0
    for i from 1 to n do
        j=i
        while (j>1) do
            res=res+1; j=j/2
    return(n)
```

7.4 Evaluating the Complexity of Algorithms

Exercise 7.16
Consider the algorithm:

```
Algo (n: integer)
   limit, j, k: integer; limit = 1; j = 1

   while (j <= n) do
      k = 1
      while (k <= limit) do
         k = k + 1
         print ("k is incremented to", k)
      j = j + 1
      limit = limit + limit
      print ("j is incremented to", j)
```

1. How many times is the condition (j <= n) tested if $n = 1$?
2. How many times does the algorithm print "j is incremented to" if $n = 5$?
3. How many times is the condition (j <= n) tested for any value of n, expressed as a function of n?
4. How many times does the algorithm print "k is incremented to" if $n = 2$?
5. How many times is the condition (k <= limit) tested if $n = 5$?
6. What is the maximum value that the variable k can reach during an execution of the 'Exam' algorithm if $n = 5$?
7. How many times does the algorithm print "k is incremented to" for any value of n, expressed as a function of n? What is the complexity class $\Theta()$ of the algorithm's complexity function?

Exercise 7.17
Consider the algorithm:

```
Algo2 (n: integer): integer
      x, y, z: integer
      x = 0
      y = 1
      z = 0
      while (y <= n) do
            if (x = y) then
                  y = y + 1
                  x = 0
            x = x + 1
            z = z + 1
      return z
```

1. What is the maximum value reached by the variable y if $n = 9$?
2. How many times is the condition (x = y) on line 7 satisfied for any value of n (as a function of n)?
3. How many times is the condition (x = y) on line 7 tested for any value of n (as a function of n)?
4. How many times is the condition (y <= n) on line 6 tested for any value of n (as a function of n)?
5. What function is computed by this algorithm?
6. What is the Θ class of this algorithm?

7.5 Solutions to Exercises

Solution of Exercise 7.2

2. If $n = 2k$, $m \times n = m \times 2k = (2 \times m) \times k$.
   If $n = 2k+1$, $m \times n = m \times (2k+1) = (2 \times m) \times k + m$.
3. Given $2^{k-1} < n \leq 2^k$. There are $1+k \simeq log_2(n)$ loop turns and a multiplication and a division by 2 in each turn, plus possibly an addition. As such, at worst $3 \cdot \log_2(n)$ operations.
4. multiplication by 2: offsetting to the left <<
   division by 2: offsetting to the right >>
   test if a binary number is odd: look at the least significant bit: $n\%2$

Solution of Exercise 7.3

1. It suffices to verify that all the numbers > 1 and less than the number p do not divide p, which gives the very naive algorithm:

```
def is_prime(p) :
  if p <= 1 : return False
  for i in range(2, p) :
    if p % i == 0 : return False
  return True
```

Therefore, the complexity is of $\Theta(p)$ (in the number of divisions/modulos).

To be more efficient, it is possible to test only all the numbers smaller than $(p-1)/2$ (integer division, given that primary numbers cannot be even), which always gives a complexity in $\Theta(p)$.

This bound can be improved when we observe that if $n = s \times t$, then either s or t is smaller than $\sqrt{n}$, since $n = \sqrt{n} \times \sqrt{n}$. Therefore, it is enough to test only all the numbers less than $\sqrt{n}$. Of course, there still will be useless divisions left: if a number is uneven, it is useless to test the divisibility by 4. With all the improvements, the complexity remains in the order of $\sqrt{n}$.

2. Run the program.
3. The box i ($i \geq 0$) of the table contains the truth value of the property "i is prime". The algorithm spans over the numbers larger than 2 and when a number p is prime (test `if tab[i]`), it marks as non-prime all the multiples of p until n. Since every non-prime integer has a prime divisor p smaller then itself, all non-prime integers will be correctly marked as such.
4. The number of operations of additions and of divisions carried out in each loop turn is either equal to 0 if i is non-prime, or equal to the number of multiples of i less than n otherwise, that is n/i. Therefore, the complexity is $n/2 + n/3 + n/5 + n/7 + \ldots \sim n \ln \ln n$ (difficult) that we can easily overestimate by $n \cdot (1 + \frac{1}{2} + \frac{1}{3} + \frac{1}{4} + \ldots) \sim n \ln n$.

7.5 Solutions to Exercises

We can start the second loop at i * i because all the multiples of i between $2i$ and $(i − 1)i$ are already marked before.

```
def eratosthene(n) :
  tab = [False, False] + [True] * (n - 1)
  for i in range(2, n + 1) :
    if tab[i] :
      for k in range(i * i, n + 1,i):
        tab[k] = False
  return tab
```

As for the previous algorithm, the upper bound of the for loop may be reduced to $\sqrt{n}$ since no tab[k] = False shall be executed after.

Solution of Exercise 7.7

$\Theta_1 = \{\log(n), \log(n^2)\}$; $\Theta_2 = \{\sqrt{n}\}$; $\Theta_3 = \{2n^2 + 3n, n^2 + \sqrt{n}\}$; $\Theta_4 = \{n^2\sqrt{n}\}$; $\Theta_5 = \{n^2 + \frac{1}{8}n^3\}$; $\Theta_6 = \{2^n, 2^{n+4}\}$; $\Theta_7 = \{4^n\}$.

Solution of Exercise 7.8

$log_2(log_2(n)) \ll log_2(n) = log_{10}(n) \ll \sqrt{n} \ll n \ll n \cdot log_2(n) \ll n \cdot \sqrt{n} \ll n^2 \ll n^3 \ll 2^n \ll 3^n \ll n! \ll n^n$.

Solution of Exercise 7.9

1. If $f(n) \in O(g(n))$, then $g(n) \in \Omega(f(n))$: yes
2. If $f(n) \in \Omega(g(n))$, then $g(n) \in O(f(n))$: yes
3. $n \in O(n), n \in \Theta(n), n^2 \in O(2^n)$: yes, yes, yes
4. $n \in O(n^2), n \in \Theta(n^2), n^2 \in \Theta(2^n)$: yes, no, yes
5. $n^2 \in O(n), n^2 \in \Theta(n), \sqrt{n}+n \in \Theta(n)$: no, no, yes
6. $3 \cdot log_2(n) \in \Theta(log_2(n)), n \cdot log_2(n) \in O(n^2), n + log(n) \in O(n)$:yes,yes,yes
7. If $f(n) \in \Theta(g(n))$, then $g(n) \in \Theta(f(n))$: yes
8. If $f(n) \in O(g(n))$, then $g(n) \in O(f(n))$: no
9. If $f(n) \in O(h(n))$ and $g(n) \in O(h(n))$, then $f(n) + g(n) \in O(h(n))$:yes
10. If $f(n) + g(n) \in O(h(n))$, then $f(n) \in O(h(n))$ and $g(n) \in O(h(n))$: yes ($f(n)$ and positive $g(n)$).
11. If $f(n) + g(n) \in \Theta(h(n))$, then $f(n) \in \Theta(h(n))$ and $g(n) \in \Theta(h(n))$: no

Solution of Exercise 7.12

For $n = 10^6$: the computer from 25 years ago needs $(50 \times 10^6 \times \log_{10} 10^6)/10^7 = 30$ s, while the modern computer $10^{12}/10^9 = 1000$ s.
For $n = 10^7$, 350 s versus 10^5 s, around 27 h.
And for $n = 10^8$, 4000 s, around one hour versus 10^7 s, or 115 days.

After one hour of calculations, on the older computer: $50 \times n \times \log_{10} n = 3600 \times 10^7$ gives $n \sim 10^8$. In the modern computer with a quadratic algorithm: $n^2 = 3600 \times 10^9$ gives $n \sim 1,9.10^6$, the older computer can treat a larger amount of data (by a factor 100).

Solution of Exercise 7.14

1. The while (i < n) loop turns $\lceil \log n \rceil$ times, the for j loop always turns n times, the total number of additions is $n \lceil \log n \rceil \in \Theta(n \log(n))$.
2. The while (i < n) loop turns $\lceil \log n \rceil$ times, the while (j < n) loop always turns $\lceil \log n \rceil$ times, the total number of additions is $(\lceil \log n \rceil)^2 \in \Theta(\log(n)^2)$.
3. For each value of i, the for j loop turns i times. The variable i takes the values: $n, \frac{n}{2}, \frac{n}{2^2}, \ldots, \frac{n}{2^p}$ with $p = \lfloor \log(n) \rfloor - 1$. Since $\sum_{i=1}^{p} \frac{n}{2^i} < \sum_{i=1}^{\infty} \frac{n}{2^i} = 2n$, the complexity is in $O(n)$.

Solution of Exercise 7.15

1. At each iteration, f1 performs an assignment, an addition and a multiplication. Let c be the (constant) total cost of these three operations. We count the number of iterations of the for j loop: for each i we have exactly i iterations. This gives $\varphi(n) = \sum_{i=1}^{n} \sum_{j=1}^{i} c = \sum_{i=1}^{n} ci = cn(n+1)/2 \in \Theta(n^2)$. We can add the cost of maintenance operations for the two loops, the complexity remains quadratic.
2. Each iteration of the while loop has a constant cost c. The number of iterations of the while loop is equal to the number of times one can divide n by 2 before reaching 1, i.e. $\log_2 n$. We therefore have $\varphi(n) = c \log_2 n \in \Theta(\log n)$.
3. We already determined (question 2) that the internal loop while has a cost $c \log_2 j$. Since it is nested in a for loop, the complexity is given by:

$$\varphi(n) = \sum_{j=1}^{n} c \log_2 j = c(\log_2 1 + \log_2 2 + \log_2 3 + \ldots + \log_2 n)$$
$$= c \log_2(1 \cdot 2 \cdot 3 \ldots \cdot n)$$
$$= c \log_2(n!) \in O(n \log n)$$

Solution of Exercise 7.16

1. Twice. Once for $j = 1$ (test is true, loop continues), and once for $j = 2$ (test is false, loop ends).
2. Once for each j, so five times.
3. It is tested $n + 1$ times. The first n times for $j = 1, 2, 3, \ldots, n$, the test is true and the loop continues; the last time for $j = n + 1$, the test is false, and the loop ends.
4. Three times. Once for $j = 1$ (limit = 1) and twice for $j = 2$ (limit = 2).
5. For each value of $j = 1, 2, 3, 4, 5$, the test is performed one more time than the value of $limit$, which is respectively 1, 2, 4, 8, 16. So, we have: $(1 + 1) + (2 + 1) + (4 + 1) + (8 + 1) + (16 + 1) = 36$ times.
6. It will be in the cycle for $j = 5$ when $limit$ is 16. The maximum value of k will then be 17 (starting from 1 and incrementing sixteen times).
7. For each value of $j = 1, 2, 3, \ldots, n$, the loop from lines 8–11 is executed 2^{j-1} times since that's the value of $limit$. So we have $1 + 2 + 2^2 + 2^3 + \ldots + 2^{n-1} = 2^n - 1$ times. The complexity class is $\Theta(2^n)$ (exponential).

Introduction to Recursion

How Different Approaches to the Same Problem May Lead to Better Complexity

An algorithm is said to be **recursive** if it makes a call to itself. In other terms, the procedure to solve the problem for a given instance I includes the resolution of the same problem for another instance I' (generally having smaller size than I). The same procedure is then applied to solve the problem on the instance I': a call is made to solve the problem on a sub-instance I'' of I', and so on. This generates a chain (or in general a tree) of **recursive calls**.

Every recursive algorithm must include a **base case**, that is a case in which an answer can be provided/returned without making any further recursive call. You understand that otherwise the chain of recursive calls would never end. Furthermore, the algorithm must be designed in such a way to guarantee that a base case is always attained sooner or later.

Generally, base cases correspond to very small sizes of the instance, like 0 or 1. This is why recursive calls are generally made on instances whose size are smaller than the original instance: by reducing the size of the instance at each call, in principle you will eventually reach a base case.

Sometimes recursive algorithms are not faster than an equivalent iterative one or may use more memory space, there are however some situations in which the most efficient algorithm to solve a problem is a recursive one or for functions that cannot be defined other than recursively (e.g. the Ackermann function).

Recursion is also unavoidable when you handle data structures that are intrinsically recursive. An exemple are linked chains (or linked lists) in which each element of the chain contains the address of the next element of the chain (a non-empty **chain** can be recursively defined as a first element to which a chain is attached). Another exemple are tree-like structures where each node v contains the addresses of the subtrees of v (a non-empty **tree** can be recursively defined as a node called root to which some **trees** are attached).

Recursion is a powerful tool in programming and algorithm implementation, but beginners often fail to grasp all its potential. When you write a recursive algorithm you should imagine that you are delegating someone else to solve a subproblem for you and you must trust that person to return to you the correct solution to that subproblem. Then you only have to worry about how to construct the solution for your own instance using the solution of the subproblem that has been returned to you.

In this chapter we will try to make you familiar with the mechanism of recursion by studying several examples. We will also learn some techniques to evaluate the complexity of a recursive algorithm.

8.1 Factorial

We want to to write an algorithm (function) returning the factorial of a given integer n. A first approach is inspired by the following formula defining the factorial:

$$n! = 1 \cdot 2 \cdot \ldots \cdot n = \prod_{i=1}^{n} i.$$

This yields a simple iterative algorithm (where there is no use of recursion)

Algorithm 8.1: Factorial by iteration

```
1  FactIter (n: integer): integer
2      i, res : integer
3
4      res = 1
5      for i from 1 to n do
6          res = res * i
7      return (res)
```

The time complexity of algorithm FactIter is clearly in $\Theta(n)$ (a loop turning n times containing a block of constant cost), its space complexity is constant (4 bytes for the variable i).

Alternatively, we can also consider the recursive definition of factorial:

$$n! = \begin{cases} 1 & \text{if } n = 0 \\ n \cdot (n-1)! & \text{otherwise} \end{cases}$$

Whenever you have a recursive formula, you can simply immediately translate it into a recursive algorithm almost verbatim:

8.1 Factorial

> **Algorithm 8.2:** Factorial by recursion
>
> 1 FactRec (n: **integer**): **integer**
> 2   **if** (n == 0) **then return**(1)
> 3   **else return** (n * FactRec(n-1))   //FactRec(n-1) is a recursive call
> 4   //on a smaller istance

▶ While the above algorithm is correct, we want to point out that it would work even without the `else` of line 3. Indeed, after a `return` in the `if` part, an `else` is never necessary. Remember that a `return` always cause the termination of the function (and the end of the algorithm if it is a return for the first call) so, as you can check, the algorithm will do the same thing with or without the `else`.

We want to compute the complexity function $\varphi(n)$ of this algorithm, that is, the number of elementary operation s executed to compute $n!$. The methods presented so far do not apply to recursive functions. When you have a recursive algorithm, you can always try to write a recursive expression for the complexity function. In this case it is very easy, indeed:

- if $n = 0$, the algorithms executes only a comparaison (n == 0) and a return (2 elementary operations),
- if $n > 0$, the algorithm executes precisely 5 elementary operation s (the comparison n == 0, the subtraction $n-1$, a multiplication, the recursive call and a return) *in addition to all elementary operation s executed for the computation of* `FactRec(n - 1)`, which are counted by $\varphi(n-1)$.

The function φ hence satisfies:

$$\varphi(n) = \begin{cases} 2 & \text{if } n = 0 \\ 5 + \varphi(n-1) & \text{otherwise} \end{cases}$$

In this case it is easy to determine a closed form for $\varphi(n)$ by computing it step by step:

$$\varphi(n) = 4 + \varphi(n-1)$$
$$= 5 + 5 + \varphi(n-2)$$
$$= \ldots$$
$$= 5 + 5 + 5 + \ldots + 5 + \varphi(0)$$
$$= 5n + 2$$

The time complexity of this algorithm is linear, like for `FactIter`.

Note that we might have evaluated the Θ class of the complexity function without computing the function itself. Indeed, you can just say that if $n = 0$ the algorithm executes just a constant number of elementary operation s, while if $n > 0$ it executes a constant number of elementary operation s plus all the elementary operation s for the computation of `FactRec(n - 1)`. So $\varphi(n)$ satisfies:

$$\varphi(n) = \begin{cases} c & \text{if } n = 0 \\ d + \varphi(n-1) & \text{otherwise} \end{cases}$$

for appropriate integer constants c and d. This yields $\varphi(n) = dn + c$, which is obviously in $\Theta(n)$.

8.1.1 Space Complexity of Recursive Algorithms, Tree of Recursive Calls

Suppose you want to compute 5! using the function implemented by the algorithm FactRec. The initial call `FactRec(5)` is clearly made from outside the function itself (the initial call always needs to be made from another function/module). A process in charge to compute 5! is then launched. The process makes a call to `FactRec(4)` and then puts itself on hold waiting for the return of the solution of that subproblem. Analogously, that proves in charge to compute 4! makes a call to `FactRec(3)` and waits for the return of the solution of that subproblem, and so on, until a call to `FactRec(0)` is made (within the call `FactRec(1)`).

These recursive calls can be represented by a tree in which every node contains a call and node u is parent of a node v if the call in v is made within the call in u. The part (a) of Fig. 8.1 shows the tree of recursive calls (top-down) for this specific example. In this case, the tree is simply a thread-like tree because the function includes only one recursive call. But, when the procedure includes more than one recursive call you will obtain a non-degenerated tree.

Fig. 8.1 Call tree of FactRec(5). (**a**) Top-down of the calls. (**b**) Bottom-up of the returns

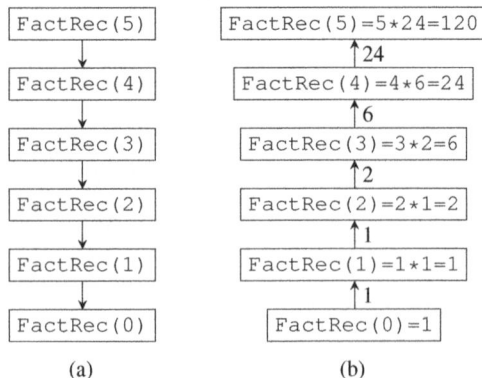

8.2 Exponentiation

The part (b) of Fig. 8.1 illustrates the bottom-up mechanism of the returns. The value 0 of the parameter corresponds to the base case of the algorithm, in which the value 1 is returned to the process in charge of computing FactRec(1). This process can now do its part of the job : multiplying the value 1 returned by FactRec(0) by the value of n, which is also 1, and return the result 1 to the process that had called it, that is, FactRec(2). The process in charge of computing FactRec(2) can now multiply the value 1 returned by FactRec(1) by the value of n, which is 2, and return the result 2 to the process that had called it, that is FactRec(3). This bottom-up mechanism continues until the process in charge to compute FactRec(5) receives the answer 24 from the process in charge to compute FactRec(4), it multiplies it by $n = 5$ and returns the final result, 120, to the function that made the initial call.

The machine needs to keep track not only of the process that is currently active but also of all the processes that are in an idle state, waiting for the return of other processes. A specific part of the memory called **stack** handles this mechanism. Processes are added to the stack at the moment of their call and removed from the stack when they return and terminate. The stack is a **last-in-first-out (LIFO) structure**, the last process added to the stack is the first to be removed from it (and the only one that can be removed from it). At a given moment, several processes are present in the stack and this occupies some memory space that needs to be taken into account when evaluating the space complexity of the algorithm.[1]

For the algorithm FactRec, at one point in time during the computation of $n!$, up to $n + 1$ processes (from FactRec(n) to FactRec(0)) are stacked. This counts for an amount of memory that is proportional to n. The space complexity of FactRec is in $\Theta(n)$, this is worse than the complexity of FactIter, which is in $\Theta(1)$. From a time complexity point of view there is no reason to prefer FactIter to FactRec, as both of the have the same time complexity, but FactIter runs using constant memory, while FactRec needs an amount of memory proportional to the value of the parameter n.

8.2 Exponentiation

Given a real number $x > 0$ and an integer $n \geq 0$ we want to compute x^n. Since x^n is the result of n multiplications by x, the problem can easily be solved by the following iterative algorithm:

---

[1] The stack has clearly a bounded size, so in some cases, when too many recursive calls are performed, the machine can run out of space. This causes the **stack overflow** error that you might already have encountered when running recursive programs.

Algorithm 8.3: Exponentiation by iteration

```
1  ExpIter (x: real, n: integer): real
2      i: integer
3      res: real
4
5      res = 1
6      for i from 1 to n do
7          res = res * x
8      return (res)
```

The complexity of this algorithm is clearly linear, that is in $\Theta(n)$. Alternatively, you can start from the following recursive definition:

$$x^n = \begin{cases} 1 & \text{if } n = 0 \\ x \cdot x^{n-1} & \text{otherwise} \end{cases}$$

where the exponentiation x^n is defined in terms of the exponentiation x^{n-1}. Again this recursive formula can be immediately translated into a recursive algorithm:

Algorithm 8.4: Exponentiation by recursion

```
1  ExpRec(x: real; n: integer): real
2      if (n == 0) then return (1)
3      else return (x * ExpRec(x, n-1))
```

By comparing the algorithms `ExpRec` and `FactRec`, it is easy to realise that they have the same complexity in $\Theta(n)$ because they perform exactly the same number of elementary operation s.

However, for this problem recursion can actually provide a faster solution if we get inspiration from the following alternative recursive definition:

$$x^n = \begin{cases} 1 & \text{if } n = 0 \\ (x \cdot x)^{n/2} & \text{if } n \text{ is even} \\ x \cdot (x \cdot x)^{(n-1)/2} & \text{if } n \text{ is odd} \end{cases}$$

This formula naturally translates into the following recursive algorithm:

Algorithm 8.5: Fast exponentiation

```
1  ExpFast(x: real; n: integer ): real
2      if (n == 0) then return(1)
3      else if (n%2 == 0) then
4          return (ExpFast(x*x,n/2))
5      else
6          return (ExpFast(x*x,(n-1)/2) * x)
```

8.2 Exponentiation

Let us analyse the complexity function $\varphi(n)$ of ExpFast. When:

- $n = 0$, the algorithm executes just a constant number of elementary operation s;
- $n > 0$ and n is even, it executes a constant number of elementary operation s plus all the elementary operation s for the computation of ExpFast(x*x,n/2), which is expressed by $\varphi(n/2)$;
- $n > 0$ and n is odd, it executes a constant number of elementary operation s plus all the elementary operation s for the computation of ExpFast(x*x,(n-1)/2), which is expressed by $\varphi((n-1)/2)$.

therefore $\varphi(n)$ satisfies:

$$\varphi(n) = \begin{cases} c & \text{if } n = 0 \\ d_1 + \varphi\left(\frac{n}{2}\right) & \text{if } n \text{ is even} \\ d_2 + \varphi\left(\frac{n-1}{2}\right) & \text{if } n \text{ is odd} \end{cases}$$

A technique to solve this specific equation consists in studying this function when n is a power of 2. Complexity functions are monotonic functions, therefore it suffices to establish the growth rate of such functions on a specific increasing sequence (such as $n = 2^k$ for $k = 0, 1, 2, \ldots$) to deduce the growth rate of the functions on the entire set of natural integers.

Let $n = 2^k$ and note $g(k)$ the function $g(k) = \varphi(2^k) = \varphi(n)$. Since 2^k is always even for $k > 0$ and since $\varphi(2^k/2) = \varphi(2^{k-1}) = g(k-1)$, the function g satisfies:

$$g(k) = \begin{cases} c & \text{if } k = 0 \\ d_1 + g(k-1) & \text{otherwise} \end{cases}$$

You can recognise that the function $g(k)$ satisfies the same recursive equation as the complexity function of FactRec or ExpRec. Consequently a closed form for g is $g(k) = d_1 k + c \in \Theta(k)$. Since $g(k) = \varphi(n)$ and $k = log_2 n$, we deduce:

$$\varphi(n) = d_1 log_2 n + c \in \Theta(log n).$$

The algorithm ExpFast is much faster than ExpRec or ExpIter.

We note that the strategy used in the algorithm ExpFast can also be implemented by an iterative algorithm.

Exercise 8.1
Design an iterative algorithm for exponentiation based on the same strategy used for the recursive fast exponentiation.

Exercise 8.2
- Run the fast exponentiation algorithm for x = 2, n = 11.
- How many recursive calls are carried out as a function of n? And how many multiplications in the worst case?

Exercise 8.3

1. Write an algorithm as naive as possible that, given a polynomial $P(x) = a_n \cdot x^n + \ldots + a_1 \cdot x + a_0$ and a value x_0, computes $P(x_0)$ (the polynomial P evaluated at x_0). We suppose that P is described by an array containing, in the box of index i, the coefficient of the monomial of degree i. For instance, the array $P = [17, -3, 6, 8]$ represents the polynomial $P(x) = 8x^3 + 6x^2 - 3x + 17$.
2. Apply your algorithm on the polynomial $P(x) = x^4 + x^3 + x^2 + x + 1$ with $x = 3$. What do you find?
3. What is the number of additions and multiplications carried out in the execution of your algorithm on a polynomial of degree n?
4. How can you improve the complexity of your algorithm by using the binary exponentiation?
5. How can you improve the complexity of your algorithm by preserving in one variable all the successive powers of x?
6. Show that the following algorithm solves the same problem:

```
def horner(P, x) :
    res = 0
    for coeff in P[::-1] :    # runs through P from right to left
        res = res * x + coeff
    return res
```

How many additions and multiplications are carried out in the execution of this algorithm on a polynomial of degree n?

8.3 Searching

The **searching problem** (in an array) is the following:

> Given an array A of objects of a type t (for instance an array of integers) and an object x of type t, determine whether $x \in A$, that is, whether there exists a position i such that $A[i] = x$.

In some cases, we expect a simple boolean answer (true or false), in some others we want the algorithm to return the position i where x is, if such a position exists. The algorithm may return a symbolic value (like -1) if x is not present in the array.

8.3.1 Naive Search

Let us suppose initially that the array is not sorted. In this case there is no better way to do this other than using the naive algorithm that spans through the entire array and checks every single position until it finds x (or not).

Algorithm 8.6: Naive search

```
NaiveSearch (A: array of n integers, x: integer) : boolean
    for i from 0 to n-1 do
        if (A[i]==x) then return (True)
    return (False)
```

▶ The following loop shows a typical common mistake that beginners make when writing an algorithm as this one :

Algorithm 8.7: Common mistake: premature return

```
1    for i from 0 to n-1 do
2        if (A[i]==x) then return (True)
3        else return (False)
```

This algorithm is *wrong* (in the sense that it does not always return the correct answer) because it provides its answer only based on the comparison of x with the first element $A[0]$. Indeed, at the first iteration of the for loop (when $i = 0$), either $A[0]$ is equal to x and in this case the algorithm stops returning True, or $A[0]$ in not equal to x and in this case the algorithm stops returning False (a return instruction causes the termination of the algorithms and the immediate exit from it). In any case, the algorithm stops after having checked only the first position of the array and it never checks all the others. The instruction return (False) must be executed only after the for loop is completed, when you have looked at all the positions of the array and you have determined that the element x is in none of them.

Note that the complexity of the NaiveSearch algorithm is in $\Theta(1)$ in the best possible case (when x is in the first position) and in $\Theta(n)$ in the worst possible case (when x is in the last position to when x is absent). Hence in any case it is in $O(n)$ (always dominated by n). It can be proven (see Exercise 8.4) that the average complexity of the NaiveSearch algorithm is in $\Theta(n)$.

8.3.2 Binary Search

Suppose now that the elements of the array are arranged in increasing order.

The strategy of binary search is to compare the element x to search with the element in the "middle" position of the array:

- if the element in the middle position is equal to x, then x has been found and the algorithm may return True (or the middle position, where x is);
- if x is smaller than the element in the middle position, then x cannot be present in the half of the array "on the right" of the middle position and the search may continue (recursively) only on the half "on the left" of it;
- if x is larger than the element in the middle position, then x cannot be present in the half of the array "on the left" of the middle position and the search may continue (recursively) only on the half "on the right" of it;

Fig. 8.2 Binary search in an array

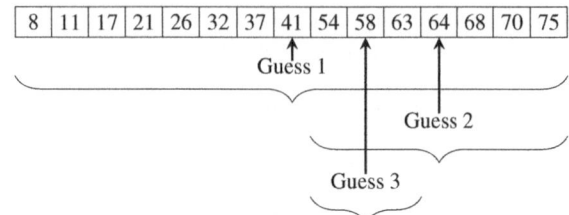

We know that any recursive algorithm must have at least one base case. What are the base cases for this algorithm? By splitting the array into smaller and smaller sections, if you do not find x during the process you will end up searching x in a subsection of size either 0 (an empty section) or 1. The element x is certainly not in an empty section so in that case you can return False. When you are searching x in a section of size 1 you simply have to verify if the only element of the section is equal to x and return True or False accordingly.

Example 8.1
Let us look what happens when searching $x = 58$ in the array of Fig. 8.2

- (Guess 1) The first guess is to look at the middle position of the whole array. That position contains the value 41, which is smaller than x, so we know that the value x cannot be in the left subarray and we can continue the search in the right subarray [54, 58, 63, 64, 68, 70, 75].
- (Guess 2) The second guess is to look at the middle position of the subarray: [54, 58, 63, 64, 68, 70, 75]. The position contains 64, which is larger than x, the algorithm then continues its search on the left part.
- (Guess 3) The third guess is to look at the middle position of the subarray: [54, 58, 63], whose middle position contains 58. The element x has been found (after 3 comparisons), the algorithm returns True.

Example 8.2
Let $A = [8, 11, 17, 26, 32, 37]$ and $x = 33$.

- (Guess 1) The middle position contains 26 (note that the position containing 17 may also be considered as the middle position because the length of the array is even, we will sort this out later), which is smaller than 33, the algorithm then continues its search of x in the (sub)array: [32, 37].
- (Guess 2) In this array the middle position contains 37, which is larger than 33, the algorithm then continues its search of x in the (sub)array: [32].
- (Guess 3) This is a subarray of size 1. The algorithm verifies that the only element is not equal to x, it can then return False as x is not present in the array.

Notice that at a given moment, the algorithm is not working on the entire array but on a specific subsection of it, so we need to identify such specific subsection in the algorithm. To do so, we will use two cursors begin and end where begin designates the first position of the subsection, while end designates the position

8.3 Searching

immediately after the last position of the subsection.[2] Initially begin has the value 0 while end has the value n (size of the array). The middle position of the current subsection is then simply the arithmetical average of the values of begin and end.

For instance, if begin has the value 15 and end the value 22, the current subsection is $A[15], A[16], \ldots A[21]$ of size $22 - 15 = 7$. The middle position is given by the expression $(15+22)/2 = 18$ (the division by 2 is an integer division), which is indeed the middle position of that section of size 7 of the array. If begin has the value 13 and end the value 19, the current subsection is $A[13], A[16], \ldots A[18]$ of size $19-13 = 6$ the middle position is given by the expression $(13+19)/2 = 18$, which is indeed the middle position of that section of size 6 of the array, defining a left half of size 3 and a right half of size 2.

After all these considerations we can draft the algorithm:

Algorithm 8.8: Binary search

```
1   BinarySearch (A: array of n integers; x, begin, end: integer) : ▷
        ▷ boolean
2       mid: integer
3
4       if (end-begin==0) then return (False)    // the array is empty
5       if (end-begin==1) then                   // the array has size 1
6           return (x==A[begin])
7       mid = (begin + end)/2                    // this is an integer division
8       if (x < A[mid]) then                     // is x in the left half?
9           return(BinarySearch(A,x,begin,mid-1))
10      else
11          if (x > A[mid]) then                 // is x in the right half?
12              return(BinarySearch(A,x,mid+1,end))
13          else
14              return (True)                    // x is exactly at mid!
```

Let us analyse its complexity. In the base cases, the algorithm executes a constant number of elementary operation s, in the general case it also executes one recursive call on an array whose size is approximately[3] half of the size of the original array. The complexity function $\varphi(n)$ satisfies :

$$\varphi(n) = \begin{cases} c & \text{if } n = 0 \text{ or } n = 1 \\ d + \varphi(\frac{n}{2}) & \text{otherwise} \end{cases}$$

---

[2] You may wonder why we did not choose to have the cursor end designate directly the last position of the subsection instead of the one after it. It is obviously possible to make that choice too and you will find several algorithms in which this choice has been made. The reason for our choice is that it is more consistent with Python's handling of intervals : in Python the lower bound of the interval is always considered included, while the upper bound is not. Intervals are closed on the left and open on the right. This choice also preserves the nice property that the value of the difference end - begin is always equal to the length of the current subsection.

[3] Up to one unit, as the new size could be $(n-1)/2$, this does not change the Θ class however.

With the same technique used to analyse the complexity of `FastExp` of the previous subsection we obtain $\varphi(n) = d \cdot \log_2(n) + c \in \Theta(log n)$. Binary search is mush faster than naive search but it can only be applied if the array is already sorted.

Exercise 8.4
Suppose you know that an element x is present in an array with probability p with $0 \leq p \leq 1$ and that every position is equiprobable (that is, if x is present, you have the same chance to find it in any cell of the array).

1. Compute the probability to find x at a given position i.
2. Compute the probability that x is not present in the array.
3. Deduce the average number of comparisons performed by the `NaiveSearch` algorithm to find an element x in an array size n.

Exercise 8.5
We perform binary search by splitting the array not at the middle position but rather at the position that divides the array into two parts, one approximately 1/3 of the total size and one 2/3 of the total size. What the complexity would be in the best and in the the worst case?

Exercise 8.6
1. Write a function `occurrencesNaive(T, x)` that returns the number of *occurrences* of an element x in an array T. What is its complexity in the worst case for an array of size n ?
   Now suppose that the parameter T is a ***sorted array***.
2. What can we say about the occurrences of an element x in T?
3. Write a function `findLeftmost(T, x, begin=0, end=None)` that returns, *in the most efficient possible way*, None if x does not appear in T and its leftmost position in the array otherwise. What is the complexity, in the worst case, for a array of size n?
4. Deduce a function `occurrencesDicho(T, x)` that returns the number of occurrences of x in T *in the most efficient possible way*. What is the complexity of `occurrencesDicho(T,x)` in the worst case, for an array of length n ?

Exercise 8.7
We say that an array T of n distinct elements is a *broken ring* if there exists an index k (unknown a priori) such that `T[k:] + T[:k]` is sorted in decreasing order (not necessarily strict).
For instance, T=[43,38,22,17,10,4,93,74,65] is a broken ring, since for $k = 6$ we have `T[6:] + T[:6]`=[93,74,65,43,38,22,17,10,4], a decreasing list.

1. In a broken ring, what is the maximal number of indexes i such that `T[i-1] < T[i]` ?
2. Deduce an algorithm `is_a_ring(T)` testing if T is a broken ring and having $\Theta(n)$ as complexity in the worst case.
   Now suppose that T is a broken ring.
3. Given a position i of T, how can you determine, with a test in constant time, if i is a position on left or on the right of m, where m is the position (unknown a priori) of the minimum of T?
4. Deduce an algorithm `minimum_ring(T)` as effective as possible to determine the position of the minimum of a broken ring T.
5. What is the complexity of this algorithm for an array of length n ?
6. Deduce an algorithm `maximum_ring(T)` of complexity $\Theta(log(n))$ in the worst case that returns the position of the maximum of a broken ring T.

Exercise 8.8
Compute as accurately as possible the complexity class for the recursive functions below.

1.
```
g1(n: int): int
    if (n<=0) then return(-1)
    if (n=1) then return(0)
    else return(1+g1(n/2))
```

8.4 Fibonacci Numbers

The well known **Fibonacci sequence** (named from the Italian mathematician Leonardo Fibonacci, twelfth century) $\{F_n\}_{n\geq 0}$ is defined by:

$$F_n = \begin{cases} 1 & \text{if } n = 0 \text{ or } n = 1 \\ F_{n-1} + F_{n-2} & \text{otherwise} \end{cases}$$

It is known that Fibonacci numbers have exponential growth. Indeed it can be shown that $F_n \in \Theta(\varphi^n)$, where $\varphi = \frac{1+\sqrt{5}}{2}$ is the so called **golden ratio**.

Here is an algorithm to compute the n-th Fibonacci number immediately derived from the recursive formula:

Algorithm 8.9: Fibonacci numbers

```
Fibo(n: integer): integer
    if (n == 0) or (n == 1) then return(1)
    return(Fibo(n - 1) + Fibo(n - 2))
```

Let $\psi(n)$ be the complexity function of the algorithm Fibo.

- If $n = 0$ or $n = 1$ the algorithm executes two comparisons, one boolean "or" operation and one return,
- If $n > 1$, the algorithm executes the same two comparisons, the same "or" operation, a return, two subtractions, an addition and all the elementary operation s for the computations of Fibo(n-1) and Fibo(n-2).

hence the function ψ satisfies :

$$\psi(n) = \begin{cases} 4 & \text{if } n = 0 \text{ or } n = 1 \\ 7 + \psi(n-1) + \psi(n-2) & \text{otherwise} \end{cases}$$

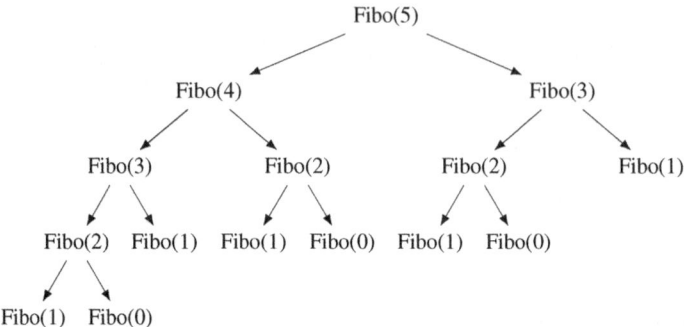

Fig. 8.3 Call tree to get the 5th Fibonacci number using recursion

By comparing the definitions of $\psi(n)$ and F_n it is clear that $\psi(n) > F_n$ for all n, so $\psi(n)$ grows at least as fast as F_n, which is in $\Theta(\varphi^n)$ (exponential). So the complexity of the algorithm Fibo is at least exponential (precisely, it is in $\Omega(\varphi^n)$).

An inspection to the tree of recursive calls shows why this algorithm is so slow. For $n = 5$:

It is apparent that in order to compute Fibo(5) the solutions of some subproblems will be computed more than once. The call Fibo(2) for instance is executed 3 times. The algorithm then wastes time recomputing something it has already computed before. This phenomenon is called **subproblem overlapping** and whenever it occurs it may have nefarious effects on the complexity. In Chap. 10 we will learn a technique to bypass this problem (Fig. 8.3).

Exercise 8.9
Create a Python program to compute the n-th Fibonacci number by the use of the following relation:

$$\begin{pmatrix} F_{n+2} \\ F_{n+1} \end{pmatrix} = \begin{pmatrix} 1 & 1 \\ 1 & 0 \end{pmatrix} \begin{pmatrix} F_{n+1} \\ F_n \end{pmatrix}$$

Optimise the algorithm by using the fast exponentiation algorithm to compute the powers of the matrix $\begin{pmatrix} 1 & 1 \\ 1 & 0 \end{pmatrix}$.

Exercise 8.10
The Tribonacci numbers are defined by

$$T_n = \begin{cases} 1 & \text{if } n < 3 \\ T_{n-1} + T_{n-2} + T_{n-3} & \text{otherwise} \end{cases}$$

1. Write a purely recursive algorithm returning the value T_n for any given integer n.
2. Write a purely iterative algorithm computing a table Tab, where $Tab[i] = T_i$ for all i will $0 \leq i \leq n$.

3. Write a purely iterative algorithm computing T_n and using only three additional integer variables instead of a table.
4. Write an algorithm based on the idea of multiplication by matrices used in exercice 8.9.

Exercise 8.11
Let's consider the following algorithm:

```
def F(n) :
    if n < 3 : return 1
    else : return 2 * F(n - 1) + F(n - 3)
```

Let $A(n)$ be number of additions carried out in the execution of F(n).

1. Give a definition of $A(n)$ by recurrence. Deduce that A is increasing.
2. Show that $A \in \Omega(2^{n/3})$ where / is the euclidean (integer) division.
3. Propose an algorithm that performs a linear number of additions to compute the same values as F(n).
4. What is the complexity of this algorithm?
5. There exists an algorithm with lower complexity?

8.5 Solution for Exercises

Solution of Exercise 8.1

Algorithm 8.10: Iterative fast exponentiation

```
FastExpIter(x: real, n: integer) : real
    exp : real

    if n==0 then return 1
    exp = 1
    while n>1 do
        if n%2==0 then
            x = x*x
            n = n/2
        else
            exp = x*exp
            x = x*x
            n = (n-1)/2
    return(exp)
```

whose Python writing could be (in an optimised way):

Program 8.1: Iterative fast exponentiation   iterfastexp.py

```
def fast_exp_iter(x,n):
    if n==0:
        return 1
    exp = 1
    while n>1:
        if n%2==1:
            exp *= x
        x = x**2
        n //= 2
    return exp*x

print(fast_exp_iter(2,5))
print(fast_exp_iter(2,6))
```

Solution of Exercise 8.3

1. For a polynomial $P(x) = a^n \cdot x^n + \ldots + a_1 \cdot x + a_0$, contained in an array P with P[i] containing the coefficient a_i.

```
def evalPoly(P, x) :
    res = 0
    for i in range(len(P)) :
        res += P[i] * (Exponentiation(x,i))
    return res
```

2. Note that by calling Exponentiation(x,i) for increasing values of i, we often compute the same power of x several times.
3. For each iteration of the loop, there is an addition, a multiplication and an exponentiation. We suppose that Exponentiation(x,i) uses i multiplications. So in the i-th iteration, $2 + i$ elementary operations are performed. In total, if n is the degree of the polynomial P, we have $\sum_{i=0}^{n}(2+i) = 2(n+1) + \frac{n(n+1)}{2}$, yielding a number of elementary operations performed in the order of n^2.
4. If we uses fast exponentiation (x**i uses $log(i)$ elementary operations) so there are $2(n+1) + \sum_{i=1}^{n}(ln(i)) = 2(n+1) + ln(n!)$ operations carried out, the complexity will then be of the order $n \cdot log(n)$.
5. The algorithm computes the value of $P(x)$ by using Horner's decomposition of a polynomial : $P(x) = (\ldots((a_n \cdot x + a_{n-1}) \cdot x + a_{n-2})\ldots) \cdot x + a_0$.
   1 addition and 1 multiplication per each loop turn. So $2(n+1) \in \Theta(n)$ operations to evaluate a polynomial of degree n.

Solution to Exercise 8.4

Since all positions are equiprobable, the probability to find x at a certain position i of A is p/n. We can then compute the probability in each case, occurring to the position where x is :

	Comparisons	Probability
Best case ($A[0] = x$)	1	p/n
Case ($A[1] = x$)	2	p/n
Case ($A[2] = x$)	3	p/n
$\vdots$	$\vdots$	p/n
Case ($A[n-2] = x$)	$n-1$	p/n
Worst case ($A[n-1] = x$ ou $x \notin A$)	n	$p/n + (1-p)$

$$C(n) = \frac{p}{n} \cdot \sum_{i=1}^{n} i + (1-p)n$$

$$= \frac{p}{n} \cdot \frac{n.(n+1)}{2} + (1-p)n$$

$$= \frac{pn + p + 2n - 2pn}{2}$$

$$= \frac{(2-p)n + p}{2}$$

We can observe that $C(n)$ is in $\mathcal{O}(n)$ and that the coefficient of n is larger when p is smaller, which can be easily explained.

Solution to Exercise 8.6

1.
```
def occurrencesNaive(T,x) :
    res = 0
    for i in range(len(T)) :
        if T[i] == x : res += 1
    return res
```

Complexity in $O(n)$.

2. They are all adjacent to each other.
3.
```
def findLeftmost(T,x,begin=0,end=None) :
    if end == None : end = len(T)
    if end-begin == 0 : return None
    half = (begin+end) // 2
    if (x == T[half] and (half == 0 or x != T[half-1])) :
        return half
    elif x <= T[half] :
        return findLeftmost(T,x,begin,half)
    else :
        return findLeftmost(T,x,half+1,end)
```

Complexity in $\Theta(log(n))$ in the worst case.

4. Note that finding the leftmost occurrence by dichotomy (in $O(\log n)$) and then performing a loop to span over all the segment of x's would not provide an optimal algorithm. The complexity would be linear in the worst case (because the while loop my turn up to $O(n)$ times. There is a solution in $O(\log n)$ that uses dichotomy to compute both the leftmost and the rightmost occurrence of x, then computes the difference between those two:

```
def findRightmost(T,x,begin=0,end=None) :
    if end == None : end = len(T)
    if end-begin == 0 : return None
    half = (begin+end) // 2
    if (x == T[half] and (half == len(T) - 1 or x != T[half+1])) :
        return half
    elif x < T[half] :
        return findRightmost(T,x,begin,half)
    else :
        return findRightmost(T,x,half+1,end)

def occurrencesDicho(T,x) :
    i_pre = findLeftmost(T,x)
    if i_pre == None :
        return(0)
    else :
        return (findRightmost(T,x,i_pre) - i_pre + 1)
```

Complexity in $\Theta(log(n))$ in the worst case.

8.5 Solution for Exercises

Solution to Exercise 8.7

1. The condition is true at index k only, thus answer is 1.
2.
```
def is_a_ring(T) :
    found_wrong = False
    for i in range(len(T)) :
        if T[i-1] < T[i] :
            if found_wrong : return False
            found_wrong = True
    return True
```

3. Given that T is a broken ring with T[k:] + T[:k] sorted in decreasing order, and m is the position of the minimum, we necessarily have $m = k-1$, i.e. m is the index of the last element of T[:k]. Therefore $i \leq m$ if and only if $T[0] \geq T[i]$.

4.
```
def minimum_ring(T,begin=0,end=None) :
    if end == None : fin = len(T)
    if end == begin : return None
    if end == begin+1 : return deb
    half = (end+begin)//2
    if T[0] < T[half] :
        return minimum_ring(T,begin,half)
    else :
        return minimum_ring(T,half,end:v)
```

5. Complexity in $\Theta(log(n))$ in the worst case

6.
```
def maximum_ring(T) :
    m = minimum_ring(T)
    return None if m == None else 0 if m == len(T) - 1 else m+1
```

Solution to Exercise 8.8

1. The complexity function of g1 satisfies

$$\varphi(n) = \begin{cases} c & \text{if } n \leq 1 \\ d + \varphi(n/2) & \text{otherwise} \end{cases}$$

This is the same equation as the one satisfied by the complexity function of the binary search. We saw that its solution is: $\varphi(n) = d \log_2 n + c \in \Theta(\log n)$. This can also be computed by changing the variable n to 2^k and by setting $\varphi(n) = \varphi(2^k) = \psi(k)$ so that:

$$\psi(k) = \begin{cases} c & \text{if } k \leq 0 \\ d + \psi(k-1) & \text{otherwise} \end{cases}$$

Then solve step-by-step for $\psi(k)$ (as we did for the complexity function for the factorial).

Solution to Exercise 8.9

Program 8.2: Fast Fibonacci by Matrix Fast Exponentiation   fastfibo.py

```
def mult_mat(m1, m2):
    """A function to multiply two 2x2 matrices"""
    return [ [m1[0][0] * m2[0][0] + m1[0][1] * m2[1][0],
              m1[0][0] * m2[0][1] + m1[0][1] * m2[1][1]],
             [m1[1][0] * m2[0][0] + m1[1][1] * m2[1][0],
              m1[1][0] * m2[0][1] + m1[1][1] * m2[1][1]] ]


def mult(m, v):
    """A function to multiply 2x2 matrix by a 2D vector"""
    return [ m[0][0] * v[0] + m[0][1] * v[1],
             m[1][0] * v[0] + m[1][1] * v[1] ]



f = [ [1, 1], [1, 0] ]

def exp(a, n):
    """Fast exponentiation of a 2D matrix"""
    if n == 1:
        return a
    m = exp(mult_mat(a, a), n // 2)
    if n % 2 == 0:
        return m
    else:
        return mult_mat(a, m)

v = [1, 1]

def fibo(n):
    if n<2:
        return v[n-1]
    return mult(exp(f,n-1),v)[0]


for i in range(0, 100):
    print(fibo(i))
```

Solution to Exercise 8.11

1.
$$A(n) = \begin{cases} 0 & \text{if } n < 3 \\ A(n-1) + A(n-3) + 1 & \text{otherwise} \end{cases}$$

if $n \geq 3$, $A(n-3) + 1 > 0$, so $A(n) > A(n-1)$.

2. Since A is increasing, for all n 3, $A(n-1) > A(n-3)$, therefore the recursive relation implies that

$$\forall n \geq 3, A(n) > 2A(n-3)$$

from which we deduce that $A \in \Omega(2^{n/3})$ since $f(n) = 2^{n/3}$ is precisely such that $f(n) = 2f(n-3)$.

3. Given the similarity with Fibonacci, we can use a list of values to stock the terms already calculated:

```
def F_2(n) :
    tab = [1] * (n+1)
    for i in range (4,n+1) :
        tab[i] = 2 * tab[i-1] + tab[i - 3]
    return tab[n]
```

but of course, it is even better to not preserve useless values, therefore it suffices to have three variables , just to memorise the three most recent values.

4. The number of additions is $n - 3$ for $n \geq 3$, but the size of integers increase linearly, therefore quadratic complexity in fact.

   The memory used is of $n + 1$ integers. Likewise, their sizes must be taken into account, so the complexity in memory $\Theta(n^2)$.

   If we only store the three final values, the complexity in memory (in number of occupied bits) will be linear in n.

5. We observe that for $n \geq 4$ we have

$$\begin{bmatrix} F(n) \\ F(n-1) \\ F(n-2) \end{bmatrix} = \begin{bmatrix} 2 & 0 & 1 \\ 1 & 0 & 0 \\ 0 & 1 & 0 \end{bmatrix}^{n-3} \cdot \begin{bmatrix} 1 \\ 1 \\ 1 \end{bmatrix}$$

therefore, we can use an algorithm based on fast exponentiation of matrices, for example

```
def F(n) :
  if n < 3 : return 1
  else :
    M = [ [2,0,1], [1,0,0], [0,1,0]]
    M = fast_exp ( M, n - 3 )
    R = mult_matrices( M, [ [1], [1], [1] ] )
    return R[0][0]
```

The Sorting Problem

A Problem Admitting a Wide Range of Possible Approaches

The **sorting problem** can be stated as follows. Given an array A of size n whose elements belong to a totally ordered set,[1] permute the elements in such a way that: $A[0] \leq A[1] \leq \cdots \leq A[n-1]$.

Note that the most general statement of the sorting problem can be given on a wider class of arrays, namely arrays containing objects of a structured type that you may want to sort with respect to a particular attribute of the object, generally referred to as *key* (which must belong to a totally ordered set). Imagine for instance a list of pairs of float numbers representing points in the two-dimensional space that you want to sort with respect to their abscissa.

We will write our algorithms for arrays containing integers, they can of course be easily modified if the objects to be sorted (or their keys) belong to any other totally ordered set (float numbers with the natural order, strings with the lexicographic order...).

The sorting problem clearly has a huge number of applications not only because sorting a set of data is a very frequent operation, but also because several problems have an easier solution (a more efficient algorithms) if the array is sorted (think for instance of binary search).

In addition to the computing time, other criteria may determine the choice of the sorting algorithm that is most appropriate for your needs. The first is obviously space, especially if the array to sort has a very large size. In particular, we give the following definition characterising the algorithms whose amount of memory used is a constant that does not depend on the size of the data.

---

[1] A set is totally ordered if, given any two distinct elements of the set, it is always possible to establish which one of the two is larger than the other.

© The Author(s), under exclusive license to Springer Nature Switzerland AG 2024
R. Mantaci, J.-B. Yunès, *Basics of Programming and Algorithms,*
Principles and Applications, Compact Textbooks in Mathematics,
https://doi.org/10.1007/978-3-031-59801-2_9

> **Definition 9.1 (In-Place Sorting)**
>
> A sorting algorithm is said **in-place** if it uses just $\Theta(1)$ memory.

In some cases, especially when you are not dealing with a set of data that is fixed in time, but rather with a dynamical database where new elements may be added in time, it is interesting to have algorithms that do not have to restart the sorting process from zero after each insertion. This leads to the following definition.

> **Definition 9.2 (Online Sorting)**
>
> A sorting algorithm is said **online** if it can be executed as data arrive without waiting for all the elements to be known.

An online sorting algorithm is one that will work if the elements to be sorted are provided one at a time, with the understanding that the algorithm must keep the sequence sorted as more and more elements are added in. The algorithm can process its input piece-by-piece in a serial fashion, that is, in the order that the input is fed to the algorithm, without having the entire input available from the beginning. In contrast, offline algorithms must be given the whole problem data from the beginning, as they presume that they know all the elements in advance.

> **Definition 9.3 (Stable Sorting)**
>
> A sorting algorithm is said to be **stable** if it preserves the relative order of equal elements (or of elements having equal key).

The concept of stability does not make much sense for simple/primitive data in which the sorting key is the value of the element itself. If an array of integers contains two or more repeated values, the order in which these repeated values appear in the final sorted array does not make any difference.

On the other hand, stability makes more sense for structured data. Imagine for instance you have a database (an array) in which each position contains an employee information sheet including several pieces of information concerning a given employee of a large company. For each employee there may be information such as name, address, year of birth.... Suppose you want to sort the array in such a way that at the end the employees are sorted by year of birth and you want employees having the same year of birth sorted by name in lexicographic order. You will have to sort the array twice, first by sorting the data according to the name key (in lexicographic order) and then by sorting the data according to the year_of_birth key. However, in order to obtain the desired result, it is essential that the algorithm applied for the second sorting is stable, because it needs to preserve the relative order established by the first sorting (that is, names increasing lexicographically).

Two classical iterative algorithms belonging to the family of the so-called *elementary* sorting algorithms will be presented firstly, some other algorithms based on more clever strategies (in particular, divide-and-conquer) and having better time complexity will follow.

9.1 Selection Sort

We present **Selection Sort** by selection of the minimum, it is also possible to implement this algorithm by selection of the maximum.

Idea of the algorithm: if the array has size n, we perform $n-1$ "passes" on it: $P_0, P_1, \ldots, P_{n-2}$ (note that the numbering of the passes starts from 0). When we perform the pass P_i, the first i positions of the array contain already elements in increasing order due to the previous passes. We then look for the minimum element among the remaining elements $A[i], A[i+1], \ldots, A[n-1]$ and place it in its correct position by swapping it with the element at position i.

Example 9.1
We want to sort $A = [6, 3, 5, 2, 8, 4]$ with selection sort. Since $n = 6$, five passes will be necessary.

First pass ($i = 0$). Compute the minimum of $[A[0], A[1], A[2], A[3], A[4], A[5]]$ (the entire array). This minimum is 2 (at position 3), we swap it with the element at position $i = 0$, the array becomes $A = [2, 3, 5, 6, 8, 4]$.

Second pass ($i = 1$). Compute the minimum of $[A[1], A[2], A[3], A[4], A[5]]$. This minimum is 3 (at position 1), we swap it with the element at position $i = 1$ (a trivial swap in this case), the array remains $A = [2, 3, 5, 6, 8, 4]$.

Third pass ($i = 2$). Compute the minimum of $[A[2], A[3], A[4], A[5]]$. This minimum is 4 (at position 5), we swap it with the element at position $i = 2$, the array becomes $A = [2, 3, 4, 6, 8, 5]$.

Fourth pass ($i = 3$). Compute the minimum of $[A[3], A[4], A[5]]$. This minimum is 5 (at position 5), we swap it with the element at position $i = 3$, the array becomes $A = [2, 3, 4, 5, 8, 6]$.

Fifth pass ($i = 4$). Compute the minimum of $[A[4], A[5]]$. This minimum is 6 (at position 5), we swap it with the element at position $i = 4$, the array becomes $A = [2, 3, 4, 5, 6, 8]$.

Note that no further pass is needed, necessarily the last element (the maximum of the array) will already be in its final position.

This strategy translates into the following algorithm which, for each $i = 0, \ldots, n-2$, simply determines the minimum in $A[i], \ldots, A[n-1]$ with the basic algorithm seen in Sect. 7.2.2 and then swaps it with $A[i]$.

> **Algorithm 9.1: Selection sort**

```
1  SelectionSort(A: array of n integers)
2      i, j, posmin : integer
3      tmp : integer   // an auxiliary variable tmp is needed to swap
4
5      for i from 0 to n-2 do
6          posmin = i
7          for j from i+1 to n-1 do
8              if (A[j] < A[posmin]) then
9                  posmin = j
10         tmp = A[posmin]      //
11         A[posmin] = A[i]     // swap
12         A[i] = tmp           //
```

Exercise 9.1
Write the Selection Sort algorithm variant in which the selected element is the maximum and not the minimum.

9.1.1 Complexity of Selection Sort

In some cases you may want to conduct a finer analysis of the complexity and separately count each kind of operations such as comparisons or assignments. Note that a swap is equivalent to three assignments. In some situations, certain operations are in practice more time consuming than others and you have to distinguish the operations that are more relevant for the complexity in the context.

Comparisons for instance, can be considered in constant time when you are making comparisons of objects that are represented in the memory with a fixed size, like integers on four bytes or float in double precision on eight bytes, but that is no longer true and certainly more costly for comparisons of objects like strings of characters or even integers of unlimited length like in Python. This is the case for the comparison of line 8, where we are comparing elements of the array.

On the other hand, assignments, corresponding to reading and writing of the memory, can take more time in case of storage in external memories. Even assignments are not all equal: assignments in swaps involving elements of the array that can be very large in size, should be distinguished for instance from the assignments of lines 6 and 9 of Selection Sort involving just integers (positions). Let us evaluate this way the time complexity of Selection Sort.

One swap is performed at each iteration of the for i loop, for a total of $n-1$ swaps, the same holds true for the initialisation of the variable $posmin$ in line 6. The comparison A[j] < A[posmin] of line 8 will be executed $n-1$ times during the first pass, $n-2$ times during the second pass, and so on, down to one time on the last pass, for a total of $\sum_{i=1}^{n-1} i = n(n-1)/2$ times. In the best case, the update of variable $posmin$ in line 9 will never be executed (this happens when the array is already sorted) and in the worst case it will be executed every time the comparison

A[j] < A[posmin] is performed, that is, $n(n-1)/2$ times (this happens when the array is sorted in a decreasing or weakly decreasing order). We can resume all this in the following table:

	posmin=i	A[j]<A[posmin]	posmin=j	swaps
Best case	$n-1$	$n(n-1)/2$	0	$n-1$
Worst case	$n-1$	$n(n-1)/2$	$n(n-1)/2$	$n-1$

In all cases, the number of comparisons is always quadratic, so overall Selection Sort runs in $\Theta(n^2)$. On the other hand, it always executes a linear number of swaps, i.e., a linear number of assignments involving elements of the array, which makes it interesting in a context where such assignments are time consuming.

The space complexity of Selection Sort is constant ($\Theta(1)$). The algorithm Selection Sort is an in-place algorithm. However, it is not online, because it needs to know the entire array before performing the first pass, which computes the minimum of all elements of the array. It is not stable either, because a swap may modify the relative order of equal elements. A simple example of this is the array [7, 7, 4], the first pass swaps the 4 at position 2 with the 7 at position 0, inverting the other of the two 7's.

9.2 Insertion Sort

The idea of the algorithm is inspired by the method sometimes used to sort the playing cards that we receive from the dealer, when we insert one by one the cards we receive in the sequence of the previously received cards that we have in our hand and that we have already sorted. As for Selection Sort, this algorithms performs $n-1$ passes on the array $P_1, P_2, \ldots, P_{n-1}$ (note that unlikely for Selection Sort the numbering of the passes starts from 1). When the algorithm performs the pass P_i, the first i elements of the array have already been sorted by the previous passes so it inserts the element $A[i]$ in the sorted sequence $A[0] \leq \cdots \leq A[i-1]$. The insertion is done by comparing the element $A[i]$ with its left neighbour and by swapping it with this neighbour until $A[i]$ reaches its final place.

Example 9.2
We want to sort $A = [6, 2, 5, 3, 8, 4]$ with insertion sort. Since $n = 6$, five passes will be necessary:

First pass ($i = 1$) insert $A[1] = 2$ in the sorted subarray $[A[0]] = [6]$. After one swap the array becomes $A = [2, 6, 5, 3, 8, 4]$.
Second pass ($i = 2$) insert $A[2] = 5$ in the sorted subarray $[A[0], A[1]] = [2, 6]$. After one swap the array becomes $A = [2, 5, 6, 3, 8, 4]$.
Third pass ($i = 3$) insert $A[3] = 3$ in the sorted subarray $[A[0] - A[2]] = [2, 5, 6]$. After two swaps the array becomes $A = [2, 3, 5, 6, 8, 4]$.
Fourth pass ($i = 4$) insert $A[4] = 8$ in the sorted subarray $[A[0] - A[3]] = [2, 3, 5, 6]$. No swap is necessary the array remains $A = [2, 3, 5, 6, 8, 4]$.

Fifth pass ($i = 5$)   insert $A[5] = 4$ in the sorted subarray $[A[0] - A[4]] = [2, 3, 5, 6, 8]$. After three swaps the array becomes $A = [2, 3, 4, 5, 6, 8]$.

This idea is translated into the following algorithm:

Algorithm 9.2: Insertion sort

```
1  InsertionSort(A:array of n integers)
2     i, j: integer
3     temp: integer   // temp is of the same type as the elements
4
5     for i from 1 to n-1 do
6        j = i
7        while ((j > 0) and (A[j] < A[j-1])) do
8           temp = A[j]     //
9           A[j] = A[j-1]   // swap
10          A[j-1] = temp   //
11          j = j-1
```

▶ We draw your attention on the comparison j>0 of line 7.

The condition A[j]<A[j-1] (the element to insert is smaller than its left neighbour) is the one that logically determines whether or not the while loop needs to continue, but without the test j>0 the program will produce a fatal bug every time the element to insert needs to be inserted in the first position because it is smaller than all elements on its left.

Indeed, if the while loop was regulated only by the condition A[j]<A[j-1], when the element has reached the initial position 0 and hence j has the value 0, the algorithm would test whether $A[0]$ is smaller than $A[-1]$. Position -1 is not in the range of positions of the array, so a reference to $A[-1]$ does not make any sense for the machine and this would make the program crash.[a]

In this case when j has the value 0, the boolean condition j > 0 has the value False, the machine does not need to test the second condition A[j] < A[j-1] because it deduces that the result of the boolean and will be False.

In similar situations in which you have a while loop where the index of an array is modified, you should always include a condition that checks that the index remains within the range of the array and that no reference to something that does not exists is made.

---

[a] In Python, if A is an array or list, $A[-1]$ does make sense, because it always designates the element in the last position of the array, however exchanging the element that you are inserting with the one in the last position of the array is certainly not what you want to do here.

9.2 Insertion Sort

9.2.1 Complexity of Insertion Sort

If we want to evaluate the time complexity of this algorithm we must take into account that the number of swaps executed at each pass depends on the content of the array, not just on its size, we must then analyse the best and the worst case.

The best case occurs when the condition $A[j] < A[j-1]$ is never true, in this case no swap will be executed. This happens when the elements are already sorted in increasing order. For each pass, a first comparison of the value of j with 0 is executed, this comparison will always have the value True so the comparison of $A[i]$ with $A[i-1]$ is also executed. This comparison will have the value False so the while loop will never start. In the best case we must count only a total of $n-1$ comparison of the value of j with 0 and $n-1$ comparison of of $A[i]$ with $A[i-1]$).

In the worst case, the algorithm needs to bring every element at the beginning of the array. This happens when the array is sorted in the opposite order. During the i-th pass the algorithm performs i comparisons A[j]<A[j-1] and the same number of swaps and decrements of j. Thus the total number of each of these three operations is $\sum_{i=1}^{n-1} i = n(n-1)/2$. The comparisons j>0 is performed once more at each iteration (when j=0), for a total of:

$$\frac{n(n-1)}{2} + n - 1 = \frac{n(n-1) + 2(n-1)}{2} = \frac{(n+2)(n-1)}{2}.$$

This can be summed up in the following table:

	j = i	j > 0	A[j] < A[j-1]	swaps	j = j-1
Best case	$n-1$	$n-1$	$n-1$	0	0
Worst case	$n-1$	$(n+2)(n-1)/2$	$n(n-1)/2$	$n(n-1)/2$	$n(n-1)/2$

In the worst case the complexity of the algorithm Insertion Sort is quadratic in terms of comparisons, like SelectionSort. Furthermore the number of swaps is also quadratic in the worst case (while SelectionSort always performs a linear number of swaps).

In the best case the complexity is linear, which is a strong point for Insertion Sort. In practice, the experience shows that for small arrays (in this context we consider small an array of size less than 15), Insertion Sort beats even algorithms having a complexity in $\Theta(n \log n)$, like Merge Sort and Quick Sort that we will see later. It is then possible to optimise these algorithms so that, when the length of the array is smaller than 15 we sort using Insertion Sort and when the length is larger than or equal to 15 we keep calling recursively the original algorithm (see Exercice 9.10). Sorting functions in many libraries use the tricky calling different sorting algorithms depending on the size of the array, one example one TimSort in Python.

It is not too hard to evaluate the average complexity of Insertion Sort. Indeed the number of swaps necessary to sort an array A containing the integers $\{1, 2, \ldots, n\}$ corresponds to the number of inversions of the permutations $A[0], A[1], \ldots A[n-$

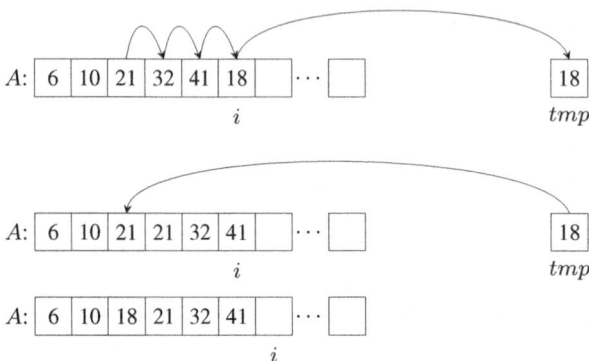

Fig. 9.1 i-th step of insertion sort

1]. The distribution of the statistics of number of inversions in permutations is well studied and it is expressed by the sequence of **Mahonian numbers**, for which a closed formula is known [15]. Using the Mahonian numbers as probabilities for each complexity case, and using their symmetry property, one can obtain that the average complexity of Insertion Sort is also quadratic.

Insertion Sort uses $\Theta(1)$ memory so it works in place.

Insertion Sort is an online algorithm because data can be treated (inserted) as long as they are fed to the algorithm and any new arrival does not necessitate restarting from zero.

Finally, it is also a stable algorithm because entries of the array are treated from left to right and an element is swapped with its left neighbour only if it is strictly smaller than it.

There are two possible optimisations for Insertion Sort. The first one allows to divide by three the number of assignments involving entries of the array (recall that each swap makes three of them). It consists in a version in which the element $A[i]$ to be inserted is first copied in a variable, and then a `while` loop *shifts* of one position to the right all the entries of the array on the left of $A[i]$ that are larger than $A[i]$. The shifts create a free cell where $A[i]$ must be inserted. A shift only needs one assignment involving entries of the array versus the three of a swap (Fig. 9.1).

The second optimisation allows to reduce the number of comparisons needed to determine the position where $A[i]$ must be inserted. This position can be computed by a recursive algorithm which is a variant of the binary search (Exercise 9.2). The number of comparisons of two entries of the array during the i-th pass is no longer linear, but logarithmic. Once you have determined the position where $A[i]$ must be inserted with the above algorithm, you can implement the shifts with a `for` loop which makes comparisons of integers, unlike a `while` loop that makes comparisons of entries of the array. (Exercise 9.3).

Exercise 9.2 (Position by Dichotomy)
Write a function:

FindPosition(A: array of n integers, x: integer):integer

which, given a sorted array A and a value x, computes by dichotomy (in $O(\log n)$) the position of the array A where the value x should be inserted to preserve the sorting.

Exercise 9.3 (Insertion Sort by Dichotomy and Shifts)
Write a function InsertionByShifts(A: array of n integers) sorting the array A by Insertion Sort with the following algorithm:
for each $i = 1, 2, \ldots n - 1$, determine using dichotomy the correct position where the element at position of i must be inserted in the sorted sequence $A[0], A[1], \ldots A[i-1]$,
then shift on the right the elements of the sequence larger than the element to insert before placing the element itself in its final position.

9.3 Merge Sort

Merge Sort is an algorithm based on a recursive strategy that allows to sort an array of size n faster than the two previous algorithms, as its time complexity is in $\Theta(n \log n)$ in all cases. We split the array into two halves (if n is odd, one of the two halves will contain an extra element). We sort each half independently (recursively, using Merge Sort), then we merge the two halves that have just been sorted.

This strategy is implemented in the following algorithm in which you will recognise some features already applied in the algorithm of Binary Search in Sect. 8.3.2 (the use of cursors *begin* and *end*, for instance). Note that we took out of the main algorithm the part of the procedure to merge the two sorted halves, we will implement that in a separate procedure Merge.

Algorithm 9.3: Merge sort

```
1  MergeSort (A: array of n integers; begin, end: integer)
2      m: integer            // variable for the middle position
3
4      if (end - begin > 1) then   // |A|<2, nothing to do
5          m = (begin + end)/2     // the middle position
6          MergeSort(A, begin, m)  // sort left half
7          MergeSort(A, m, end)    // sort right half
8          Merge(A, begin, m, end) // merge sorted halves
9                                  // A[begin...m-1] and A[m...end-1]
```

▶ We said that every recursive algorithm must have at least one base case, so you may wonder where is the base case for MergeSort.

The base case corresponds to the case *end − begin* ≤ 1. Indeed, as noted in the commentaries of the algorithms, if the (section of the) array to be sorted is reduced either to an empty section, or to a section containing only one element, there is nothing to do because an array of size 0 or 1 is already sorted. However in an imperative programming language you cannot write "do nothing", so the empty base case is implicit here, since something will be done only if *end − begin* > 1.

Let's write now the procedure Merge. It should be clear that Merge is not a sorting algorithm but just a procedure that, given an array A and two consecutive sections *A[begin]*, ..., *A[m − 1]* and *A[m]*, ..., *A[end − 1]* of the array that are *already sorted*, merges them into a unique sorted sequence and place this sequence in the positions from *begin* to *end − 1* (Figs. 9.2 and 9.3).

Initially, the procedure copies the section *A[begin]*, ..., *A[m − 1]* in an array L (for left) and the section *A[m]*, ..., *A[end − 1]* in an array R (for right). It then uses three cursors: *i* to run through the array L, *j* to run through the array R and *k* to run through the array A. The core of the algorithm is a loop that at each iteration compares *L[i]* and *R[j]* and then copies back in the array A the smaller of the two. The cursor of the array of the element that has been copied (L or R) is then moved by one position to the right to make it ready for the next comparison. This loop continues as long as there are still elements to be compared in L and in R.

When all the elements either in L or in R have been copied back to A, the remaining elements of the other array must be copied as well. The pseudo-code of Merge includes two additional loops to do that. Clearly, only one of the two loops will be performed during a specific execution of the algorithm.

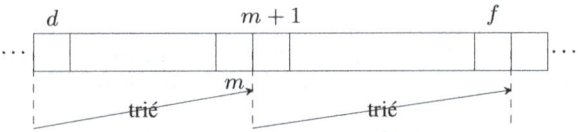

Fig. 9.2 Merge sort: before the merge

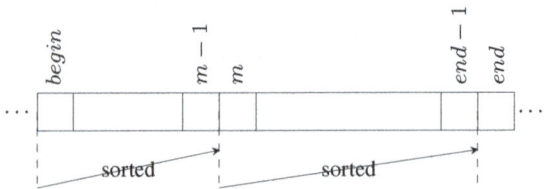

Fig. 9.3 Merge sort: before the merge

9.3 Merge Sort

Algorithm 9.4: Merge

```
1  Merge (A: array of n integers; b, m, e: integer)
2      L: array of m-b integers
3      R: array of e-m integers
4      i,j,k: integer
5
6      for k from b to m-1 do
7          L[k-b] = A[k]           //copy A[b],...,A[m-1] in L
8      for k from m to e-1 do
9          R[k-m] = A[k]           //copy A[m],...,A[e-1] in R
10     i = 0
11     j = 0
12     while (i < m-b) and (j < e-m) do //the loop with the comparisons
13         if (L[i] <= R[j]) then
14             A[k] = L[i]
15             i = i+1
16         else
17             A[k] = R[j]
18             j = j+1
19         k = k+1
20     while (i < m-b) do //if there are still elements of L to copy
21         A[k] = L[i]
22         i = i+1
23         k = k+1
24     while (j < e-m) do //if there are still elements of R to copy
25         A[k] = R[j]
26         j = j+1
27         k = k+1
```

9.3.1 Time Complexity of Merge and Merge Sort

A constant number of operations is required to place each element of the section $A[begin], \ldots, A[end-1]$ in its final position, therefore the time complexity of Merge is in $\Theta(end - begin)$, that is, Merge runs in a time proportional to the size of the resulting sorted section of the array. When Merge is called by MergeSort to sort an array of size n its time complexity is then proportional to n.

Let us now evaluate the time complexity of MergeSort. When $n = 0$ or 1, the algorithm executes just a constant number of elementary operation s; when $n > 1$ the algorithm makes two recursive calls on arrays of size $n/2$, whose complexity is expressed by $2\varphi(n/2)$, and a call to Merge having linear cost. The complexity function $\varphi(n)$ of MergeSort then satisfies :

$$\varphi(n) = \begin{cases} c & \text{if } n = 0 \text{ or } n = 1 \\ 2\varphi(\frac{n}{2}) + dn & \text{otherwise} \end{cases}$$

where dn represents the linear cost of Merge.

To solve this recurrence let us suppose that n is a power of 2, say $n = 2^k$ and denote $g(k) = \varphi(2^k) = \varphi(n)$. We can rewrite the recurrence as:

$$g(k) = \begin{cases} c & \text{if } k = 0 \\ 2g(k-1) + d2^k & \text{otherwise} \end{cases}$$

Therefore:

$$\begin{aligned} g(k) &= 2g(k-1) + d2^k \\ g(k-1) &= 2g(k-2) + d2^{k-1} \\ g(k-2) &= 2g(k-3) + d2^{k-2} \\ &\vdots \\ g(2) &= 2g(1) + d2^2 \\ g(1) &= 2g(0) + d2^1 \\ g(0) &= c. \end{aligned}$$

Now we multiply every equation for an appropriate power of 2, namely we multiply the second equation by 2, the third equation by 2^2 and so on, this way we create equal terms in opposite sides of the equations that we will eliminate by summing them all up:

$$\begin{aligned} g(k) &= 2g(k-1) + d2^k \\ 2g(k-1) &= 2^2 g(k-2) + d2^k \\ 2^2 g(k-2) &= 2^3 g(k-3) + d2^k \\ &\vdots \\ 2^{k-2} g(2) &= 2^{k-1} g(1) + d2^k \\ 2^{k-1} g(1) &= 2^k g(0) + d2^k \\ 2^k g(0) &= c2^k \end{aligned}$$

by summing all the equations we obtain:

$$g(k) = c2^k + dk2^k.$$

We revert to n and φ, since $n = 2^k$ we have $k = \log_2 n$, so:

$$\varphi(n) = cn + dn\log_2 n \in \Theta(n \log n).$$

9.3.2 Space Complexity and Other Features of Merge Sort

While the elementary algorithms `SelectionSort` and `InsertionSort` require $\Theta(1)$ memory, `MergeSort` uses $\Theta(n)$ memory (the two arrays L and R). So, unlike the other two algorithms, it does not sort the array "in-place".

9.3 Merge Sort

It is possible to implement an "in-place" version of MergeSort that merges the two parts by inserting the elements of the right part into the left one by performing shifts, we basically insert the elements of the second section into the first using the same strategy as Insertion Sort. The time complexity of this algorithm however is in $\Theta(n^2)$ in the worst case.

The algorithm Merge Sort is not on-line. Sorting the array with Merge Sort after insertion of a new element necessitates a full execution of the algorithm.

It can be checked that Merge Sort is stable because of the comparison L[i] <= R[j] of line 13. In case of two equal elements, one in L and one in R, the one in L is copied first in the original array. A strict test L[i] < R[j] would make the algorithm non stable.

Exercise 9.4

1. Apply manually the algorithm of merge sort to the table [4,2,5,6,1,4,1,0]. Count the precise number of comparisons carried out.
2. The following is a Python program version (of linear complexity) of the function Merge(A1, A2) merging two sorted arrays A1 and A2.

```
def Merge(A1, A2):
    res = []
    i = 0
    j = 0
    nbInv = 0 # NEW
    while (i < len(A1) and j < len(A2)):
        if A1[i] <= A2[j]:
            res += [ A1[i] ]
            i += 1
        else:
            res += [ A2[j] ]
            j += 1
    for k in range(i, len(A1)):
        res += [ A1[k] ]
    for k in range(j, len(A2)):
        res += [ A2[k] ]
    return res, nbInv
```

Recall that a *inversion* of A is a couple of elements A[i] < A[j] in the wrong order, meaning that the positions verify i > j.

Modify the previous function into a function nbInversionsBetween(A1, A2) that counts the inversions in the table A1+A2 (supposing that A1 and A2 are sorted).

3. Deduce from it a program nbInversions(A) that computes the number of inversions of an array A of size n in time $\Theta(n \log n)$.

Exercise 9.5
The **Natural Merge Sort**, proposed by D. Knuth, is a variation of merge sort that takes advantage of pre-sorted sections of the array, called "monotonies".
A decomposition of an array T into monotonies is a sequence of subarrays $T[0 : i_1], T[i_1 : i_2], \ldots, T[i_{k-1} : len(T)]$, all sorted, and whose concatenation is T. With the habitual convention used by Python, $T[a, b]$ designates the subarray that starts at position a et terminates at position $b - 1$.
For example, $[1, 3, 6, 4, 5, 9, 8, 2, 7]$ can decomposed into $[[1, 3, 6], [4, 5, 9], [8], [2, 7]]$, or in terms of subarray bounds (indices), $[(0, 3), (3, 6), (6, 7), (7, 10)]$.

1. Write a function monotonies(T) that returns a list M representing a decomposition of T into monotonies in terms of subarray bounds (so if $T = [1, 3, 6, 4, 5, 9, 8, 2, 7]$ we want the list of pairs $[(0, 3), (3, 6), (6, 7), (7, 10)]$ and *not* the actual list of subarrays). What is its complexity?
2. Write an (iterative) algorithm NaturalMergeSort(T) which, after computing the list M of the bounds of the monotonies of T, sorts the array T by merging the first monotony with the second, then the resulting monotony with the third, and so on, until you get a single monotony (and therefore a sorted array).
   Implement the algorithm with a loop where appropriate calls to the procedure Merge(T: array of n integers; d, m, f: integer) are made. Recall that a call Merge(T, d, m, f) merges the sections $T[d], T[d + 1], \ldots, T[m - 1]$ and $T[m], T[m + 1], \ldots, T[f - 1]$.
3. What is its worst-case and best-case complexity?
4. Write another version of NaturalMergeSort(T) that performs the mergings somewhat like the regular merge sort. Run a first pass on the list of monotonies and merge pairwise the first with the second, then the third with the fourth, and so on (if the number of monotones is odd, the last one will not be merged with any other). After this pass, the number of monotonies will be halved, and the same process is repeated until having a single monotony.
   For this version, it is recommended to update the M list of monotones each time a merging is performed. Both an iterative and a recursive algorithms can be proposed.

Exercise 9.6
Let A be an array containing at least two integers. We want to compute the distance between the two closest elements in A (that is, the smallest possible value of $|A[i] - A[j]|$ for all pairs (i, j) where $0 \leq i \neq j < length(A)$.

1. Write a naive algorithm in $O(n^2)$ that solves the problem.
2. Write an algorithm in $O(n \log n)$ that solves the problem.
3. Can we use the idea of the algorithm found in question 2 to calculate the difference between the two farthest elements in A (i.e., the largest possible value of $|A[i] - A[j]|$)?
4. Can question 3 be solved by an algorithm with a strictly better complexity than $O(n \log n)$?

9.4 Quick Sort

Quick Sort is a recursive algorithm having complexity in $\Theta(n \log n)$ in the best case but $\Theta(n^2)$ in the worst case. In the average case, it runs in $\Theta(n \log n)$.

The idea is to partition the array by choosing an element $A[p]$ of the array called **pivot** and then rearranging the array so that all the elements smaller than the pivot are on its left and all elements larger than the pivot are on its right. If the array has repeated values, the algorithm may choose to put elements equal to the pivot either all on the left of it or all on the right of it.

9.4 Quick Sort

Note that after this rearrangement the pivot is in its final position of the sorting process. We then start again the same procedure on the two sections on the left and on the right of the pivot without having to deal with it anymore.

The choice of the pivot may have an influence on the complexity of the algorithm but this will be discussed later. For the moment, let us suppose that the pivot is chosen via a function called ChoosePivot that given an interval $[begin, \ldots, end[$ of the array, returns (in constant time, regardless of how) a position between $begin$ and $end - 1$. To fix the ideas you may assume for the moment that ChoosePivot always returns $begin$, that is, it always chooses as pivot the first element of the array (or of the section $[begin, \ldots, end[$ of the array). We will see later that is some cases this might not be a wise choice.

The algorithm makes a call to the function

Partition(A, begin, end, indexpivot)

that rearranges the section $A[begin], \ldots A[end - 1]$ of the array using the element $A[indexpivot]$ as pivot, that is, it rearranges the section of the array in such a way that all the elements smaller than the pivot are on its left and all elements larger than or equal to the pivot are on its right. Furthermore, the procedure also returns the new position of the pivot after the partitioning process (we need to know that position for the recursive calls made immediately after the call of Partition).

Algorithm 9.5: Quick sort

```
1  QuickSort(A:array of n integers; begin, end: integer)
2      indexpivot: integer
3
4      if (end-begin > 1) then
5          indexpivot = ChoosePivot(begin, end)
6          indexpivot = Partition(A, begin, end, indexpivot)
7          QuickSort(A, begin, indexpivot)
8          QuickSort(A, indexpivot+1, end)
```

Initially, the Partition algorithm temporarily places the pivot in the first position of the section to be partitioned, i.e. at the position $begin$, by swapping it with the element in that positon (if we assume that ChoosePivot selects $begin$ as position of the pivot, this swap has no effect). It then uses two cursors i and j initialised at $begin + 1$ and $end - 1$ respectively. With these two cursors it performs a loop that preserves the following property: after every iteration, the positions on left of i contain values smaller than the pivot and the positions on the right of j contain values larger than the pivot as illustrated in Fig. 9.4.

To do so, the algorithm checks the current values of $A[i]$ and of $A[j]$. If $A[i]$ is smaller than the pivot then it is placed already on the correct side of the array, there is nothing to do other than increasing i to analyse the element at the next position on the right. Analogously, if $A[j]$ is larger than the pivot then it is already located on

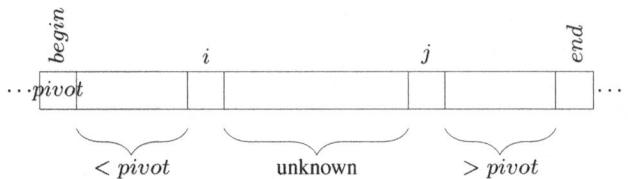

Fig. 9.4 During a partition step in QuickSort

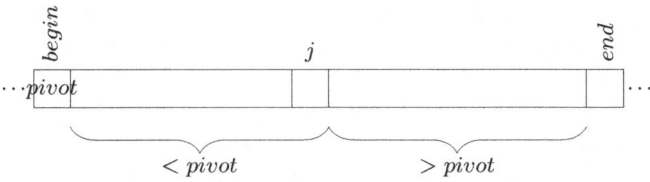

Fig. 9.5 End of partition step in QuickSort

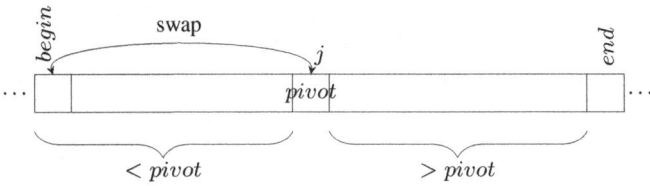

Fig. 9.6 Placing the pivot in QuickSort

the correct side of the array, there is nothing to do other than decreasing j to analyse the element on the left. In the remaining case, both $A[i]$ and $A[j]$ are on the wrong side and it suffices to swap them to bring both of them on the correct side.

At every iteration either i is increased by 1 or j is decreased by one (or both things), at some point the two cursors must cross each other, that is, j becomes smaller than i. At that point the section $A[begin + 1, \ldots, end - 1]$ has been partitioned as expected, it is composed of a section of values smaller than the pivot followed by a section of values larger than the pivot, see Fig. 9.5. Note that elements of these sections are not sorted.

The only thing left to do is to place the pivot in its final position, to do so it suffices to swap it with the rightmost element of the section of elements smaller than the pivot. This element is in position j, which is also the value to return because it is precisely the final position of the pivot, see Fig. 9.6.

This yields the following algorithm:

Algorithm 9.6: Partition in Quick Sort

```
1   Partition(A:array of n integers; begin, end, indexpivot : integer): ▷
        ▷ integer
2   i, j: integer
3   tmp: integer
4
5   tmp = A[begin]         // swap the pivot with the first element
6   A[begin] = A[indexpivot]
7   A[indexpivot] = tmp
8   i = begin + 1          // position the two cursors
9   j = end - 1
10  while (j >= i) do
11      if A[i] < A[begin] then
12          i = i + 1
13      else if A[j] > A[begin] then
14          j = j-1
15      else    // if you get here, A[i] and A[j] must be swapped
16          tmp = A[i]
17          A[i] = A[j]
18          A[j] = tmp
19          i = i + 1
20          j = j - 1
21  tmp = A[begin]  // final swap to put pivot in final positon
22  A[begin] = A[j]
23  A[j] = tmp
24  return(j)
```

9.4.1 Complexity of Quick Sort

The time complexity of Partition is in $\Theta(end - begin)$, that is, Partition runs in a time proportional to the size of the section of the array it has to rearrange. When Partition is called by QuickSort to sort an array of size n, its time complexity is then proportional to n. Then, two recursive calls are made. If k is the final position of the pivot, we make one call on a section of the array of size k and another on a section of the array of size $n - k - 1$, because we do not include the pivot in any future calls.[2]

---
[2] This -1 term in $n - k - 1$ is one of the reasons that make Quick Sort faster than Merge Sort in most cases.

So, if we evaluate the complexity of Partition with a term dn where d is a constant, we can write the following recursive formula:

$$\varphi(n) = \begin{cases} c & \text{si } n = 0, 1 \\ dn + \varphi(k) + \varphi(n - k - 1) & \text{otherwise} \end{cases}$$

Suppose that the pivot partitions the array into two sections of equal size. T his occurs when the pivot is the median value of the array.[3] In this case the function φ satisfies:

$$\varphi(n) = \begin{cases} c & \text{si } n = 0, 1 \\ dn + 2\varphi(\frac{n-1}{2}) & \text{otherwise} \end{cases}$$

This shows that in this case Quick Sort is even faster than Merge Sort, as we find the same kind of recursion (with an improving term -1 in $\varphi(\frac{n-1}{2})$) that was not present for Merge Sort). This is the best case for Quick Sort and its complexity is in $O(n \log n)$.

Suppose that the pivot partitions the array into two sections one of which is empty, this occurs when the pivot is the minimum or the maximum of the array. In this case the function φ satisfies:

$$\varphi(n) = \begin{cases} c & \text{si } n = 0, 1 \\ dn + \varphi(n - 1) & \text{otherwise} \end{cases}$$

This recursive equation can easily be solved:

$$\begin{aligned} \varphi(n) &= dn + \varphi(n-1) \\ &= dn + d(n-1) + \varphi(n-2) \\ &\vdots \\ &= d(n + (n-1) + \ldots + 1) \\ &= d\frac{n(n+1)}{2} \end{aligned}$$

This is the worst case for QuickSort and it is in $\Theta(n^2)$.

Notice that if our strategy to choose the pivot is to always take the first element of the section, when the array is already sorted from the beginning, the algorithm will always choose the minimum of the section as pivot, one of the two parts of the partition will be empty and we are in the worst case! So the algorithm will make the highest possible number of operations in the case when in principle you would expect it would have the least to do.

---

[3] This seems in principle a very strong hypotheses, especially if we assume that we keep being lucky by having perfect equal-sized partitions at all stages (recursive calls) of the algorithm.

9.4 Quick Sort

Experimentally, the strategy of choosing a pivot at random (you take as *indexpivot* an integer drawn at random in the interval [*begin, end*[) works equally well, and avoids that the worst possible case coincides with the case where the array is already sorted from the beginning.

It is possible to prove that the average complexity of Quick Sort is in $O(n \log n)$. An argument in favour of this (but not a proof of it) is that even for very skewed partitions, the algorithm may remain in $O(n \log n)$. Imagine for instance a case where the partition always puts only one thousandth of the elements on one side and 999 per thousand on the other side. It is not difficult to prove that the algorithm will perform at most a number of operations in the order of $n \log_{\frac{1000}{999}} n$. See Exercise 9.8.

Exercise 9.7 (Execution of Quick Sort)

Let A be the following array: 7 1 5 6 2 3 10 8 0 9 4

Describe the execution of the following variants of quick sort on the table A.

1. Variant with auxiliary memory, you have two lists in which you can separate the elements smaller than the pivot from the elements larger than the pivot. Take always the first element as pivot.
2. *Idem*, but always choosing the median element as pivot
3. Variant "in place", you cannot use auxiliary lists hand have to swap the elements the way it has been presented in the courseL The pivot always being the first element.

In each case, precisely count the number of comparisons carried out.

Exercise 9.8 (Skewed Partitions may Lead to $\Theta(n \log n)$)

Let α be a real number with $0 < \alpha < \frac{1}{2}$. Suppose the procedure Partition always partitions the array into two sections, one of size $\alpha \cdot n$ and one of size $(1 - \alpha) \cdot n$ (including the pivot in any of those two sections). If α is very close to 0, this gives a very biased partition at all levels.

1. Add the nodes of depth 2 and 3 in the following tree of the recursive calls where QS(n) represents a call of Quick Sort over an array of size n (we are only interested in the size of the subarrays here). Suppose $\alpha^3 n$ is still larger than 1.

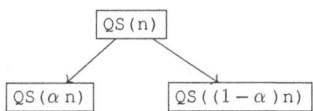

2. What is the height of the complete tree? (How many levels does it have?)
3. What is the cumulative cost of all the calls to the procedure Partition made at any level of the tree?
4. Conclude that the complexity of Quick Sort is $O(n \log n)$ in this case.

Exercise 9.9 (Complexity of Quick Sort)

1. Evaluate the number of element comparisons carried out by quick sort (with pivot T[0]) in the following cases:

   - C[n] = [1, 2, ..., n-1, n];
   - D[n] = [n, n-1, ..., 2, 1];
   - M[k] = [2**k] + M[k-1] + [i+2**k for i in M[k-1]] (with M[0] = [1]).

2. Give other examples of tables of size 7 for which the complexity of quick sort is the same as for C[7]. Same question for M[2].
3. What is the number of vertices of the tree of recursive calls of quick sort for a table of length n whose elements are all distinct? What can we conclude concerning its minimal height? and its maximum height?
4. Give a boundary as precise as possible of the cumulative number of comparisons carried out by the recursive calls of depth p.
5. Deduce the complexity in time of quick sort in the best and in the worst case (always assuming that all the elements are distinct).

Exercise 9.10 (Quick Sort Improvements)

1. Write a *recursive* function EnhancedQuickSort in which the arrays of size strictly less than 15 (and therefore also the *sections having size strictly less than 15* in arrays of any size) are sorted using Insertion Sort. Arrays (or sections of arrays) having size larger than or equal to 15 will be sorted with the usual partition strategy of Quick Sort.
2. Write a *recursive* function IncompleteQuickSort based on the Quick Sort model, but in which an array is not sorted if its size is strictly less than 15 (and therefore sections of an array having size strictly less than 15 are not sorted either). In general, this function therefore returns an unsorted array.
3. Write a function SedgewickSort which sorts the array returned by IncompleteQuickSort using Insertion Sort.
4. Compare the time of computation of EnhancedQuickSort and SedgewickSort with other sorting algorithms that you have previously implemented.

9.5 Is $n \log n$ Optimal?

The following table recapitulates complexity and properties of the sorting algorithms presented so far:

	Best Case	Worst Case	Average	In-place	Online	Stable
Selection Sort	$\Theta(n^2)$	$\Theta(n^2)$	$\Theta(n^2)$	Yes	No	No
Insertion Sort	$\Theta(n)$	$\Theta(n^2)$	$\Theta(n^2)$	Yes	Yes	Yes
Merge Sort	$\Theta(n\log n)$	$\Theta(n\log n)$	$\Theta(n\log n)$	No ($\Theta(n)$)	No	Yes
Quick Sort	$\Theta(n\log n)$	$\Theta(n^2)$	$\Theta(n\log n)$	Yes	No	No

9.5 Is $n \log n$ Optimal?

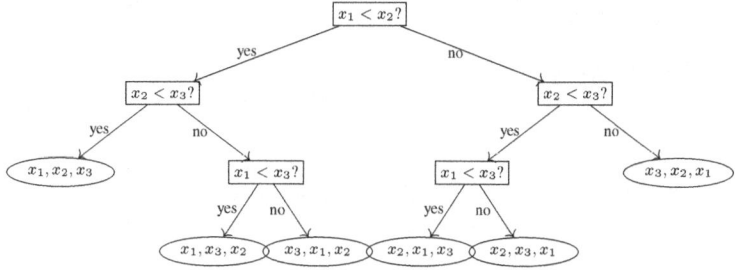

Fig. 9.7 Decision tree for sorting an array of three elements

At this point you may wonder : "Is it possible to do better in terms of time complexity ? Is it possible to sort n elements faster than in $\mathcal{O}(n \log n)$ in the worst case?"

The answer is "no" for algorithms sorting the array using comparisons.[4]

The proof of this fact uses the so-called **decision trees**. Suppose we want to sort a sequence of elements $x_1, x_2, \ldots, x_n$. The corresponding decision tree is a binary tree in which each internal node (that is a node that is not a leaf) corresponds to a comparison ($x_i < x_j$?) between two elements. Based on the answer of this comparison, we can determine the relative position of the elements x_i and x_j in the sorted array. After a certain number of comparisons, it is then possible to deduce the order of all elements in the sorted array and we place the resulting sequence in a leaf of the tree. The decision tree therefore has exactly $n!$ leaves (one for each possible permutation). Figure 9.7 gives the example of the decision tree for $n = 3$.

The height h of the decision tree is equal to the maximal number of comparisons that are needed to sort any array of size n, that is, the number of comparisons executed in the worst case. A binary tree of height h has at most 2^h leaves (this happens for a *complete* binary tree in which each internal node has exactly two children and the leaves are all at the same depth). Hence for the decision tree we have : $n! \leq 2^h$. By taking logarithms we deduce $h \geq \log_2(n!)$. It is possible to show that $\log_2(n!) \in \Theta(n \log n)$ (see Exercise 9.11). Consequently, the number of comparisons needed to sort an array of size n is at least of the order of $n \log n$ in the worst case.

Exercise 9.11
Show that $\log_2(n!) \in \Theta(n \log n)$.

---

[4] This obviously raises an additional question: "how is it possible to sort an array without making comparisons between its elements?" We will answer to this question in the next section.

9.6 Sorting in Linear Time

9.6.1 Counting Sort

Suppose we know that the entries in the array to be sorted (or their keys) belong to a discrete finite interval.[5] Without loss of generality, we can assume that the interval is $[0, m-1]$ because for any finite discrete interval I of size m it is possible to establish an order-preserving bijection between I and $[0, m-1]$, you will just have to keep a conversion table of size m that associates an integer in $[0, m-1]$ with each element of the original interval.

Sorting the array without comparisons is then possible by introducing an array of counters $C[0..m-1]$ in which each cell $C[k]$ counts the number of elements of the array that are equal to k (or whose key is equal to k). The resulting algorithm is called **Counting Sort**.

We start by giving a simpler version of the algorithm for arrays containing integers. Each counter $C[k]$ gives you the length of the segment of elements equal to k in A when sorted, so the array A can be refilled from left to right knowing exactly for each position i which integer goes in the cell $A[i]$ of the sorted array. Notice that this process *overwrites* the entries of the array with others.

Algorithm 9.7: Counting sort

```
1   CountingSortForInt (A: array of n integers; m: integer)
2       C: array of m integers
3       i, k : integer
4
5       for k from 0 to m-1 do          // initialisation of the counters
6           C[k] = 0
7       for i from 0 to n-1 do          // counting
8           C[A[i]] = C[A[i]]+1
9       i = 0
10      for k from 0 to m-1 do          // putting back the integers in A
11          while (C[k]>0) do
12              A[i] = k
13              C[k] = C[k] - 1
14              i = i +1
```

If you are sorting objects of a given class `object` with respect to an integer key whose values are between 0 and $m-1$, you cannot overwrite an element with another having the same key because the two elements are not equal. You need to use an additional array B to copy the objects in the right order.

---

[5] This is a quite restrictive hypothesis, you need to know beforehand that the elements of the array belong to a discrete set (this excludes the floats for instance) and that they are all in a bounded range between two values a and b with $a < b$. Some exemples: sorting according to age (an integer between 0 and 130) or according to the country (an integer between 0 and 300).

9.6 Sorting in Linear Time

Some little further manipulations on the array C can be convenient (they do not modify the Θ class of the overall complexity). First, we use an array of length $m+1$ instead of m, we set $C[0] = 0$ and we keep it this way until the end of the algorithm. We make a *shift* of the counters in the sense that the occurrences of the key i are counted by counter $C[i + 1]$ and not $C[i]$. Then, we cumulate all the values in this array by adding to each counter the sum of all the previous ones.

After these manipulations, each counter $C[i]$ contains the starting position of the section of entries having key i in the sorted array, that is, the position where the first entry having key equal to i must be inserted in B. So you can simply go through the elements of the array A from left to right with a simple for loop, at each iteration the array C will tell you in which case of B you should put the the current element. Obviously, you have to keep each of these counters updated by increasing it by 1 every time you make a writing in B.

Algorithm 9.8: Counting Sort

```
1   CountingSort (A: array of n objects; m: integer): array of n objects
2       C: array of m integers
3       B: array of n objects
4       i, k : integer
5
6       for k from 0 to m-1 do              // initialisation if needed
7           C[k] = 0
8       for i from 0 to n-1 do              // counting
9           C[key(A[i])+1] += 1
10      for k from 1 to m do                // cumulating the values
11          C[k] = C[k] + C[k-1]
12      for i from 0 to n-1 do              // putting the integers in B
13          B[C[key(A[i])]] = A[i]
14          C[key(A[i])] += 1
15      return B
```

The time complexity of these algorithms is in $\Theta(n + m) = \Theta(\max(n + m))$ because they include loops of length n and of length m. If m is small with respect to n, the complexity is in $\Theta(n)$, linear with respect to the size of the array. This algorithm is interesting when you are sorting large arrays whose entries (or their keys) belong to a small range, typically an array with a lot of repetitions. If m is $\Omega(n \log n)$ (at least of the order of $n \log n$) you should use Merge Sort or Quick Sort instead.

The space complexity of the simpler version is $\Theta(m)$ (the space for the array C). For the general version, you need to add the space for the array B in $\Theta(n)$ and the final complexity is in $\Theta(n + m) = \Theta(\max(n + m))$.

Exercise 9.12 (An Application of the Partition Procedure: Flag Sort)
The problem of the *Dutch flag* is the following: the table to be sorted contains three types of elements: the blues, the whites, and the reds, and we need to sort them by color.

1. If all the elements of the same color are identical it suffices to count them. Write an algorithm in $O(n)$ time and $O(1)$ space that returns the sorted table.
   From now on we suppose that all the elements of the same color are not identical, therefore it is not sufficient to count them.
2. We recall that a sorting algorithm is *stable* if it preserves the order of the initial table for the elements of the same key (in this case, color). Propose a linear and stable algorithm (but not in place) to solve this problem.
3. Propose a linear algorithm in place (but not stable) in the case where there are only two colors (blue and red).
4. How do we adapt the previous algorithm in the case where the table contains one single white element, in its first box?
5. Generalize the algorithm of the question 3 in the case of three colors. For this, we will maintain the following invariant:

   the table consists of 4 consecutive segments, one blue, one white, one unexplored, et one red.

   Use three cursors to represent the boundaries between these segments.

Note: To our knowledge there does not exist an algorithm simultaneously linear, stable and in place for this problem; however, it is possible to lightly modify the algorithm of question 5 to obtain a stable algorithm and in place (but therefore not linear).

9.6.2 Radix Sort

Like Counting Sort, **Radix Sort** is a non-comparative sorting algorithm that sorts data in linear time. The algorithm performs the sort by grouping items based on their digits, it processes each digit in the numbers, from the least significant to the most significant. The principle of **Radix Sort** is the following:

- Given an array of n numbers to sort, we first perform a stable sort (for the moment it does not matter how) with respect to their units digit (we place first those elements whose units digit is 0, then those whose units digit is 1 and so on).
- then we sort again the array sorted at the previous step according to the tens digit, again using a stable sort,
- then we sort according to the hundreds digit,
- and so on...

The following procedure, which implements this algorithm, assumes that each element of the array T has d digits. The "i-th digit" is defined as the i-th digit from the right (so the "first digit" is the units):

9.6 Sorting in Linear Time

Algorithm 9.9: Radix sort

1 RadixSort (T: **array of** n **integers**, d: **integer**)
2   **for** i **from** 1 **to** d **do**
3   use a stable sort to sort T with respect to the i-th digit

Example 9.3
Let us apply Radix Sort to the following array (for $d = 4$):

Initial array	5998	1445	2114	9479	6566	8680	2680	6016	6592	2422
Sort by units	8680	2680	6592	2422	2114	1445	6566	6016	5998	9479
Sort by tens	2114	6016	2422	1445	6566	9479	8680	2680	6592	5998
Sort by hundreds	6016	2114	2422	1445	9479	6566	6592	8680	2680	5998
Sort by thousands	1445	2214	2422	2680	5998	6016	6566	6592	8680	9474

Note that the algorithm would not work if we use a sorting algorithm that is not stable. Note also that it is not necessary that all integers in the array have the same number of digits, it suffices to make them all of the same length by adding zeroes appropriately at the beginning.

If the sorting algorithm used to sort relatively to each digit has a complexity in $\Theta(f(n))$ (it doesn't matter what the function f is), the complexity of **Radix Sort** if obviously in $\Theta(d \cdot f(n))$, where d is the number of digits of the largest of all numbers to be sorted. The value d can be considered a constant (it does not depend on the size n of the array) and therefore the complexity of Radix Sort will be the same as the complexity of the algorithm used to sort according to a digit, i.e. $\Theta(f(n))$.

We can easily define a function Digit(p, i: integer): integer which computes the value of the i-th decimal digit of the integer p. For the sake of uniformity, the least significant digit (the first digit) is numbered by 1. This is simply the function that returns $\frac{p}{10^{i-1}}$ mod 10:

Algorithm 9.10: Extracting a digit

1 Digit(p: **integer**, i: **integer**): **integer**
2   **return** (p/(Exp(10,i-1) % 10)

9.6.3 Bucket Sort

To perform each sort relative to the i-th digit (for any i between 1 and d), we will use **Bucket Sort**. The idea is that we have ten buckets : $S[0], S[1], \ldots, S[9]$, in which we distribute the elements (if we are working in base 10, but we may be working in any other base). In the bucket $S[k]$, we will place the elements of the array whose

i-th digit is k. Each bucket $S[k]$ will be a list of integers (a simple list in Python, a linked list in other languages).

For instance, the state of the ten buckets $S[0], S[1], \ldots, S[9]$ after a distribution of the elements of the array A of the previous example according to the units digit is:

Bucket	Elements
$S[0]$	[8680, 2680]
$S[1]$	[]
$S[2]$	[6592, 2422]
$S[3]$	[]
$S[4]$	[2114]
$S[5]$	[1445]
$S[6]$	[6566, 6016]
$S[7]$	[]
$S[8]$	[5998]
$S[9]$	[9479]

We can write a procedure
`Distribute(A:array of n integers, i:integer, S:array of 10 lists)`
which iterates through the array A and places each element in the appropriate bucket (i.e. $A[j]$ goes into the $S[k]$ bucket if its i-th digit is k).

Algorithm 9.11: Distribute elements to appropriate bucket

```
1  Distribute (A: array of n integers, i: integer, S: array of 10 lists)
2      for j from 0 to n-1 do
3          add A[j] to S[Digit(A[j],i)]
```

This algorithm is clearly in $O(n)$.

We now write a procedure
`Recompose (S: array of 10 lists): array of n integers)`
which receives the array S of the ten buckets where the elements have been distributed and returns an array containing the elements of the array sorted relatively to the i-th digit.

Algorithm 9.12: Recompose buckets to an array

```
1  Recompose (S: array of 10 lists): array of n integers
2      A=[]
3      i=0
4      for k from 0 to 9 do
5          for t from 0 to length(S[k])-1 do
6              A[i] = S[k][t]
7              i = i+1
```

This procedure is also clearly in $O(n)$ and takes into account the considerations about stability. Therefore, the time complexity of the Bucket Sort algorithm resulting from the concatenation of the Distribute and Recompose is in $\Theta(n)$. Its space complexity is also $\Theta(n)$ (the total space occupied by the buckets). Consequently both the space and the time complexities of Radix Sort are in $\Theta(d \cdot n) = \Theta(n)$ if we use Bucket Sort to sort the numbers by digits. So Radix Sort sorts the array in linear time.

Then the final version of Radix Sort could be:

Algorithm 9.13: Radix sort

```
1  RadixSort (A: array of n integers, d: integer): array of n integers
2      S: tab[0..9] of lists
3      for i from 1 to d do
4          Distribute(A,i,S)
5          A = Recompose(S)
6      return A
```

Exercise 9.13
Use a Radix Sort to sort an array of strings in lexicographic order.
Hint: Use 26 buckets. Consider short strings ending with space characters if needed.

9.7 Solutions to Exercices

Solution to Exercise 9.4

1.

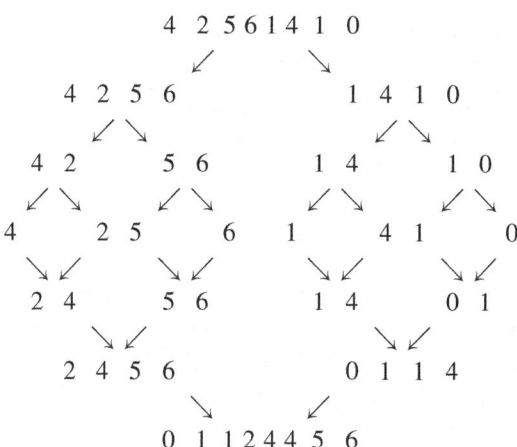

2.
```
def nbInversionsBetween(A1, A2):
  res = []
  i = 0
  j = 0
  nbInv = 0 # NEW
  while (i < len(A1) and j < len(A2)):
    if A1[i] <= A2[j]:
      res += [ A1[i] ]
      i += 1
    else:
      res += [ A2[j] ]
      j += 1
      nbInv += len(A1) - i # NEW
  for k in range(i, len(A1)):
    res += [ A1[k] ]
  for k in range(j, len(A2)):
    res += [ A2[k] ]
  return res, nbInv
```

3.

Solution to Exercise 9.6

1.
```
Closest1(A: array of n integers): integer
  i, j: integer
  min = |A[0] - A[1]|
  for i from 0 to n-2 do
    for j from i+1 to n-1 do
      if (|A[i] - A[j]| < min) then min = |A[i] - A[j]|
  return (min)
```

2. We sort the array (with merge sort, in $O(n \log n)$), and then we only need to check the differences of adjacent elements (in $O(n)$).

```
Closest2(A: array of n integers): integer
  i: integer
  MergeSort(A)
  min = |A[0] - A[1]|
  for i from 1 to n-2 do
    if (|A[i+1] - A[i]| < min) then min = |A[i+1] - A[i]|
  return (min)
```

3. Yes, we sort the array in $O(n \log n)$, and then we return the difference between $A[n-1]$ (the maximum) and $A[0]$ (the minimum).

```
Farthest(A: array of n integers): integer
  MergeSort(A);
  return (A[n-1] - A[0]);
```

9.7 Solutions to Exercices

4. Yes, we can compute the minimum and maximum of A using the standard min and max algorithms that find the min and max of A in $O(n)$, and then we return their difference.

Solution to Exercise 9.7

1. With the first element as pivot:

```
                    T = [7, 1, 5, 6, 2, 3, 10, 8, 0, 9, 4]
                                   pivot = 7
              T = [1, 5, 6, 2, 3, 0, 4]                    T = [10, 8, 9]
                        pivot = 1                             pivot = 10
T = [0]           T = [5, 6, 2, 3, 4]                    T = [8, 9]      T = []
↱ [0]                   pivot = 5                         pivot = 8       ↱ []
              T = [2, 3, 4]        T = [6]          T = []    T = [9]
                pivot = 2           ↱ [6]            ↱ []      ↱ [9]
        T = []     T = [3, 4]                              ↱ [8, 9]
         ↱ []      pivot = 3                            ↱ [8, 9, 10]
                   T = [4]
                    ↱ [4]
                  ↱ [3, 4]
               ↱ [2, 3, 4]
            ↱ [2, 3, 4, 5, 6]
         ↱ [0, 1, 2, 3, 4, 5, 6]
                  ↱ [0, 1, 2, 3, 4, 5, 6, 7, 8, 9, 10]
```

2. With the median element as pivot:

```
                    T = [7, 1, 5, 6, 2, 3, 10, 8, 0, 9, 4]
                                   pivot = 5
          T = [1, 2, 3, 0, 4]                      T = [7, 6, 10, 8, 9]
               pivot = 2                                  pivot = 8
    T = [1, 0]          T = [3, 4]              T = [7, 6]          T = [10, 9]
     pivot = 0           pivot = 3               pivot = 6           pivot = 9
  T=[]   T=[1]       T=[]   T=[4]            T=[]   T=[7]         T=[]   T=[10]
   ↱[]    ↱[1]        ↱[]    ↱[4]             ↱[]    ↱[7]          ↱[]    ↱[10]
      ↱ [0, 1]            ↱ [3, 4]                ↱ [6, 7]            ↱ [9, 10]
             ↱ [0, 1, 2, 3, 4]                         ↱ [6, 7, 8, 9, 10]
                          ↱ [0, 1, 2, 3, 4, 5, 6, 7, 8, 9, 10]
```

3. In the "in place" variant, the order of elements changes a lot more because of the swaps. Let us suppose that the pivot is kept in first position until the end of the partitioning. The left and right partitions are expanded until two elements that should be swapped are found. Finally, the pivot is swapped with the last element of the left partition.

   We can detail the partitioning using brackets to represent the two parts of a partition:

Start	<u>7</u>	[]1	5	6	2	3	10	8	0	9	4[]
Expanding partitions	<u>7</u>	[1	5	6	2	3]	10	8	0	9	4[]
Exchange 10 et 4	<u>7</u>	[1	5	6	2	3	4]	8	0	9	[10]
Expanding partitions	<u>7</u>	[1	5	6	2	3	4]	8	0	[9	10]
Exchange 8 et 0	<u>7</u>	[1	5	6	2	3	4	0]	[8	9	10]
Exchange pivot and 0	[0	1	5	6	2	3	4]	<u>7</u>	[8	9	10]
Next:	[[]<u>0</u>	[1	5	6	2	3	4]]	7	[8	9	10]
To the left, nothing to do	[0	[1	5	6	2	3	4]]	7	[8	9	10]
Etc	[0	[[]<u>1</u>	[5	6	2	3	4]]]	7	[8	9	10]
	[0	[1	[5	6	2	3	4]]]	7	[8	9	10]
	[0	[1	[[3	4	2]	<u>5</u>	[6]]]]	7	[8	9	10]
	[0	[1	[[[2]	<u>3</u>	[4]]	5	[6]]]]	7	[8	9	10]
	[0	[1	[[2	3	4]]	5	[6]]]]	7	[8	9	10]
	[0	[1	[2	3	4	5	6]]]	7	[8	9	10]
	0	1	2	3	4	5	6	7	[[]8	[9	10]]
	0	1	2	3	4	5	6	7	[8	[[]<u>9</u>	[10]]]
	0	1	2	3	4	5	6	7	[8	[9	<u>10</u>]]
	0	1	2	3	4	5	6	7	8	9	10

Solution to Exercise 9.12

1.
2.
```
BLUE, WHITE, RED = 0, 1, 2
def flag(T) :
  blues,whites,reds=[],[],[]
  for color,content in T:
    if color == BLUE:
      blues.append((color,content))
    elif color == WHITE:
      whites.append((color,content))
    else:
      reds.append((color,content))
  return blues+whites+reds
```

9.7 Solutions to Exercices

3. Solution 1:

   We will maintain the following invariant:

   the table consists of 3 consecutive segments, one blue, one unexplored and a red.

   The `i` cursor represents the boundary between the blue segment and the unexplored segment. The `j` cursor represents the boundary between the unexplored segment and the red segment.

   ```
   def flag(T) :
     i=0
     j= len(T)-1
     while i <= j :
       if T[i] == BLUE :
         i += 1
       elif T[j] == RED :
         j -= 1
       else :
         T[i], T[j] = T[j], T[i]
     return T
   ```

   Solution 2:

   We will maintain the following invariant:

   the table consists of 3 consecutive segments, one blue, one red and one unexplored.

   The `i` cursor represents the boundary between the blue segment and the red segment. The `j` cursor represents the boundary between the red segment and the unexplored segment.

   ```
   def flag(T) :
     i=0
     j= 0
     while j <= len(T)-1:
       if T[i] == BLUE :
         T[i], T[j] = T[j], T[i]
         i += 1
         j += 1
       else :
         j += 1
     return T
   ```

4.
5.
```
def flag(T) :
  i = 0
  j = 0
  k = len(T)-1
  while j <= k :
    if T[j] == BLUE :
      T[i], T[j] = T[j], T[i]
      i += 1
      j += 1
    elif T[j] == WHITE :
      j += 1
    else :
      T[j], T[k] = T[k], T[j]
      k -= 1
  return T
```

Solution to Exercise 9.13

This solution is implemented in Python:

Program 9.1: Sort strings with radix sort   radixstring.py

```
1  def bucket_for(s, i):           # ' '< 'a'< 'b'< ...< 'z'
2      # add phantom space at the end...
3      c = s[i].lower() if i<len(s) else ' '
4      if c==' ':                  # space is the lesser
5          return 0
6      return ord(c)-ord('a')+1 # get index from ascii code
7
8  def distribute(t, i):
9      buckets = [[] for _ in range(27)]
10     for j in range(len(t)):
11         buckets[bucket_for(t[j],i)].append(t[j])
12     return buckets
13
14 def recompose(buckets):
15     return [e for l in buckets for e in l]
16
17 def radix_sort(t, d):
18     for i in range(d):
19         t = recompose(distribute(t,d-i-1))
20     return t
21
22 l = [ "hello", "bicycle", "tomatoe", "apex", "zoo", "warning",
```

9.7 Solutions to Exercices

```
23            "bucket", "sort", "radix", "Australia" ]
24
25   max_len = 0
26   for s in l:
27       max_len = max_len if len(s)<max_len else len(s)
28
29   print(l)
30   l = radix_sort(l,max_len)
31   print("Sorted: ",l)
```

Note that we defined the sorting order through the function bucket_for, in which we also add phantom spacings at the end of strings if necessary (remind that Radix Sort needs all elements to be of the same length).

More on Recursion

And How to Eliminate it when it Becomes a Burden

10

Recursion, as we have previously said, is a powerful concept in computer science and programming that allows us to solve complex problems by breaking them down into smaller, more manageable subproblems. In this chapter we present some more advanced techniques and strategies that enhance our problem-solving capabilities.

We will explore three key concepts: **divide and conquer**, **dynamic programming**, and **tail recursion**. These techniques build upon the foundation of recursion and provide us with additional tools to tackle a wider range of problems efficiently and effectively. By understanding and harnessing the power of these approaches, we will be able to optimise our code, improve algorithmic efficiency, and solve increasingly complex problems.

Divide and conquer is a fundamental strategy that involves breaking down a problem into smaller subproblems, solving each subproblem independently, and then combining the solutions to obtain the final result. It is a top-down approach that allows us to conquer complex problems by dividing them into more manageable pieces. By leveraging the principle of recursion, divide and conquer enables us to solve problems efficiently and elegantly. We will explore various examples of this strategy that demonstrate its effectiveness.

Dynamic programming, on the other hand, takes a different approach. It focuses on solving problems by breaking them down into overlapping subproblems and solving each subproblem only once, storing the results for future reference. This bottom-up approach allows us to avoid redundant computations and dramatically improves the efficiency of our algorithms. Dynamic programming is particularly useful when dealing with optimisation problems and problems that exhibit overlapping substructures.

Tail recursion, lastly, is a technique that optimises recursive functions by eliminating unnecessary stack operations, thereby reducing memory usage and improving overall performance. By transforming recursive calls into iterative loops, tail recursion allows us to solve problems that would otherwise exhaust the available stack space.

Throughout this chapter, we will provide comprehensive explanations, examples, and practical implementations of these advanced recursion techniques. By the end, you will be better equipped with a diverse set of tools to approach even the most intricate computational challenges.

10.1 Divide and Conquer Algorithms and the Master Theorem

The strategy called **Divide and Conquer** is a paradigm that allows to implement recursive algorithms that in some cases turn out to be very efficient.

The divide-and-conquer approach to solve a problem on a given instance I can be resumed as follows:

- first, recursively[1] solve the same problem on some smaller sub-instances of I (divide);
- then "combine" the partial solutions of the subproblems found in the previous step in order to obtain a global solution for the instance I (conquer).

The operations allowing to "combine" partial solution into global solutions are specific to the problem that is being solved.

We have already met some exemples of divide-and-conquer algorithms.

One is binary search in which we split the array that must be searched into two halves, we solve the problem for one of the two halves and then we simply return for the entire array the same result we obtained for one of its two halves (strictly speaking, there is nothing to "combine" in this case).

Another typical exemple of divide-and-conquer algorithm is Merge Sort presented in Sect. 9.3. As for binary search, the strategy of Merge Sort starts by splitting the array to be sorted into two halves, then each of the two halves is sorted separately (recursively, using Merge sort) and finally the two sorted parts are merged into a unique sorted sequence. For Merge Sort, the "combining" part is the merging of the two sorted halves (partial solutions of the two subproblems) into one.

In general, a divide-and-conquer algorithm solves the problem on a number a of sub-instances of size n/b, where a and b are two integer constants that depend on the problem at hand. Then you certainly recognise that the complexity functions of a divide-and-conquer algorithms satisfy recurrences of the form:

$$\varphi(n) = \begin{cases} c & \text{if } n \leq n_0 \\ a\varphi(\frac{n}{b}) + f(n) & \text{otherwise} \end{cases}$$

---

[1] That is, by using the same algorithm.

10.1 Divide and Conquer Algorithms and the Master Theorem

where:

- $\frac{n}{b}$ represent the size of the sub-instances of the subproblems solved by the recursive calls;
- a represents the number of subproblems solved (that is, the number of recursive calls);
- n_0 is an integer constant representing the maximal instance size for which the problem can be solved without further recursive calls (typically $n_0 = 0$ or $n_0 = 1$) and c a constant representing the number of elementary operations in these base cases;
- $f(n)$ represents the costs of "combining" the partial solutions computed by the recursive calls in order to compute the global solution.

The **Master Theorem** for the resolution of recurrences allows to determine the asymptotic behaviour (in terms of $\Theta()$) of functions satisfying precisely this kind of recursion.

This is a statement of the Master Theorem in a simplified form.[2]

Theorem 10.1 (Master Theorem)
Let $T(n)$ be a function satisfying the recursion:

$$T(n) = \begin{cases} c & \text{if } n \leq n_0 \\ aT(n/b) + f(n) & \text{otherwise} \end{cases}$$

for integer constants a, b, c and n_0 and suppose that $f(n) \in \Theta(n^k)$ for a real number k, then:

(case **"small f"**) if $k < \log_b a$, then $T(n) \in \Theta(n^{\log_b a})$;
(case **"medium f"**) if $k = \log_b a$, then $T(n) \in \Theta(n^k \log n)$;
(case **"large f"**) if $k > \log_b a$, then $T(n) \in \Theta(n^k)$.

In other terms the Master Theorem allows to compute the Θ class of $T(n)$.

Example 10.1
As a first application, we can evaluate again the complexity of Binary Search using the Master Theorem.
Binary Search makes one call on a sub-instance whose size is the half of the size of the original one, so we have $a = 1$ and $b = 2$. The number of elementary operations executed to reconstruct the global solution (the answer for the entire array) from the partial solution (the answer for the half) is constant, hence $f(n) \in \Theta(1) = \Theta(n^0)$, so $k = 0$.

---

[2] An extended form of the Master Theorem allows to solve a wider class of recurrences.

Since $\log_b a = \log_2 1 = 0 = k$ we are in the case "f medium" case and we can deduce $\varphi(n) \in \Theta(n^{\log_b a} \log n) = \Theta(n^0 \log n) = \Theta(\log n)$.

Example 10.2
As another application of the Master Theorem we can evaluate again the complexity of Merge Sort using the Theorem.
The algorithm makes two calls on two sub-instances whose size is the half of the size of the original one, so we have $a = 2$ and $b = 2$, the cost of operations executed to reconstruct the global solution (the answer for the entire array) from the two partial solutions is $\Theta(n) = \Theta(n^1)$ (complexity of the Merge function), so $k = 1$.
Since $\log_b a = \log_2 2 = 1 = k$ we again are in the "f medium" case and we can deduce that the complexity function of the algorithms in the worst case is in $\Theta(n^{\log_2 2} \log n) = \Theta(n^1 \log n) = \Theta(n \log n)$.

Exercise 10.1 (Master Theorem)
Using the Master Theorem, determine the complexity class of the following functions :

1. $A(n) = 2 A(n/4) + 1$
2. $B(n) = 2 B(n/4) + \sqrt{n}$
3. $C(n) = 2 C(n/4) + n$
4. $D(n) = 2 D(n/4) + n^2$
5. $E(n) = 5 E(\frac{n}{3}) + n^2$
6. $F(n) = F(\frac{9n}{10}) + n$

10.2 More Divide and Conquer Algorithms

10.2.1 Minimum of an Array

The divide-and-conquer paradigm can also be applied to implement an alternative way to compute the minimum of an array. The idea is to split the array into two halves and recursively compute the minimum of each of the halves. The global solution can be deduced by simply comparing the two partial solutions and returning the smaller of the two.

Algorithm 10.1: Minimum of an array

```
1   MinDac(A: array of n integers; begin, end: integer): integer
2       middle: integer
3       minL, minR: integer
4
5       if (end - begin == 1) then
6           return A[begin]
7       middle = (begin + end)/2
8       minL = MinDac(A, begin, middle)
9       minR = MinDac(A, middle, end)
10      if (minL < minR) then
11          return(minL)
12      else
13          return(minR)
```

10.2 More Divide and Conquer Algorithms

The complexity function of MinDac obviously satisfies:

$$\varphi(n) = \begin{cases} c & \text{if } n \leq 1 \\ 2\varphi(\frac{n}{2}) + d & \text{otherwise} \end{cases}$$

where the constant d represents that cost of the "combining" part that in this case consists simply in a comparison and therefore is in $\Theta(1) = \Theta(n^0)$.

We can apply the Master Theorem with $a = 2$, $b = 2$ and $k = 0$. Since $k = 0 < 1 = \log_2 2 = \log_b a$ we are in the case "small f" and we deduce $\varphi(n) \in \Theta(n)$. So the time complexity of the algorithm MinDac is linear, like the classical iterative algorithm to compute the minimum of an array.

10.2.2 Longest Freezing Period

Suppose you have an array A of n integers representing the daily maximum temperature (in Celsius degrees) in a location over a period of n days. You want to compute the length of the longest freezing period, i.e. the maximum number of consecutive days in which the temperature remained below zero.

You can obviously do that in $\Theta(n)$ with a simple for loop using a counter and another variable to store the current maximal length but we are going to implement an algorithm based on divide and conquer.

The divide-and-conquer algorithm splits the array into two halves and recursively computes the length of the longest freezing period in each of the two halves. In order to determine the length of the longest freezing period in the entire array, the algorithm still needs to compute the length of the longest freezing period overlapping the transition point between the two halves (the middle point) and finally return the maximum among these three lengths.

The computation of the length of the longest freezing period overlapping the transition point between the two halves takes two while loops: one that starts from the middle and keeps moving on the right as long as negative numbers are met, and another one that starts from the middle and keeps moving on the left as long as negative numbers are met.

Algorithm 10.2: Longest freezing period

```
LfpDac(A: array of n integers; begin, end: integer): integer
    middle, i, lfpL, lfpR, lfpM: integer

    if (end - begin == 1) then
        if (A[begin] < 0) then
            return (1)
        else
            return (0)
    middle = (begin + end)/2
    lfpL = LfpDac(A, begin, middle)
```

```
11      lfpR = LfpDac(A, middle, end)
12      i = middle
13      while (i<end) and (A[i]<0) do
14         lfpM = lfpM +1
15         i = i+1
16      i = middle -1
17      while (i >= begin) and (A[i]<0) do
18         lfpM = lfpM +1
19         i = i -1
20      return(Max(lfpL, lfpM, lfpR))
```

The two while loops have a complexity in $\Theta(n)$ in the worst case, so in the worst case the function $f(n)$ expressing the complexity of the combining part of the algorithm is in $\Theta(n^1)$. We can apply the Master Theorem with $a = 2$, $b = 2$ and $k = 1$. Since $k = 1 = \log_2 2 = \log_b a$ we are in the case "medium f" and we deduce the algorithm LfpDac has a complexity in $\Theta(n \log n)$, hence it is slower than the equivalent iterative algorithm.

However, it is worth to note that a divide-and-conquer algorithm solving the problem in linear time also exists. It suffices to modify the above algorithm in such a way that—instead of returning just an integer representing the length of the longest freezing period in the interval $[begin, end - 1]$—it returns a triplet (lfpB, lfp, lfpE) where:

- lfpB represents the length of the longest freezing period starting on day $begin$ in the interval $[begin, end - 1]$;
- lfp represents the length of the longest freezing period in the interval $[begin, end - 1]$ (this is the same value returned by the LfpDac algorithm);
- lfpE represents the length of the longest freezing period ending on day $end - 1$ in the interval $[begin, end - 1]$.

Surprisingly, although this algorithm appears to do more work than LfpDac because it returns more information, it turns out to be faster than LfpDac. Indeed, if you compute the triplet (lfpBL, lfpL, lfpEL) for the left half $[begin, middle - 1]$ and the triplet (lfpBR, lfpR, lfpER) for the left half $[middle, end - 1]$, it is possible to reconstruct the triplet (lfpB, lfp, lfpE) for the entire section $[begin, end - 1]$ in constant time (See Exercise 10.2).

In this case the function $f(n)$ expressing the complexity of the combining part of the algorithm is constant, i.e. in $\Theta(n^0)$. Having $a = 2$, $b = 2$ and $k = 0$ since $k = 0 < \log_2 2 = \log_b a$ we are in the case "small f" and we deduce that this version of the algorithm has a complexity in $\Theta(n)$, the same as the equivalent iterative algorithm.

10.2 More Divide and Conquer Algorithms

Exercise 10.2
Write a divide-and-conquer algorithm
`LfpDacLin(A: array of n integers; begin, end: integer)`,
having linear complexity (in $O(n)$) and returning a triplet of integers (`lfpB`, `lfp`, `lfpE`) where:

- `lfpB` represents the length of the longest freezing period in the interval $[begin, end - 1]$ and starting on day $begin$;
- `lfp` represents the length of the longest freezing period in the interval $[begin, end - 1]$ (this is the same value returned by the `LfpDac` algorithm);
- `lfpE` represents the length of the longest freezing period in the interval $[begin, end - 1]$ and ending on day $end - 1$.

Hint When you are computing the triplet for the entire period $[begin, end - 1]$ from the triplets for the two halves (computed recursively), you may want to distinguish the case where all days of either of the two halves are freezing.
Verify that the complexity of your algorithm is linear using the Master Theorem.

10.2.3 Karatsuba's Multiplication

The **Karatsuba algorithm** (from the Rusiian mathematician Anatolii Alexevich Karatsuba is a very efficient divide-and-conquer algorithm that can be applied for the multiplication of two integers written in any base B (see [13]). Let x and y be two integers that we want to multiply. Without loss of generality we can suppose that both numbers have n digits and that n is even (if it's not the case, we can add the appropriate number of 0s at their beginning).

The usual algorithm to multiply two integers having n digits requires a quadratic number ($\Theta(n^2)$) of multiplications of digits: indeed you have to multiply each digit of y by all digits of x. Then you have to perform a linear number ($\Theta(n)$) of additions. However, additions have lower cost with respect to multiplications, so in this problem we will focus on counting just the number of multiplications.

Let x_0 be the number formed by the first $n/2$ digits of x and x_1 be the number formed by the last $n/2$ digits of x. Formally, $x_0 = x/B^{n/2}$ and $x_1 = x \mod B^{n/2}$. Define analogously y_0 and y_1. For instance if $x = 1234$ and $y = 5678$ then $x_0 = 12$, $x_1 = 34$, $y_0 = 56$ and $y_1 = 78$.

Clearly $x = x_0 B^{n/2} + x_1$ and $y = y_0 B^{n/2} + y_1$ so:

$$x \cdot y = x_0 y_0 B^n + (x_0 y_1 + x_1 y_0) B^{n/2} + x_1 y_1 \qquad (10.1)$$

This formula suggests already the following divide-and-conquer algorithm:

- split the two numbers x and y into two halves x_0, x_1 and y_0, y_1 as explained above and compute the four multiplications $x_0 y_0, x_0 y_1, x_1 y_0$ and $x_1 y_1$;
- use the results of these four multiplications to compute the result of the multiplication of x by y via the Eq. 10.1.

Note that in Eq. 10.1 there seem to be two further multiplications:

- the multiplication of $x_0 y_0$ by B^n and
- the multiplication of $(x_0 y_1 + x_1 y_0)$ by $B^{n/2}$,

However, a multiplication of a number by a power of the base B is an operation having a much lower complexity than a generic multiplication. One of the first things we learn at elementary school is that to multiply a number by a power of 10, it suffices to add some 0's at the end of the number. In a computer (where the base is $B = 2$) multiplications of a number by a power of 2 are implemented simply by shifting the digits of the number, which can be performed in linear time (like additions). Hence the cost of multiplications by a power of the base B is irrelevant with respect to the cost of generic multiplications.

Therefore the algorithm described above reduces the problem of multiplying two numbers having n digits to four multiplications of two numbers having $n/2$ digits, then its complexity function obviously satisfies:

$$\varphi(n) = \begin{cases} c & \text{if } n \leq 1 \\ 4\varphi(n/2) + f(n) & \text{otherwise} \end{cases}$$

where $f(n)$ represents the (linear) cost of the additions and shifts that have to be performed to combine the four products $x_0 y_0$, $x_0 y_1$, $x_1 y_0$ and $x_1 y_1$ to obtain xy.

We can apply the Master Theorem with $a = 4$, $b = 2$ and $k = 1$. Since $k = 1 < 2 = \log_2 4 = \log_b a$, we are in the case "small f" and we deduce $\varphi(n) \in \Theta(n^2)$. So the algorithm we just described would have quadratic complexity, exactly like the classical multiplication algorithm that we usually apply.

Karatsuba's algorithm, however, is based on a further observation, namely the identity :

$$x_0 y_1 + x_1 y_0 = (x_0 + x_1)(y_0 + y_1) - x_0 y_0 - x_1 y_1.$$

From this identity we deduce that, if we have already computed $x_0 y_0$ and $x_1 y_1$, we need only one extra multiplication (and some further additions or subtractions) in order to compute $x_0 y_1 + x_1 y_0$, i.e. the multiplication $(x_0 + x_1)(y_0 + y_1)$. Thanks to this observation we obtain the Karatsuba algorithm (see [13]), which reduces the multiplication of two numbers having n digits to *three* multiplications of two numbers having $n/2$ digits,

Algorithm 10.3: Karatsuba's multiplication

```
1  Karatsuba(x, y: integers): integer
2      if (x < 10 or y < 10) then
3          return x * y                    // traditional multiplication
4
5      n = max(digits(x), digits(y))       // digits() returns the length
```

10.2 More Divide and Conquer Algorithms

```
6       m = n / 2
7
8       x0, x1 = x / 10 ^ m, x % 10 ^ m    // compute the four halves
9       y0, y1 = y / 10 ^ m, y % 10 ^ m
10
11      z0 = karatsuba(x0, y0)             // 3 recursive calls
12      z1 = karatsuba(x1 + x0, y1 + y0)
13      z2 = karatsuba(x1, y1)
14
15      // combining the result of the three subproblems of size M/2
16      return (z0 * 10 ^ (m * 2)) + ((z1 - z2 - z0) * 10 ^ m) + z2
```

whose complexity function satisfies :

$$\varphi(n) = \begin{cases} c & \text{if } n \leq 1 \\ 3\varphi(n/2) + f(n) & \text{otherwise} \end{cases}$$

We can apply the Master Theorem with $a = 3$, $b = 2$ and $k = 1$. Since $k = 1 < \log_2 3 = \log_b a$ we are in the case "small f" and we deduce $\varphi(n) \in \Theta(n^{\log_2 3})$. Since $\log_2 3 \approx 1.585$, the Karatsuba is faster than the classical multiplication algorithm that we learnt in elementary school.

10.2.4 Stooge Sort

Stooge Sort is a recursive sorting algorithm issued of the divide-and-conquer strategy. Although as we will see it is not very performant, it provides a perfect example of a divide-and-conquer algorithm that does not simply divide the input into two parts.

The algorithm first checks if the last element of the array is smaller than the first element and in that case it swaps them. Then, if the size n of the array is larger than 2, it divides the array into three parts each having a size equal to $n/3$ (up to one unity) and recursively sorts the first two-thirds and the last two-thirds of the array. Finally, it sorts the first two-thirds again. In other terms, if we note k the result of the division $n/3$, then the algorithm:

- first sorts the section $A[0, \ldots, 2k - 1]$ (the first two thirds);
- then sorts the section $A[k, \ldots, n - 1]$ (the last two thirds);
- finally sorts the section $A[0, \ldots, 2k - 1]$ (the first two thirds) again.

The algorithm correctly sorts the array. Indeed after the first sorting of the section $A[0, \ldots, 2k - 1]$, the k largest elements of the array are certainly in the section $A[k, \ldots, n]$. Hence, after the sorting of the section $A[k, \ldots, n - 1]$, these k largest elements reach their final position in the last third $A[2k, \ldots, n - 1]$, therefore the section $A[0, \ldots, 2k-1]$ contains now the $2k$ smallest elements of the array (not in order) and the final sorting of this section will place them in the right position.

Here's the pseudocode:

Algorithm 10.4: Stooge sort

```
1   StoogeSort(A:array of n integers; begin, end: integer)
2       if A[end-1] < A[begin] then
3           swap(A[begin], A[end-1])
4       if end - begin > 2 then
5           k = (end - begin)/3           //k is 1/3 of the size
6           StoogeSort(A, begin, end-k)   //sort the first 2/3 of the array
7           StoogeSort(A, begin+k, end)   //sort the last 2/3 of the array
8           StoogeSort(A, being, end-k)   //sort the first 2/3 again
```

The time complexity of Stooge Sort can be analysed using the Master Theorem. Let $T(n)$ be the time complexity of sorting an array of size n. The Stooge Sort algorithm divides the array into three parts and recursively sorts the first two parts, then the last two parts, and finally the first two parts again. Thus, it makes three recursive calls on arrays whose size is $2/3$ of the original one. The time complexity can be expressed as follows:

$$T(n) = 3T\left(\frac{2n}{3}\right) + O(1)$$

or

$$T(n) = 3T\left(\frac{n}{\frac{3}{2}}\right) + O(1)$$

Using the Master Theorem with $a = 3$, $b = 3/2$, and $f(n) \in O(1)$ so $k = 0$, we have $k = 0 < \log_b a = \log_{\frac{3}{2}} 3$, we are in the case "small f" and hence:

$$T(n) = \Theta(n^{\log_{\frac{3}{2}} 3}).$$

Note that, since $3 > \frac{9}{4}$, we have $\log_{\frac{3}{2}} 3 > \log_{\frac{3}{2}} \frac{9}{4} = 2$, therefore the complexity of Stooge Sort is worse than quadratic, so it is slower than the elementary sorting algorithms Selection Sort and Insertion Sort.

Exercise 10.3
In this exercise, we want to implement an algorithm that, given an array of n integers with $n \geq 2$ returns a couple containing the largest and the second-largest element of the array. As a complexity measure we take the number of comparisons between two elements in the array performed in the worst case.

1. Give an iterative algorithm, specify when your algorithm has the worst-case, and calculate the number of comparisons it performs in this case. This number should not exceed $2n - 3$.

Fig. 10.1 L-shape tiling of a square

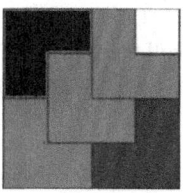

2. Give a *recursive* algorithm based on the Divide and Conquer principle. Your algorithm should not execute more than 2 comparisons (between array elements) for each recursive call.
3. Evaluate the order of magnitude of the complexity function $\varphi(n)$ of your algorithm using the Master Theorem.
4. For a more precise calculation of the number of comparisons performed by your algorithm, assume that n is a power of 2 (say, $n = 2^k$) and define:

$$g(k) := \text{\# comparisons made by the algorithm on an array of size } 2^k.$$

Write the recurrence equation satisfied by $g(k)$ and solve it.
Then, in the found formula, replace 2^k with n to express this number of comparisons as a function of n and compare it with $2n - 3$ (optimal bound for the iterative algorithm in question 1). Which algorithm performs fewer comparisons?

Exercise 10.4 (Tiling with L-Shaped Tiles)

Consider a square grid of size n in which a cell i, j is "forbidden" ($1 \leq i \leq n$ and $1 \leq j \leq n$). We assume that n is a power of 2 ($n = 2^k$ for some $k \geq 1$).
We want to tile the grid (excluding the forbidden cell) with L-shaped tiles.
Figure 10.1 is an example of a solution where the forbidden cell is the white one in the top right corner.

- Propose a method based on the "divide and conquer" strategy to reduce the resolution of the initial problem to the resolution of several similar subproblems on smaller input data.
- Evaluate the number of recursive calls made by the algorithm in terms of k and deduce the same number in terms of n.
- Find the complexity of this algorithm in terms of n using the Master Theorem.

10.3 Dynamic Programming

As we have seen in Sect. 8.4 where we gave an algorithm to compute the Fibonacci numbers, some recursive algorithms present the unpleasant phenomenon that we called "subproblem overlap", that is, calls to solve again the same subproblem are performed at several moments of the execution of the algorithm and this causes a waste of time because the same calculations will be repeated all over again.

The paradigm of **Dynamic Programming** allows to overcome this phenomenon and it is based on the following idea : if we store somewhere the solution of a subproblem the first time we calculate it, then when the same subproblem needs to be solved again, we will just retrieve its solution from where we stored it, rather than computing it again.

This idea presumes then that we keep a table (**lookup table**) containing in each cell the solution of one of the subproblems that we will need to solve. There are two possible way to implement this strategy: memoisation and tabulation.

10.3.1 Memoisation (Top Down)

The memoised algorithm for a problem is similar to the recursive version with a small modification that looks into a lookup table, called **memoisation table**, before computing solutions. We initialise a lookup array with all cells containing a symbolic value undef representing the fact that the solution to that specific subproblem is not yet known.[3] Whenever we need the solution to a subproblem, we first look at the corresponding cell in the lookup table. If the cell still contains the initial value undef then we make the recursive call, calculate the value and put the result in the lookup table so that it can be reused later. If instead a precomputed value is already there (the cell contains another value than undef), then we return directly that value, without performing again the computation.

The memoised version of the algorithm is still a recursive algorithm, however, unlike the original algorithm, it makes a recursive call to solve a given subproblem only the first time the solution of that subproblem is needed. As most recursive algorithms, it works top-down, i.e., to compute the solution for a given value of the argument it starts making calls for smaller and smaller values of the argument.

As an example, we will illustrate this principle on the recursive algorithm Fibo that we implemented in Sect. 8.4 and that we recall here.

Algorithm 10.5: Fibonacci number

```
1  Fibo(n: integer): integer
2     if (n == 0) or (n == 1) then return(1)
3     return(Fibo(n - 1) + Fibo(n - 2))
```

To write the memoised version of this algorithm we need to define a table whose size (and whose number of dimensions, as we will see in the next example) depends on the problem. In this case we need to memoise all the solutions of the subproblems $Fibo(i)$ for $i = 0, 1, \ldots, n$ so we need an array of integers of size $n + 1$.

The lookup table can be introduced either as a global variable (a global variable is accessible from any function of the program, so it will be accessible in particular by the memoised function) or as a parameter of the memoised function. In both cases,

---

[3] In practice, undef can be set equal to None for a language like Python that allows to use such a null value universally compatible with objects of any type. In other programming languages that are stricter regarding typing, if the table contains integers then undef must be an integer too. Typically, in this case one sets undef equal to an integer value that cannot be the solution of a subproblem. For instance, if your solutions are positive numbers you can simply set undef equal to -1.

10.3 Dynamic Programming

the lookup table needs to be initialised outside the memoised function by setting all cells equal to **undef**.

In the first case (table as a global variable) the algorithm will look like this:

Algorithm 10.6: Fibonacci, memoisation

```
1  T: array of n+1 integers
2
3  FiboMemo (n: integer): integer
4      for i from 0 to n do
5          T[i] = undef
6      return(FiboAux(n))
7
8  FiboAux (n: integer): integer
9      if (T[n] == undef) then
10         if (n == 0) or (n == 1) then
11             T[n]=1
12         else
13             T[n] = FiboAux(n - 1) + FiboAux(n - 2)
14     return(T[n])
```

And this is the version with the table T as parameter:

Algorithm 10.7: Fibonacci: memoisation

```
1  FiboMemo (n: integer): integer
2      T: array of n+1 integers
3      for i from 0 to n do
4          T[i] = undef
5      return(FiboAux(n, T))
6
7  FiboAux (n: integer, T array of n+1 integers ): integer
8      if (T[n] == undef) then
9          if (n == 0) or (n == 1) then
10             T[n]=1
11         else
12             T[n] = FiboAux(n - 1,T) + FiboAux(n - 2, T)
13     return(T[n])
```

While we have seen that the number of calls made by the original Fibo algorithm grows exponentially, the number of calls made by the FiboAux algorithm (and hence by FiboMemo) grows linearly. The following is the tree of recursive calls made by FiboAux to compute the Fibonacci number of rank 5. Compare it with the tree of the purely naive recursive algorithm in Fig. 8.3.

Only the calls in bold font actually produce new recursive calls, all the others do not and return immediately a value, either because they deal with base cases (the calls FiboAux(1) and FiboAux(0)) or because the same call has already been made in the computations (and hence the corresponding value is in the table already and be simply returned).

Fig. 10.2 Call tree of FiboAux

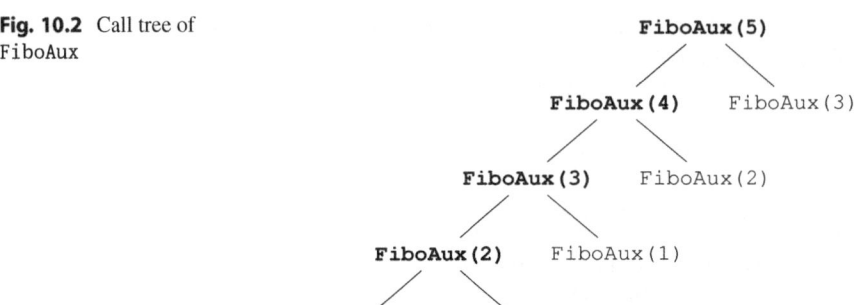

For instance, the call FiboAux(3) made by FiboAux(5) (the right child of FiboAux(5) in the tree) does not produce any new call, since it takes place after the call FiboAux(3) made by FiboAux(4) (the left child of FiboAux(4) in the tree, in bold). All calls in the left subtree are obviously made before those in the right subtree (Fig. 10.2).

It can be easily deduced that the total number of calls to FiboAux for an arbitrary n is $2n - 1$, therefore the complexity is linear.

10.3.2 Tabulation (Bottom-Up)

The tabulated version of the program builds the table in a bottom-up fashion and returns the last entry from the table. For example, for the Fibonacci numbers, we first calculate F_0, then F_1, then F_2, and so on and we store them in the table as long as they are computed. The tabulated program is a purely iterative version of the original recursive algorithm that simply fills up the table bottom-up.

Algorithm 10.8: Fibonacci, tabulation

```
1  FiboTab (n: integer): integer
2      T[0]=1
3      T[1]=1
4      for i from 2 to n do
5          T[i] = T[i-1] + T[i-2]
6      return(T[n])
```

Note the this algorithm does not make any recursive call at all (because it is purely iterative) and clearly has a time complexity in $\Theta(n)$.

10.3 Dynamic Programming

10.3.3 Binomial Coefficients

Binomial coefficient $B_{n,k} = \binom{n}{k}$ with $n, k \geq 0$, are defined by the following recursive formula:

$$B_{n,k} = \begin{cases} 0 & \text{if } n < 0 \text{ or } k < 0 \text{ or } k > n \\ 1 & \text{if } k = 0 \text{ or } k = n \\ B_{n-1,k} + B_{n-1,k-1} & \text{otherwise} \end{cases}$$

This formula immediately yields the following recursive algorithm.

Algorithm 10.9: Binomial by recursion

```
1  Binom (n, k: integer): integer
2      if (n < 0) or (k < 0) or (k > n) then return(0)
3      if (k == 0) or (k == n) then return(1)
4      return(Binom(n-1, k) + Binom(n-1, k-1))
```

However this algorithm does present subproblems overlapping. This is apparent already at the second level of the recursive calls, since the call `Binom(n-2, k-1)` will be made both in the execution of `Binom(n-1, k)` and of `Binom(n-1, k-1)`. It is easy to prove that the complexity of this algorithm is in $\Omega(\binom{n}{k})$. Since binomial coefficients grow exponentially, the complexity of `Binom` is at least exponential.

We then write an algorithm using the dynamic programming paradigm of tabulation. Note that for this problem we need to store all the solutions of all subproblems `Binom(i, j)` with $0 \leq i \leq n$ and $0 \leq j \leq k$, hence the table T needs to be a two-dimensional array with $n + 1$ rows and $k + 1$ columns. The table cells in this case can all be initialised with the value 0. The tabulated algorithm fills the cells of this table in the standard order : from the top row (row 0) to the bottom row (row n) and each row is filled from the left (column 0) to the right (column k). In fact, only the cells containing non-zero values needs to be filled. The algorithm computes the first $n + 1$ rows and the first $k + 1$ columns of the **Pascal triangle**. If i is larger than k, only the first $k + 1$ cells of the i-th row need to be computed, this is managed with an appropriate upper bound for the `for j` loop of line 11.

Algorithm 10.10: Binomial, tabulation

```
1  BinomTab (n, k: integer): integer
2      i, j: integer
3      T: matrix of (n+1) x (k+1) integers
4
5      for i from 0 to n do
6          for j from 0 to k do
7              T[i,j] = 0
8      T[0,0]=1
```

```
9        for i from 1 to n do
10           T[i,0]=1
11           for j from 1 to min(k, i-1) do
12               T[i, j] = T[i-1, j] + T[i-1,j-1]
13           if (i <= k) then
14               T[i,i]=1
15       return(T[n,k])
```

For instance, a call to `BinomTab(6,3)` produces the following table:

$$\begin{pmatrix} 1 & 0 & 0 & 0 \\ 1 & 1 & 0 & 0 \\ 1 & 2 & 1 & 0 \\ 1 & 3 & 3 & 1 \\ 1 & 4 & 6 & 4 \\ 1 & 5 & 10 & 10 \\ 1 & 6 & 15 & 20 \end{pmatrix}$$

and returns the value $T[6, 3] = 20$.

The complexity of this algorithm is then in $\Theta(nk)$, so it is polynomial versus the exponential complexity of the trivial recursive algorithm `Binom`.

Exercise 10.5
Super Mario must traverse a field of size $n \times m$ going from cell $[0, 0]$ in the top-left corner of the field to cell $[n - 1, m - 1]$ in the bottom-right corner. Each cell (i, j) contains a bonus $B[i, j]$ gained if Super Mario passes on that cell, the matrix $B[i, j]$ of size $n \times m$ is a given data of the problem. Movement is allowed only to the right (East) and downwards (South).
We note $V(i, j)$ the maximum possible total bonus that can be totalised to go from cell $[0, 0]$ to cell $[i, j]$, that is, the sum of the bonuses of the cells along the best possible path from cell $[0, 0]$ to cell $[i, j]$. We aim to calculate the value $V(n - 1, m - 1)$.

1. Give a recursive expression for $V(i, j)$ in terms of $V(-, -)$ for two parameters having smaller values than i and j, respectively.
   Hint: Consider the cells *from which* one can arrive to the cell $[i - 1, j - 1]$.
2. Give the pseudocode of the recursive function that computes $V(i, j)$ using this formula (the function can then be called for $i = n - 1$ and $j = m - 1$).
3. Show with a small example that this function solves overlapping subproblems.
4. Give the pseudocode of the memoised version of the function and evaluate its complexity in time and space.

Exercise 10.6
We have a box of Lego with all pieces having the same width and depth, but having varying heights of all possible integers, (theoretically) an unlimited quantity of pieces of each kind. We want to calculate the number $T(n, k)$ of possible ways to build a tower of height n using k pieces.[a]
For instance:

---

[a] This is the number of compositions of the integer n having k parts.

10.3 Dynamic Programming

Input: n=5; k=3;
Output: 6 (since there are 6 possible towers, as listed in the table below):

[3, 1, 1]	[1, 3, 1]	[1, 1, 3]
[1, 2, 2]	[2, 1, 2]	[2, 2, 1]

1. Give a recursive expression for $T(n, k)$ in terms of $T(-, -)$ for two parameters having smaller values than n and/or k.
   Hint: Consider the last piece added to the towers that are a solution.
2. Give the pseudocode of a recursive function derived from this formula that computes $T(n, k)$.
3. Show with a small example that this function solves overlapping subproblems
4. Give the memoised version of the function.

10.3.4 On the Order of the Filling of the Memoisation Table

If you are using tabulation, the order in which the table is filled depends on the problem and is not necessarily strictly bottom-up as in all the examples we have seen so far. In fact, you need to make sure that when you fill a cell of the table, all the other cells on which this cell depends have been filled already.

Suppose for instance we have the following "kayak problem".

You are doing water rafting on kayaks going downstream along a creek. There are n stations along the creek, the departure is station 0, the arrival is station $n - 1$. At any station i you can rent a kayak that you can return at any station downstream (a station j with $j > i$). We have a price table Price[-,-] such that for all pair of stations (i, j) with $j > i$, the cost to rent a kayak at station i and return it at station j is given in Price[i,j]. However, the cheapest way to go from station i to station j may not be the direct way. It may be cheaper to rent a kayak at i, return it at an intermediary station k with $i < k < j$, then rent another kayak at station k and return it at station j.

We want to determine the cost of the cheapest way to go from the departure station to the arrival station.

For instance if you have four stations and the following price table :

$$\begin{bmatrix} 0 & 10 & 20 & 35 \\ - & 0 & 15 & 22 \\ - & - & 0 & 8 \\ - & - & - & 0 \end{bmatrix},$$

then the cheapest way to go from station 0 to station 3 will be to change kayak at station 2. This will cost Price[0, 2] + Price[2, 3] = 20 + 8 = 28. All the other solutions have a higher cost:

- if we never change kayak, the cost will be Price[0, 3] = 35,

- if we change kayak at station 1, the cost will be Price[0, 1] + Price[1, 3] = 10 + 22 = 32,
- if we change kayak at station 1 and again at station 2, the cost will be Price[0, 1] + Price[1, 2] + Price[2, 3] = 10 + 15 + 8 = 33.

To solve the problem we define a function $C(i, j)$ which, if $j > i$, computes the lowest possible cost to go from station i to station j. The answer to our problem can then be obtained by a call to $C(0, n - 1)$.

We can give a recursive expression for $C(i, j)$. The base case (except for the case when $j < i$ and $C(i, j)$ is undefined) is when $j = i$. In this case, obviously, we have $C(i, j) = 0$.

In the general case ($j > i$), the optimal solution is:

- either the solution with no stops, renting a kayak at station i and returning it at station j without changes, the relative cost is given by Price[i, j];
- or a solution that changes kayak at least once at a station k between i and j (therefore $i < k < j$) and that goes from i to k in the cheapest possible way and then from k to j in the cheapest possible way, the corresponding cost is given by $C(i, k) + C(k, j)$.

We deduce the recursive expression:

$$C(i, j) = \begin{cases} 0 & \text{if } j = i \\ \min(\text{Price}[i, j], \min_{i<k<j}(C(i, k) + C(k, j))) & \text{if } j > i \end{cases}$$

A recursive program using this formula would certainly suffer of (heavy) subproblem overlapping so it is a good idea to write rather a memoised version using tabulation.

The Fig. 10.3 shows the cells on which a given cell (i, j) depends (the shaded ones in the picture).

Fig. 10.3 The kayak problem, dependence of a cell

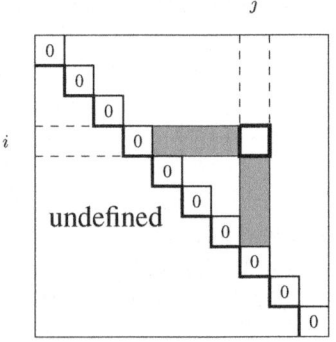

Fig. 10.4 The kayak problem, scanning the cells

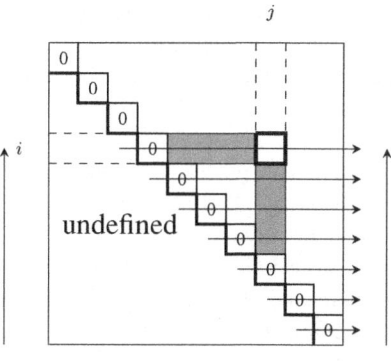

Fig. 10.5 The kayak problem, alternative scanning

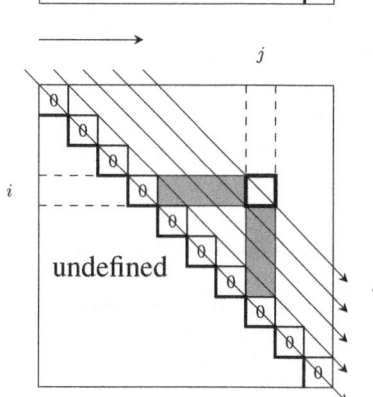

In this case filling the table in the usual manner (from the top row to the bottom row, and each row from left to right) would not work. Not all the necessary cells would be filled when we need to fill cell (i, j) (namely, those in the j-th column below row i).

An appropriate order would be to fill up the table starting from the bottom row and going up, rows can still be filled from left to right as illustrated in Fig. 10.4.

An alternative way would be to fill the table diagonal after diagonal, starting from the diagonal $j = i$ and moving north-east is depicted in Fig. 10.5.

In both cases the answer to our problem will be the value in the cell $(0, n-1)$ of the table.

Exercise 10.7
Implement the appropriate for loops that fill up the memoisation table of size $n \times n$ for the "kayak" problem by diagonals, as illustrated at the end of the above subsection.

10.4 Tail Recursion

Tail recursion is a special form of recursion where the recursive call is the last operation performed in the function, and the result of the recursive call is immediately returned. Tail recursion is useful because it allows the compiler or interpreter to optimise the function by converting it into an iterative loop. This eliminates the overhead of function calls, stack frames, and return values, which can lead to improved performance and reduced memory usage.

However, not all recursive functions are tail recursive. In some cases, the recursive call is not the last operation in the function, and the result of the recursive call needs to go through other computations before being returned. This type of recursion is called non-tail recursion, and it cannot be optimised by the compiler into an iterative loop.

One technique for transforming some non-tail recursive functions into tail-recursive functions is to use accumulators. An accumulator is a variable that is used to accumulate the partial results of the computation as the function recurses. Instead of returning a value directly, the function updates the accumulator and passes it along with the recursive call. The accumulator is initialised with an initial value and updated at each recursive call. When the base case is reached, the final value of the accumulator is returned as the result of the function.

Here is an example of a non-tail-recursive function for computing the factorial of a number:

Algorithm 10.11: Factorial by recursion

```
1  FactRec(n: integer):integer
2      if n == 0 then
3          return(1)
4      else
5          return(n * FactRec(n-1))
```

This function is not tail recursive because it performs an additional multiplication operation after the recursive call. We can eliminate this non-tail recursion by using an accumulator:

Algorithm 10.12: Factorial with tail recursion

```
1  FactorialAcc(n, acc:integer): integer
2      if n == 0 then
3          return(acc)
4      else
5          return(FactorialAcc(n-1, n*acc))
6
7  Factorial(integer n): integer
8      return(FactorialAcc(n, 1))
```

In this version, the `FactorialAcc` function takes an additional argument `acc` to accumulate the result of the computation. The base case simply returns the accumulator value, while the recursive case multiplies the accumulator by the current value of n and passes the result along with the decremented n to the next recursive call.

10.4 Tail Recursion

The `Factorial` function simply calls `FactorialAcc` with an initial accumulator value of 1 (which is the value returned by the classic Factorial function in the base case). This version `FactorialAcc` is tail recursive (no operations are performed between the recursive calls and the returns) and can be optimised by the compiler or interpreter into an iterative loop. Basically the program is translated into:

Algorithm 10.13: Iterative equivalent function

```
1   acc = 1
2   while n>0 do
3       acc = n*acc
4       n -= 1
5   return(acc)
```

▶ Beware that although the values computed by `FactRec` and by `FactorialAcc` are the same, they are not computed in the same way! In the case of the standard `FactRec`, the value is computed bottom-up, i.e. from `FactRec(0)` returning 1, to `FactRec(1)` returning $1 * 1 = 1$, to `FactRec(2)` returning $2 * 1 = 2, \ldots$, up to `FactRec(n)` returning $n * (n-1)! = n!$.
In the case of the accumulated version, the value is obtained top-down, during the recursive descent: initially the accumulator contains $n * 1$, then $n(n-1)$, then $n(n-1)(n-2)$, $\ldots$, down to $n(n-1) \ldots 3 \cdot 2 \cdot 1$ and when returning we just send back the final value.
That works either ways only because the multiplication operation is commutative.

However this transformation cannot be applied to every recursive function (we already said that a general recursive scheme cannot be transformed into an iterative one). To realise this, let us compare the behaviour of the two following functions.

Let f be the function defined by $f(0) = 1$, $f(n) = nf(\frac{n}{2})$ if n is even and $f(n) = f(\frac{n-1}{2})$ otherwise. This function is not tail recursive because it performs an additional multiplication operation after the recursive call in the case when n is even. It is possible to write a final recursive function equivalent to f using an accumulator.

Algorithm 10.14: f with tail recursion

```
1   fAcc(n, acc:integer): integer
2       if n == 0 then
3           return acc
4       else
5           if (n %2 == 0) then
6               return fAcc(n/2, n*acc)
7           else
8               return fAcc((n-1)/2, acc)
```

A call to fAcc(n, 1) returns the value of $f(n)$ for all n. It is immediate to deduce an equivalent iterative algorithm:

Algorithm 10.15: Iterative version of f

```
1  fIter(n, acc:integer): integer
2      acc = 1
3      while n > 0 do
4          if (n %2 == 0) then
5              acc = n * acc
6              n = n/2
7          else
8              n = (n-1)/2
9      return(acc)
```

We can simplify this pseudocode because, when n is even, the integer division $(n-1)/2$ is equal to the integer division $n/2$:

Algorithm 10.16: Iterative version of f

```
1  fIter(n, acc:integer): integer
2      acc = 1
3      while n > 0 do
4          if (n %2 == 0) then
5              acc = n * acc
6          n = n/2
7      return(acc)
```

Consider now the function g defined by $g(0) = 1$, $g(n) = ng(\frac{n}{2})$ if n is even and $g(n) = 1 + g(\frac{n-1}{2})$ otherwise. Let's try to apply the same strategy to find a tail recursive version of g using accumulators.

Algorithm 10.17: g with tail recursion (incorrect)

```
1  gAcc(n, acc: integer): integer
2      if n == 0 then
3          return acc
4      else
5          if (n %2 == 0) then
6              return(gAcc(n/2, n*acc))
7          else
8              return(gAcc((n-1)/2, 1+acc))
```

However, this function gAcc is not equivalent to g.

For instance, $g(10) = 10 \cdot g(5) = 10(1 + g(2)) = 10(1 + 2(g(1))) = 10(1 + 2(1 + g(0))) = 10(1 + 2 \cdot 2) = 50$.

10.4 Tail Recursion

On the other hand, $gAcc(10, 1) = gAcc(5, 10) = gAcc(2, 11) = gAcc(1, 22) = gAcc(0, 23) = 23$.

The reason why the method works with f but not with g is that f only performs multiplications while g performs multiplications and additions. As we noted after presenting the tail recursive version for the factorial, the classic recursive function and the accumulated function do not compute the result in the same way. The order in which operations are performed is changed. If a functions performs only one kind of operations (like multiplications for Factorial and for f), we obtain the same result both way as long as the operation is commutative. When a function performs two kind of operations (like g, performing multiplications and additions) we also need some properties of associativity between the two operations or the result computed by the two functions will differ.

Sometimes more than one accumulator is needed. Here is another example computing the n-th Fibonacci number with a tail recursive algorithm using two accumulators.

Algorithm 10.18: Fibonacci with tail recursion

```
1  Fib_acc(n, acc1, acc2: integer): integer
2      if n == 0 then
3          return acc1
4      else
5          return Fib_acc(n-1, acc2, acc1+acc2)
6
7  Fib(n: integer): integer
8      return Fib_acc(n, 1, 1)
```

In this algorithm, the fib_acc function uses tail recursion to compute the n-th Fibonacci number. The base case returns the current value of $acc1$, while the recursive case updates $acc1$ and $acc2$ and passes them along with $n - 1$ to the next recursive call. The Fib function simply calls fib_acc with initial values of $acc1 = 1$ and $acc2 = 1$.

Exercise 10.8
Consider the following recursive function:

Algorithm 10.19: Mysterious recursion

```
1  Recursion(m, n : integer): integer
2      if (m == 0 || n == 0) then return 1
3      else return (2 * recursion(m-1, n+1))
```

1. What does this function return for any pair of integers (m, n)?
2. Give an accumulated version of this function.
3. Deduce an equivalent iterative function.

Exercise 10.9
Generalise the method seen for the Fibonacci numbers to write a tail recursive function to compute the so called "Tribonacci" numbers, defined by:

$$T(n) = \begin{cases} 1 & \text{if } n < 3 \\ T(n-1) + T(n-2) + T(n-3) & \text{otherwise} \end{cases}$$

Hint Use three accumulators.

10.5 Solutions to Exercises

Solution of Exercise 10.1

1. We can apply the Master Theorem with $a = 2, b = 4$, and $k = 0$.
   Since $\log_b a = \log_4 2 = 1/2 > 0 = k$, we are in the "small f" case.
   Thus, $A(n) \in \Theta(n^{\log_b a}) = \Theta(n^{\log_4 2}) = \Theta(\sqrt{n})$.
2. Here $a = 2, b = 4$, and $k = 1/2$.
   Since $\log_b a = \log_4 2 = 1/2 = k$, we are in the "medium f" case.
   Thus, $B(n) \in \Theta(n^{\log_b a} \log n) = \Theta(\sqrt{n} \log n)$.
3. Here $a = 2, b = 4$, and $k = 1$.
   Since $\log_b a = \log_4 2 = 1/2 < 1 = k$, we are in the "large f" case.
   Thus, $C(n) \in \Theta(f(n)) = \Theta(n)$.
4. Here $a = 2, b = 4$, and $k = 2$.
   Since $\log_b a = \log_4 2 = 1/2 < 2 = k$, we are in the "large f" case.
   Thus, $D(n) \in \Theta(f(n)) = \Theta(n^2)$.
5. Here $a = 5, b = 3$ and $k = 2$.
   Since $\log_b a = \log_3 5 < 2 = k$, we are in the "large f" case.
   Thus, $E(n) \in \Theta(f(n)) = \Theta(n^2)$.
6. Here $a = 1, b = \frac{10}{9}$ (you have to write the recursion by writing $T_5(n)$ as a function of $T_5(\frac{n}{b})$ for a certain b, here $b = \frac{10}{9}$), and $k = 1$.
   Since $\log_b a = \log_{\frac{10}{9}} 1 = 0 < 1 = k$, we are in the "large f" case.
   Thus, $F(n) \in \Theta(f(n)) = \Theta(n)$. Notice that the result would be the same for any $0 < b < 1$.

Solution of Exercise 10.3

1. The variable max1 contains the largest element, the variable max2 contains the second-largest element.

```
TwoMax(T:tab of n integers) : couple of integers
    if (T[0] > T[1]) then
        max1 = T[0]
        max2 = T[1]
    else
        max1 = T[1]
```

10.5 Solutions to Exercises

```
7       max2 = T[0]
8    for i from 2 to n-1 do
9       if (T[i] > max1) then
10          max2 = max1
11          max1 = T[i]
12      else
13          if (T[i] > max 2) then
14              max2 = T[i]
15   return(max1, max2)
```

The loop runs $n - 2$ times and makes at most two comparisons per iteration, which amounts to $2(n - 2) = 2n - 4$, plus the initial comparison between $T[0]$ and $T[1]$, resulting in $2n - 3$.

2. The DPR algorithm has two base cases : $n = 2$ and $n = 3$:

```
1  TwoMaxDPR(T: tab of n integers; d, f: integer): couple of integers
2     if (f == d+2) then
3         if (T[d] > T[d+1]) then return(T[d], T[d+1])
4         else return(T[d+1], T[d])
5     else
6        if (f == d+3) then
7            (max1g, max2g) = TwoMaxDPR(T, d, d+2)
8            if (T[d+2] > max1g) then return (T[d+2], max1g)
9            else
10               if (T[d+2] > max2g) then return (max1g, T[d+2])
11               else return      (max1g, max2g)
12       else
13          m=(d+f)/2
14          (max1g, max2g) = TwoMaxDPR(T, d, m)
15          (max1d, max2d) = TwoMaxDPR(T, m, f)
16          if (max1g > max1d) then
17              if (max1d > max2g) then return (max1g, max1d)
18              else return (max1g, max2g)
19          else
20              if (max1g > max2d) then return (max1d, max1g)
21              else return (max1d, max2d)
```

At most two comparisons per recursive call.

3.

$$\varphi(n) = \begin{cases} c & \text{if } n = 2 \\ 2\varphi(n/2) + d & \text{otherwise} \end{cases}.$$

(c and d are two constants).
We have $a = 2$, $b = 2$, $\log_b a = \log_2 2 = 1 > 0 = k$. Case "$f$ small".
So, $\varphi(n) \in \Theta(n^{\log_2 2}) = \Theta(n)$.

4. If $k = 1$ ($n = 2$) the algorithm makes one comparison. If $k > 1$ we must count all the comparisons made in the two recursive calls on the two halves (each of

size 2^{k-1}), plus the two comparisons made by the main call itself. Therefore:

$$g(k) = \begin{cases} 1 & \text{if } k = 1 \\ 2g(k-1) + 2 & \text{otherwise} \end{cases}.$$

so,

$$\begin{aligned}
g(k) &= 2(g(k-1)) + 2 \\
&= 2^2 g(k-2) + 2^2 + 2 \\
&= 2^3 g(k-3) + 2^3 + 2^2 + 2 \\
&\vdots \\
&= 2^{k-1} g(1) + 2^{k-1} + 2^{k-2} + \ldots + 2 \\
&= 2^{k-1} + 2^{k-1} + 2^{k-2} + \ldots + 2 \\
&= 2^{k-1} + 2^k - 2
\end{aligned}$$

The last equality is justified by the identity:

$$2^{k-1} + 2^{k-2} + \ldots + 2 + 1 = \sum_{i=0}^{k-1} 2^i = 2^k - 1$$

Since $2^k = n$ and $2^{k-1} = n/2$, the number of comparisons as a fonction of n is $\frac{1}{2}n + n + 2 = \frac{3}{2}n + 2$, which is smaller than $2n - 3$ for $n > 7$, so the DPR algorithm makes fewer comparisons than the iterative one.

Solution of Exercise 10.4

We immediately think at the idea of splitting the room into four quadrants NE, NW, SE, SW (see Fig. 10.6) and solve the problem on each of them.

However, the divide-and-conquer strategy works when you reduce the resolution of a problem on the original instance to the resolution of the exact same problem

Fig. 10.6 Splitting into quadrants

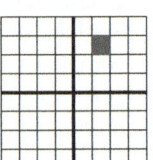

Fig. 10.7 Forbidden cells after splitting into quadrants

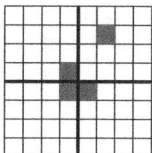

to smaller instances. The problem here stipulates that there is a forbidden cell in the room to be tiled and three of the quadrants do not have such a cell, we need to introduce a forbidden cell for each of them.

The three cells to be declared forbidden for the other three quadrants are always in the 2-by-2 square at the center of the room. Their choice depends obviously on the quadrant where the original forbidden cell lies. The Fig. 10.7 shows the choice in case the original forbidden cell is in the NE quadrant. Notice that these three cells leave the space for exactly one tile that can be placed at the end, after the four quadrants have been tiled.

Assume we have:

- a function Quadrant(p,q,l,i,j), which, given a square-shaped section C of the grid with the top-left corner at (p, q) and side length 2^l, and given a cell (i, j) in C, returns the quadrant of C in which (i, j) is located (write the pseudocode of this function, it's simple arithmetic involving the parameters p,q,l,i,j);
- a function PlaceTile(i,j,dir) which, for a cell (i, j) and a direction $dir \in \{NE, NW, SE, SW\}$, places a tile with its "hollow" (the missing cell to make it a square) on cell (i, j) and positioned in direction dir relative to the tile itself.

The main function Tiling(p,q,l,i,j) will tile a square with the top-left corner at (p, q), with a side length of 2^l, and the cell (i, j) is forbidden.

We start by calculating the quadrant where the forbidden cell is with a call to dir = Quadrant(p,q,l,i,j), this will also give the orientation in which we will have to place the last tile in the middle.

If l=1, we place the tile with the correct orientation: PlaceTile(i,j,dir).

Otherwise, we divide the problem into four subproblems: one for each quadrant. For the quadrant containing the forbidden cell, we make a recursive call while keeping the same cell as forbidden. For each of the other three quadrants, we mark the center cell as forbidden. These three cells form an L-shape that we can tile with a call to PlaceTile (at the end, for example).

So, there are four cases to write depending on the value of dir. In the following solution the code is given only for the case : dir=NE. You can try to find smart formulas using a coding of the four possible directions with vectors having component either 1 or −1 that allow to unify the four cases.

```
1  Tiling(p,q,l,i,j : integer)
2     dir = Quadrant(p,q,l,i,j)
3     if (l == 1) then
4        PlaceTile(i,j,dir)
```

```
    else
        m=2**(l-1)
        if (dir == NE) then
            Tiling(p, q+m, l-1, i, j)        // NE quadrant
            Tiling(p, q, l-1, p+m-1, q+m-1)  // NW quadrant
            Tiling(p+m, q, l-1, p+m, q+m-1)  // SW quadrant
            Tiling(p+m, q+m, l-1, p+m, q+m)  // SE quadrant
            PlaceTile(p+m-1, q+m, dir)       // Place the last tile
        if (dir == NW) then
            ...
```

Let $c(k)$ be the number of recursive calls to tile a square of side length 2^k. We make four recursive calls on four squares having side length 2^{k-1} so we have $c(k) = 4(c(k-1))$, and hence $c(k) = 4^k$. Since $k = \log_2 n$, the number of calls in terms of n is: $4^{\log_2 n} = (2^{\log_2 n})^2 = n^2$.

By the Master Theorem: we make four recursive calls on squares having size $n/2$ and `PlaceTile` has constant cost so we have the recursion:

$$T(n) = \begin{cases} c & \text{if } n = 2 \\ 4T(n/2) + c & \text{if } n > 2 \end{cases}$$

Here $a = 4$, $b = 2$, and $k = 0$, we are in the case "small f", hence $T(n) \in \Theta(n^{\log_2 4}) = \Theta(n^2)$.

Solution of Exercise 10.5

1. A cell $[0, j]$ on the row 0 can be reached only from the cell $[0, j-1]$ on its left. A cell $[i, 0]$ on the column 0 can be reached only from the cell $[i-1, 0]$ above it. In all other cases you can reach a cell $[i, j]$ either from the cell $[i, j-1]$ on its left or from the cell $[i-1, j]$ above it, you just have two check which one of the two brings more points, then add the bonus of the cell $[i, j]$.

$$V(i, j) = \begin{cases} B[0, 0] & \text{if } i = j = 0 \\ V(0, j-1) + B[0, j] & \text{if } i = 0 \\ V(i-1, 0) + B[i, 0] & \text{if } j = 0 \\ max(V(i-1, j), V(i, j-1)) + B[i, j] & \text{otherwise} \end{cases}$$

2.
```
VRec(i, j: integer): integer
    if (i == 0) and (i == 0) then
        return (B[0][0])
    if (i == 0) then
        return(VRec(0,j-1) + B[0][j])
    if (j == 0) then
```

```
7        return (VRec(i-1,j) + B[i][0])
8        return (max(VRec(i-1,j), VRec(i,j-1)) + B[i][j])
9
10  VRec(n-1,m-1)
```

3.
4. The following memoised version has complexity $\Theta(nm)$ both in time (the two nested for loops) and space (size of the memoisation table).

```
1
2   VMemo(n, m: integer): integer
3     VTable : matrix of size n x m of integers
4
5     VTable[0][0] = B[0][0]
6     for j in range(1, m) do
7       VTable[0][j] = VTable[0][j-1] + B[0][j]
8     for i in range(1, n) do
9       VTable[i][0] = VTable[i-1][0] + B[i][0]
10      for j in range(1, m) do
11        VTable[i][j] = max(VTable[i][j], VTable[i][j]) + B[i][j])
12    return(VTable[n-1,m-1])
```

Solution of Exercise 10.6

1. Base cases.
   If $n = 0$ and $k = 0$, we have $T(n,k) = 1$ (the only solution is the empty tower).
   If $k = 0$ or $k > n$, we have $T(n,k) = 0$ (no solution exists).
   General case ($0 < k \leq n$).
   If the last piece added to a solution has a height of h, then under this piece there is a tower of $(k-1)$ pieces with a height of $(n-h)$. These towers are counted by $T(n-h, k-1)$ and h can vary from 1 to n. Therefore, we have:

$$T(n,k) = T(n-1,k-1) + T(n-2,k-1) + \ldots + T(0,k-1) = \sum_{h=0}^{n-1} T(h,k-1)$$

Since we established that $T(n,k) = 0$ if $k > n$, we can simplify this sum by eliminating the zero terms as follows: $\sum_{h=k-1}^{n-1} T(h, k-1)$ (although this simplification was not essential for the rest of the exercise). The formula is then:

$$T(n,k) = \begin{cases} 1 & \text{if } n = 0 \text{ and } k = 0 \\ 0 & \text{otherwise, if } k = 0 \text{ or } k > n \\ \sum_{h=k-1}^{n-1} T(h, k-1) & \text{otherwise} \end{cases}$$

2.

```
1  TRec(n, k: integer): integer
2    res: integer
3    if (n == 0) and (k == 0) then
4      return (1)
5    if (k == 0) or (k > n) then
6      return(0)
7    res = 0
8    for h from k-1 to n-1 do
9      res += TRec(h, k-1)
10   return (res)
```

3. For example, we have:

$$T(6,4) = T(3,3) + T(4,3) + T(5,3)$$

But

$$T(5,3) = T(2,2) + \mathbf{T(3,2)} + T(4,2)$$

and

$$T(4,3) = T(2,2) + \mathbf{T(3,2)}$$

So, in this example, there is overlapping at the level of the subproblem $T(3,2)$ (and $T(2,2)$ also).

4. The following memoised version has time complexity $\Theta(n^2 k)$ because there are $O(nk)$ entires of the table to compute (precisely $(n+1) \times (k+1)$ and each entry is compute by a loop (the for h loop) that turns up to n times.

The space complexity is in $O(nk)$ (the size of the memoisation table is $(n+1) \times (k+1)$).

```
1  TMemo(n, k: integer): integer
2    TTable : matrix of size (n+1) x (k+1) of integers
3
4    TTable[0][0] = 1
5    for j in range(1, k) do
6      TTable[0][j] = 0
7    for i in range(1, n) do
8      TTable[i][0] = 0
9      for j in range(1, k) do
10       for h from k-1 to n-1 do
11         res += TTable[h][k-1]
12       TTable[i][j] = res
13   return(TTable[n,k])
```

Trees as Data Structures

How Using Non-linear Data Structures can Lead to More Efficient Algorithms (in Particular for the Searching Problem)

Linear structures like arrays or (linked) lists present the inconvenience that at least one of the function to access (search), insert or remove an element have complexity $\Theta(n)$ in the worst case. Non-linear structure like **trees** allow to perform this operations in logarithmic time.

Trees serve as valuable mathematical structures with a wide range of applications in various fields, including computer science, graph theory, and data analysis. They are a fundamental and versatile data structure that plays a pivotal role in computer science and programming. Trees provide an intuitive way to represent and analyse hierarchical relationships, making them an essential tool for solving problems related to classification, organisation, and optimisation as well as an elegant solution to various computational challenges.

Throughout this chapter, we will provide clear definitions, intuitive explanations, and practical implementations of general trees and in particular of binary search trees and binary heaps. We will discuss the algorithms and techniques for implementing, constructing, manipulating, and traversing these tree structures effectively. Additionally, we will explore the time and space complexity analysis of various operations on these data structures, enabling you to make informed decisions about their usage and performance in real-world applications.

Binary heaps, another variation of binary trees that prioritise the ordering of elements based on their values. Binary heaps are complete binary trees, meaning they are perfectly balanced except for the deepest level, which is filled from left to right. They possess the heap property, which dictates that for any node in the heap, its value is either greater than or equal to (in the case of a max-heap) or less than or equal to (in the case of a min-heap) the values of its children. Binary heaps are widely used in priority queues and provide efficient solutions for managing and organising data with prioritised access requirements.

Moving on, we encounter **binary search trees** (BSTs), an important type of tree that exhibits an ordered hierarchical structure. In a BST, each node contains a key or value, with the property that the key of any node in the left subtree is less than the key of the node itself, while the key of any node in the right subtree is greater. This ordering property enables efficient searching, insertion, and deletion operations, making BSTs a valuable tool for maintaining sorted data and implementing efficient data retrieval algorithms.

A special case of BSTs are the **AVL trees**, named after their inventors Adelson-Velsky and Landis (see [2]). They are self-balancing binary search trees designed to maintain their structural balance during insertion and deletion operations. An AVL tree has the ability to ensure that the heights of the left and right subtrees of any node differ by at most one, thus guaranteeing logarithmic time complexity for search, insertion, and deletion operations. To achieve this balance, AVL trees employ rotations and rebalancing techniques when necessary, adjusting the tree structure to maintain optimal performance. By mitigating the effects of skewed or unbalanced trees that we can have with generic BSTs, AVL trees offer reliable and efficient data storage solutions in scenarios with a dynamically changing dataset.

11.1 Definitions

First, let us establish the foundations by defining some basic concepts related to trees. The properties and characteristics of trees, such as depth, height, and the arrangement of nodes and edges, offer insights into the structure and behaviour of complex systems, enabling efficient algorithm design and data manipulation.

In mathematics, a tree is a fundamental type of object that exhibits a hierarchical structure and is often used to model relationships or hierarchies among elements. Formally, an **undirected tree** can be defined as a connected acyclic graph, meaning it is a collection of nodes (also known as vertices) connected by edges, where there are no cycles (loops) present. In our context, we are rather interested in **directed trees**, where each edge is directed from the higher node in the hierarchy (parent) to the lower (child).

11.1.1 Key Components and Basic Properties of a Tree

The individual elements within a tree are represented by **nodes**. Each node may contain data or other associated attributes, depending on the context of the tree. The connections between nodes are represented by directed **edges**. An edge connects two nodes and represents a relationship (parent-to-child) or link between them. The **root** of a tree is the unique node that does not have any incoming edges. Every other node has exactly one incoming edge (every node except the root has at exactly one parent).

Trees are intrinsically recursive structures, a subtree of a tree is a tree itself. For this reason, in mathematics, a tree can also be defined recursively, building upon simpler components of trees. A recursive definition of a tree can be formulated based on the concept of attaching subtrees to a new root.

11.1 Definitions

Here is a recursive definition of a tree:

Base Cases: An empty set is considered a tree called the **empty tree** and noted Λ.

A single node with no subtrees is considered a tree by itself (a **singleton tree**).

Recursive Case: A tree is formed by attaching one or more subtrees to a new root node. Each subtree is itself a tree that follows the same recursive definition. Root nodes of subtrees of a given node are called **children nodes**.

Each non-root node in a tree has a single parent node, which is the node directly above it in the hierarchy. This implies that for a given node there is a unique path connecting the root of the tree to that particular node.

Conversely, a node may have zero or more child nodes, which are the nodes directly below it in the hierarchy. **Leaf nodes**, also known as terminal nodes or external nodes, are the nodes in a tree that do not have any child nodes. They represent the endpoints or leaves of the hierarchical structure.

The **depth of a node** in a tree is the number of edges along the unique path from the root to that particular node. The root node is at depth 0, and the depth increases as we move further away from the root.

The **height of a tree** is the maximum depth among all its nodes. It represents the longest path from the root to any leaf node in the tree. Since the root node is at depth 0, the height of a singleton tree is 0.

The height of a non-empty tree T of root node r having subtrees $T_1, T_2, \ldots, T_k$ clearly can be defined recursively as:

$$h(T) = 1 + \max_{i=1}^{k} h(T_i), \tag{11.1}$$

the additional 1 counts the extra level of depth between the root and its children.

Note that the height of the empty tree has to be defined equal to -1 (negative 1). If we apply the above recursive formula 11.1 to a singleton tree S, imagining it as a node to which two empty trees are attached, we get:

$$0 = h(S) = 1 + \max(h(\Lambda), h(\Lambda)) = 1 + h(\Lambda)$$

which implies $h(\Lambda) = -1$.

The **arity of a tree** is the the maximum number of children that any node in the tree can have. It represents the degree of branching or the maximum number of branches that emanate from a single node or the largest possible size of a brotherhood in the tree.

A **binary tree** is a tree having an arity of 2, each node can have at most two children. Similarly, a ternary tree has an arity of 3, allowing each node to have up to three children.

11.2 Implementation of Trees in Memory

The memory implementation of non-linear data structures like trees needs to take into account that, in addition to the content of the data structure, the links relating the data (that is, the hierarchical structure or the parent-child relation in the case of a tree) need to be represented in some way.

11.2.1 Implementations by Arrays

If the tree has n nodes (numbered from 0 to $n-1$) each containing one element, we can represent a tree T as an object having two attributes that are arrays of size n:

- T.content is an array of elements such that, for any node i, the case T.content[i] contains the value of the element stored in node i.
- T.parent is an array of integers such that, for any node i, the case T.parent[i] contains the number (index) of the parent node of i. By convention, the root of the tree has itself as parent.

Example 11.1
In the following tree, the label (index) affected to each node may represent the order in which new nodes have been added to an initially empty tree: The corresponding .content array is:

61	11	22	14	18	17	10	36	48	80	15	51	21	35	20
0	1	2	3	4	5	6	7	8	9	10	11	12	13	14

and the .parent array is:

0	0	0	1	1	0	5	3	5	8	8	3	8	8	4
0	1	2	3	4	5	6	7	8	9	10	11	12	13	14

In the implementation by arrays, it is easy to "move up" in the tree, indeed we can do it in $\Theta(1)$ thanks to the information parent[i]. On the other hand, it is more difficult to "go down" in the tree, that is, to access the children of a node. This requires a traversal of the array parent and therefore a time $O(n)$.

A way to circumvent this problem is to add more information for each node, thus allowing to access the children in $O(1)$. For exemple, a binary tree with n nodes containing integers may be implemented with an array T of n quadruplets (arrays of length 4) where for each $i \in \{0, \ldots, n-1\}$ the quadruplet T[i] is composed by:

1. T[i][0]: the integer value stored in the node i.
2. T[i][1]: the parent the node i (equal to i itself if i is the root).
3. T[i][2]: the left child of the node i (equal to -1 if it does not exist).
4. T[i][3]: the right child of the node i (equal to -1 if it does not exist).

11.2 Implementation of Trees in Memory

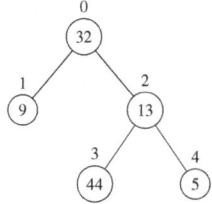

Fig. 11.1 A tree

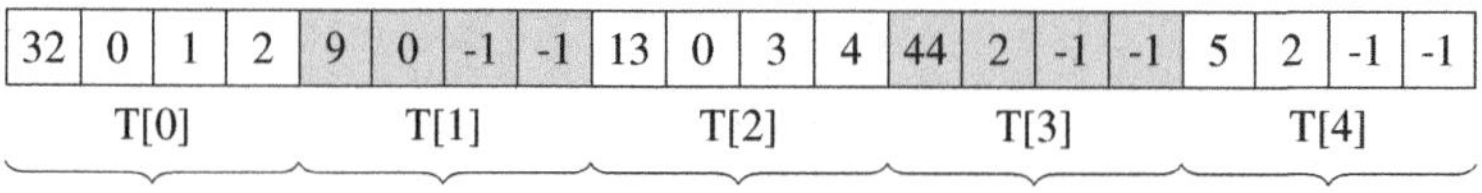

32	0	1	2	9	0	-1	-1	13	0	3	4	44	2	-1	-1	5	2	-1	-1
T[0]				T[1]				T[2]				T[3]				T[4]			

Fig. 11.2 Tree nodes as quadruplets

Example 11.2
The tree in Fig. 11.1 is represented by the array of five quadruplets in Fig. 11.2.

This can easily be generalised to trees having an arity larger than 2. It can be a bit more delicate to implement for trees whose arity is not known or may change through time.

11.2.2 Implementation by References/Pointers

Arrays are implemented in memory using contiguous memory cells, ensuring that all elements are stored adjacent to each other. Consequently, knowing the memory address of the first element is sufficient to compute the address of any other element using indexing, thus granting direct access. Indexing involves simple shifts based on the size of the array's elements, allowing for efficient memory access. Arrays are stored in memory in a compact manner.

On the other hand, **referencing** or **memory addressing** enables the storage of data in a dispersed, non-compact manner. This is evident in data structures such as linked lists or linked chains, where each element is associated with a reference to the memory address of the next element in the list. To achieve this, a suitable data structure, representing a link in the chain, is used to encapsulate the pair element-reference.

In linked lists or chains, the elements are not stored in adjacent memory cells. Instead, it can be likened to a scavenger hunt where at each location you find a candy along with an indication of where the next one can be found. This approach linearises the data in memory, as opposed to the spatial linearisation in the case of arrays. The following figure gives a possible depiction of a linked list containing the element 1, 2, 3, 4, 5, 6 (in this order).

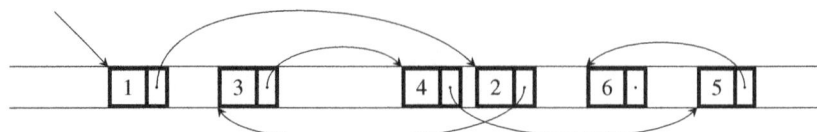

Fig. 11.3 A list scattered in memory

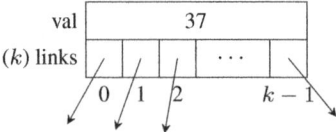

Fig. 11.4 A node of a tree having arity k

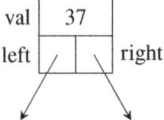

Fig. 11.5 A node of a binary tree

The same underlying principle used for linked chains can also be applied to implement trees (Fig. 11.3).

11.2.2.1 The Arity of the Tree Is Known

If the arity is k, we can implement a node N of a tree as an object having two attributes:

- N.val (val for "value") where we store an element, and
- N.links which is an array of size k of trees (in fact, an array of references of subtrees), where for all i, the case N.links[i] contains the reference of the i-th child of the node N. If a node has less than k children, the rightmost cells of the links array will be null.

Each node of the tree therefore has a structure as shown in Fig. 11.4.

In the particular case of binary trees, to implement the links to the children, we do not use an array of size two, but directly two named attributes:

- N.left containing the reference of the left child and
- N.right containing the reference of the right child.

Here is how to imagine a node of a binary tree (Fig. 11.5):

11.2 Implementation of Trees in Memory

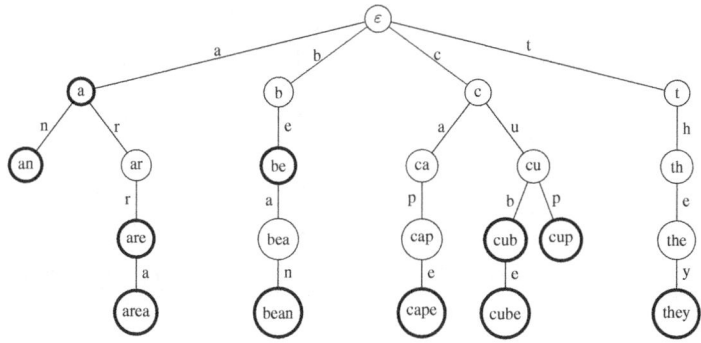

Fig. 11.6 A lexicographic tree

Exercise 11.1 (Lexicographic Trees)
Lexicographic trees can be used to implement dictionaries. The lexicographic tree of L is a tree where:

- each node corresponds to a word w on the alphabet A (not necessarily a word in the dictionary);
- each edge corresponds to a letter a from the alphabet A (such an edge will be labeled by a);
- the root corresponds to the empty word;
- if a node N of the tree corresponds to the word w, then the child of N accessible via the outgoing edge labeled by a (if it exists) corresponds to the word wa;
- all the leaves of the tree, as well as possibly some of the internal nodes of the tree (but not necessarily all!), represent the words of the dictionary

Figure 11.6 shows the lexicographic tree of the little dictionary containing the eleven words {a, an, are, area, be, bean, cape, cub, cube, cup, they}. We have indicated inside each node N the corresponding word, however this is redundant and hence unnecessary: the labels of the edges composing the path from the root to N give the same word. The thick/marked nodes correspond to the words in the dictionary (so this is essential information), note for instance that the words "cap" and "the" are not in this dictionary.
We will assume that each node of a lexicographic tree includes an array of 26 links (labeled from a to z) corresponding to the 26 potential children. It also need to include a boolean field for the marking.

1. Write an algorithm to check if a given word is present in the dictionary.
2. Write an algorithm to add a new word to the dictionary.

11.2.2.2 The Arity of the Tree Is not Known, the *Left-Child Right-Sibling* Implementation

If the arity of the tree is not known in advance or if it is too large, we can use the following implementation, which allows us to represent trees of any arity with only two links (references) in each node.

The first of these two links, .firstch (for "first-child") contains the address of the first (leftmost) child of the node. The second of these two links will be denoted .rightsib and it contains the address of the sibling of the node immediately on its right. The figure below shows a tree represented by "first-child right-sibling".

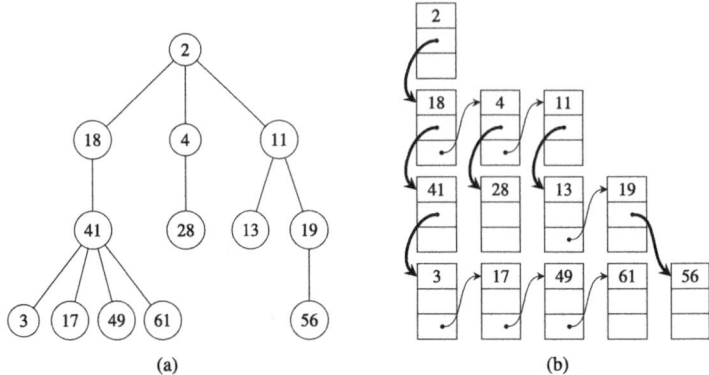

Fig. 11.7 The left-child right-sibling implementation of a tree of arbitrary arity. (**a**) A tree. (**b**) Its implementation

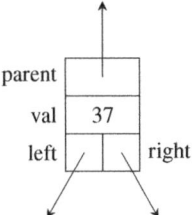

Fig. 11.8 A node of a binary tree with parenting

We notice that we no longer have direct access from each node to all its children, but only to its leftmost child. One reaches the other children as sibling of the first child, by following the right-sibling links (Fig. 11.7).

For all of the implementations presented in this subsection, once you have defined the type/structure of a node, you can define a tree as an object containing the reference of its root node, since once you have access to the root, you have access to the whole tree. Note that in this implementation both a node and a tree are of the same type (the value of both is a reference to a node), a tree is equivalent to a node (its root).

11.2.3 The .parent Attribute

For all the structures presented in Sect. 11.2.2, and in particular for the binary trees, the descent towards the children of a node is "easy", but from a given node there is no easy way to go up to its parent. To overcome this, each of the node structures presented can be equipped with an additional `parent` attribute which is a link to the parent of the node. This attribute will have be initialised correctly when creating the node (Fig. 11.8).

This is how a node of a binary tree looks like with the `parent` attribute:

11.3 Tree Traversal

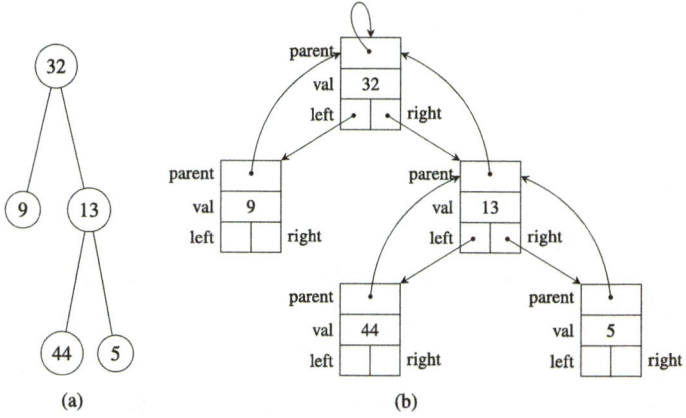

Fig. 11.9 A tree with parenting. (**a**) A tree. (**b**) Its implementation

And here is an example of a small tree with this implementation. Note that the `parent` of the root "points" to the root itself (it contains the address of the root node itself) (Fig. 11.9):

11.3 Tree Traversal

The first question that immediately arises is: how to traverse a tree, i.e. how to "visit" each of its nodes to perform some kind of operations[1] in each of them ? By definition, trees are recursive structures (a subtree of a tree is a tree itself), so it makes sense that a good number of algorithms on trees are recursive. Iterators make it easy to browse lists/arrays with loops, but in general you cannot do loops like "for all nodes of the tree" if the tree is represented using nodes with references. If you need to browse through a tree it is convenient to use recursion.

11.3.1 Depth-First Traversal

In **depth-first search** (DFS), the strategy of the traversal is to go deep as much as possible in the tree until you reach a leaf and then you backtrack to the closest branching point and from there you visit the nodes of the next branch. We remind that we call "visiting" the moment at which we perform some sort of operation on the node. There are three variants that share this common approach to traverse a tree: pre-order, post-order and in-order, where "pre-", "post-" and "in-" refer to the moment the root is visited (before, after or "in the middle" of the subtrees).

---

[1] Such operation may simply be displaying/printing the value stored in the node, or modifying the content of the node, for instance.

Fig. 11.10 A small binary tree

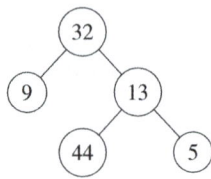

11.3.1.1 Pre-order

Let T be a tree with root r and subtrees $T_1, T_2, \ldots, T_k$. **Pre-order traversal** first visits the root r (we emphasise that in practice this "visit" will be a very precise operation, for example print(T.val), and then traverses recursively and in pre-order the subtrees $T_1, T_2, \ldots, T_k$ (Fig. 11.10).

So for a tree of arity k, if the visit consists in displaying the values stored in the nodes, we have the following algorithm. Note that for an empty tree (base case of the recursion), the algorithm does nothing.

Algorithm 11.1: Pre-order traversal

```
1  PreOrder (T: tree)
2    if (T != null) then
3      print(T.val)
4      for i from 1 to k do
5        PreOrder(T.links[i])
```

▶ Note that the (implicit) base case of this algorithm is the case when the tree is empty. In this case the algorithm does nothing. The empty tree is the only base case for most recursive algorithms on trees. It is a common mistake for beginners to add other useless base cases (such as, the tree is a singleton). You should always check if additional base cases are really necessary for your algorithm. If a function does the right thing (or returns the right answer) for the empty tree and if your recursive case is correct, then most of the time the function will do the right thing for any tree.

In the particular case of binary trees this becomes:

Algorithm 11.2: Pre-order traversal of a binary tree

```
1  PreOrder(T: binarytree)
2    if (T != null) then
3      print(T.val)
4      PreOrder(T.left)
5      PreOrder(T.right)
```

11.3 Tree Traversal

For example, the pre-order of the small tree:
will display:

```
1  32 9 13 44 5
```

11.3.1.2 Post-order

To traverse a tree T in **post-order**, we first recursively traverse in post-order the subtrees $T_1, T_2, \ldots, T_k$ and then visit the root:

Algorithm 11.3: Post-order traversal

```
1  PostOrder (T: tree)
2    if (T != null) then
3      for i from 1 to k do
4        PostOrder(T.links[i])
5      print(T.val)
```

In the particular case of binary trees this becomes:

Algorithm 11.4: Post-order traversal of a binary tree

```
1  PostOrder (T: binarytree)
2    if (T != null) then
3      PostOrder(T.left)
4      PostOrder(T.right)
5      print(T.val)
```

For example, Post-order traversal of the small tree in the example will display:

```
1  9 44 5 13 32
```

11.3.1.3 In-order

The **In-order** makes mostly sense for binary trees, nevertheless it can be defined for trees of any arity.

To traverse T in In-order, we first recursively traverse in In-order the first subtree T_1, then we visit the root and finally we traverse recursively and in In-order the subtrees $T_2, T_3, \ldots, T_k$:

Algorithm 11.5: In-order traversal

```
1  InOrder(T: tree)
2    if (T != null) then
3      InOrder(T.links[1])
4      print(T.val)
```

```
5       for i from 2 to k do
6           InOrder(T.links[i])
```

In the particular case of binary trees this becomes much more symmetric:

Algorithm 11.6: In-order traversal of a binary tree

```
1   InOrder(T: binarytree)
2       if (T != null)
3           InOrder(T.left)
4           print(T.val)
5           InOrder(T.right)
```

For example, the In-order traversal of the small tree in the example will display:

```
1   9 32 44 13 5
```

Exercise 11.2
Give the display obtained by performing a pre-order, post-order or in-order traversal of the tree in the figure in Example 11.1.

Exercise 11.3
A binary tree can be represented by a triplet $(-, -, -)$ whose first component is the value at the root, the second is the triplet representing the left subtree and the third the triplet representing the right subtree. For instance the representation of the small tree in the example is : $(32,(9),(13,(44),(5)))$ (note that for a leaf we simplify the triplet $(value, empty, empty)$ with the expression $(value)$).
Modify one of the three procedures of depth-first traversal so that it also displays parentheses and commas representing the hierarchical relation of the nodes.

Exercise 11.4
Write an algorithm `TreeToList(T: binary tree): list` that, given a binary tree, produces the list of elements of the tree obtained by traversing the tree in in-order. Evaluate its complexity.

Exercise 11.5
Trees can also be used to represent arithmetical expressions.
A single operand x (a constant) is represented by a singleton tree containing the value of x in its unique node.
If op is a (binary) operator and E_1 and E_2 are two expressions, then the expression $E_1\ op\ E_2$ is represented by the tree whose root contains the operator op and has the tree representing E_1 as left subtree and the tree representing E_2 as right subtree.
For instance:

- $2 * 3 + 4$ is represented by the tree of Fig. 11.11a,
- $2 * (3 + 4)$ is represented by the tree of Fig. 11.11b.

Fig. 11.11 Syntax trees. (**a**) $2 * 3 + 4$. (**b**) $2 * (3 + 4)$

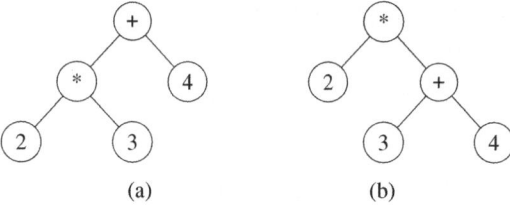

(a)   (b)

Given a binary tree representing an arithmetical expression, write four algorithms to :

1. display the expression in prefix notation;
2. display the expression in suffix notation (see also Exercise 5.6) ;
3. display the expression in infix notation; for this question you may have to add parentheses, do not worry if some of them are not necessary like in $(2 * 3) + 4$;
4. compute the value of the expression (for instance the value of $2 * 3 + 4$ is obviously $6 + 4 = 10$).

11.3.2 Breadth-First Traversal

One prominent technique for traversing a tree is breadth-first traversal. This approach allows us to systematically explore a tree's nodes layer by layer, starting from the root and moving outward in a breadth-first manner. Also known as **level-order traversal**, this technique ensures that we visit all nodes at a given depth before moving on to the next depth level.

Unlike depth-first algorithms that are naturally implemented using recursion, the breadth-first traversal algorithm is an iterative algorithm that operates using a queue data structure, which ensures that the node are explored layer by layer. A **queue** (a first-in-first-out linear structure) is used to maintain the list of the nodes that have already been visited (and in the order in which they have been visited) but whose children must yet be visited.[2]

The algorithm begins by enqueueing the root node and then iteratively follows these steps until the queue becomes empty:

- Dequeue the front node from the queue, visit it, and process its data or perform any desired operations.
- Enqueue all the children (if any) of the dequeued node, maintaining the order in which they appear from left to right.

By adhering to this approach, breadth-first traversal guarantees that we process the nodes in a level-wise manner. This characteristic makes it particularly useful for tasks that require exploring hierarchical relationships or determining the shortest

---

[2] In PYTHON, a queue can be implemented with a simple list. The insertions in the queue (enqueueing) is realised with a call to the method .append, the deletions (dequeueing) with a call to the method pop(0) (see Chap. 5 in the PYTHON section).

path between nodes, finding the minimum or maximum depth of a tree, counting nodes at each level, or detecting patterns based on layer proximity.

Algorithm 11.7: Breadth-first traversal of a tree

```
1  BFTraversal (T: tree)
2      Q : queue //initally empty
3      Enqueue(Q,T)  //enqueue the root
4      while (not(isEmpty(Q))) do
5          u = Dequeue(Q)
6          Visit(u)
7          for all children v of u do
8              Enqueue(Q,v)
```

The breadth-first traversal algorithm finds wide application across numerous domains, in particular when applied to general graphs (not just trees) in fields like network routing and web crawling. Its usage finds relevance also in biological studies, such as analyzing genetic relationships and studying the spread of diseases.

Exercise 11.6
Inspired by the structures seen in Chap. 5, implement BFT for a binary tree represented as an array of quadruplets as shown in Sect. 11.2.2.

11.4 Recursive Functions on Trees

In this section we want you to get familiarised with writing some (simple) recursive functions on trees. To simplify, we will only consider binary trees but it is straightforward to realise how these algorithms can be generalised for trees of any arity.

11.4.1 Computation of the Size of a Tree

Let T be a binary tree implemented by a class having attributes `val`, `left`, `right`. We want a function `Size(T: tree): integer` that returns the size (the number of nodes) of the tree T.

$Size(T)$ satisfies the following recursive definition:

$$Size(T) = \begin{cases} 0 & \text{if } T \text{ is empty} \\ 1 + Size(T.right) + Size(T.left) & \text{else} \end{cases}$$

from which we can easily deduce an algorithm that returns the size of a tree T.

11.4 Recursive Functions on Trees

> **Algorithm 11.8:** Size of a binary tree

```
1  Size(T: tree): integer
2      if (T == null) then return (0)
3      return (1 + Size(T.right) + Size(T.left))
```

For example, you can verify that if T is a singleton (it only has one node, its root), the function correctly returns the value 1 as $1 + Size(\Lambda) + Size(\Lambda) = 1 + 0 + 0$.

What is the time complexity of this algorithm?

The function makes a call for each node in the tree. Each call has a cost in $\Theta(1)$. So if the size of the tree is n, the complexity of the function is in $\Theta(n)$; in other words, we calculate $Size(T)$ in time $\Theta(Size(T))$.

Exercise 11.7
Define a Size algorithm to compute the number of nodes of a tree of arity k. What is the complexity of this algorithm then?

11.4.2 Computation of the Height

Let T be a binary tree implemented by a class with attributes val, left (left child), right (right child).

We want a function Height that returns the height of the tree, *i.e.* the longest path from the root to a leaf.

We have seen that $Height(T)$ satisfies the following recursive definition:

$$Height(T) = \begin{cases} -1 & \text{if } T \text{ is empty} \\ 1 + \max(Height(T.right), Height(T.left)) & \text{else} \end{cases}$$

from which we can easily deduce an algorithm that returns the height of a tree T.

> **Algorithm 11.9:** Height of a tree

```
1  Height(T: tree): integer
2      hleft, hright: integer
3      if (T == null) then return(-1)
4      hleft = Height(T.left)
5      hright = Height(T.right)
6      if (hleft > hright) then return (1+hleft)
7      return (1+hright)
```

Note that this function correctly returns the value 0 for a singleton tree.

▶ You must not write:

   Algorithm 11.10: Bad algorithm for the height

```
1  Function Height(T: tree): integer
2    if (T == null) then return(-1)
3    if (Height(T.left) > Height(T.right)) then
4      return(1 + Height(T.left))
5    return(1 + Height(T.right))
```

Indeed this program would uselessly make twice each recursive call.

The structure of the program is exactly the same as that of the algorithm for Size. The function makes one call for each node in the tree and each call is $\Theta(1)$. If therefore the size of T is n the complexity of the function Height is in $\Theta(Size(T)) = \Theta(n)$.

11.4.3 Another Exemple

Let T be a binary tree implemented by a class with attributes val, left (left child), right (right child) and suppose that the attribute val is an integer. We want a function SumEvens(T: tree): integer that returns the sum of the even integers stored in the tree T.

- If the root of the tree contains an even number, then this number contributes to the sum and the two sums of the even numbers in the left and right subtrees must be calculated.
- if in the root of the tree there is an odd number, then this number does not contribute to the sum, it is only necessary to calculate the two sums of the even numbers in the left and right subtrees.

We can therefore deduce an algorithm that returns SumEvens for a tree T.

   Algorithm 11.11: Sum even numbers in a binary tree

```
1  EvenSum (T: tree): integer
2    if (T == null) then return (0)
3    sumsubtrees = EvenSum(T.right) + EvenSum(T.left)
4    if (T.val % 2 == 0) then return (T.val + sumsubtrees)
5    else return(sumsubtrees)
```

As in the other two cases, the function makes a call for each node of the tree. Each call is in $\Theta(1)$. So the complexity of the function is in $\Theta(n)$.

Exercise 11.8
Let A be a binary tree implemented by a class having attributes `val`, `left`, `right`. The `.val` field contains integers.

1. Write an algorithm that returns the number of nodes in the tree that contain a negative value.
2. Let v be an integer value. Write an algorithm that returns the sum of the values stored in the tree that are smaller than v.
3. Write an algorithm that returns the sum of all even values contained in nodes of the tree having two children that also contain an even value.
4. Write an algorithm that returns the sum of all values contained in nodes having an even depth. The root is at depth 0, its grandchildren (if they exist) at depth 2, and so on... Don't forget to handle the cases where one (or both) children of a node are null, as in these cases some grandchildren do not exist...
5. We define the cost of a path from the root to a leaf as the sum of the integers contained in the nodes along the path. Write a recursive algorithm that, given a binary tree, returns the minimum weight of a path from the root to a leaf.
6. Write a recursive algorithm that, given a binary tree, exchanges the right and left children of each node in the tree.

11.5 Heaps and Priority Queues

Heaps are binary trees that satisfy two particular properties, one concerning their shape and the other concerning their content. The property on the shape in particular makes it very easy to implement heaps in memory. Indeed, a single array with the content is enough to implement a heap, while we have seen that in general, this is not sufficient for a generic tree.

Both properties make heaps the ideal structure for representing so-called **priority queue**.

A **priority queue** is a set of data (numerical or belonging to a totally ordered set), variable over time, on which only two operations must be performed: the addition of a new element and the removal of the minimal element (the element having highest priority), this operation will be called *MinRemoval*.

What happens in a priority queue is similar to what happens, for example, in the processor of a multi-user computer which simultaneously receives many requests: to open an application, to save a file, to open an Internet link, to move a directory... An operating system will sequentially execute these requests one after the other but not necessarily in the order in which it received them. Some are more important than others and therefore have higher priority. Each request is therefore assigned a value expressing its priority, in general a smaller number corresponds to a higher priority. The operating system must therefore "manage" the list/queue of requests waiting to be processed, i.e.:

add   to a priority queue any new request that arises, using the priority value of the requests as key;
remove   from the queue the request with the minimum priority value (which therefore has maximum priority) to process it (execute the request).

Note that if we chose to implement a priority queue using an array, we would have two options :

- either keeping this array sorted according to the priority of the elements so that the minimum is always in the initial position, but then with each new addition the array would have to be re-arranged, which would cost no less than $O(n)$ (one insertion in sorted list, as in Insertion Sort).
- or keeping this array in disorder, but then for each removal of the minimum it will be necessary to search the minimum of the array, which would cost no less than $O(n)$.

In both cases, removing the minimum requires shifting the elements that follow it, which also requires $O(n)$ time in the worst case, so if you use an array, at least one of the two operations will be in $O(n)$. We will see that using heaps we can perform these two operations in $O(\log n)$ (where n is the size of the heap) in the worst case, very quickly then.

11.5.1 Definition of Heaps

We will first give the formal definition of heap and then we will explain and comment on this definition.

> **Definition 11.1**
>
> A binary tree T of height h is a heap (more precisely, a **min-heap**) if it satisfies the following two properties:
>
> shape   For any integer p with $0 \leq p < h$, there are exactly 2^p nodes of depth p. Moreover, the nodes of depth h (these must be leaves) are placed "as left as possible".
>
> content   For any node N of T, the item contained in N is smaller (or more precisely, its key has a smaller priority value) than the items contained in its two children (if these exist).

The first part of the "shape" property tells us that for each $p < h$, we have exactly the maximum number of nodes of depth p that a binary tree can have. In other terms, all "levels" of depth, except possibly the last one, must be "complete". The second part of the "shape" property simply tells us that the nodes of depth h are the leftmost leaves. In other words, schematically a heap always has the following shape:

For example, the only possible shape of a heap of size 10 is:

11.5 Heaps and Priority Queues

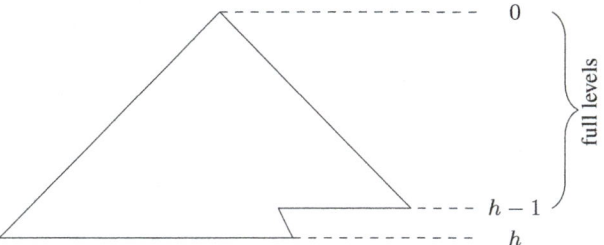

Fig. 11.12 Shape of a heap

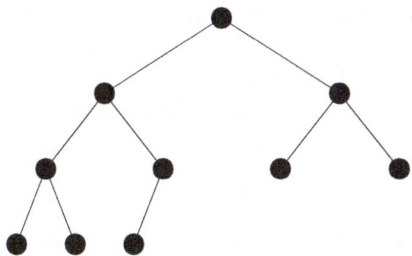

Fig. 11.13 The shape of a heap of size 10

And here is a with possible filling for a heap of size 10. We can check that the element of each node is smaller than the elements in its children (Fig. 11.12):

▶ **Remark 11.1** An important consequence of the "shape" property is also that the height h of a heap is always in $\Theta(\log_2 n)$ where n is the size of the heap (Fig. 11.13).

The following two remarks are consequences of "content" property.

▶ **Remark 11.2** Note that in a min-heap, the minimum is always at the root.

▶ **Remark 11.3** Furthermore, the values contained in the nodes that we encounter in any path from the root to a leaf are inincreasing order.

We obtain the definition of **max-heap** by modifying the "content" property by imposing that for any node N of T, the element contained in N is *larger* than the elements contained in its two children (if they exist).

Exercise 11.9
Give an example of a max-heap of size 12.

Exercise 11.10
Give a max-heap containing the elements of the min-heap of Fig. 11.14.

Fig. 11.14 An example of heap of size 10

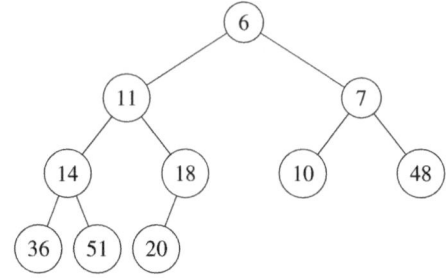

11.5.2 Implications on Heap Implementation in Memory

Let us number the nodes of the heap level by level, from left to right.

Note that with this numbering, if a node bears the number i, then its children (if they exist) bear the numbers $2i+1$ and $2i+2$, and conversely, if a node has number $i > 1$ then its parent has number $(i-1)/2$ (integer division). This is a consequence of Property 1.

But then the parenthood relation is perfectly known and we don't need a Parent array to memorise it, the array Content alone characterises (almost) completely the heap. We will come back later to address the "almost". Below is the Content array for the above heap.

Exercise 11.11
Modify BFS to obtain an algorithm that takes as argument a heap implemented as collection of nodes having attributes val, left and right and returns an array in which every cell i contains the value of the heap stored in the node number i.

Exercise 11.12
Write a PYTHON program that given an array representing a heap, displays the content of a heap level by level using BFS. For instance, for the heap of size 10 from the previous example (Fig. 11.15), the program is expected to print:

```
6
11 7
14 17 10 18
36 51 20
```

Now modify the program so that it inserts the necessary spacing to place each (non-leaf) node in the position in the middle of its two children. For instance, for the heap of size 10 from the previous example (Fig. 11.15), the program is expected to print:

```
            6
      11         7
   14    17    10    18
  36 51 20
```

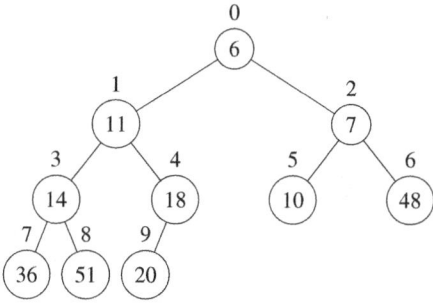

Fig. 11.15 Numbering nodes in a heap

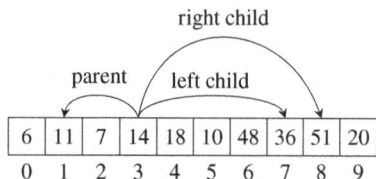

Fig. 11.16 Parenthood and childhood relations in a heap as an array

11.5.3 Insert and MinRemoval in Heaps

Before presenting the algorithms, we will show on some examples how we perform the operations of insertion and removal of the minimum (Fig. 11.16).

Let T be the heap of size 10 from the previous example (Fig. 11.15) and let $x = 9$. we want to insert x into T while making sure that what we get after the insertion is still a heap (Fig. 11.17).

Initially, the new element is placed in the leftmost "unused" leaf. If the deep most level is already complete, then this is the first leaf in the following level. The tree obtained satisfies Property 1 on the form, but not necessarily Property 2 on the content. To correct this, the element x is compared with the element y contained in its parent node, if x is smaller than y, they must be swapped. We will continue with a loop while that brings x up to its final place as long as the parent contains a larger element. This operation is called **upward percolation**.

For MinRemoval, you need to write an algorithm that removes the value at the root from the heap (while ensuring that what you get after the removal is still a heap) and returns that value (Fig. 11.18).

Phase 1. We start by storing this value in a variable min that we will return at the end. Then we overwrite the element at the root with the element of the rightmost (last) leaf and we remove that leaf.

Phase 2. Once again, the resulting tree satisfies Property 1 on form, but not necessarily Property 2 on content. To correct this, we compare the element at the root x with its two children, if x is larger than the minimum of the two, then x and

Fig. 11.17 Insertion of 9

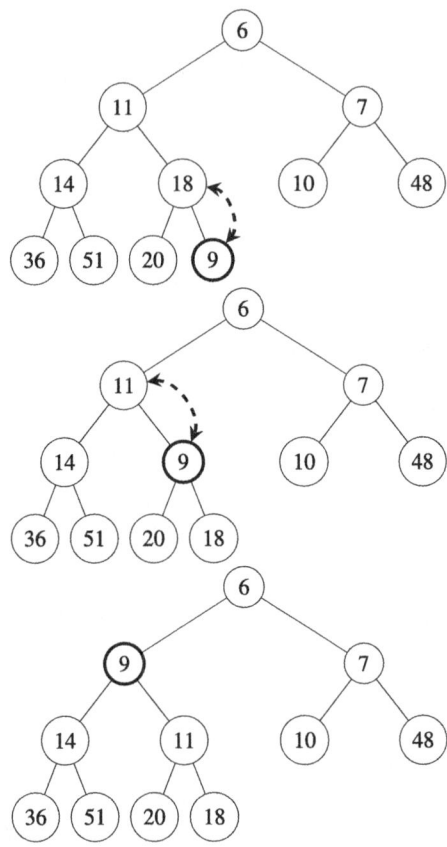

this minimum must be swapped. We continue like this with a loop `while` which brings the element x down to its final place (**downward percolation**). Note the during downward percolation, the element is always swapped with the smaller of its two children (Fig. 11.19).

Both for Insertion and for MinRemoval, we will therefore have to execute a `while` loop that at each iteration makes a swap (in $\Theta(1)$). This loop turns at most h times, where h is the height of the heap, because at each iteration we go up or down of one level of depth.

These operations can therefore be executed in $O(h) = O(\log n)$. We will see in the next section how to write the corresponding algorithms after a complement on the in-memory implementation.

11.5.4 A Step Back to the Aspect of the Implementation

It must be taken into account that a heap changes size over time because new elements are added while minimal elements are removed over time.

Fig. 11.18 Removal of the minimum in a heap, phase 1. (**a**) Record the minimum. (**b**) Move last value to the root. (**c**) Delete last node

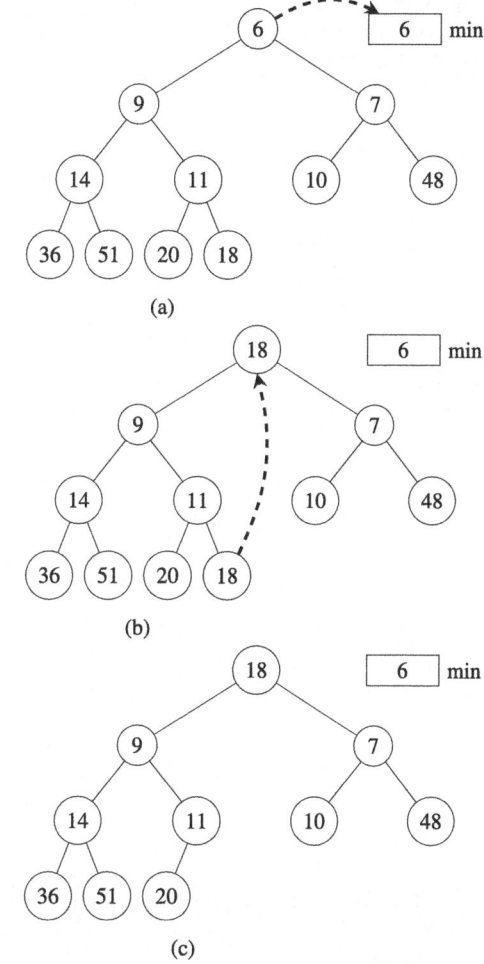

In PYTHON this is not a problem because arrays have variable size (they actually are implemented as dynamic lists), but in other languages like C or JAVA, an array such as Content is a static structure, in particular its size is fixed at the beginning, so it cannot take account of size variations due to insertions and deletions.

Therefore in principle you should use linked lists to represent the array in one of those languages, but if you absolutely want to use arrays, a basic solution is to define a class with two attributes:

- Content, which is an array of (constant) size, say, $nMax$.
- Size, which is an integer variable and is always equal to the current size of the heap.

Fig. 11.19 Removal of the minimum in a heap, phase 2, downward percolation

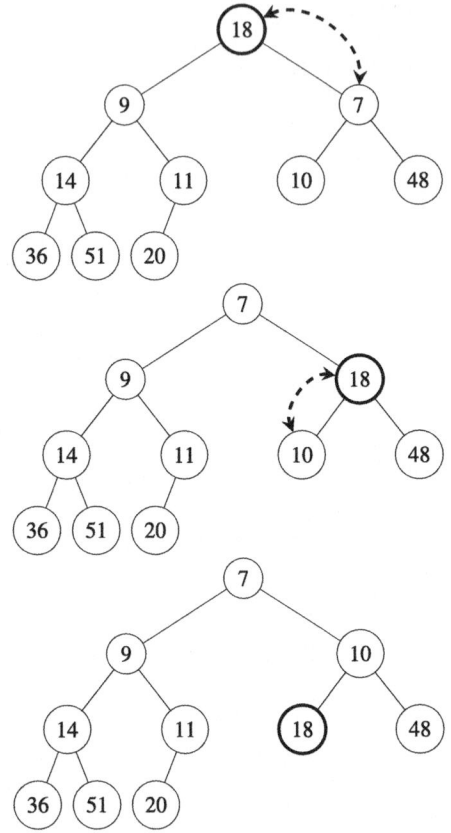

Algorithm 11.12: Heap class structure

1 Heap **class**
2   self.Content: **array of** nMax elements;
3   self.Size: **integer**;

With an object of this class we can represent any heap of size less than or equal to $nMax$ and obviously that implies that you have to manage the issue of potential overflow. In such a case, when the array is totally full, the size of the heap is generally doubled by copying the array in the first half of another array twice its size.

The Size attribute is initialised to 0 when an empty heap is created and it is updated by an increment at each addition (insertion) and by a decrement at each removal of the minimum element. If we work with arrays where the first cell is numbered by 0, the value of the attribute Size is the position in the array of the first unused leaf, while the cell T.Size - 1 of the array contains the last element currently in the heap (in the deepest, rightmost leaf).

11.5 Heaps and Priority Queues

On the right of the cell Size - 1 we might still have values but they are only the "traces" left by elements that were stored in these nodes when the heap was larger, but that by now have been either deleted in the current heap, or moved to other upper nodes. Only the Size attribute is valid for determining which cells of the table correspond to the nodes of the heap.

Therefore if T is a heap:

- T.Content designates an array (in which we find the content of the nodes),
- T.Size designates its size and therefore,
- T.Content[0] denotes the item at the root of the heap;
- T.Content[T.Size-1] designates the item in the last leaf, *i.e.* the deepest and rightmost leaf.

11.5.5 Insertion in a Heap

We are ready to write the algorithm for inserting an x element in a heap T. The version provided is for the implementation of a heap as an object of the class of the previous subsection. We leave as exercice the adaptation to PYTHON, where you do not need to keep track of the actual size of the heap and you can uses lists and their method such as append and delete. We use the function Swap(A, i, j) that swaps the values in position i and j of an array A.

Algorithm 11.13: Insert in a heap

```
1  InsertHeap (T: heap; x: element)
2     posx: integer              // to track the position of x
3
4     if (T.Size == nMax) then resize the heap first
5     T.Size = T.Size+1          // we make a new place,
6     T.Content[T.Size-1] = x    // we place x there
7     posx = T.size-1
8     // while the parent contains a larger element, we swap
9     while (posx>0) and (x<T.Content[posx/2]) // upward percolation
10        Swap(T.Content, posx, posx/2)
11       posx = posx/2
```

We have already noticed that the loop while runs at most h times where h is the height of the tree. At each iteration it executes operations in $\Theta(1)$. So the complexity of the algorithm is $O(h) = O(\log n)$.

11.5.6 MinRemoval in a Heap

For the removal of the minimum one must be a little more careful. In fact, the **downward percolation** is a slightly more delicate operation than the upward one.

For insertion (**upward percolation**), at each step of the loop we just need to compare an element with its parent, for deletion (downward percolation) we first need to determine which of the two children contains the minimal value, then, if this minimum is smaller than the value x, we must swap x with the contents of this child.

However, it must be taken into account that not all nodes have two children. Leaves for example have none but there may also be a node (and only one) with only one child (see for example the node that contains the value 18 in the example heap of size 10). This case will therefore have to be treated separately.

A node bearing the number i has two children if its right child exists, that is to say that $2i + 2$ is smaller than $T.Size$. The while loop must then check this condition, and then determine the child that contains the minimum value and exchange it with x if it is less than x. We will therefore exit the loop in two cases:

- either because x is already in the right place. In this case there is nothing more to do.
- or because the node containing x does not have two children.
  This second case can be further distinguished into two sub-cases:
  – either x is in a leaf, in which case x cannot go any further down and therefore there is nothing to do in this case either.
  – or x is in a node with only one child (the left one, and this child will be a leaf). In this case, it is only necessary to check if this child contains a value smaller than x and in this case swap them.

To resume, at the exit of the loop while, you just have to check if a left child exists (the condition is $2i + 1 < T.Size$) and if it contains a value smaller than x, we make a last exchange. This gives the following algorithm:

Algorithm 11.14: Removal of the minimum in a heap

```
1  MinRemovalHeap (T: heap): element
2      x, left, right: element
3
4      if (T.Size == 0) then
5          return (null)
6      else
7          // Phase 1
8          min = T.Content[0];      // we store in min
9          T.Content[0] = T.Content[T.size-1]; // root <= last leaf
10         T.Size = T.Size-1;       // we free up a place at the end
11         // Phase 2 (downward percolation)
12         posx = 0;
13         while (2*posx+2 < T.size)       // while a right child exists
14             x = T.Content[posx];
15             left = T.Content[2*posx+1];
16             right = T.Content[2*posx+2];
17             if ((left > x) and (right > x))  // if x greater than both
18                 return(min);               // x is in its place, end
```

11.5 Heaps and Priority Queues

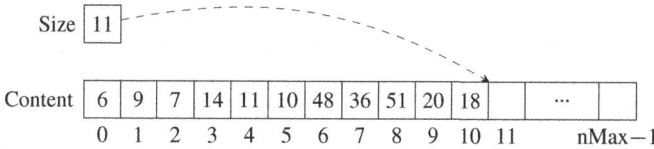

Fig. 11.20 A heap in an array

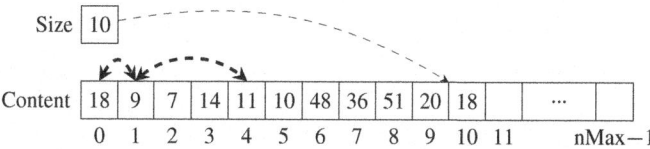

Fig. 11.21 A heap in an array

```
19      else
20        if (left < right)           // which of the two children
21          smallerchild= 2*posx +1   // contains the min
22        else
23          smallerchild= 2*posx + 2
24        Swap (T.Content, posx, smallerchild)
25        posx = smallerchild         // x is now in that position
26      // check if a single left child with smaller content exists
27      if ((2*posx+1<T.size) and (T.Content[posx]>T.Content[2*posx+1]))
28        Swap (T, posx, 2*posx+1)
29      return(min);
```

The complexity analysis is the same as for Insert, so in $\Theta(\log n)$.

11.5.6.1 An Example of MinRemoval on the Array Content

Here is a heap with 11 nodes before a call to MinRemoval. The arrow is only symbolic, Size is not a pointer but a simple integer, however it acts a bit like a pointer here (Figs. 11.20, 11.21, and 11.22).

MinRemoval starts to work. The 6 is overwritten by the value 18 found in the last node, the size is decremented (see the following figure).

We note that the old copy of 18 is still in position 10, but for the algorithms it no longer exists, because we will never reference a cell beyond the cell T.Size-1.

The thick arrows indicate the swaps that will make 18 percolate down to its final place.

Here is the same heap at the end of MinRemoval. It has now 10 elements (nodes). The old 18 is still in the Content array, but formally it is no longer in the heap. In particular, it will be overwritten when this cell will be used for an insertion (T.Size will again be incremented again to 11 at this time).

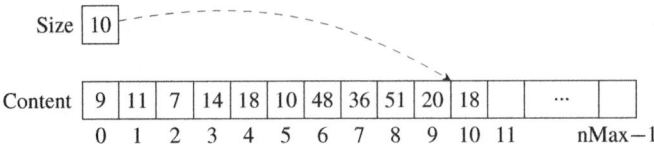

Fig. 11.22 A heap in an array

Exercise 11.13
Draw all the heaps containing the values {1, 2, 3, 4} and then all those containing the values {1, 2, 3, 4, 5}.

Exercise 11.14
Where can we find the second smallest element in the heap? And the third smallest?

Exercise 11.15
Normally, the only removal allowed in a heap is the removal of the minimum at the root. However, in some cases, we need to remove the element in the node number i (while obtaining a new heap after this deletion).
Show how to modify the algorithm MinRemoval(T) to obtain an algorithm
$$\text{Remove(T: heap; i: integer)}$$
which, given a heap T and an integer $i < T.Size$, deletes the item T.Content[i] ensuring that T is still a heap after deletion.

Exercise 11.16
Say what the following algorithm does. Give its complexities in time and space.

Algorithm 11.15: Mystery algorithm

```
1   Mystery (A: array of n  elements)
2       i: integer
3       T: heap
4
5       for i from 0 to n-1 do
6           InsertHeap(T, A[i])
7       for i from 0 to n-1 do
8           A[i] = MinRemovalHeap(T)
```

11.6 Binary Search Trees (BST)

The most common operations performed on a set of data are: inserting a new item, deleting an item, and searching for an item in the set to establish if it is part of it or not. It therefore makes sense to look for ways to represent the data so that these operations can be performed quickly.

As for the priority queues, we note that a linear data structure such as an array would not be suitable:

11.6 Binary Search Trees (BST)

- either we keep this array sorted, this would facilitate the search since it could be done by dichotomy (in $O(\log n)$), but at each new insertion the table would have to be re-ordered, which would not cost less that $O(n)$;
- or we keep this array in disorder, but then the search would cost no less than $O(n)$.

In both cases, the deletions require left shifts of the elements following the deleted element, which may also take $O(n)$ time in the worst case. In the end, there would always be at least one (or even two) of the three operations which would require linear time $O(n)$.

We will see that with **Binary Search Trees** (BST) we can execute these three operations in $O(h)$ (where h is the height of the tree) in the worst case. Unfortunately, the height of an BST is not bounded by $O(\log n)$ like in heaps. We can just say that $h \in O(n)$ (where n is the size of the tree), because obviously $h < n$.

We will see later (Sect. 11.7) that it is possible to define "balanced" BSTs having the additional property that $h \in \log n$.

11.6.1 BST Definition

Definition 11.2

A binary tree T is a BST if it satisfies the following property:
For any node N of T, the nodes of the left subtree of N contain smaller values than the one contained in N, the nodes of the right subtree of N contain larger values than the one contained in N.

Obviously, the objects stored in the nodes of the tree may be more complex than simple numerical values, as long as the ordering property of BST is true for a specific key of such objects (Fig. 11.23).

Fig. 11.23 Binary search tree property

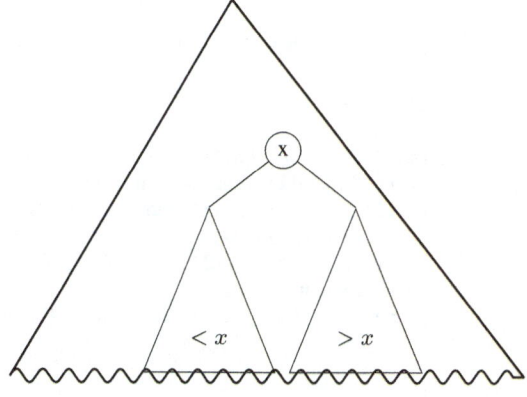

▶ The property must be true for all the nodes of the two *subtrees* and not just for the two children. This is a common mistake. The following tree is *not* a BST, although for all node N, the left child of N contains a smaller value and the left child a larger value than the one contained in N, but in a BST the value 8 cannot be in the left subtree of a node containing 4.

Here are two examples of BST, the second is a thread-like (degenerate) tree with height $h = n - 1 \in \Theta(n)$:

If a BST contains repeated values, an (arbitrary) convention must be made about the side (right or left) where these duplicates must be placed. Our convention will be to put them in the right subtree. The property defining the BSTs becomes:

For any node N of T, the nodes of the left subtree of N contain values smaller than the one contained in N while the nodes of the right subtree of N contain values larger than *or equal to* the one contained in N.

Exercise 11.17
Where can we find the smallest element of a BST? And the maximum?
Write an iterative algorithm in $O(h)$ which returns the address of the node where the minimum value contained in a (non-empty) BST is found.
Write a recursive algorithm in $O(h)$ that does the same thing.
Justify that the complexity of your algorithms is in $O(h)$.

11.6.2 Testing That a Binary Tree Is a BST

To test whether a tree is a BST using the definition can be quite heavy. For every node N of the tree, you need to compute the maximum $maxl$ of its left subtree and the minimum $minR$ of its right subtree and then verify that $maxl < N.val \leq minR$). The computation of the maximum of a minimum in a BST can be done in $O(h)$, where h is the height of the tree (see Exercise 11.17). Such an algorithm would make n calls (one for each node) and each call would cost $O(h)$, so the total cost would be $O(hn)$, which is $O(n \log n)$ at the best.

▶ Note that the following algorithm in $O(n)$ would be *wrong*:

Algorithm 11.16: (wrong) Test if a tree is a BST

```
1  IsBST (T: tree);boolean
2    if (T==null) then return (true)
3    if (T.left != null) and  (T.left.val >= T.val) then
4      return (false)
5    if (T.right != null) and  (T.right.val < T.val) then
6      return (false)
7    return(IsBST(T.left) and IsBST(T.right))
```

11.6 Binary Search Trees (BST)

Fig. 11.24 Not a BST

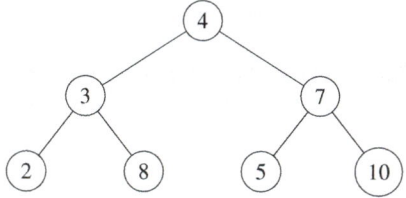

This algorithm simply tests that each node contains a value larger than the value in its left child (if it exists) and smaller than (or equal to) the value in its right child and finally it tests that both subtrees of each node are BST. However, this is not sufficient as we have pointed out in a previous alert. For instance this algorithms would return `true` for the tree in Fig. 11.24, while we have already noted that this tree is not a BST.

However, an algorithm testing if a tree is a BST and having complexity in $O(n)$ exists and it is based on the following proposition.

> **Proposition 11.1**
> *A binary tree is a BST if and only if the in-order traversal of the tree produces a non-decreasing sequence.*

This proposition can be easily proved by induction (on the size of the tree).

The list produced by the in-order traversal can be obtained in $O(n)$ (Exercise 11.4). On the other hand, the verification that a list is non-decreasing can also be performed in $O(n)$, we can therefore deduce the following algorithm in $O(n)$ that tests whether a binary tree is a BST.

Algorithm 11.17: Test if a tree is a BST

```
1  IsBST (T: tree): boolean
2      L: list
3
4      if (T==null) then return (true)
5      L=TreeToList(T)
6      for i from 0 to length(L)-2 do
7          if L[i]>L[i+1] then return (false)
8      return (true)
```

Exercise 11.18
By adapting the in-order traversal algorithm, give a purely recursive algorithm that checks whether a binary tree is a BST.

Hint : return a couple made of a list and a boolean.

Exercise 11.19 (Sometimes More Is Less)
Let T be a binary tree implemented by pointers. Each node is therefore an object with an attribute .val where we store an element and .left and .right. containing the reference of the left child and the right child, respectively.

1. Write a recursive algorithm that returns true if T is a BST and false otherwise and that is not based on the in-order traversal as presented in this section. You can rather use the functions MinBST and MaxBST returning the min and the max of a BST respectively.
2. Evaluate the complexity of your algorithm.
3. Write a recursive algorithm in $O(n)$ that returns a triplet (bst, max, min) where

   - bst is a boolean having the value true if T is a BST and false otherwise;
   - max is the maximum value contained in the tree and
   - min is the minimum value contained in the tree.

4. Evaluate the complexity of the second algorithm.

Exercise 11.20 (Another Way)
Write a recursive algorithm that returns true if T is a BST and false otherwise and that uses the functions

- IsBST(T: BST) that returns true if T is a BST and false otherwise;
- IsBSTmin(T: BST; x: element) that returns true if T is a BST containing values all larger than x and false otherwise;
- IsBSTmax(T: BST; x: element) that returns true if T is a BST containing values all smaller than x and false otherwise;
- IsBSTbound(T: BST; x, y : element) that returns true if T is a BST containing values all larger than x and smaller than y and false otherwise;

Evaluate the complexity in time and space of the algorithm.

11.6.3 Search in a BST

Let T be a BST and x an element. The search algorithm for x in T should return:

- the address of the node containing x, if x is present in the tree T;
- null, if x is not present in the tree T.

The BST property allows searching recursively using the dichotomy method. Indeed, apart from the case where T is empty (in which the algorithm returns the value null), it suffices to compare x with the value stored at the root (T.val):

- if $T.val = x$ the address to return is the address of the root (so T itself);
- if $T.val > x$, it is useless to search for x in the right subtree, it suffices to continue the search only in the left subtree;

11.6 Binary Search Trees (BST)

- and conversely, if $T.val < x$, it is useless to search for x in the left subtree, it suffices to continue the search only in the right subtree.

We simply deduce the following recursive algorithm:

Algorithm 11.18: Search in a BST

```
1  SearchBST (T: BST, x:element): node
2      if (T == null ) or (T.val == x) then
3          return (T)
4      else
5          if (x < T.val) then
6              return (SearchBST(T.left, x))
7          else
8              return (SearchBST(T.right, x))
```

The returned object is indicated as a node type because we return the (address of the) node containing x.

What is the time complexity of this algorithm?

Notice that unlike other algorithms such as Size or Height (seen in Sect. 11.4), for each node N the algorithm performs *at most one* recursive call on either one of its two children, and not on both.

Moreover, with each recursive call, we move down one level deeper in the tree because we make a call on one of the two subtrees. So SearchBST performs at most one recursive call for each depth level. Since each recursive call only performs comparisons or function calls, the total cost of each call remains in $O(1)$.

There will be at most h calls, so we can conclude that the algorithm SearchBST is in $O(h)$.

11.6.4 Insertion in a BST

Let T be a BST and x a new element that we want to insert into T.

We note that there is only one place (only one node, precisely a leaf) where x can be inserted, and this place is only determined by the value of x.

For instance, the value $x = 16$ could be inserted in the BST on the left of Fig. 11.25 only as the left child of the node containing 18.

To preserve the BST property during the insertion of x in a non-empty BST T, it will be necessary to compare x with $T.val$. If x is smaller than $T.val$ then x must be inserted into the left subtree, otherwise it must be inserted into the right subtree.

When we find an empty place (and this may happen immediately if the given tree is empty) we create a new node where we place the value x. This node is a leaf, therefore both its children are null. If we are including a parent attribute, we can handle that information by staying "a step behind" (if the tree is not empty we do the creation of the new node when we have landed on its parent). We do the creation of a new node with a call to the constructor of the Node class, like new(Node(x, null, null, p)),[3] which will create a new node containing x in the val field, with left and right equal to null, and p in the parent field.

Algorithm 11.19: Insertion in a BST

```
1  InsertionBST (T: BST, x: element):
2    if (T == null) then
3      T = new(Node(x, null, null, null));
4    else
5      if (x < T.val) then
6        if (T.left == null) then
7          T.left = new(Node(x, null, null, T));
8        else
9          InsertionBST(T.left, x)
10     else
11       if (T.right == null) then
12         T.right = new(Node(x, null, null, T));
13       else
14         InsertionBST(T.right, x)
```

The complexity analysis is the same as for SearchBST. The algorithm makes at most one call that costs $O(1)$ for each level of the tree. The complexity is therefore in $O(h)$.

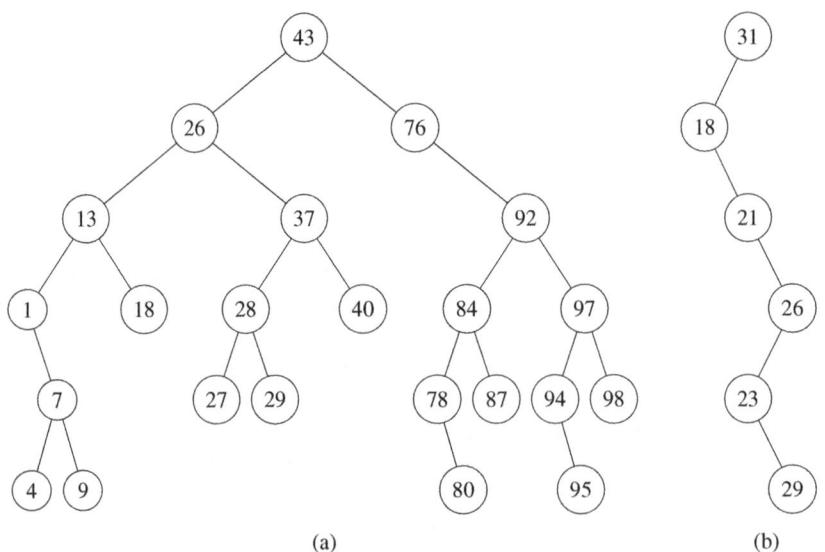

Fig. 11.25 Two BSTs. (a) A BST. (b) A degenerated BST

---

[3] In many languages new is the name of the function called to create a new object.

11.6 Binary Search Trees (BST)

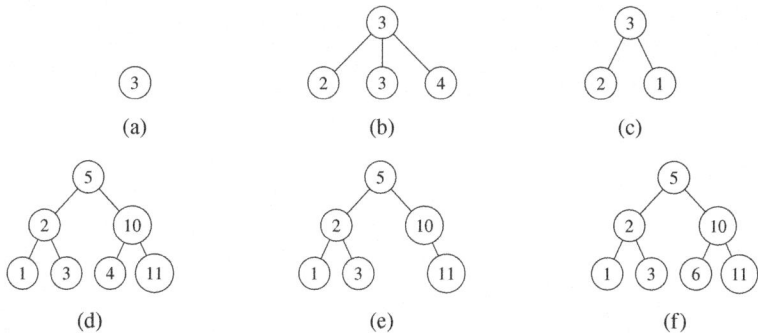

Fig. 11.26 Which ones are BSTs?

Exercise 11.21
Which BST we get if we insert in an initially empty BST the values 1, 2, 3, 4, 5, 6, 7, 8, 9 (in that order)? What if we insert 1, 2, 9, 3, 8, 7, 6, 4, 5 (in that order)?

Exercise 11.22
How many different shapes of threadlike BST of size n are there?

Exercise 11.23 (Binary Search Trees)

1. Among the trees in Fig. 11.26, which ones are Binary Search Trees (BSTs)? Justify.
2. Draw BSTs of all possible heights for the set of keys {1, 2, 3, 4, 5, 6, 7}.
3. How many BSTs of a given shape are there for a fixed set of n values?
4. Starting with an empty tree, insert the nodes with labels 5, 9, 4, 2, 7, 1, 6, 3, and 8 using the insertion algorithm for a BST.

11.6.5 Deletion in a BST

The deletion is the most complicated of the three basic algorithms for BSTs but it has the same complexity as search and insertion.

First of all it will be necessary to locate x in the (nonempty) tree T.[4] This is done by comparing x to the value at the root and making the appropriate recursive call on the left or on the right subtree. If one of these subtree is found empty, then x was not present in the tree and the algorithm does nothing.

The base (and the main) case of the recursion occurs when you land on the node where x is stored. Three cases must be distinguished:

1. x is in a leaf;

---

[4] We assume in this section that T is nonempty. You can otherwise include in the deletion algorithm an initial condition if (T != null).

Fig. 11.27 BST for exemples of deletions

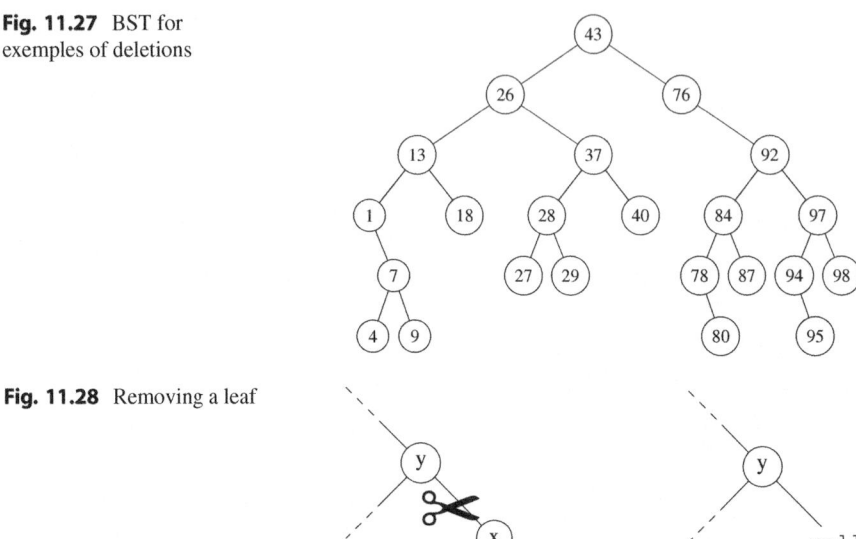

Fig. 11.28 Removing a leaf

2. x is in a node with only one child;
3. x is in a node with two children.

11.6.5.1 The Element x Is in a Leaf

It is the simplest case. If N is the leaf that contains x, to delete N it suffices to simply "cut" the link from the parent of N to N and free the memory space allocated to this leaf.[5] The resulting tree obviously remains a BST. To do this, it will first be necessary to check whether N is the left child or the right child of its parent, to determine which of the two links of its parent must be cut (set equal to null). There is a special case when the tree T contains only on node containing x, in this case T becomes the empty tree.

For example, if we look at the BST on the Fig. 11.27, the value 18 can be removed from the BST simply by modifying the value of the left attribute of the node which contains 13 (the parent of the node that contains 18).

11.6.5.2 The Element x Is in a Node N with Only One Child

This case is also relatively simple. All you have to do is to "lift-up" the only subtree of N of one level. This can be done by coping in N the values of the attributes of its only child. Then, if this only clild had children, we must update their parent attribute to reflect that now their parent, is now N (Fig. 11.28).

---

[5] In most languages, all memory dynamically allocated by a call of the function new should be explicitly freed when it is no longer used, we will not insist on this aspect, most languages have a function free doing just that.

11.6 Binary Search Trees (BST)

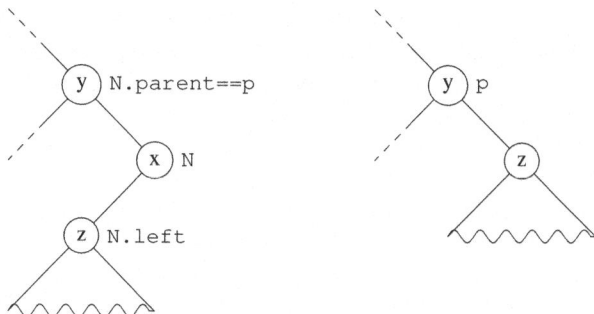

Fig. 11.29 Removing a node with one child

Note that this operation preserves the property of the BSTs. The only place where the tree has been modified is for the right subtree of $N.parent$. However, the new right subtree of $N.parent$ contains larger values than $N.parent.val$, since these elements were already in the right subtree of $N.parent$ before the deletion of x.

In the figure we illustrated the case where only the right subtree exists. A symmetric case of this is the deletion of 1 in the BST of Fig. 11.27. The right subtree of the node N containing 1 becomes the left subtree of its parent, the node containing 13. This is done by copying in the node N the attributes `val`, `left` and `right` of the node that contains 7. Furthermore the attribute `parent` of the nodes containing 4 and 9, as their parent is now the node N (the node that contained 1 before its deletion). Note that the node that used to contain the only child of N (the node that contained 7 before the deletion of 1 in our exemple) becomes redundant and the memory allocated to it should be freed up in programming langages that require that (Fig. 11.29).

11.6.5.3 The Element x Is in a Node with Two Children

This is the most complicated case. Suppose for example that we want to remove the value 92 from the BST of Fig. 11.27. The value 92 must be eliminated, but the node containing it must be preserved, otherwise the tree will be disconnected. The value contained in this node must therefore be replaced with some other value v already in the BST.

After that, the node containing the old copy of the value v that replaces x must be eliminated, so as not to create a false duplicate. One might get the impression that by doing so one has only shifted the problem from the deletion of x to the deletion of v, but we will see that deleting the node containing the old copy of v is always very simple.

Note that if we want to preserve the property of the BSTs, we cannot replace 92 with just any value. In fact, we realise that only two values are the possible candidates for this substitution : 87 and 94. What is special about these two values? They are the immediate predecessor and the immediate successor of 92 in the BST and therefore they are the only values which, if placed in the node N which contains

92, guarantee that everything in the left subtree of N remains smaller (or equal) than $N.val$ and everything in the right subtree of N remains larger than $N.val$.

The two candidates are respectively the maximum of the left subtree of N and the minimum of the right subtree of N.

The algorithm will therefore adopt one of these two strategies to choose which of these two values should replace the one to be deleted. In the following we will make the convention that we always choose the minimum of the right subtree, although a random choice of one of the two strategies every time it is needed may lead to more balanced trees.

To delete an element in a node N having two children, the algorithm will therefore have to:

- compute the value $minR$, minimum of the right subtree of N,
- replace N.val with $minR$ and then
- delete the value $minR$ from the right subtree of N.

We only need a function that computes the value of the minimum of a BST, we call this function on N.right, we copy the returned value $minR$ into N.val and then we make a call to DeletionBST(N.right, minR) in order to delete the old copy of $minR$ from N.right.

With the call DeletionBST(N.right, minR) we did not just shift the problem of deletion to another value. The deletion of the value $minR$ is easy to do because the node containing the minimum of a BST has no left child. If this node had a left child, this left child would contain a smaller value, contradicting the fact that the node contains the minimum. This node therefore has 0 or 1 child, the deletion of the value it contains falls into one of the two "easy" cases, it can therefore be carried out as done in those cases without any further function calls.

From these considerations we can write the following algorithm. As usual, we have tried to write the algorithm in a form that can be easily translated in the most commonly used languages (such as PYTHON, C of JAVA). Some adjustments may be needed according to the language you choose. In languages that require it you should include the **free** instructions (see the warning at the end of this paragraph), in PYTHON you might have to rewrite the procedure as a function that returns the tree obtained from the deletion of x from T (as currently written, the algorithm modifies the tree itself and does not return anything).

▶ In some programming languages, any dynamically allocated memory (such as the memory allocated for nodes when you call the function **new**) must be explicitly freed when it is no longer in use, otherwise that memory would remain locked and unusable in the future. These languages include a function normally called **free** that receives a parameter corresponding to a memory address (a pointer) and that frees up the memory located at that address. In these languages, it will

11.6 Binary Search Trees (BST)

therefore be necessary to explicitly ask for a `free` before terminating the algorithm in the "leaf" and "node with a single child" cases.

Algorithm 11.20: Deletion in a BST

```
1   DeletionBST (T: BST, x: element)
2     if (x == T.val) then //if we have found x
3       if (T.left == null) and (T.right == null) then //leaf
4         if (T.parent == null) then T = null //T had only one node
5         else if (T.parent.left = T) then T.parent.left = null
6              else T.parent.right = null
7              free(T) //for languages that require it
8       else
9         if !((T.left != null) and (T.right != null)) then //only one▷
             ▷ child
10          if (T.left != null) then onlychild = T.left
11          else onlychild = T.right
12          T.val = onlychild.val
13          T.left = onlychild.left
14          T.right = onlychild.right
15          if (onlychild.left != null) then
16             onlychild.left.parent = T
17          if (onlychild.right != null) then
18             onlychild.right.parent = T
19          free(onlychild) //for languages that require it
20        else //two children
21            T.val = MinValBST(T.right)
22            DeletionBST(T.right, T.val)
23    else //we look for x recursively
24      if (x < T.val) then
25        if (T.left != null) then
26          DeletionBST(T.left,x)
27      else
28        if (T.right != null) then
29          DeletionBST(T.right,x)
```

Algorithm 11.21: Compute the minimum value in a BST

```
1   MinValBST(T: BST): element
2     p: node
3     p = T
4     while (p.left != null) do
5        p = p.left
6     return(p.val)
```

11.6.5.4 Analysis of the Complexity of `DeletionBST`

In the two "easy" cases, in addition to the initial recursive calls made to locate x and having a cost $O(h)$, you just have to do some tests and modify a few links, which costs $O(1)$, so the total cost of deletion in these two cases is $O(h)$.

In the third case, in addition to the $O(h)$ for the recursive calls, you have to add the cost to compute the minimum of the right subtree (complexity in $O(h)$) and then the cost of the call to delete the minimum from the right subtree (complexity in $O(h)$), so the total complexity in the third case remains in $O(h)$.

Therefore `DeletionBST` is always in $O(h)$.

We note that it is possible to define a function `DeletionMinBST` that deletes the minimum of a BST and returns its value performing only one loop in $O(h)$. This function can be called instead of `ValMinBST` in the case of a node having two children, this would allow to economise $O(h)$ elementary operations with respect to the proposed solution that first computes the minimum and then deletes it.

Exercise 11.24
Write a version of `DeletionBST` that uses the function `DeletionMinBST` described at the end of the previous section. The case in which the minimum of the right subtree is in its root may have to be treated as special.

Exercise 11.25
Write a sorting algorithm that sorts an array of size t in time $O(t \log t)$ using a BST. There are two algorithms that satisfy these conditions but adopt two totally different strategies, try to find both.

11.7 AVL Trees

We have seen that with BSTs we can implement the three operations of insertion, deletion and search in $O(h)$ (where h is the height of the tree) in the worst case. Unfortunately, the height of an BST is not in $O(\log n)$ (where n is the size of the tree) like for heaps. We can just say that $h \in O(n)$, since obviously $h < n$.

The object of this section will be to define "balanced" BSTs having the property that $h \in O(\log n)$.

Ideally, we would like to work with BSTs that are as balanced as possible, maybe shaped like heaps, which would ensure that the nodes are all as close as possible to the root. This would minimise the height and ensure that it is in $O(\log n)$.

Unfortunately, manipulating BSTs that also satisfy the heap shape property is not easy. We will have to make a compromise by working with BSTs that will be sufficiently balanced to guarantee the property $h \in O(\log n)$.

11.7.1 Definition and Properties

Definition 11.3

If N is a node of a binary tree T, we call **balance factor** of N the quantity $\delta(N)$ defined as the difference between the height of the left subtree of N and the height of the right subtree of N:

$$\delta(N) = Height(N.left) - Height(N.right).$$

11.7 AVL Trees

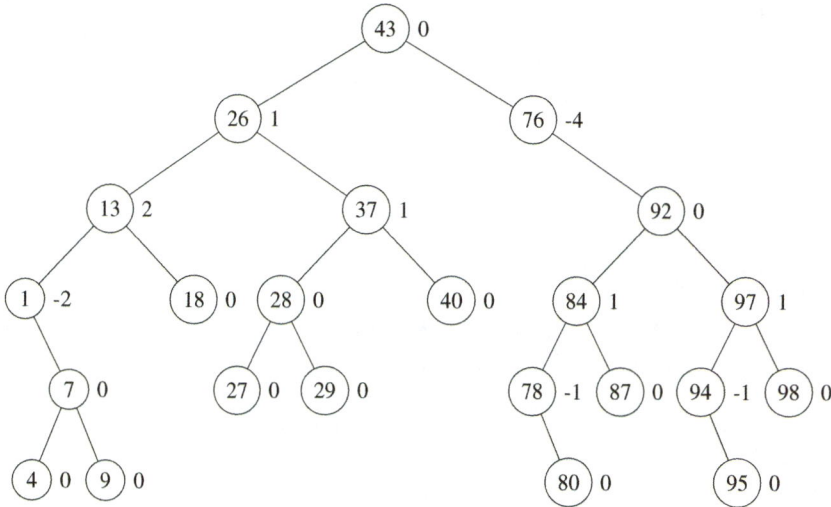

Fig. 11.30 A BST with its balance factors

▶ The balance factor is well defined as the difference in the *heights* of the two sub-trees and *not* as the difference of the balance factors of the two children (this is a common error). In the calculations, you should not forget that the height of the singleton tree (consisting only of the root) is 0 and that the height of the empty tree is -1.

The following figure shows the BST already used in previous sections indicating the balance factor of each node (Fig. 11.30).

For example, the balance factor of the node containing 76 is equal to -4 because its (empty) left subtree has height -1 and its right subtree has height 3, so we have $\delta = (-1) - (3) = -4$.

Take note that:

- A balance factor $\delta(N) = 0$ means that the two subtrees of N have the same height.
- A balance factor $\delta(N) = k > 0$ means that the left subtree of N is k levels higher than its right subtree.
- A balance factor $\delta(N) = k < 0$ means that the right subtree of N is k levels higher than its left subtree.

Exercise 11.26
Compute the balance factor of the nodes of the thread-like BST presented in Fig. 11.25b.

Fig. 11.31 Not an AVL

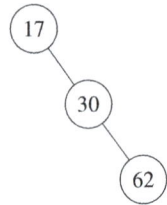

Definition 11.4

A **binary search tree** is said to be an **AVL** tree or simply an AVL[6] if the balance factor of each node has an absolute value smaller than or equal to 1:

$$|\delta(N)| \leq 1 \text{ for all node } N.$$

So the only allowed values for the balance factor in an AVL are: $-1, 0, 1$. As a result, the BST in the previous figure is not an AVL tree.

Even though the AVLs are not perfectly balanced, it is understandable that the condition that defines them implies a quite good amount of balancing on these trees. In any case, the balance condition of the AVLs is sufficient for our purposes, as stated in the following theorem, which will be given without the proof.

Theorem 11.1
If T is an AVL then : $Height(T) \in O(\log(Size(T)))$.

If we use an AVL instead of a simple BST, the operations of search, insertion and deletion will therefore cost a time in $O(\log n)$, if n is the size of the tree (Fig. 11.31).

The issue now is that insertions and deletions (as programmed for BSTs) can break the condition on balance factors that defines AVLs. For example if we insert 17, 30 and 62 in an initially empty BST, the tree obtained will not be an AVL (the balance factor of the root is -2).

We will see that each time an insertion or a deletion breaks the AVL property (that is, as soon as at least one node has a balance factor equal to 2 or -2), it is possible to rebalance the tree with operations that transform the tree while preserving the property of the BSTs and restoring the property on the balance factors.

These operations are called **rotations** and they are executed in constant time (in $\Theta(1)$), so they can be performed (if necessary) after each insertion or deletion operation with negligible cost relative to the cost of the operation itself (which is in $O(\log n)$).

---

[6] The name "AVL tree" comes from the names of the two inventors, Adelson-Velsky and Landis (see [2]). We will use the shortcut "AVL" instead of "AVL tree".

11.7 AVL Trees

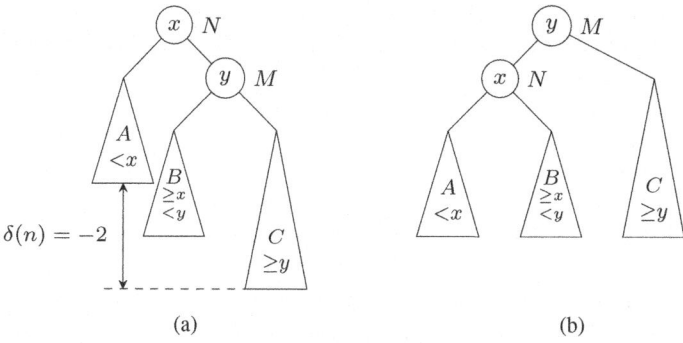

Fig. 11.32 Left rotation in an AVL. (**a**) Before. (**b**) After

Exercise 11.27

1. Is the subtree of the BST in Fig. 11.27 whose root is the node containing 92 an AVL?
2. If we insert the value 82 in this tree with `InsertionBST`, is the resulting tree an AVL?
3. Which nodes had their imbalance modified following the insertion of 82?
4. In general which nodes can have their imbalance modified following the insertion of a new value?

Exercise 11.28
Find a recursive algorithm in $O(n)$ that checks if a Binary Search Tree (BST) (without height or balance factor fields on the nodes; for each node, we only know its value and its children) is an AVL tree.

11.7.2 Rotations

The two operations `LeftRotation` and `RightRotation` (or simply LR and RR) allow to rebalance the tree when necessary. They are symmetrical to each other so we will only describe the left rotation.

If at some point the right subtree of a node becomes too high ($\delta(N) = -2$) you have to apply a *left rotation* around the node N. This operation is illustrated in the Fig. 11.32

If M denotes the right child of N, this operation can be broken down as follows:

- it flips the edge (N, M) so that M becomes the parent of N and N the left child of M;
- in its descent, N brings down its left subtree A;
- in its ascent, M brings up its right subtree C;
- B, the left subtree of M, is detached from M and is attached to N as its right subtree.

Let us verify that this operation preserves the BST property (if a node contains a value x then its left subtree contains only values smaller than x and its right subtree only values larger than x).

The only nodes in the tree whose left and right subtrees have been modified by the rotation are N and M, so we just need to check that the property is still preserved for these two nodes.

- The left subtree of N has not changed so it contains elements smaller than the element x stored in N.
- The elements in B, new right subtree of N, were in the right subtree of N before the rotation, so they contain elements larger than the element x stored in N.
- The new left subtree of M contains:
  - the element x which is certainly smaller than the element y contained in M, because M was in the right subtree of N before the rotation;
  - the elements of A, which are smaller than x and therefore smaller than y, because they were in the left subtree of N before the rotation;
  - the elements of B, which were already in the left subtree of m and are therefore smaller than y.
- The right subtree of M has not changed, so it contains elements larger than the item y contained in M.

In practice, it must be taken into account that the node N has in principle a parent (unless it is the root of the tree) and therefore modifications of attributes of the parent of N must be made too. For example if N is the right (resp. left) child of its parent, then after the rotation this right (resp. left) child must become M.

We will write a rotation algorithm in the case where the implementation of the tree provides that each node also has an attribute .parent containing the reference of the parent.

Algorithm 11.22: Rotation in an AVL

```
1   LR (T: BST; N: node):
2       P, M, B : node
3
4       P = N.parent
5       M = N.right
6       if (P!=null) then
7           if (N == P.left) then
8               P.left = M
9           else
10              P.right = M
11      else
12          T=M
13
14      B = M.left
15      N.right = B
16      N.parent = M
17      M.left = N
```

11.7 AVL Trees

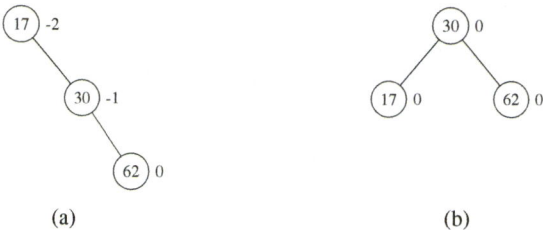

Fig. 11.33 A left rotation. (**a**) Before rotation. (**b**) After rotation at node 17

Fig. 11.34 A non sufficient left rotation. (**a**) Before rotation. (**b**) Wrong AVL after simple left rotation at node 17

```
18      M.parent = P
19      B.parent = N
```

As you can see, a rotation only performs some comparisons and assignments, therefore its complexity is in $\Theta(1)$.

If you are not carrying a parent attribute You can check that a left rotation around the root is enough to rebalance the BST obtained by inserting 17, 30 and 62 into an initially empty BST. In this particular case, N is the node containing 17, M the node containing 30, C the tree containinig only 62, while A and B are empty (Fig. 11.33).

However, you can check that the left rotation does not succeed in rebalancing the following tree (obtained by inserting 17, 62 and 30 in an initially empty BST) (Fig. 11.34):

Indeed we are in the presence of the only case where a (simple) left rotation is not sufficient. This happens in the case where $\delta(N) = -2$ and $\delta(N.right) = 1$. In this case, you have to perform what is called a *double left rotation* (Fig. 11.35).

Definition 11.5

A double left rotation around a node N is the sequence of a (simple) right rotation around the right child of N followed by a (simple) left rotation around N.

For example, for the tree obtained by inserting 17, 62 and 30 in an initially empty BST, we first apply a right rotation around the node containing 62, this way we will

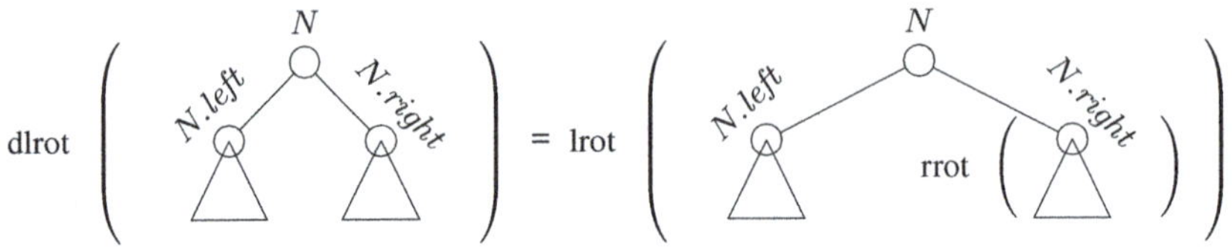

$$\text{dlrot}\left(\begin{array}{c}N\\ N.\textit{left}\quad N.\textit{right}\end{array}\right) = \text{lrot}\left(\begin{array}{c}N\\ N.\textit{left}\quad \text{rrot}\left(\begin{array}{c}N.\textit{right}\end{array}\right)\end{array}\right)$$

Fig. 11.35 A double left rotation in an AVL

obtain the tree of the previous example, and we know that a left rotation around the root will be enough to rebalance it.

The double left rotation pseudocode is immediate:

Algorithm 11.23: Double rotation in an AVL

```
1  DLR (T: BST; N: node):
2      RR(T, N.right)
3      LR(T, N)
```

▶ **Remark 11.4** There is, of course, the symmetric case of this, where $\delta(n) = 2$ and $\delta(n.left) = -1$. In this case it is necessary to perform a double right rotation. A double right rotation around a node n is the sequence of a (simple) left rotation around the left child of N followed by a (simple) right rotation around N.

11.7.3 Rebalancing

We can now easily write a function that rebalances the tree by applying the correct rotation in each case. This pseudocode assumes that we have a function `delta` returning the balance factor of a given node. We will discuss in the next section how to implement efficiently such function.

Algorithm 11.24: Rebalancing an AVL

```
1   rho(T: BST; N: node):
2       if (delta(N) == -2) then
3           if (delta(N.right) < 1) then
4               LR(T, N)
5           else
6               DLR(T, N)
7       else
8           if (delta(n) == 2) then
9               if (delta(n.left) > -1) then
10                  RR(T, N)
11              else
12                  DRR(T, N)
```

11.7 AVL Trees

So to get the InsertionAVL and DeletionAVL algorithms, we just call the rho function at the end of the algorithms InsertionBST and DeletionBST respectively. This call, made just before the end of these procedures, will rebalance the tree and ensure that the AVL property about balance factors is preserved at all times.

Note that this call to rho will be placed just at the end of the procedures and therefore it will take place after the recursive call is made on one of the two subtrees. The rebalancing is therefore done in the "bottom-up" phase of the recursion. In other words, when we call rho for the rebalancing of a node, we have already rebalanced its subtrees. This remark allows us to justify the correctness and the complexity of our algorithms.

11.7.4 Complexity and Implementation Issues

We want the complexity of the rebalancing function to be irrelevant (in constant time) so that the complexity of InsertionAVL and DeletionAVL remains in $O(h) = O(\log n)$.

The complexity of the function rho is given by the complexity of the function delta, since all the other operations are in $\Theta(1)$. If we want rho to be in constant time we must find a way to implement the function delta also in constant time.

One way would be to equip each node with an attribute .balfact that would contain the (integer) value of the node's balance factor. This way we would have access to this information in $O(1)$, since the delta function would simply be:

Algorithm 11.25: Delta

```
1  delta (N: node): integer
2      return (N.balfact)
```

However, when each insertion, each deletion and each rotation modifies the value of the balance factor of certain nodes, their attributes .balfact must then be updated. This update can be a little complicated, so we will choose another implementation that on the one hand guarantees that the cost of rho remains constant and on the other hand allows easier updates.

Instead of equipping each node N with an attribute .balfact for the balance factor, we will equip it with an attribute .h that will contain the (integer) value of the height of the sub-tree having the node N as root. We will use the definitions of height and of balance factor to do all the operations, including updates, in $O(1)$. The function delta will be simply written as :

Algorithm 11.26: Delta with height

```
1  delta (N: node): integer;
2      return (N.left.h - N.right.h); // balance factor is the difference
```

3   // of the heights of the two subtrees

We can write a version of UpdateHeight in constant time based on the definition of height and therefore that computes the height of a tree depending on to the heights of its two subtrees *without making a recursive call* but simply by consulting the .h attributes of the two children. Care must be given to managing the cases where the subtrees could be empty (null) since in this case, the reference to the attribute .h of an object does not exist and that would cause an error. If both subtrees exist, we can consult their .h, calculate their max and add 1. If exactly one of two subtrees is non-empty, N.h will be the height of the non-empty subtree plus 1.

Algorithm 11.27: Updating height in AVL

```
1  UpdateHeight (N: node): integer
2    if ((N.left==null) and (N.right==null)) then    //singleton case
3       N.h=0
4    else if (N.left==null) then                     //only right child
5       N.h = N.right.h + 1
6    else if (N.right==null) then                    //only left child
7       N.h = N.left.h + 1
8       else N.h = max(N.left.h, N.right.h) + 1      //general case
```

The update of the height will also be performed in the bottom-up phase of the recursion ; this guarantees that when we call rho (and therefore delta) on a node N, the .h attributes of its two children have already been updated and therefore contain the correct value, which makes it possible to recalculate the correct values of the balance factor and the height of N.

Since rotations modify also the height of some subtrees, some calls to UpdateHeight must be done in the procedures of the rotations. For instance, two calls need to be added at the end of LR: a call UpdateHeight(N) and a call to UpdateHeight(M), because N and M are the only nodes whose height may change after a rotation. The calls UpdateHeight(N) must be done before the call UpdateHeight(M) because N is a children of M after the rotation and therefore we need to know N.h to compute correctly M.h.

11.7.5 Insertions in AVL

We can now write easily the insertion algorithm in the AVLs, as a variation of the algorithms InsertionBST.

Algorithm 11.28: Insertion in an AVL

```
1  InsertionAVL (T: AVL, p: node, x: element):
2  InsertionBST (T: BST, x: element):
3    if (T == null) then
```

11.7 AVL Trees

```
4            T = new(Node(x, null, null, null, 0)); //note the 5th parameter
                 ▷ for the height, initialised as 0
5           else
6             if (x < T.val) then
7               if (T.left == null) then
8                 T.left = new(Node(x, null, null, T, 0));
9               else
10                InsertionAVL(T.left, x)
11            else
12              if (T.right == null) then
13                T.right = new(Node(x, null, null, T,0));
14              else
15                InsertionBST(T.right, x)
16          rho(T)                      // we rebalance in O(1)
17          UpdateHeight(T);             // we update the height in O(1)
```

We insist on the fact that the algorithm rebalances the nodes in the bottom-up phase and therefore from the deepest node (among those where there is a 2 or -2 balance factor) to the shallowest.

The complexity of this algorithm is the same as the complexity of InsertionBST since all the operations that we have added are in $\Theta(1)$.

It is interesting to note that in the case of insertion, if we rebalance first the deepest unbalanced node (which is what the algorithm does), then automatically all the nodes having a 2 or -2 balance factor and located above (closer to the root) will be rebalanced automatically too. In other words, the rho function will really have to do some work only once for each insertion. Only one rotation (simple or double) is always sufficient to rebalance the tree after an insertion.

Exercise 11.29
Here is a list of 14 items.

$$27, 62, 37, 13, 8, 21, 71, 52, 90, 40, 54, 57, 30, 15.$$

1. Build the AVL tree by inserting the values in the given order. Draw the tree after each insertion, detailing the tree modifications necessary each time.
2. Write the list given by the infix traversal of the obtained tree. What property does it have? Is this still the case for all AVLs? Is this always the case for a class of trees wider than AVLs?

11.7.6 Deletions in AVL

Like in the case of the insertion, the algorithm for the deletion in AVL's can be obtained from the algorithm DeletionBST by adding the appropriate calls to rho and UpdateHeight.

Like for insertion, you certainly will have to call rho and UpdateHeight at the end of the each call of the DeletionAVL procedure. Furthermore, more rebalancing and updates of heights may be necessary in the step when you delete the minimum

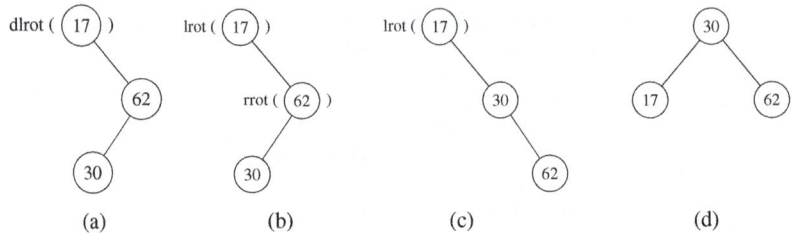

Fig. 11.36 A double left rotation in an AVL. (**a**) Before rotation. (**b**) Sub-rotations. (**c**) After right rotation. (**d**) After left rotation

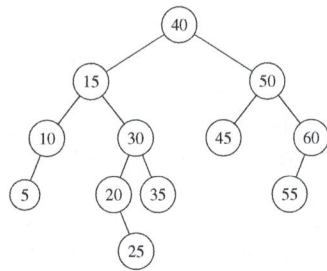

Fig. 11.37 A tree

of the right subtree and these depend on the way you have implemented this part of the algorithm. The implementation is left to the reader (Fig. 11.36).

Exercise 11.30

1. Give the AVL tree obtained by deleting 45 from the tree in Fig. 11.37.
2. Give the AVL tree obtained by deleting 30 from the tree obtained in the previous question.

11.8 Solutions to Exercises

Solution of Exercise 11.1

1.

```
LexSearch (s: string; T: tree): boolean
  p: tree
  p = T
  for i from 0 to length(s)-1 do
    if (p.links[s[i]] == null) then return(false)
    else p = p.links[s[i]];
  return (p.marked);
```

11.8 Solutions to Exercises

2.
```
LexInsertion (s: string; T: tree)
  p: tree;
  p = T;
  for i from 0 to length(s)-1 do
    if (p.links[s[i]] == null) then
        p.links[s[i]] = new(tree);
    p = p.links[s[i]];
  p.marked = true;
```

Solution of Exercise 11.8

1.
```
NumNeg(T: tree): integer
  onchildren : integer
  if (T == null) then
      return(0)
  onchildren = NumNeg(T.fg) + NumNeg(T.fd)
  if (T.val < 0) then
      return (1 + onchildren)
  return (onchildren)
```

2.
```
SumSmaller(v: integer T: tree): integer
  onchildren : integer
  if (T == null) then
      return(0)
  onchildren = SumSmaller(v, T.fg) + SumSmaller(v, T.fd)
  if (T.val < v) then
      return (T.val + onchildren)
  return (onchildren)
```

3.
```
EvenEven(v: integer T: tree): integer
  onchildren : integer
  if (T == null) then
      return(0)
  onchildren = EvenEven(T.fg) + EvenEven(T.fd)
  if (T.val%2 == 0) then
     if (T.fg != null) and  (T.fd != null) then
        if (T.fg.val%2 == 0) and (T.fd.val%2 == 0) then
           return (T.val + onchildren)
  return (onchildren)
```

4.

```
EvenDepth(T: tree): integer
   onchildren : integer
   if (T == null) then
       return(0)
   ongrandchidren = 0
   if (T.fg != null) then
       ongrandchidren += EvenDepth(T.fg.fg) + EvenDepth(T.fg.fd)
   if (T.fd != null) then
       ongrandchidren += EvenDepth(T.fd.fg) + EvenDepth(T.fd.fd)
   return (T.val+ ongrandchidren)
```

5.

```
MinPath(T: tree): integer
   onchildren : integer
   if (T == null) then
       return(0)
   onchildren = min (MinPath(T.fg), MinPath(T.fd))
   return (T.val+ ongrandchidren)
```

6.

```
Mirror(T: tree): integer
   tmp : tree
   if (T != null) then
      tmp = T.fg
      T.fg = Mirror(T.fd)
      T.fd = Mirror(tmp)
```

Solution of Exercise 11.20

```
IsBST(T: BST): boolean
   if (T == null) then return(true)
   return(IsBSTmax(T.left, T.val) and IsBSTmin(T.right, T.val))

IsBSTmax(T: BST; x: element): boolean
   if (T == null) then return(true)
   if (T.val >= x) then return(false)
   return(IsBSTmax(T.left, T.val) and IsBSTbound(T.right, T.val, x))

IsBSTmin(T: BST; x: element): boolean
   if (T == null) then return(true)
   if (T.val <= x) then return(false)
   return(IsBSTbound(T.left, x, T.val) and IsBSTmin(T.right, T.val))

IsBSTbound(T: BST; x, y: element): boolean
   if (T == null) then return(true)
   if ((T.val <= x) or (T.val >= y)) then return(false)
   return(IsBSTbound(T.left, x, T.val) and IsBSTbound(T.right, T.val, y))
```

Solution of Exercise 11.28

A hint before you look at the solution below : write a recursive function that returns:

- the value -2 if the tree is unbalanced (not an AVL).
- the height (≥ -1) of the tree if the tree is indeed an AVL.

```
IsAVL(T: tree): integer
   hl, hr: integer
   if (A == null) then return-1

   hl = IsAVL(T.left)
   hr = IsAVL(T.right)
   if (hl == -2) or (hr == -2) or (|hr - hl| > 1) then
       return(-2)
   else
       return(1 + max(hl, hr))
```

Complexity in $O(n)$ (n recursive calls, each with $O(1)$ cost).

Hashing   12

Back to the Searching Problem

Hashing is one of the fundamental techniques used in computer science to store, retrieve, and search for data. It is used in a wide range of applications, from indexing databases and file systems to implementing hash tables in programming languages. In this chapter, we will explore the basics of hashing, including its definition, implementation and analysis.

Hashing technique is used to map data of arbitrary size (e.g. arbitrarily long strings of characters) to data of fixed size (like integers). The fixed-size data is called a **hash value** or a **hash code**, and it is typically used as an index into an array or a table. The process of mapping data to hash values is called **hashing**, and the function that performs the mapping is called a **hash function**.

A hash function takes a key as input and returns a hash value as output. The hash value is typically an integer (or a bit string) that is computed based on the contents of the key. The hash function should be deterministic, meaning that it should always return the same hash value for the same key. It should also be efficient, meaning that it should be able to compute the hash value quickly.

Hashing is often used in conjunction with **hash tables**, which are data structures that allow for efficient insertion, deletion, and retrieval of data. A hash table can be imagined as an array of buckets, in each bucket we store one (or more) element(s). The size of the array and the size of the image set of the hash function h are the same: there is one bucket for every possible value of h. When we use a table of size m, frequently we use a hash function that first converts a key in some (very large) integer N and then computes N mod m, thus obtaining a number included between 0 and $m-1$, the bucket having the number N mod m is the bucket in which the element will be stored (in principle, see next paragraph) and eventually searched later.

Regardless of the hash function you choose, you will always have to handle **collisions** that happen when two different keys have the same hash value. Depending on the way these collisions are handled, there are two ways to implement hash tables: **separate chaining** and **open addressing**.

12.1 Separate Chaining

In separate chaining each bucket is implemented as a dynamic list, which means that we create a linked list for each bucket, and insert each key (or each pair (key, data)) into the appropriate list. With separate chaining, collisions are simply handled by adding the incoming element to the bucket (list) where all other elements with the same hash value are stored. The procedures of searching, inserting, retrieving or deleting a key/data are reduced to the analogous operation on linked lists. In Python the objects of the class list with their methods append(x), pop(), pop(i) and insert(x,i) are ideal to implement a bucket without having to bother with the details in the manipulation of linked lists.

Here is an example of hashing with separate chaining and a collision. Suppose we have a hash table with $m = 5$ buckets, and we want to insert the following 6 keys: 12, 23, 34, 45, 56, 67. To map the keys to the buckets we can use as hash function: $h(k) = k \mod 5$. Here are the mappings for each key:

$$h(12) = 2$$
$$h(23) = 3$$
$$h(34) = 4$$
$$h(45) = 0$$
$$h(56) = 1$$
$$h(67) = 2$$

Notice that both 12 and 67 map to bucket 2, which creates a collision. Here is what the resulting hash table would look like:

Bucket	List
0	45
1	56
2	12 → 67
3	23
4	34

Note that the keys 12 and 67 are stored in the same bucket, but they are in a linked list, which allows us to retrieve them separately.

As new elements are added to the table and the buckets become larger, the performances of the algorithms for searching, insertion and deletion may deteriorate. It is possible to monitor whether the table becomes too full by monitoring the ratio

12.1 Separate Chaining

n/m where n is the number of keys currently present in the table and m is the size of the table (the number of buckets). This ratio is called **load factor** or **fill ratio** of the table and gives you the average number of key/data present in a bucket, therefore the average cost of a search, an insertion or a deletion in the table will be in $O(n/m)$.

If, as the result of an insertion, the load factor exceeds a certain threshold previously set (typically equal to 2), the insertion algorithm is programmed to start fresh by creating a new table of larger size (typically twice the size of the previous one) and redistribute the element in the new table using a hash function that hashes the integers using the integer $2m$ instead of m to compute the modulo (rehashing).

If you want to insert a new key, say 21, in the following table, the ratio n/m would become 11/5, which is higher than 2:

Bucket	List
0	45 → 90
1	56
2	12 → 67 → 47 → 82
3	23 → 38
4	34

A new table of size 10 is created and the elements rehashed with the hash function mod 10, then the key 21 is inserted in this new table:

Bucket	List
0	90
1	21
2	12 → 82
3	23
4	34
5	45
6	56
7	67 → 47
8	38
9	

By applying resizing and rehashing whenever needed, we keep the average size of a bucket not larger than 2, therefore the average cost of a research, an insertion or a deletion will be in $O(2) = O(1)$, that is, in constant time.

It would seem however that some insertions would be much more costly than others. When an insertion requires rehashing and hence the creation of a new table, the cost of such insertion would be quite high because you need to count also the operations needed to redistribute the elements in the new table. These operations are in $O(n)$. However, consider that if you are performing a rehashing in which you have to redistribute n elements in the new table, you have already performed at least n insertions in the table (or even more if some deletion has already also occurred). So the cost in $O(n)$ of the construction of the new table and rehashing can be distributed over those n of insertions, by increasing their constant cost of an additional constant term. We say that the **distributed complexity** of the algorithms remains in $O(1)$.

Symmetrically, resizing for a smaller table may be appropriate when the load factor of the table becomes too low.

Exercise 12.1
Write the programs in Python that realise insertion, deletion and search in a hash table implemented with separate chaining. The following parameters can be entered by the user:

- m, the initial size of the table;
- α_{max}, the maximal load factor, if the load factor becomes larger than this value, an upsizing of the table needs to be performed;
- α_{min}, the minimal load factor, if the load factor becomes smaller than this value, a downsizing of the table needs to be performed.

initial size of the table as well as the maximal and the minimum load ratio accepted

12.2 Hashing with Open Addressing

Hashing with open addressing is another common technique used for implementing hash tables. In this method, each bucket can contain only one element. The implication is that collisions must be resolved by finding alternative locations in the table. These alternative locations are obtained by "probing" a sequence of possible indices. The same sequence obviously needs to be used when inserting and when searching.

Since each bucket contains at most one element, the load factor α of a hash table implemented with open addressing is always smaller than or equal to 1. Another implication is that the hash table may eventually get completely full. In that case rehashing the elements in a new larger hash table is mandatory before performing any further insertion.

12.2.1 Insertion in Tables with Opening Addressing

If a collision occurs and a bucket is found occupied when trying to insert a new element in the table then we continue searching for a vacant bucket within the hash table. This search can be made starting from the occupied slot and then by moving of one slot to the right (circularly, we consider that on the right of the last slot there

12.2 Hashing with Open Addressing

is the first one) until an empty case is found[1] and the element can be inserted there. This method is called **linear probing**.

For example, let's consider the hash function $h(k) = k \bmod 8$, and we want to store five key-value pairs, $(11, A)$, $(19, B)$, $(17, C)$, $(21, D)$ and $(27, E)$.

Initially, the hash table will be empty, but after inserting the first element $(11, A)$, the key is hashed to bucket 3.

Bucket	0	1	2	3	4	5	6	7
Content	---	---	---	(11, A)	---	---	---	---

Next, when we hash the second element $(19, B)$, the key also hashes to bucket 3 and it collides with the first key. As this slot is occupied, we search for the next available slot in the table, starting from index 3, and the element gets inserted at index 4.

Bucket	0	1	2	3	4	5	6	7
Content	---	---	---	(11, A)	(19, B)	---	---	---

When hashing the third element $(17, C)$, the key hashes to index 1, which is empty, and the key-value pair gets inserted at index 1, then $(21, D)$ is hashed in bucket 5:

Bucket	0	1	2	3	4	5	6	7
Content	---	(17, C)	---	(11, A)	(19, B)	(21, D)	---	---

When it is time to insert $(27, E)$, the key hashes to index 3 we find this slot is occupied, we search for the next available slot in the table, starting from index 3, and the key gets inserted at index 6. The hash table will be as follows:

Bucket	0	1	2	3	4	5	6	7
Content	---	(17, C)	---	(11, A)	(19, B)	(21, D)	(27, E)	---

The following algorithm for the insertion of a new element x in a hash table T assumes that n is a global variable whose value is kept equal to the number of elements present in the table and that `isAvailable(i: integer): boolean` is a function that returns True if and only if the slot i of the table T does not contain already an element. Note that the algorithm starts by checking if the insertion of the element x would make the table overflow, and in this case it operates a rehashing. The `while` loop performs the linear probing.

---

[1] An empty slot can always be found because a full table is resized and rehashed before any attempt of a new insertion.

Algorithm 12.1: Insertion in a hash table

```
1  Insert(T: hashtable of size m; x: element)
2    if n == m then
3      Rehash(T, 2*m)
4    i = hash(key(x))
5    while not (isAvailable(i)) do
6      i = (i+1) % m
7    T[i] = x
8    n = n+1
```

12.2.2 Searching in Tables with Opening Addressing

Searching needs to take into account the strategy used by the insertions. We look for the key in the hash table using the same hash function. So, when searching the element of key k, you start checking the bucket $h(k)$. If the bucket is occupied by some other element, you start looking at the positions on its right one by one, until either you find the element you were looking for, or you find an empty[2] slot, in that case you can conclude that the element is not in the table (otherwise it would be in one of the inspected compartments). The algorithm needs also to take into account the case of a completely full table where the element to be searched is not present. In this case you will never find an empty slot nor you will find the element and your loop may run forever. You need hence to count the number of probings and stop when they become more than m (the size of the table) because it means you have checked all the boxes without finding the element.

We write the algorithm is such way that it returns the number of the bucket containing the element if the element is present and the value -1 if the element is not present.

Algorithm 12.2: Searching in a hash table

```
1  Search(T: hashtable of size m; x: element): integer
2    i = hash(key(x))
3    probing = 0
4    while not (isEmpty(i)) and (probing <= m) do
5      if T[i] == x then
6        return(i)
7      i = (i+1) % m
8      probing = probing +1
9    return(-1)
```

---

[2] As we will see, we will have to define "empty" with care.

12.2 Hashing with Open Addressing

For instance, the algorithm correctly detects that the element of key 27 is present in the table

Bucket	0	1	2	3	4	5	6	7
Content	---	---	(17, C)	---	(11, A)	(19, B)	(21, D)	(27, E)	---

by starting the search from the bucket $h(27) = 3$ and inspecting successively the buckets 4, 5, and 6 (where the algorithm finds it and returns 6). It also correctly detects that the element of key 43 is not present in the table by starting the search from the bucket $h(43) = 3$ and inspecting successively the buckets 4, 5, and 6, and 7 where it finds an empty bucket.

However this algorithm may fail if some deletions have occurred. Imagine for instance the element $(19, B)$ gets deleted before you search for the element of key 27. The `while` loop would stop at the (now empty) slot number 4 and would return `False` even is the element is present in the table.

To solve this issue it suffices to implement appropriately the deleting algorithm.

12.2.3 Deletion in Tables with Opening Addressing

Deletion is also possible in open addressing. When we need to delete a key from the table, rather than simply removing the element, we typically mark the slot as "deleted" with a dedicated value different than the one used indicating slots that have been empty from the beginning. During subsequent insertions a slot marked as "deleted' is treated as an available slot, like the empty ones, but during future searches is will be recognised as different than a bucket that has always been empty therefore coming across such a marked slot will not interrupt the `while` loop of the search.

Algorithm 12.3: Deletion in a hash table

```
1  Delete(T: hashtable of size m; x: element)
2      i = Search(T,x)
3      if i != -1 then
4          T[i]= Deleted
```

For example, we want to delete the element of key 19 from the hash table of the above example, we mark the slot as deleted (symbolically noted as *Del*). Now, the hash table looks as follows:

Bucket	0	1	2	3	4	5	6	7
Content	---	---	(17, C)	---	(11, A)	Del	(21, D)	(27, E)	---

If now we search for 27 in the hash table, we start from the bucket $h(27) = 3$ and we find that the slot is occupied, we then move to the next slot, which is marked as *Deleted*, and we continue our search to the next slot. There we find another key-value pair $(21, D)$. As they are not equal, we continue our search to the next bucket (index 6) where we finally find the key-value pair $(27, E)$ and correctly return 6.

This also explains why we used two different functions `isAvailable` and `isEmpty` in the insertion and in the search respectively. The former function returns `True` if the slot is either empty (it has never received any element) or deleted (it used to contain an element that now has been deleted). The latter function returns `True` only if the slot has always been empty.

12.2.4 Complexity of Search, Insertion and Deletion with Open Addressing

The complexity of search, insertion, and deletion in hashing with open addressing depends on several factors, including the load factor, the size of the hash table, and the choice of the probing strategy.

One of the key factors that affect the performance of open addressing is the load factor of the hash table. When the load factor is low, the number of collisions is also low, and the number of probes required to insert or retrieve an element is minimal. However, as the load factor increases, the number of collisions also increases, leading to a higher number of probes required to insert or retrieve an element.

Another factor that affects the performance of open addressing is the choice of the hash function. A good hash function should distribute the keys evenly across the hash table, reducing the likelihood of collisions. However, designing a good hash function can be a challenging task, especially when dealing with complex data structures or non-uniform data distributions.

Moreover, open addressing suffers from the problem of **clustering**, where a series of collisions result in clusters of filled slots in the hash table. This phenomenon can cause long probing sequences, slowing down the operations performed on the hash table.

The choice of the probing strategy can also affect the complexity of search, insertion, and deletion in open addressing. Linear probing, for example, is simple and easy to implement, but it can lead to clustering and degraded performance when the load factor is high. **Quadratic probing** and **double hashing** can mitigate the clustering problem, but they require more computation per probe.

If you are searching or are trying to insert an element x using linear probing, then for any $i = 1, 2, \ldots, m$, the i-th bucket to be probed will be bucket $(h(x) + i - 1) \bmod m$. When you use quadratic probing, the i-th bucket to be probed will be bucket $(h(x) + (i-1)^2) \bmod m$.

Double hashing is a technique used in open addressing hash tables to resolve collisions. With double hashing, in addition to the (primary) hash function h_1 another secondary hash function h_2 is used. When a collision occurs, we probe a different bucket using the secondary hash function. When you use double hashing, the i-th bucket to be probed will be bucket $(h_1(x) + ih_2(x)) \bmod m$.

12.2 Hashing with Open Addressing

The secondary hash function is designed to produce a different index for each key, even if they hash to the same index using the primary hash function. A good secondary hash function that avoids clustering is the function $h_2(key) = R - (key \mod R)$ where R is a prime number less than the size of the hash table and relatively prime to the size of the hash table.

Assuming a hash table of size m and a load factor α, the worst-case complexity of search, insertion, and deletion in open addressing is $O(m)$. This occurs when the hash table is completely full (i.e., $\alpha = 1$), and every slot in the table is probed before finding an empty slot or the searched element.

In practice, however, the average-case complexity of search, insertion and deletion in open addressing is much better. Assuming a good hash function and a low load factor, the average-case complexity of these operations is $O(1)$. This is because most lookups can be performed in a single probe, and most insertions and deletions require only a small number of probes.

If we make the (strong) assumption that the hashing function will evenly distribute items into the slots of a hash table and moreover that each item to be hashed has an equal probability of being placed into a slot, regardless of the other elements already placed, then the following theorem can be proved (but we will not give the proof here).

> **Theorem 12.1**
> In a hash table with open addressing, with load factor $\alpha < 1$ and with hash function assumed to be uniform the average number of probings for a failed search is at most $\frac{1}{1-\alpha}$ while the average number of probings for a successful search is at most $\frac{1}{\alpha} \ln \frac{1}{1-\alpha}$.

Exercise 12.2
Consider a hash table of size 10, and the hash function $h(k) = k \mod 10$. Insert the following key-value pairs:

$(10, A), (25, B), (17, C), (5, D), (13, E), (22, F), (18, G), (16, H), (19, I)$.

Show the resulting hash table.

Exercise 12.3
Consider the hash table from the previous exercise. Suppose we want to delete the key-value pair $(17, C)$. Show the resulting hash table after deletion. Give the sequence of the probes made for the search of the pair $(16, H)$ and then for the search of the pair $(19, I)$.

List of Figures

Fig. 1.1	von Neumann architecture of a computer	4
Fig. 1.2	Solving $ax^2 + bx + c$ over $\mathbb{R}$ (flowchart)	6
Fig. 2.1	A standard PyCharm window	10
Fig. 3.1	Flowchart basic nodes. (**a**) Start of execution. (**b**) Instruction/Statement. (**c**) Output	34
Fig. 3.2	Flowchart of a simple sequence of instructions	35
Fig. 3.3	More flowchart nodes. (**a**) End of execution. (**b**) Test	35
Fig. 3.4	Flowchart of a `for` iteration	36
Fig. 3.5	If-then-else flowcharts. (**a**) If-then-else. (**b**) If-then	40
Fig. 3.6	Flowchart of a `while`	45
Fig. 3.7	Possible flowchart for a `break` in a `for`	46
Fig. 3.8	Possible flowchart for a `continue` in a `for`	48
Fig. 5.1	A list used as a stack	93
Fig. 5.2	A list as a queue	95
Fig. 5.3	Negative indexing	97
Fig. 5.4	A variable in Python	99
Fig. 5.5	Two variables and two objects of the same value	99
Fig. 5.6	Two variables and one object	100
Fig. 5.7	Two variables and one object	101
Fig. 5.8	Two variables and two list objects. (**a**) Before `append`. (**b**) After `append`	102
Fig. 5.9	A possible list implementation in Python	118
Fig. 6.1	Drawing of $\sin(x)$ with short segments	137
Fig. 6.2	Drawing of $\sin(x)$ with long segments	137
Fig. 6.3	Drawing saved in an image file	138
Fig. 6.4	Label a drawing	139
Fig. 6.5	Controlling the thickness of a drawing	140
Fig. 6.6	Multiple drawings on the same picture	141
Fig. 6.7	Axis scaling	142
Fig. 6.8	Removal in the Sierpiński carpet	152
Fig. 6.9	A Sierpiński carpet after some recursions	152
Fig. 6.10	Monte-Carlo picking to get π=3.1482666666666668	155

Fig. 7.1	$f(n) \in O(g(n))$	171
Fig. 7.2	$f(x) = x$ and $g(x) = x^2 - 6$	172
Fig. 7.3	$g(x) = 2x + 4 \in O(f(x))$	172
Fig. 7.4	Complexity of sequential composition, B_1 then B_2	177
Fig. 7.5	Complexity of a loop including a block of instructions	178
Fig. 8.1	Call tree of `FactRec(5)`. (**a**) Top-down of the calls. (**b**) Bottom-up of the returns	190
Fig. 8.2	Binary search in an array	196
Fig. 8.3	Call tree to get the 5th Fibonacci number using recursion	200
Fig. 9.1	i-th step of insertion sort	216
Fig. 9.2	Merge sort: before the merge	218
Fig. 9.3	Merge sort: before the merge	218
Fig. 9.4	During a partition step in QuickSort	224
Fig. 9.5	End of partition step in QuickSort	224
Fig. 9.6	Placing the pivot in QuickSort	224
Fig. 9.7	Decision tree for sorting an array of three elements	229
Fig. 10.1	L-shape tiling of a square	253
Fig. 10.2	Call tree of `FiboAux`	256
Fig. 10.3	The kayak problem, dependence of a cell	260
Fig. 10.4	The kayak problem, scanning the cells	261
Fig. 10.5	The kayak problem, alternative scanning	261
Fig. 10.6	Splitting into quadrants	268
Fig. 10.7	Forbidden cells after splitting into quadrants	269
Fig. 11.1	A tree	277
Fig. 11.2	Tree nodes as quadruplets	277
Fig. 11.3	A list scattered in memory	278
Fig. 11.4	A node of a tree having arity k	278
Fig. 11.5	A node of a binary tree	278
Fig. 11.6	A lexicographic tree	279
Fig. 11.7	The left-child right-sibling implementation of a tree of arbitrary arity. (**a**) A tree. (**b**) Its implementation	280
Fig. 11.8	A node of a binary tree with parenting	280
Fig. 11.9	A tree with parenting. (**a**) A tree. (**b**) Its implementation	281
Fig. 11.10	A small binary tree	282
Fig. 11.11	Syntax trees. (**a**) $2 * 3 + 4$. (**b**) $2 * (3 + 4)$	285
Fig. 11.12	Shape of a heap	291
Fig. 11.13	The shape of a heap of size 10	291
Fig. 11.14	An example of heap of size 10	292
Fig. 11.15	Numbering nodes in a heap	293
Fig. 11.16	Parenthood and childhood relations in a heap as an array	293
Fig. 11.17	Insertion of 9	294
Fig. 11.18	Removal of the minimum in a heap, phase 1. (**a**) Record the minimum. (**b**) Move last value to the root. (**c**) Delete last node	295

Fig. 11.19	Removal of the minimum in a heap, phase 2, downward percolation	296
Fig. 11.20	A heap in an array	299
Fig. 11.21	A heap in an array	299
Fig. 11.22	A heap in an array	300
Fig. 11.23	Binary search tree property	301
Fig. 11.24	Not a BST	303
Fig. 11.25	Two BSTs. (**a**) A BST. (**b**) A degenerated BST	306
Fig. 11.26	Which ones are BSTs?	307
Fig. 11.27	BST for exemples of deletions	308
Fig. 11.28	Removing a leaf	308
Fig. 11.29	Removing a node with one child	309
Fig. 11.30	A BST with its balance factors	313
Fig. 11.31	Not an AVL	314
Fig. 11.32	Left rotation in an AVL. (**a**) Before. (**b**) After	315
Fig. 11.33	A left rotation. (**a**) Before rotation. (**b**) After rotation at node 17	317
Fig. 11.34	A non sufficient left rotation. (**a**) Before rotation. (**b**) Wrong AVL after simple left rotation at node 17	317
Fig. 11.35	A double left rotation in an AVL	318
Fig. 11.36	A double left rotation in an AVL. (**a**) Before rotation. (**b**) Sub-rotations. (**c**) After right rotation. (**d**) After left rotation	322
Fig. 11.37	A tree	322

List of Python Interactive Sessions (REPL)

1	An interactive Python session	xi
2.1	Hello world	11
2.2	Basic arithmetic	12
2.3	Floating-point arithmetic	13
2.4	Fallacies of arithmetic on floats	14
2.5	Integer division	14
2.6	Types	15
2.7	Arithmetic on complex	15
2.8	Type conversion	16
2.9	Math functions	17
2.10	Signature violation	18
2.11	Use of a math function	19
2.12	On-the-fly help	19
2.13	Help of a module	19
2.14	Use of variables	21
2.15	Assignment	23
2.16	Deleting a variable	23
2.17	None	24
2.18	Assignment	24
2.19	Undefined variable error	25
2.20	Sequential composition	26
2.21	Compound or parallel assignment	26
2.22	Booleans	27
2.23	Tests	27
2.24	Some arithmetic expression	28
2.25	Approximation of π	28
2.26	Computing decades	28
2.27	Approximation of π	29
2.28	Approximation of π	29
3.1	Canonical printing of typed values	39
3.2	f-strings	39

© The Author(s), under exclusive license to Springer Nature Switzerland AG 2024
R. Mantaci, J.-B. Yunès, *Basics of Programming and Algorithms,
Principles and Applications*, Compact Textbooks in Mathematics,
https://doi.org/10.1007/978-3-031-59801-2

3.3	Format in f-strings	39
4.1	Local variable	58
4.2	Exception not catched	61
4.3	Documenting a function	65
5.1	Tuples	84
5.2	Tuples	84
5.3	Length of a tuple	88
5.4	Extracting elements of a tuple	88
5.5	Labeled tuples	89
5.6	Lists	90
5.7	More lists	90
5.8	Concatenation of lists	90
5.9	List repetition	91
5.10	Initializing a long list	91
5.11	Accessing elements of a list	91
5.12	Length of a list	92
5.13	Extracting elements from a list	92
5.14	Modifying a list	92
5.15	List as a stack	94
5.16	List as a queue	95
5.17	Removing or deleting an element from a list	96
5.18	Is an element in a list or not?	96
5.19	Clearing a list	96
5.20	Sorting a list	96
5.21	Copying a list	97
5.22	Negative indexing	97
5.23	Slicing a list	98
5.24	Slicing defaults	98
5.25	Slice step	98
5.26	Negative step	98
5.27	`id` of an object	99
5.28	Two variables with two objects of the same value	99
5.29	Are objects the same?	100
5.30	Two equivalent objects	100
5.31	Assignment	100
5.32	Mutable objects and variables	101
5.33	Two variables and two objects	101
5.34	Looping over sequences	102
5.35	Zip sequences	103
5.36	Multi-dimensional and comprehension list	105
5.37	Triangular structure	105
5.38	Ternary expression	106
5.39	if-else vs ternary expression	106
5.40	Printing a tuple	107
5.41	List is usable in place of a tuple	107

5.42	Wrong data is usable	108
5.43	Constructing a dictionary	108
5.44	Constructing a dictionary	108
5.45	Accessing data in dictionary	108
5.46	Keys can be of any type	109
5.47	Modifying a dictionary	109
5.48	Iterating over a dictionary	109
5.49	Classes	111
5.50	Labeled cards	120
5.51	52 cards deck	121
5.52	52 cards, using `range`	121

List of Programs

1	A program	xi
1.1	Solving a polynomial of degree 2 over $\mathbb{R}$	7
3.1	Hello program	32
3.2	Approximations of π	33
3.3	Formatted code	34
3.4	Iterations with a range	36
3.5	Interactive approximation of π	38
3.6	if-then-else	41
3.7	if-then	41
3.8	Approximation of π	41
3.9	if else if else if else if	42
3.10	`elif`	42
3.11	if-else and assignment	43
3.12	Conditional expression	43
3.13	while loop	44
3.14	Input validation	44
3.15	`break`	46
3.16	While to replace break	47
3.17	Sum of prime numbers	49
3.18	Final approx. of π	50
3.19	Final approx. of π	50
3.20	π to the 4th decimal place	51
3.21	Controlled validation	51
3.22	Asking for continuation	52
3.23	Validation loop using a `break`	52
3.24	Loops and `break`	53
4.1	Binomial	56
4.2	Binomial using function	56
4.3	Definition of a function	57
4.4	Several parameters	58
4.5	A procedure	59

4.6	A function returning a value	59
4.7	Stop in case of bad input	60
4.8	Error handling with None	60
4.9	Try-except block	61
4.10	Example of a try-except	61
4.11	Closure	62
4.12	Effect of a closure	62
4.13	Context dependent	63
4.14	Modifying a global variable	64
4.15	Bad usage of variable in closure	64
4.16	Local hides global	65
4.17	Module of approximation functions	66
4.18	Main module using external functions	66
4.19	Cosines for different units	67
4.20	Cosine for different units	68
4.21	Parameter default value	68
4.22	Keyword arguments	69
4.23	Factorial as iteration	70
4.24	Factorial as recursion	71
4.25	Bad recursion	71
4.26	Recursion limit in Python	73
4.27	With functions	76
4.28	Module of series for π and e	77
4.29	Program to compute n-th approximation of π and e	77
4.30	Module to get user input	78
4.31	Program to compute n-th approximation of π and e	78
4.32	Binary representation of a decimal	79
4.33	Tournament method for min and max	79
4.34	Pascal triangle	80
4.35	Pascal triangle by recursing on pattern	80
4.36	Factorial, iteration as recursion	81
5.1	Passing a tuple to a function	85
5.2	Return a tuple	85
5.3	Error handling with tuples	86
5.4	Walrus operator	87
5.5	Sum of n first primes	105
5.6	Type Point	111
5.7	Objects with methods	112
5.8	Point with methods for polar	113
5.9	Polar/Cartesian	115
5.10	Printing objects	116
5.11	Comparing tuples	118
5.12	Comparing points	119
5.13	Comparing points in any n-D space	119
5.14	Reverse Polish calculator	120

List of Programs

5.15	Generating a deck of 52 cards	121
5.16	A robot playing the Battle game	122
5.17	3×3 matrix multiplication	123
5.18	A primitive implementation of a chained list	124
6.1	Wall clock measure	128
6.2	Repeating experiments	129
6.3	CPU time	130
6.4	Wall clock vs CPU clock on inputs	131
6.5	Shuffling a list	132
6.6	Syracuse	133
6.7	Number of loops in Syracuse	133
6.8	Number of multiplications in Syracuse	133
6.9	Number of tests in Syracuse	134
6.10	Number of tests in Syracuse	135
6.11	Generate data to plot	136
6.12	Plot some data	136
6.13	Save picture as an image file	138
6.14	Adding labels on axis	138
6.15	Changing colours	139
6.16	Changing the thickness	140
6.17	Adding labels on axis	141
6.18	Logarithmic scale on y-axis	142
6.19	Write data into a file	144
6.20	Reading a file, iterating over the lines of text	146
6.21	Stripping strings	146
6.22	Splitting strings into list of words	147
6.23	Splitting strings into list of words	148
6.24	Generating a pseudo-random sequence	149
6.25	Illusion of randomness	150
6.26	Measure time to sort shuffled lists	152
6.27	Average and standard deviation	153
6.28	Average and standard deviation on-the-fly	153
6.29	Measure Python sort execution time	154
6.30	π by Monte-Carlo	156
6.31	Drawing a Sierpiński carpet	157
8.1	Iterative fast exponentiation	202
8.2	Fast Fibonacci by Matrix Fast Exponentiation	206
9.1	Sort strings with radix sort	240

List of Algorithms

1	Sum of elements of an array	x
7.1	Sum of elements of an array	165
7.2	Minimum of an array	167
7.3	Example	178
7.4	Sum of matrices	179
8.1	Factorial by iteration	188
8.2	Factorial by recursion	189
8.3	Exponentiation by iteration	192
8.4	Exponentiation by recursion	192
8.5	Fast exponentiation	192
8.6	Naive search	194
8.7	Common mistake: premature return	195
8.8	Binary search	197
8.9	Fibonacci numbers	199
8.10	Iterative fast exponentiation	201
9.1	Selection sort	212
9.2	Insertion sort	214
9.3	Merge sort	217
9.4	Merge	219
9.5	Quick sort	223
9.6	Partition in Quick Sort	225
9.7	Counting sort	230
9.8	Counting Sort	231
9.9	Radix sort	233
9.10	Extracting a digit	233
9.11	Distribute elements to appropriate bucket	234
9.12	Recompose buckets to an array	234
9.13	Radix sort	235
10.1	Minimum of an array	246
10.2	Longest freezing period	247
10.3	Karatsuba's multiplication	250

© The Author(s), under exclusive license to Springer Nature Switzerland AG 2024
R. Mantaci, J.-B. Yunès, *Basics of Programming and Algorithms,
Principles and Applications*, Compact Textbooks in Mathematics,
https://doi.org/10.1007/978-3-031-59801-2

10.4	Stooge sort	252
10.5	Fibonacci number	254
10.6	Fibonacci, memoisation	255
10.7	Fibonacci: memoisation	255
10.8	Fibonacci, tabulation	256
10.9	Binomial by recursion	257
10.10	Binomial, tabulation	257
10.11	Factorial by recursion	262
10.12	Factorial with tail recursion	262
10.13	Iterative equivalent function	263
10.14	f with tail recursion	263
10.15	Iterative version of f	264
10.16	Iterative version of f	264
10.17	g with tail recursion (incorrect)	264
10.18	Fibonacci with tail recursion	265
10.19	Mysterious recursion	265
11.1	Pre-order traversal	282
11.2	Pre-order traversal of a binary tree	282
11.3	Post-order traversal	283
11.4	Post-order traversal of a binary tree	283
11.5	In-order traversal	283
11.6	In-order traversal of a binary tree	284
11.7	Breadth-first traversal of a tree	286
11.8	Size of a binary tree	287
11.9	Height of a tree	287
11.10	Bad algorithm for the height	288
11.11	Sum even numbers in a binary tree	288
11.12	Heap class structure	296
11.13	Insert in a heap	297
11.14	Removal of the minimum in a heap	298
11.15	Mystery algorithm	300
11.16	(wrong) Test if a tree is a BST	302
11.17	Test if a tree is a BST	303
11.18	Search in a BST	305
11.19	Insertion in a BST	306
11.20	Deletion in a BST	311
11.21	Compute the minimum value in a BST	311
11.22	Rotation in an AVL	316
11.23	Double rotation in an AVL	318
11.24	Rebalancing an AVL	318
11.25	Delta	319
11.26	Delta with height	319
11.27	Updating height in AVL	320
11.28	Insertion in an AVL	320

12.1	Insertion in a hash table	332
12.2	Searching in a hash table	332
12.3	Deletion in a hash table	333

References

1. W. Ackermann, Zum Hilbertschen Aufbau der reellen Zahlen. Math. Ann. **99**, 118–133 (1928)
2. G.M. Adelson-Velski, E.M. Landis, An algorithm for organization of information. Dokl. Akad. Nauk SSSR **146**, 263–266 (1962)
3. G. Boole, *The Mathematical Analysis of Logic: Being an Essay Towards a Calculus of Deductive Reasoning* (Macmillan, Barclay, & Macmillan, Cambridge, 1847)
4. T. Cormen, C. Leiserson, R. Rivest, C. Stein, *Introduction to Algorithms*, 4th edn. (MIT Press, 2022)
5. W. Dijkstra, Goto statement considered harmful. CACM **11**, 125–133 (1968)
6. L. Euler, De summis serierum reciprocarum. Euler Archive - All Works, 41 (1740)
7. L. Fibonacci, L.E. Sigler, *The Book of Squares/Leonardo Pisano Fibonacci; An Annotated Translation into Modern English by L.E. Sigler* (Academic Press, Boston, 1987)
8. D. Goldberg, What every computer scientist should know about floating-point arithmetic, in *1991 Issue of Computing Surveys*, chapter D (Association for Computing Machinery, 1991)
9. C.A.R. Hoare, Quicksort. Comput. J. **5**(1), 10–16 (1962)
10. C.A.R. Hoare, An axiomatic basis for computer programming. Commun. ACM **12**(10), 576–580 (1969)
11. IEEE, IEEE standard for binary floating-point arithmetic. Technical report, New York. Note: Standard 754–1985 (1985)
12. IEEE-754, *60559-2020 — ISO/IEC/IEEE International Standard — Floating-point Arithmetic* (Institute of Electrical and Electronics Engineers, 2020)
13. A. Karatsuba, Y. Ofman, Multiplication of multidigit numbers on automata. Sov. Phys. Dokl. **7**, 595 (1962)
14. D.E. Knuth, *The Art of Computer Programming*, 3rd edn. (Addison-Wesley, 1997)
15. P.A. Macmahon, The indices of permutations and the derivation therefrom of functions of a single variable associated with the permutations of any assemblage of objects. Am. J. Math. **35**, 281 (1913)
16. M. Matsumoto, T. Nishimura, Mersenne twister: A 623-dimensionally equidistributed uniform pseudorandom number generator. ACM Trans. Model. Comput. Simul. **8**(1), 3–30 (1998)
17. N. Metropolis, S. Ulam, The Monte Carlo method. J. Am. Stat. Assoc. **44**, 335 (1949)
18. H. Rogers, *Theory of Recursive Functions and Effective Computability* (MIT Press, Cambridge, MA, 1987)
19. A.M. Turing, On computable numbers, with an application to the Entscheidungsproblem. Proc. Lond. Math. Soc. **s2-42**(1), 230–265 (1937)
20. J. von Neumann, First draft of a report on the EDVAC. Technical report, 1945
21. J.W.J. Williams, Algorithm 232: Heapsort. Commun. ACM **7**(6), 347–348 (1964)

© The Author(s), under exclusive license to Springer Nature Switzerland AG 2024
R. Mantaci, J.-B. Yunès, *Basics of Programming and Algorithms, Principles and Applications*, Compact Textbooks in Mathematics,
https://doi.org/10.1007/978-3-031-59801-2

Index

A
Abstract data type (ADT), 93, 116
Ackermann, W., 72
Adelson-Velsky, G., 274
Algorithm, ix, x, 161, 162
    analysis, ix
Algorithmic, *see* Algorithm
Al-Khwārizmī, M., ix
Alternative, 40
Anemic domain model, 110
Arithmetic and logical unit (ALU), 4
Arity, *see* Tree
Array, *see* List
Assignment, 23
    compound, 26
    parallel, 26
Average complexity, 168
AVL, 274, 312, 314
    balance factor, 312
    deletion, 321
    insertion, 320
    rebalancing, 318
    ρ, 318
    rotation, 315

B
Balance factor, *see* AVL
Base case, 187
Basic instruction, 5
Benchmarking, 127
Best case, 167
Binary heap, 273
Binary Search, 195, 197
    complexity, 245
Binary Search Tree (BST), 300, 301, 314
    definition, 301
    deletion, 307
    insertion, 305
    search, 304
Binary tree, *see* Tree
Binomial, 55
Boole, G., 27
Boolean, 27
Bound, 57
Bound (local) variable, 57
Bound variable, 58
Bucket Sort, 233

C
Call by value, 85
Central processing unit (CPU), 4
Class, 111
Clock
    CPU clock, 130
    wall clock, 128
Closure, 62
Coding, x
Collatz conjecture, 132
Command, 10
Command line mode, 32
Comment, 33, 65
Compiler, 5
Complexity
    average, 168
    best case, 167
    big-O, 170
    big-Omega, 174
    big-Theta, 172
    constant, 167
    dominance, 170
    growth rate, 170
    insertion sort, 215
    linear, 167, 168
    logarithmic, 178

master theorem, 245
Merge Sort, 219
O, 170
Ω, 174
optimality, 228
Quick Sort, 225
recursion, 190
selection sort, 212
space, 164, 167
Θ, 172
time, 164
worst case, 167
Comprehension list, 104
Computer, 4
Conditional branching, 5
Conditional expression, 43
Constant, 167
Constructor, 111
Control flow, 5, 31
  alternative, 5, 40
  function call, 5
  loop, 5
Control unit (CU), 4
Counting operations, 132
Counting Sort, 230
Curry, H., 55
Curry-Howard correspondence, 55

D
Data encapsulation, 112
Data structure
  ADT, 93
  dictionary (*see* Dictionary)
  FIFO, 95
  heap, 289, 290
  immutable, 83
  LIFO, 93
  list, 89
  object (*see* Object)
  priority queue, 289
  queue, 95
  stack, 93
  tuple, 83
Data type, 15
Decision tree, *see* Tree
Declarative paradigm, 3
Default value, 67
Depth-first search, 281
Deserialisation, 147
Dichotomy, 217
Dictionary, 83, 107, 108
  items, 109
  iteration, 109

keys, 109
values, 109
Dijkstra, E., 45
Distributed complexity, 330
Divide and conquer, 163, 243, 244
Docstring, 65
Document, 65
Documentation, 65
Dominance, 170
Downward percolation, 294, 297
Drawings, 136
Dynamic programming, 163, 243, 253

E
Elementary operation, 164
Empty list, 90
EOL, 150
EPOCH, 128
Error, *see* Exception
Error handling, 59
Escaping, 39
Euler, L., 20, 66
Exception, 61
  handling, 61
Exponentiation, 191
Expression, 9
Extension, 104

F
Factorial, 56, 188
Fast multiplication, 249
Fetch, 4
Fibonacci
  numbers, 199
Fibonacci sequence, 199, 253
Fibonacci, L., 199
Field, 112
File format, 143
First-In-First-Out (FIFO), 95
Floating-point, 12, 13
Flowchart, 5
  break, 46
  continue, 48
  iteration, 36
  sequence, 34
  test, 35
Formal languages theory, 147
Fractal, 151
Free variable, 62
Function, 55, 59
  Ackermann, 72
  call, 72

Index

documentation, 65
primitive recursive, 72
prototype, 18
pure, 63
recursive, 70
return value, 166
tail recursive, 75
type (*see* Type)
Function call, *see* Control flow, 57
Functions
    `abs`, 20
    `append`, 113
    `close`, 144
    closure, 62
    `copy`, 97
    `del`, 23, 95, 96
    `fill`, 152
    `gcd`, 18
    `help`, 19
    `id`, 99
    `input`, 38
    `len`, 88, 92
    `open`, 144, 145
    parameters, 57
    `plot`, 137, 141, 151
    `print`, 21, 39, 150
    `process.time_ns`, 130
    `quit`, 11, 60
    `randint`, 74, 150
    `range`, 37, 121, 136
    `read`, 144
    `savefig`, 138
    `scatter`, 151
    `seed`, 150
    `show`, 137
    `shuffle`, 103, 132
    `sort`, 151
    `split`, 147
    `strip`, 146, 147
    `sum`, 105
    `time_ns`, 128
    `type`, 15
    `write`, 144, 145
    `zip`, 103

G
Golden ratio, 199
Greedy approach, 163
Gregory, J., 20

H
Hash, 327
    clustering, 334
    collision, 327
    double hashing, 334
    fill ratio, 329
    linear probing, 331
    load factor, 329
    quadratic probing, 334
Hash code, 327
Hash function, 327
Hashing, 327
    deletion, 333
    insertion, 330
    open addressing, 330
    searching, 332
Hashmap, *see* Dictionary
Hash table, 327
Hash value, 327
Heap, 289, 290
    insert, 297
    insertion, 293
    max-heap, 291
    min-heap, 290
    percolation, 293
    removal, 293, 297
Hiding, *see* Variable
Howard, W., 55

I
Identation, 37
Identifier, 9, 21, 22, 24
Immutable, 84
Immutable data structure, 83
Imperative paradigm, 3
In-order, 283
In-order traversal, 283
In-place, 210
Indentation, 37
Index, 91
    slice, 97
Initialiser, 111
Input, 38
Insertion Sort, 213
    complexity, 215
Instruction, 3–5
Integer, 12
Integer division, 14
Integrated Development Environment (IDE), 9
Intension, 104
Interactive mode, 9, 10
Interpreter, 5
Invariant method, 163
Iteration, 35
Iteration statement, 35

K

Karatsuba algorithm, 249
Karatsuba, A.A., 249
Kayak problem, 259
Keyboard
    reading, 38
Keywords
    break, 45–47
    continue, 45, 48
    elif, 42
    else, 40–42
    except, 61
    False, 27
    for, 34–37, 46, 48, 70–72, 76, 102, 146
    if, 28, 40–42
    import, 16, 17, 67
    None, 23, 24, 60
    return, 57
    then, 40
    True, 27
    try, 61
    while, 28, 44, 45, 54, 70, 76
    with, 144

L

Labeled tuples, 89
Landis, E., 274
Last-in-first-out (LIFO) structure, 93, 191
Leibniz, G.W., 20
Level-order traversal, 285
Lexical closure, 62
Lexicographic tree, 279
Linear, 167
Linear Congruential Generator (LCG), 149
Linear-Feedback Shift Registers (LFSR), 149
Linked list, 117
List, 83, 89, 93, 95
    append, 93
    chain, 187
    clear, 96
    comprehension, 104
    copy, 97
    in, 96
    index, 91
    insert, 94
    length, 92
    linked, 117
    pop, 93
    remove, 95
    shuffle, 132
    sort, 96, 132
Literal, 14
    string, 38

Local, 58
Logarithmic complexity, 178
Lookup table, 254
Loop, *see* Control flow, 35
    break, 45
    continuation, 48
    continue, 45
    for, 34
    while, 43
Loop invariant, 163

M

Mahonian numbers, 216
Map, *see* Dictionary
Marshalling, 147
Master Theorem, 245
Max-heap, 291
Memoisation, 254
Memoisation table, 254
Memory addressing, 277
Memory cell, 4
Merge Sort, 217
    complexity, 219, 246
    space complexity, 220
Mersenne, M., 149
Method, 111, 112
Min-heap, 290
Modules, 9, 16, 66
    collections, 89
    math, 17, 38, 67
    matplotlib, 136, 142
    numpy, 136
    pyplot, 138, 151, 152
    random, 74, 103, 132, 149
    sympy, 49
    time, 128
    import, 16
    math, 16
Monte-Carlo, 151
Mutable sequence, 89

N

Naive Search, 194
Name, 21–23
Natural Merge Sort, 222
Negative indexing, 97
None, 23, 24, 60
Numerical analysis, 14

O

Object, 21, 83, 110
    __init__, 111

method, 112
self, 111
__str__, 116
Object Oriented Programming (OOP), 83, 110
Observer effect, 128
Online, 210
Open addressing, see Hashing
Operation, 5
  counting, 132
  elementary, 164
Operators
  ", 39
  " ", 65
  %, 12, 14
  %=, 25
  ', 39
  **, 12
  *=, 25
  *, 12
  *, 91
  ,, 21, 26, 57, 90
  -=, 25
  -, 12
  -, 110
  //=, 25
  //, 14
  /=, 25
  /, 12–14
  :=, 87
  :, 57, 97
  ;, 26
  <=, 27
  <, 27
  ==, 27, 100
  =, 23, 25
  >=, 27
  >, 27
  [], 84, 90
  and, 27
  array[index], 109
  in, 96
  is, 100
  not, 27
  or, 27

P
Parameter, 57, 166
  default value, 67
  keyword, 69
  positional, 69
Parameter passing, 55
Pascal triangle, 257
Percolation, 293

Pivot, 222
Pokémon Go, 176
Polish Postfix Notation, 94
Positional argument, 20, 69
Positional parameter, 69
Post-order, 283
Post-order traversal, 283
Pre-order traversal, 282
Primitive recursive functions, 72
Priority queue, 289
Problem, 3, 161
  instance, 3, 161
Procedure, 59
Processor, 4
Program, 3, 4, 31
Programming, ix, x, 3
Programming language, 3, 5
Programming paradigm, 3
Prompt, 11
Prototype, 18
Pseudo-random number generator (PRNG), 148
Pseudo-random numbers, 148
Pseudocode, 162
Pure function, 63
Python, 7, 9
  abs, 20
  append, 113
  close, 144
  code structure, 36
  comment, 33
  conditional expression, 43
  copy, 97
  del, 23, 95, 96
  documentation, 17
  fill, 152
  function, 55
  gcd, 18
  help, 19
  id, 99
  indentation, 37
  input, 38
  len, 88, 92
  None, 57
  open, 144, 145
  plot, 137, 141, 151
  print, 21, 39, 150
  process.time_ns, 130
  quit, 11, 60
  randint, 74, 150
  range, 37, 121, 136
  read, 144
  savefig, 138
  scatter, 151

seed, 150
show, 137
shuffle, 103, 132
sort, 151
split, 147
statement, 24
strip, 146, 147
sum, 105
time_ns, 128
type, 15
variable, 21
while, 43
write, 144, 145
zip, 103

Q

Queue, 95, 285
　dequeue, 95
　enqueue, 95
　is_empty, 95
　priority, 289
Quick Sort, 222, 223
　complexity, 225
　pivot, 226

R

Radix Sort, 232, 233
RAM, 4
Ramanujan, S., 21
Random, 148
Range, 37
Read-Evaluate-Print Loop (REPL)
　close session, 11
　mode, 10
Reading keyboard, 38
Record, 83
Recursion, 70, 71
Recursive call, 187
　complexity, 190
　tree, 200
Recursivity, 187, 243
　base case, 187
Referencing, 277
Remainder of the integer division, 14
Resource, 144
return, 59
Returning value, 55
Reverse Polish Notation, 94
Rotations, 314
Russian Peasant, 169

S

Script, *see* Program
Script mode, 32
Search, 194
　Binary Search, 195
　Naive Search, 194
　searching problem, 194
Searching problem, 194
Seed, 149
Seemodule, 16
Selection Sort, 211
　complexity, 212
self, 111
Separate chaining, 328
Sequence, 102
Serialisation, 147
Shuffle, 132
Side effect, 23
Sierpiński carpet, 151
Sierpiński, K., 151
Sieve of Eratosthenes, 169
Signature, 18
Slicing, 97
Software
　ADA, 6
　ASSEMBLY, 6
　BASH, 11
　BASIC, 6
　C, 6, 295, 310
　C++, 6
　CMD, 11
　EMACS, 32
　FORTH, 94
　FORTRAN, 6
　GO, 6
　GOOGLE DOCS, 32
　HASKELL, 6
　JAVA, 6, 295, 310
　KOTLIN, 6
　LIBREOFFICE, 32
　LINUX, 9
　LISP, 6
　MACOS, 9
　MATHEMATICA, 6
　MATLAB, 6
　MS-WORD, 32
　PASCAL, 6
　PHP, 6
　PYCHARM, 9, 11, 32
　PYTHON, x, xi, 3, 6, 7, 9–18, 21, 22, 24, 27, 28, 31–33, 36–38, 40–44, 49, 61, 64, 68, 70–73, 83, 85, 87–89, 93, 97–99, 102–105, 108, 110–112, 116, 127,

128, 130, 136, 144, 146, 149–151,
285, 292, 295, 297, 310
VIM, 32
VISUAL STUDIO CODE, 9, 11, 32
WINDOWS, 9
Sort
  algorithm comparisons, 228
  Bucket Sort, 233
  Counting Sort, 230
  Insertion Sort, 213
  Merge Sort, 217
  Quick Sort, 222, 223
  Radix Sort, 232
  Selection Sort, 211
  Stooge Sort, 251
Sort by counting, 230
Sorting
  linear time, 230
  online, 210
  in place, 210
  stability, 210
Sorting optimality, 228
Sorting problem, 209
Source file, 31, 32
Space complexity, 163, 167
Space-time tradeoff, 164
Stable, 210
Stack, 73, 93, 191
  is_empty, 93
  pop, 93
  push, 93
Stack overflow, 73, 191
Statement, 9, 24
Stooge Sort, 251
  complexity, 252
Storage, 21
String
  formatted, 39
  f-string, 39
  interpolated, 39
String interpolation, 39
Structure, 83
Subproblem overlapping, 200
Swap, 27
Syracuse sequence, 133

T

Tabulation, 256
Tail recursion, 243, 261
Tail recursive functions, 75
Terminal mode, 32
Ternary expression, 106

Text editor, 32
Time complexity, 163, 165
  function, 166
Tournament method, 74
Traversal, 281
Tree, 273
  arity, 275
  AVL (*see* AVL)
  binary, 275
  binary search (*see* Binary Search Tree (BST))
  BST (*see* Binary Search Tree (BST))
  children nodes, 275
  decision, 229
  definition, 275
  directed, 274
  edge, 274
  empty, 275
  height, 275, 287
  leaf, 275
  lexicographic, 279
  node, 274
  node depth, 275
  recursive call, 200
  root, 274
  singleton, 275
  size, 286
  traversal, 281
    depth-first search, 281
    in-order, 283
    post-order, 283
    pre-order, 282
  undirected, 274
Tuple, 83
  singleton, 85
Turing, A., 72
Two's complement, 165
Type, 9, 15
  bool, 27
    and, 27
    comparisons, 27
    False, 27
    not, 27
    or, 27
    True, 27
  complex, 15
  conversion, 16
  float, 13, 15, 19
  int, 15, 16, 21, 38, 165
  NoneType, 24
  size, 164
  string, 38

U
Unknown, 21
Unmarshalling, 147
Upward percolation, 293, 298

V
Value, 23
Variable, 9, 21, 57
    assignment, 23
    bound, 57
    control, 37
    definition, 23
    deletion, 23
    free, 62
    hiding, 65
    identifier, 22
    lifetime, 58
    local, 58
    name, 22
    None, 24
    swap, 27
Variable hiding, 65
Variable lifetime, 58

W
Wall clock, 128
Walrus operator, 87
While loop, 44
Word processor, 32
Worst case, 167

SPRINGER NATURE

GPSR Compliance

The European Union's (EU) General Product Safety Regulation (GPSR) is a set of rules that requires consumer products to be safe and our obligations to ensure this.

If you have any concerns about our products, you can contact us on ProductSafety@springernature.com

In case Publisher is established outside the EU, the EU authorized representative is:

Springer Nature Customer Service Center GmbH
Europaplatz 3
69115 Heidelberg, Germany

The manufacturer's authorised representative in the EU is Springer Nature Customer Service Centre GmbH, Europaplatz 3, 69115 Heidelberg, Germany. If you have any concerns regarding our products, please contact ProductSafety@springernature.com

Printed and bound by CPI Group (UK) Ltd, Croydon, CR0 4YY

25/03/2026

02078188-0018